LULA

This English-language edition first published by Verso 2024

First published as *Lula: Biografia, Volume 1*

1 3 5 7 9 10 8 6 4 2

Verso
UK: 6 Meard Street, London W1F 0EG
US: 388 Atlantic Avenue, Brooklyn, NY 11217
versobooks.com

Verso is the imprint of New Left Books

ISBN-13: 978-1-80429-492-5
ISBN-13: 978-1-83929-806-0 (UK EBK)
ISBN-13: 978-1-83929-496-3 (US EBK)

British Library Cataloguing in Publication Data
A catalogue record for this book is available from the British Library

Library of Congress Cataloging-in-Publication Data

Names: Morais, Fernando, author. | Mier, Brian, translator.
Title: Lula : a biography / Fernando Morais ; translated by Brian Mier.
Other titles: Lula. English.
Description: English-language edition. | London ; New York : Verso, 2024. | Includes index.
Identifiers: LCCN 2024012325 (print) | LCCN 2024012326 (ebook) | ISBN 9781804294925 | ISBN 9781804294963 (ebk)
Subjects: LCSH: Lula, 1945- | Presidents—Brazil—Biography. | Brazil—Politics and government—2003- | Brazil—Politics and government—1985-2002. | Partido dos Trabalhadores (Brazil)—History. | Political corruption—Brazil. | Money laundering—Brazil.
Classification: LCC F2538.5.L85 M6613 2024 (print) | LCC F2538.5.L85 (ebook) | DDC 981.06/5092 [B]—dc23/eng/20240325
LC record available at https://lccn.loc.gov/2024012325
LC ebook record available at https://lccn.loc.gov/2024012326

Typeset in Minion by Hewer Text UK Ltd, Edinburgh
Printed and bound by CPI Group (UK) Ltd, Croydon CR0 4YY

Contents

Political Party and Public Agency Abbreviations vii
Map of ABC, São Paulo x

1. Sergio Moro orders Lula's arrest but he decides not to turn himself in to the Federal Police. "They'll have to come for me" 1
2. While searching Lula's home, the Federal Police stick a bug under his couch to secretly record conversations with his wife 15
3. GloboNews network runs a fake story—"Lula Will Resist Arrest!"—and its ratings rise by 694 percent 25
4. Emídio learns that the Federal Police had not one but several spies filming everything that happened inside the union hall 41
5. After standing up to the neighbors and the Federal Police, the people spend 581 days yelling greetings to Lula. He can't see them from his cell, but he can hear them 53
6. A hacker named Red opens to the gates of hell, and the Supreme Court buries Moro and the Car Wash investigation. Lula steps out of prison as a presidential candidate 79
7. Jardim Lavinia, April 1980—With the police at the door to arrest him, Lula growls, "I'm sleeping, damn it! They can go fuck themselves!" 105

8. Navy intelligence intercepts communications from the Curia and reveals that Cardinal Arns asked the German Catholic Church to support the ABC Metalworkers' strike fund 117

9. After a cruel childhood in abject poverty, Lula receives the key to paradise: a diploma from SENAI technical school 129

10. Lula's fiancée makes an ultimatum: "You have to choose between the union and marriage. You can't have both" 149

11. "I know, doctor, my baby was born dead." "Be strong, Mr. Lula, because the news is worse: Your wife, Lourdes, has died too" 163

12. During his first visit to a foreign country, Lula rushes home from Tokyo: his brother is being tortured in a DOI-CODI prison 181

13. After years denigrating the political class, Lula starts building the foundation for the Workers' Party 197

14. While Lula faces the police and the bosses in ABC, Brizola tries to rebuild the Brazilian Labor Party and is blocked by Golbery 217

15. Lula brings together workers, politicians, intellectuals, and leftist activists to create the Workers' Party. Two months later, he is arrested 231

16. In the middle of the night, a polite man in a tie interrogates Lula in a cubicle in DOPS, sent by a general codenamed "the chief" 237

17. Clobbered in the polls, Lula sinks into depression and decides to abandon politics. He travels to Cuba, listens to Fidel, and returns to Brazil to win a congressional seat with the most votes in history 253

Epilogue 269

Appendix: An X-ray of the Large Communications Companies' War against Lula and His Party 277

Index 291

Political Party and Public Agency Abbreviations

ARENA: Aliança Renovadora Nacional / National Renewal Alliance—the official government political party during the Brazilian military dictatorship (1964–85)

CUT: Central Única dos Trabalhadores / Unified Workers' Central—Brazil's (and Latin America's) largest trade union center, with approximately 7.5 million members

DIEESE: Departamento Intersindical de Estatística e Estudos Socioeconômicos / Interunion Department of Statistics and Socioeconomic Studies—a research institute established by twenty trade unions in 1955 to provide accurate data on indices used by the federal government to establish minimum wage values. Over the years it has become an important source of data on a variety of issues used by labor unions to negotiate with employers.

DOI-CODI: Departamento de Operações de Informações - Centro de Operações de Defesa Interna / Information Operations Detachment - Center of Internal Information—the military dictatorship's information and political repression agency, responsible for torture and political executions of communists and union and student leaders

DOPS: Departamento de Ordem Política e Social / Department of Political and Social Order—a Brazilian secret police organ operating 1928–83 responsible for repressing antigovernment political movements. During the military dictatorship (1964–85), under the leadership of Sérgio Fleury, it operated death squads.

FIESP: Federação das Indústrias do Estado de São Paulo / São Paulo State Industry Federation—a politically powerful trade association representing 130,000 manufacturing companies

MDB: Movimento Democrático Brasileiro / Brazilian Democratic Movement—the official and only legally permitted opposition party during the Brazilian military dictatorship (1964–85)

MST: Movimento dos Trabalhadores Rurais sem Terra / Landless Rural Workers' Movement—a Marxist peasants' movement (with an estimated 1.5 million members) that fights for rural land reform by occupying unproductive land and establishing family farming communities

MTST: Movimento dos Trabalhadores Sem-Teto / Homeless Workers' Movement—one of Brazil's largest working-class housing movements; coordinates land occupations and self-managed social housing construction while working to pressure the government on urban reform

PCB: Partido Comunista Brasileiro / Brazilian Communist Party

PC do B: Partido Comunista do Brasil / Communist Party of Brazil

PDT: Partido Democrático Trabalhista / Democratic Labor Party—a center-left party that was created by Leonel Brizola in 1981, after the military dictatorship blocked him from naming his new party after Getúlio Vargas's PTB

PMDB: Partido do Movimento Democrático Brasileiro / Brazilian Democratic Movement Party—the updated name for the MDB after 1980

PSDB: Partido da Social Democracia Brasileira / Brazilian Social Democracy Party—the party of former Brazilian president Fernando Henrique Cardoso, founded in 1988, which initially emerged as part of the social democratic opposition to the military dictatorship (1964–85) and later shifted toward economically liberal conservatism

PSOL: Partido Socialismo e Liberdade / Socialism and Liberty Party—a leftist party that splintered off from the Workers' Party (PT) in 2004 and that currently has twelve elected members of congress and three mayors in office

PT: Partido dos Trabalhadores / Workers' Party

PTB: Partido Trabalhista Brasileiro / Brazilian Labor Party—founded by Getúlio Vargas in 1945, it was outlawed by the military dictatorship in 1965. When Vargas ally Leonel Brizola attempted to relaunch it in 1981, the military maneuvered to help an ally register the party name, and it has existed as an ideologically bankrupt "party for hire" ever since. In 2022, its honorary president, Roberto Jefferson—a staunch ally of Jair Bolsonaro—was arrested for shooting a female Federal Police officer during a standoff in which they tried to execute an arrested warrant for threats of violence he made against the Supreme Court.

SNI: Serviço Nacional de Informações / National Intelligence Service—an intelligence and counterintelligence organization established by Brazil's military dictatorship on June 13, 1964. Dissolved in 1990, it was replaced by the civilian Department of Intelligence.

SENAI: Serviço Nacional de Aprendizagem Industrial / National Industrial Apprenticeship Service—traditional institution of public interest; not for profit and without interference from the public administration

Map of the ABC region, the largest industrial center in Latin America

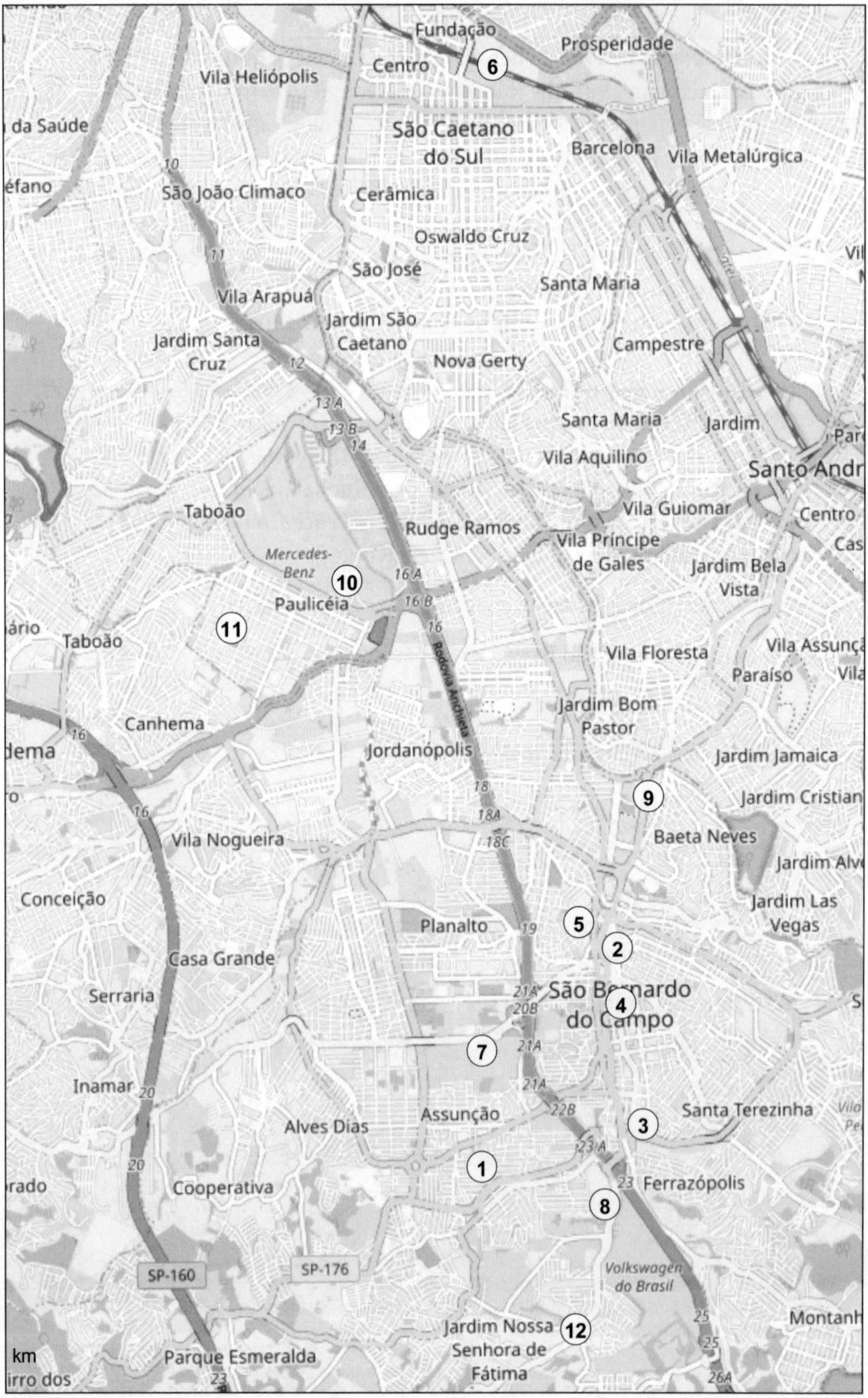

Location in Brazil

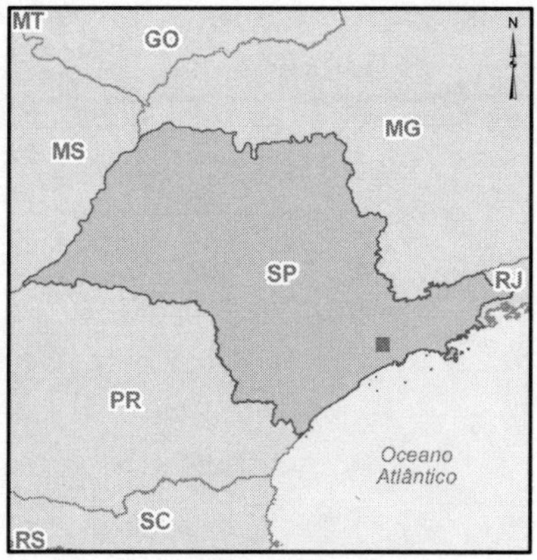

Location in the State of São Paulo

1 The house where Lula lived with Marisa

2 First headquarters of the ABC Metalworkers' Union

3 Current headquarters of the Metalworkers' Union

4 Main church of São Bernardo do Campo

5 Vila Euclides Stadium

6 Indústria Villares (factory)

7 Scania-Vabis

8 Volkswagen

9 General Motors

10 Mercedes-Benz

11 Pauliceia Cemetery

12 Rota do Frango ("Chicken route," once famous for its restaurants)

1

Sergio Moro orders Lula's arrest, but he decides not to turn himself in to the Federal Police. "They'll have to come for me"

As a listless workday at the Lula Institute drew to a close on Thursday, April 5, 2018, ex-president Dilma Rousseff, Senator Cid Gomes, Paraná senator and Workers' Party (PT) president Gleisi Hoffmann, and Lula's lawyers Valeska Teixeira and Cristiano Zanin sipped coffee and talked, while waving goodbye to the last few workers as they trickled out of the building. Tall, thin, and elegant, with the appearance of an altar boy, Zanin went out to the sidewalk in front of the building and told a group of journalists there that if the law was obeyed, there would be no immediate risk of Lula's arrest.

"Even within the perverse logic of preemptive arrest after the second appeal, the decision of the Porto Alegre Federal Regional Court should prevail," he said, "and it stipulates that an arrest can only take place after the exhaustion of all appeals within its jurisdiction, and this hasn't happened yet." Inside the institute, there was no tension, only a subdued mood of expectation. The Supreme Court had ruled against one of Lula's defense team's many writs of habeas corpus early that morning, by a vote of six to five (with Justice Rosa Weber breaking the tie). The move sought to block Lula's arrest until all his appeals could be ruled on, but its rejection opened the door for the worst-case scenario: the feared outcome that Sergio Moro, a federal judge from the city of Curitiba, Paraná, would issue an arrest warrant.

From a strictly legal perspective, after the Supreme Court ruling, everyone there knew that Lula's arrest warrant could come at any moment. The feeling, however, was that there was no reason it should happen immediately. In the squat two-story building with a basement garage, located near the Ipiranga History Museum on São Paulo's south side, the general opinion was that Moro would wait until the beginning of the following week to issue the warrant. Not everyone agreed, though. One of the dissenting voices was that of Senator Lindbergh Farias (PT / Rio de Janeiro), who had just arrived from a meeting with criminal law professor Celso Vilardi, dean of the Getúlio Vargas Foundation Law School. Vilardi, said Senator Farias, believed that arrest was imminent and that the warrant could come out as they spoke.

Lula didn't agree. Certain that he was going to be free over the weekend, he left his second-floor office, descended a spiral staircase to a short hallway with two sofas and matte glass walls, and asked for his young assistant, the sociologist Marco Aurélio "Marcola" Santana Ribeiro, if he could place a call for him to Moisés Selerges. A descendant of German immigrants, the stocky Selerges, fifty-two, who kept his head cleanly shaved and liked to wear colorful Hawaiian shirts, had worked for thirty-five years as a truck chassis painter at the Mercedes-Benz plant. He was the director of the ABC Metalworkers' Union (named after Greater São Paulo's ABC industrial region) and one of Lula's good friends.

Sitting with his back to the front door of the institute, Lula bluntly told his friend that he thought he was going to be arrested the following week. He asked him to organize a "secret barbecue" for a small group of friends that Saturday morning behind the union hall so he could relax "with some ribs and a little cachaça." As he waited for Lula to hand him back his phone, Marcola was surprised to see the lawyers, Teixeira and Zanin, storm in through the front door, looking furious. One step in front of her husband, Teixeira showed her smartphone screen revealing a headline from the news website *UOL* that was going viral around the world: "Moro Orders Lula's Imprisonment." Accustomed to Brazil's woefully lethargic judiciary, the husband/wife team hadn't imagined that the judges at Porto Alegre's Fourth Regional Federal Court (known as the TRF-4) would act in record time and, in the course of a single afternoon, authorize Moro to issue an arrest warrant. In the three final paragraphs of the ruling, published online, the judge had transformed Lula's legal rights of the accused into "concessions":

Relative to the conviction of ex-president Luiz Inácio Lula da Silva, we concede, in respect to his former office, the opportunity for him to turn himself in voluntarily to the Federal Police in Curitiba by 5:00 p.m. on 4/06/2018, at which point he will begin serving his sentence.

The use of handcuffs is prohibited under any circumstances.

The logistical details of his arrival *must* be negotiated with the Paraná Federal Police superintendent, Agent Maurício Valeixo.

Be aware that, due to the dignity of the office he held, a special room has been prepared in the Federal Police headquarters for the beginning of the sentence, in which the ex-president will be separated from the other prisoners without incurring any risk to his moral or physical integrity.

Sergio Fernando Moro
Curitiba, 4/05/2018, 5:50:10 p.m.

Lula's arrest warrant consecrated Moro as the leader of a political earthquake that had begun four years earlier with the investigation he led, the Operation Car Wash (*Lava Jato*) anti-corruption investigation, at its epicenter. Transformed into a national superhero through the support of a massive propaganda machine, the man previously known as a squeaky-voiced Paraná provincial judge, Sergio Fernando Moro, forty-five, now boasted of leading a war on corruption that was unprecedented in the history of Brazil. Under the spotlight of prime-time TV and on the covers of weekly news magazines while leading Operation Car Wash, he had convicted nearly a hundred politicians; owners, directors, and presidents of banks and private and state companies; currency speculators; marketing professionals; and even anonymous common citizens caught in the crossfire of the investigation—sentencing them to hundreds of years of prison. A constant public speaker at events for businessmen, lawyers, and police officers on five continents, the young judge puffed up his chest to brag that he had issued over 1,000 search warrants, a measure that enabled him to restore "over R$4 billion in bribes" to the public treasury.

The fury of Moro and his followers in the public prosecutor's office didn't stop there. Using laws originally created to facilitate investigations for felonies like kidnapping and rape, his use of coerced plea-bargain testimony enabled Operation Car Wash but created an additional monstrosity: the banalization of the plea bargain. Generations of

Brazilians had grown up believing that no one was sleazier or more infamous than a snitch, squealer, or informant. In Brazilian society, such a person was historically recognized as a scoundrel. This widespread disgust of the plea bargain was illustrated by the businessman Marcelo Odebrecht on camera in 2015 when, in one of his first testimonies in the Operation Car Wash investigation, he said, "Within my legacy I have values, including moral values, that I will never betray . . . When I'm at home and my daughters have a fight, I ask who did it . . . Sometimes I punish the one who snitches the most."

The hard-pressed businessman's moral code appeared sound at first, but it didn't last forever. He ended up bowing to the pressure of what Operation Car Wash investigators nicknamed "the velvet parrot's perch"—a reference to a torture instrument that was used especially during the military dictatorship. Operation Car Wash prosecutors explained the velvet parrot's perch as a process in which either the prisoner would reveal what they wanted to hear, or the prisoner would pay dearly. During the dictatorship, refusal to talk could mean the end of a prisoner's life. Operation Car Wash used the threat of abnormally long prison sentences. However, not everyone bowed to this violence. Workers' Party treasurer João Vaccari Neto spent two years in prison without opening his mouth, even when they went after his family. A top executive at Odebrecht's eponymous conglomerate held the following conversation with the author of this book, who promised to keep his name secret:

> "Why did you spend so much time in prison? What crime were you accused of?"
>
> "I wasn't accused of anything. I was held in prison because I had nothing to declare against Lula. When they discovered that I really didn't have any information that could incriminate him, they opened my cell door and said, 'You can go home now.' "

By the lethargic and bureaucratic standards of the Brazilian justice system, the rulings leading to Lula's arrest warrant were made with alarming speed. This created suspicion that they had been agreed upon in advance between three court jurisdictions. Thanks to the precision of the electronic records of votes and dispatches, we know that the clock in the Supreme Court marked 12:48 a.m. when it denied Lula's habeas corpus by a vote of six to five. Hours later, the ruling from Brasília materialized on the computers of the TRF-4 regional court in Porto Alegre. On that same day, at exactly 5:32:20 p.m., court secretary Lisélia Czarnobay sent a dispatch to the Thirteenth Federal Court in Curitiba authorizing the arrest warrant. At 5:50:10 p.m., head judge Moro issued a warrant ordering Lula's arrest. In a glaring exception to standard procedure in Brazil, in which these kinds of bureaucratic documents normally sit for months and even years in court drawers before they are acted on, Moro produced a warrant worthy of the *Guinness Book of World Records*, seventeen minutes and fifty seconds from the moment it arrived at his court.

Taken by surprise by Zanin, the group—which now included Lula Institute director Paulo Okamoto, Lula's aide Paulo André, ex-congresswoman Clara Ant, ex-minister Paulo Vannuchi, and Congressman Vicentinho (PT / São Paulo)—argued in the hallway about the next moves. Marcola stepped out onto a little courtyard decorated with plastic furniture and called Selerges to let him know about the change in plans. He said, "Bring Lula here immediately. The only place he'll be safe is at the union hall. Don't waste time at the institute. Don't take him home. Bring him to the union."

Marcola returned and gave the message to Army Reserve captain Valmir Moraes, chief of Lula's personal security team—the bodyguard service that all ex-presidents receive as a legal right—which was made up of eight military reservists. After a brief and nervous discussion, they decided that everyone would go to São Bernardo do Campo, the municipality where the Metalworkers' Union was located, except for Senator Cid Gomes of the Democratic Labor Party (PDT), who had to catch a flight back to Fortaleza that night. His quick visit to São Paulo had been fruitless. He had tried to convince Dilma Rousseff to run for Senate in Ceará, where polls were showing she had the support of 70 percent of the electorate. She had to decide immediately, since the legal deadline for moving official residence before the election season would expire in two days. Tempting as the offer was, the ex-president politely refused. Rousseff had already decided that she was going to run for office in Minas Gerais, the state of her birth where, six months later, she would bitterly finish fourth, behind three political outsiders. Still undecided as to how he would react to the news from Curitiba, Lula twisted the edges of his mustache while listening to everyone there. Captain Moraes approached and murmured in his ear: "President, it's hell out there. Let's go right now. It's not safe here. We have to leave before someone provokes some kind of incident."

The warlike scenario unfolding on the street outside the Lula Institute was a taste of what was to come for the next forty-eight hours. Along with the half dozen journalists who always loitered in front, on the sidewalk on narrow Pouso Alegre Street, a crowd was growing, comprised of curious bystanders, newspaper reporters, bloggers, and radio and TV crews that were already broadcasting live. Motorcycles zigzagged through the crowd carrying video camera operators hoping to film the ex-president. There were cameramen and photographers on the sidewalk, standing on the roofs of vans, and in three TV helicopters hovering overhead from *Globo*, *Bandeirantes*, and *Record*, all with their lenses pointed at the door of the institute's underground garage, from which Lula was expected to depart.[1]

Responding to the news that was going viral on the internet, radio, and TV, crowds for and against Lula's arrest were growing in front of the institute, blocking traffic and provoking a symphony of car horns, to the dismay of patients at neighboring São Camilo Hospital. The incident Captain Moraes feared came to pass as Lula's convoy left the building, not from the main garage exit but from a side door a hundred meters away on Gonçalo Pedrosa Street.

Seeing Senator Farias, State Congressman Emídio de Souza (PT / São Paulo), and ex-congressman Márcio Macedo (PT/Sergipe) at the institute's door, businessman Carlos Alberto Bettoni, fifty-six, emerged from a group of anti-Lula demonstrators and ran up pointing his finger and yelling, "Lula's a thief! Lula's a thief!" A group of Workers' Party supporters surrounded him, and one of them punched him in the face. Spinning around, Bettoni lost his balance, fell, hit his head on the bumper of a dump truck that was stopped in traffic, and landed on the ground, unconscious and bleeding. When he came to, he was walked to the hospital next door, where he was diagnosed with head trauma. The episode resulted in charges of attempted homicide and a twelve-day preventative imprisonment for both aggressors, Manoel Eduardo "PT Marinho" Marinho, an ex–city councilman from neighboring Diadema, and his son Leandro.

1 The main terrestrial television groups, plus SBT (Brazilian Television System).

The small convoy that followed Lula's car on the twenty-kilometer ride from the institute to the union hall drove through crowds of antagonists yelling "Lula the thief!," shooting fireworks, and kicking at the vehicles. The anti-Lula mobs had been directed there by news reports and by the commotion of the swarm of motorcycle delivery drivers and press vehicles that surrounded the convoy.

In order to lose the angry mob and the vehicles following them, Moraes ordered Lula's driver, Army paratrooper lieutenant Carlos Eduardo Rodrigues, to change the route. Instead of riding up Nazaré Avenue, which hugs the side of the Ipiranga Museum and empties on to Anchieta Highway, the group took an abrupt right turn toward Ricardo Jafet Avenue. Minutes later, at high speed, they turned onto Imigrantes Highway. This maneuver rid them of most of the press vehicles.

Sitting in the back seat of the black Chevrolet Omega, protected from view by tinted windows, Lula appeared indifferent to the commotion in the streets and the whirling rotors of the helicopters that were now flying so low it looked like they were going to crash into the vehicles. He spoke calmly with his bodyguards about the route change and, with nearly no knowledge of smartphones (it's possible he didn't even know how to use one without help), asked Moraes to place a few calls. He called his daughter, Lurian, and his sons Fábio "Lulinha" Luís, Marcus Cláudio, Luís Cláudio, and Sandro Luís. In conversations with each of them, he summarized what was happening and said he was en route to the union headquarters so that he could decide what to do. He told them not to worry, because nothing bad was going to happen to him. Between those calls, he received calls from politicians and friends, to which he repeated what he told his children: he was going to decide what to do when he got to the union.

Immediately behind the ex-president's vehicle, a black Ford Focus stayed glued to the rear bumper carrying army sergeants Ricardo Silva dos Santos, Edson Moura, Ricardo Messias de Azevedo, and Misael Melo, all members of Lula's personal security team. Behind it, a line of a half dozen vehicles carried people from the Lula Institute. One of them also carried João Pedro Stedile, Gilmar Mauro, and João Paulo Rodrigues from the Landless Rural Workers' Movement (MST). The MST leaders called their activists and asked them to head toward the union hall. As they arrived on a ring road outside São Bernardo, Captain Moraes realized that the change in route hadn't helped as much as they had thought.

Probably guided by the news helicopters, dozens of TV crew support motorcycles and vans with antennas on their roofs were waiting, engines idling, under Dr. David Capistrano da Costa Filho Viaduct.

Crossing the five kilometers between Imigrantes Highway to the union hall was like running a marathon. The commotion provoked by the motorcycles zigzagging against traffic, up and down the narrow streets of São Bernardo, brought even more people out onto the streets. Most of them were celebrating Lula's arrest. Laughing, some of the motorcyclists riled up the crowd, "It's Lula! Lula is there! Lula is getting arrested!"

The most aggressive elements of the maddened crowd didn't limit themselves to words and began hitting the hoods of the cars with Brazilian flags on poles. In the first two vehicles, six of Lula's bodyguards, all armed with semi-automatic pistols, suffered a test of nerves they'd never experienced before. Inside the Omega, Lula calmly spoke with Moraes and Rodrigues, making and receiving phone calls as if he wasn't the center of the maelstrom that had taken over the streets.

As night fell, there was still no sign that things would end well. The entire block around the union hall was filled with Lula supporters. In order to get the car to the building entrance, Rodrigues had to slowly push through a succession of human chains. Hundreds of workers, union leaders, activists, intellectuals, artists, and politicians from several states opened a path for Lula to pass through and discretely isolated all the entrances and exits to the five-story building where the last two members of his security team were waiting for him, Lieutenants Rogério dos Santos and Elias dos Reis.

As if on fire, the crowd repeated a single chorus of "Don't turn yourself in! Don't turn yourself in!"

A squad of Federal Police special forces agents lurked at a prudent distance of 200 meters from the protesters but were clearly visible. They were few in number compared to the crowd surrounding the union hall, perhaps a few dozen, but they looked threatening and ready for combat. The agents, wearing khaki camouflage uniforms and helmets, covered their faces with ninja-style balaclavas and toted German HK417 assault rifles, like those used by US special forces in Iraq and Afghanistan.

Philosopher and political activist Guilherme Boulos, leader of the Homeless Workers' Movement (MTST) and the Socialism and Liberty Party (PSOL), heard about Lula's arrest warrant at six o'clock that evening as he exited an airplane at Cumbica Airport in the São Paulo satellite city of Guarulhos. He was returning from a political tour of the Northeast, where he had traveled to discuss his pre-candidacy for the Brazilian presidency in that year's elections, which were scheduled for October. Hearing the news, he headed toward the Lula Institute. However, when he received a phone call from Marcola telling him that Lula was going to the union hall, he changed course.

The union hall was located in the same part of São Paulo's ABC region—a group of industrial satellite cities in greater São Paulo that is home to around 2.5 million people—where Boulos was originally planning to go when he landed in Guarulhos. He was already late for an assembly at the MTST's Povo Sem Medo squatters' camp—a sprawling 60,000-square-meter settlement installed in front of the Scania truck factory in São Bernardo, where 8,000 homeless families had been living for six months in nylon tents. The assembly that night started on a festive note: a celebration of the victorious dissolution of the camp. In exchange for leaving the area, which was the property of a local construction company, São Paulo state governor Geraldo Alckmin (a member of the Brazilian Social Democracy Party, PSDB) had signed a contract with Boulos to deliver 2,400 housing units to homeless families who were living in the camp.

During his ride there, Boulos called Josué Rocha, from the MTST directorate, and Andreia Barbosa, coordinator of the squatters' settlement, and suggested they announce what was going on in the assembly and propose that everyone immediately head to the union hall, which was only a kilometer away.

"This warrant is arbitrary and absurd—it's a political arrest!" yelled Boulos over the phone. "Everyone has to go to São Bernardo and guarantee democratic resistance. We can't sit back and passively accept this outrage!"

The assembly immediately approved the proposal by voice vote. Minutes later, a huge crowd blocked the already-chaotic traffic on Anchieta Highway and marched toward the union hall, which was now transformed into a bunker protecting the ex-president. The only people who stayed in the squatters' camp were the elderly, women with babies, and people with physical disabilities.

By the time Boulos made it to the union, there were around 5,000 people there, including activists, union workers, and members of the

PT, the MST, and the MTST, waving red flags and yelling, "Don't turn yourself in! Don't turn yourself in! Surround it, surround it! Don't let them take him! Lula's not leaving! The Federal Police aren't getting in!"

Upon hearing news of Moro's warrant, the PT-affiliated Unified Workers' Central trade union federation (CUT) called on social media for its members to join the crowd in front of the union hall. "We have to keep resisting and defending the greatest political leader this country has ever had," it announced. "To defend Lula is to defend democracy."

Soon, the streets surrounding the building were filled with an estimated 10,000 metalworkers and activists, who were ready to stay there until Lula decided what he wanted to do.

Despite the sturdy security barricades set up at the doors, the inside of the union hall teemed with people. Metalworkers from the old days said that even during the height of the ABC strikes in the 1970s and '80s, they hadn't seen so many people inside. Politicians, activists, and union members from across the country had arrived in groups and mixed with intellectuals, TV and movie actors, nuns, rappers, and innumerable reporters and photographers. The news site *Jornalistas Livres* (billed as "a people's collective without owners, bosses, editors, marketing, or censors") alone had managed to put eighteen young people inside the building to live stream everything with their smartphones. Apparently drawn by the news—nobody knows how—peddlers instantly appeared in the streets outside selling flags, T-shirts, and hats with "Free Lula" printed on them, and pushing carts selling mineral water, coconut water, cold beer, and cheap barbecued shish kebabs.

On the second floor, where Lula was taken, the only collective decision made was that he would sleep that night in the union hall. Moisés Selerges took on the task of improvising accommodation for the ex-president. In a hard-to-find room in the basement, the last in a labyrinth of gray hallways cutting through Eucatex room dividers, Selerges installed a platform with a double mattress, a pillow, striped sheets, and a cotton comforter with a green-and-blue floral print.[2] The union leader also went to Lula's apartment and picked up two changes of clothes, packing them in a small brown plastic suitcase. In the room next door, there was

2 "Eucatex" refers to the modular casement partitions widely used in Brazil under this brand name.

a table with ham and cheese sandwiches, cans of beer, soft drinks, and water.

Regarding the most serious and important decision—how to respond to the arrest warrant—the political circle around Lula was clearly divided. Senators Farias and Hoffmann, attorney Luiz Eduardo Greenhalgh—who had worked with Lula for thirty years—and social activists Stedile and Boulos argued that Moro's ruling should simply be ignored, transferring the problem to their adversaries. For them, the word of the day was "resist." They argued that the security forces would never commit the insanity of massacring the crowd surrounding the union hall to arrest Lula. This impasse would become a breaking story around the world and provide, in the opinion of those who favored resistance, an opportunity for international denunciation of the persecution led by Moro, the Attorney General's Office, and the Federal Police.[3] Even though this proposal came from two leaders of the PT and the leaders of the MST and MTST—the most relevant social movements in the country—lawyers Teixeira and Zanin were surprised to hear it. Although they vehemently argued, in Brazil and abroad, that Lula was a victim of "lawfare" (defined as the spurious use of the law against an adversary to destroy his reputation and delegitimize his arguments), the couple knew that disobeying the arrest warrant could cause Moro to rule him a fugitive from justice and order his preemptive imprisonment, a circumstance which would make it nearly impossible to obtain a writ of habeas corpus.

The essential question—whether to turn himself in or to resist—remained unanswered. Silent as usual, without sharing his opinion with anyone, the experienced Captain Valmir Moraes worried as he listened to the discussion. He knew that the Federal Police had no structure or training for breaking up crowds. He feared that any confrontation could turn into a bloodbath since a single bullet from an HK417 assault rifle could travel through six people. Moreover, while not everyone there knew it, the São Paulo Military Police were also on standby.

Less than a kilometer from the union hall, hidden behind the trees in a little patch of forest by the entrance ramp to Padre Fiorente Elena Viaduct on Anchieta Highway, Military Police riot-control troops were waiting in four gray buses, two troop-transport trucks, and two BearCat

3 Brazil's counterpart to the FBI.

SWAT vehicles. The Military Police, faces painted for battle, were supported by a pack of threatening-looking Rottweilers and German shepherds and armed with rifles, rubber bullets, and tear-gas-grenade launchers. All it would take was one word from the police chief in São Paulo for the police to dissolve the crowd that surrounded the hall and open a path, by force, for federal agents to enter the building and arrest Lula.

Concerned at the signs of a large riot-police presence in the area, Emídio de Souza called the governor's chief of staff, Samuel Moreira, to get more information. He was told that the Military Police were on standby by request from the Federal Police. Since it was a response to a court order, he said, the riot police had authorization to intervene if there was resistance.

As night fell, both the union hall and the streets outside became even more tightly packed. Moro's twenty-four-hour deadline was nearing, and nobody seemed to know what the outcome of the stalemate would be. Would Lula resist, or would he peacefully turn himself in to the police? Seeing the worried look on Moraes's face, Lula pulled him into a corner and gave him the first sign that he'd made up his mind. "Moraes, I'm not turning myself in. If they ordered my arrest, they're going to have to arrest me."

Afterward, he called Souza over and quietly set up a small committee with him, the lawyers, Congressman Wadih Damous (PT / Rio de Janeiro), and ex-congressman Carlos Sigmaringa Seixas (PT / Federal District) to negotiate the terms and conditions of his arrest. (Sigmaringa, known among politicians as the "only Brazilian who refused three invitations to be a Supreme Court justice," would die of cancer eight months later at the age of seventy-four.) It took the three of them an hour to arrive at the gray-and-purple São Paulo Federal Police headquarters in the Lapa neighborhood, where they were met by police superintendent Disney Rosseti and three agents. The conversation was polite but inconclusive. The PT committee explained that Lula wasn't going to voluntarily turn himself in and hoped that the police would enter the union hall to arrest him. Rosseti was worried:

"We have an arrest warrant, and we are going to execute it. We want to do this in the most peaceful way possible. Ideally, he would come here spontaneously. In fact, this is what the arrest warrant orders: that he turn himself in to the Federal Police."

Souza interrupted him. "Dr. Rosseti, this isn't going to happen. Lula isn't going to leave the union hall and turn himself in here voluntarily."[4]

The Federal Police chief politely replied, "The best solution for everyone would be for him to turn himself in. We don't want to have to conduct a difficult operation. I insist that we want to enforce this arrest warrant in the most peaceful way possible."

Sigmaringa and Damous said, "He is the ex-president of Brazil and cannot be submitted to a vexing and humiliating situation like this. We won't let him be humiliated."

"I assure you that he will not be submitted to any form of embarrassment, such as being handcuffed," Rosseti said.

Convinced that the meeting wouldn't result in any kind of agreement, the three men said goodbye, saying, "We'll go back to the union hall and explain your conditions to Lula and get back in touch with you before five o'clock tomorrow afternoon."

Even after they told Lula the news from the Federal Police chief, the politicians and activists who surrounded him, as well as the crowd both inside and outside of the union hall who refused to leave, went all night without an answer to the only thing that interested them: Would Lula resist? As midnight came and went, and collective exhaustion set in, the political tension seemed to lower a bit. Worried that if they left, they wouldn't be able to get back into the union the next day, dozens of people slept on the ground, transforming book bags and piles of old newspapers into pillows. Some politicians went back to their homes or to hotels in São Paulo, while others saw no alternative than to sleep in tiny rooms at a notorious fleabag hotel two blocks away. Lula went down into his improvised room, used one of the showers in the collective bathroom next door, lay down, and went to sleep, apparently still not knowing what he would do when he woke up the next day. For security purposes, and to guarantee that there would be images of any incident that might happen, photographer Ricardo Stuckert, who had been working with Lula since his days in the presidency, slept on a sofa next to Lula's improvised bed.

4 In Portuguese, the title "doctor" is commonly given to anyone considered to belong to a higher social class, regardless of their level of education.

2

While searching Lula's home, the Federal Police place a bug under his couch to secretly record conversations with his wife

As the sun came up, fourteen of the twenty-four hours given by Judge Moro had come and gone. Day broke with even more people in the union hall than the night before. The arrest warrant was front-page news in all of Brazil's newspapers and many of the biggest outlets around the world, and the rumor that there might be resistance had brought foreign correspondents and activists from all over the country. Traveling by car, bus, and airplane, a babel of politicians, social activists, legal scholars, priests, evangelical pastors, Buddhist monks, musicians, TV and movie stars, football legends, and mothers with babies in their arms gathered in the streets of São Bernardo do Campo. An article published online by Brazil's largest newspaper, *Folha de São Paulo*, that morning claimed, with no source, that part of the crowd was made up of "poor teenagers" who had been recruited from the periphery of São Paulo by the state public teachers union to "thicken the crowd in the protest defending Lula." One thing that was certain was that the majority of the people in the street, in disagreement with all the lawyers and some of the politicians, wanted Lula to resist rather than turn himself in quietly. For an unarmed crowd to defend against a battalion of military riot police and Federal Police special forces, however, seemed like complete madness.

Lula exuded calm. Although he had slept only four hours, he woke up in a good mood and spent an hour and a half on the treadmill and other exercise equipment that was brought there from his house, then took a shower. He put on a pair of jeans and a light-blue T-shirt, along with a blue striped jacket that Bolivian president Evo Morales had given him, and circulated through different groups, hugging people, consoling those who were crying, and making jokes with old friends whom he hadn't seen since the protests of the 1980s. From time to time, these conversations were interrupted to conduct closed-door meetings with union, social movement, and party leaders.

In a wing on the second floor, three large rooms were isolated and reserved for his family—brothers, children, in-laws, grandchildren, and others who appeared unexpectedly. It was in one of these rooms that, around noon, Lula had lunch with his relatives, telling him he still hadn't made up his mind. They urged him to turn himself in.

That afternoon, news that the water had been cut sent shock waves through the union hall. "First they cut the water, and when it starts to get dark outside, they'll cut the electricity," said Selerges, who was expecting the worst. "This could be a sign that they are going to invade the union."

Before leaving to hire a water truck with the robust Paulo "Big Paul" Caires, who was president of the National Confederation of Metalworkers (CNM), Selerges called on the people in charge of maintenance of an electrical generator set up in the building's internal courtyard. It was capable of generating 330 kilovolt-amps—enough energy to keep all the lights and air conditioners in the building running without interruption, as long as its tank was refilled.

He told the workers what to do in the case of a blackout. "Stand by the generator room door. If they cut our electricity, turn it back on, and stand here guarding it and refilling the tanks with diesel every three hours."

It was only after they rented a water tanker truck that Selerges and Paulo learned that the problem had already been solved. The state water company, SABESP, responsible for providing water to São Paulo's ABC region, had already sent two water trucks to fill the union hall's storage tanks.

Worried it would get tied up in a political scandal because a fake news story was going viral on social media that the water had been cut on purpose, the company's director issued a press release:

> SABESP declares that the supply of water to the ABC Metalworkers Union Hall in São Bernardo do Campo is functioning normally. Due

> to the large number of people in the building, it's possible that its internal water tanks haven't been able to meet the demand. SABESP is already sending water trucks to the site to guarantee the supply of water.

Less than four hours before Moro's deadline, a trickle of light at the end of the tunnel appeared as Cláudia "Claudinha" Troiano, Lula's personal secretary at the institute, called Senator Hoffman into a corner and whispered, "Tomorrow is April 7, Dona Marisa's birthday. If she were alive, she would turn sixty-eight. Why don't we organize a mass in memory of her here at the union?"

Claudinha was referring to Marisa Letícia Lula da Silva, Lula's late wife who had died of a brain hemorrhage in February of the previous year. Hoffmann saw in this idea the potential for a solution to the standoff. She met with Congressman Paulo Pimenta (PT / Rio Grande do Sul), Senator Lindbergh, Congressmen Sigmaringa and Damous, Piauí governor Wellington Dias (PT), party director Márcio Macedo, and defense lawyer Cristiano Zanin in a back room and explained Claudinha's solution.

"It would be inadmissible and unacceptable for the judge to block Lula from participating in a memorial mass for his wife, who died in such tragic circumstances," she said.

They unanimously decided to hold the mass, now transformed into an ecumenical, multi-faith event, at 11:00 a.m. the next day, which was a Saturday. All that was missing was to see if Lula would agree. Gleisi and the group quickly explained the proposal to him, and he immediately approved, even though it would mean disrespecting Moro's arrest deadline. "It's a good idea," he said.

Among those who disagreed with the idea of resistance was lawyer and former congressman José Eduardo Cardozo. As Dilma Rousseff's former minister of justice, some of Lula's supporters—non-PT members among them—mistrusted him, criticizing him for not "showing a pulse" during the abusive raids by the Federal Police (which was under his jurisdiction) during Operation Car Wash. These raids were always accompanied by hordes of TV cameras and reporters, who were often tipped off before even the defendant's defense lawyers found out what was happening. They also complained about how the Federal Police, under orders from Moro, wiretapped the offices of Teixeira Martins, the firm run by Lula's defense lawyers, for twenty-three days. Because they tapped the firm's main phone line, along with conversations about Lula's case, the Federal Police also recorded conversations with most of the firm's other clients. In all, Moro, the prosecutors, and the Federal Police listened in to 462 phone calls, totaling thirteen hours, fifty minutes, and four seconds. The conversations that mentioned Lula were transcribed by the police and sent, every day, to prosecutor Dalton Dallagnol and the rest of the Car Wash task force, along with Judge Moro himself. This enabled the judge and task force attorneys to learn about Lula's defense team's strategies in advance, enabling them to act preemptively to counter them point by point in the courtroom. It didn't, for example, look like a coincidence that Moro issued a bench warrant for Lula on March 4, 2016, during the time his lawyers were being wiretapped.

Moro and the public prosecutor's use of lawfare was in full swing at that point. Although the Supreme Court ruled to halt the wiretaps on March 16, Sergio Moro, hungry for attention, ignored the court's order and leaked to *Globo TV* parts of taped conversation between Lula and then president Rousseff in which she invited him to be his chief of staff (the conversation was ridiculed due to Lula's mispronunciation of the name of one of Dilma's staff, Messias, as "Bessias" and by the phrase he used to say goodbye, "Ciao, dear"). Warned publicly by Supreme Court justice Teori Zavascki, Judge Moro apologized. Zavascki then ordered that all of the audio tapes be destroyed; Moro refused to obey. Many PT supporters complained that, despite the fact that Moro's legal abuse ended up under investigation by the UN Human Rights Commission, the minister of justice hadn't even opened an internal investigation to find out who had participated in an act condemned by the Supreme Court.

At 6:00 a.m. on March 4, 2016—two years before Lula's arrest—the Federal Police ordered 200 agents and 30 income tax auditors to execute thirty-three search warrants and eleven bench warrants. Targets of the operations included Lula, his sons, and his grandchildren. On seeing Federal Police agent Luciano Flores at the front door of his apartment with a bench warrant, Lula told him, "I'm not leaving my home. You can either take my statement here or handcuff me and take me by force."

It wasn't a bluff. The law clearly stated that a bench warrant was only allowed when the accused refused to appear in court twice—which was not true in Lula's case. Despite this, the police tried to convince him that, "for security purposes," he couldn't make his statement there. Flores was referring to the dozens of activists who had handcuffed themselves to the front gate of Lula's apartment building in São Bernardo do Campo, who were threatening to block the Federal Police from arresting the ex-president. After negotiations with his lawyers, Lula ended up agreeing to let them take him, without handcuffs, to the Federal Police post inside Congonhas Airport. In the opinion of at least one of the lawyers, Luiz Eduardo Greenhalgh, it was thanks to the activists in São Bernardo and Congonhas Airport, where a crowd gathered in front of the Federal Police office, that Lula wasn't arrested and flown to Curitiba that day.

While Lula testified in a room in Congonhas Airport, his wife, Marisa, stayed at the apartment watching a group of seven federal agents—armed men and women in camouflage uniforms—scour every square inch of their home, from the bathroom to the kitchen, the living room, and the bedrooms in search of something they couldn't name. Mattresses were lifted up; cabinets, desk drawers, contents of closets, and houseplants were turned upside down. The police agents meticulously inspected refrigerators, and even freezer motors and stoves. Marisa watched everything with a frown, chain-smoking, without saying a word.

An identical process was simultaneously underway in their son Luís Cláudio's house and would be repeated later that week in the homes of their other three sons, Fábio, Marcos Cláudio, and Sandro. For reasons that were never explained by the Federal Police, Lula's oldest daughter, Lurian, who lived in Niterói, across the bay from Rio de Janeiro, was the only family member excluded from the police raids. Nevertheless, the terror caused by what happened to her father and brothers—police raids that were broadcast live on TV and the internet—induced panic attacks. Beginning the day after March 4, 2016, Lurian, an early mother of two sons and grandmother of a newborn baby, began waking up with a start every morning at six o'clock, regardless of what time she had gone to bed the night before, and calling the doorman on the intercom to ask if anything unusual was happening.

When the Federal Police took stock of its raids on the five homes, it announced it had seized 417 documents totaling 634 pages of paper, fifty-one electronic devices (desktop computers, smartphones, notebooks, tablets, and other devices), and seventy media storage devices (memory cards, DVDs, CDs, external hard drives, flash drives, and so on). While finishing their work in Lula's apartment at around one o'clock that afternoon, filling black cloth suitcases with papers, the federal agents took advantage of a momentary lapse in attention by Marisa to stick a tiny piece of Velcro under the living room sofa in front of the TV with a bug in it—a metal disk the size of a watch battery—that was capable of transmitting all of the sounds made in that room. Among them, naturally, would be all of the conversations in which Marisa participated. Quickly discovered by Lula's security team, the bug was deactivated before it could begin working.

To the frustration of the authorities, the inventory of that mountain of documents and objects seized showed there was no money, jewelry, valuable objects, or documents that could serve as ammunition for the war Moro and the Paraná public prosecutor's office were waging against the ex-president, his wife, and their children. The main body of material was dozens of bank receipts for installment payments and household expenses, old income tax declarations, checkbook stubs, bank statements, and receipts for domestic appliances, and an old instruction manual supplied by the Ipê fiberglass company on use and maintenance of two paddleboats. These were the toys that Marisa had bought for her grandsons that were later exhibited to the press as proof of their supposed ownership of the Atibaia country home, which became the object of another criminal investigation.

When it came to the media storage and electronic devices seized, the outcome would be no different. The only thing they found on the flash drives, CDs, DVDs, hard discs, and memory cards were images of children's birthday parties and family gatherings. Among the items seized were an iPad mini loaded with video games that belonged to Lula's young grandson Arthur, the son of Marlene and Sandro, and a flash drive with photos of his birth. Despite their content, these items remained in the custody of the Federal Police until the unexpected death of the seven-year-old boy from meningococcal meningitis in March 2019, at which time Lula had spent nearly a year in prison. Though the search warrants did not extend to Lula's daughters-in-law, the Federal Police illegally confiscated a flash drive that had the only copy of a master's thesis in administrative law that Luis Cláudio's wife Fatima had yet to submit to her university.

Indifferent to the suspicious glances with which he was received in the union hall that tense afternoon, Cardozo attributed the grievances to PT supporters who had accumulated a "ledger of problems" with him during his years in the party.

"I can guarantee that despite my many defects," he says, "these fights usually had more to do with my virtues."

He counters the claims that he was a minister who failed to "show a pulse" and colluded with the Federal Police's arbitrary actions. Although he thinks the raid on Lula's house was arbitrary, he says he couldn't punish the federal agent in charge of it because it was based on a court order.

"Look," he says, "thinking that a minister can punish a Federal Police agent because he upheld a decision made by a judge is a claim that could only come from someone who doesn't understand how Brazilian institutions work or the meaning of separation of powers."

Friday afternoon moved forward with dozens of small meetings, people crying, and others proposing physical resistance against the police. The barriers erected in front of the doors did not appear to be working very well—the union hall was becoming more and more overcrowded. As the clock struck 5, the tension in the air was almost unbearable. The deadline had passed, and Lula hadn't obeyed the arrest order. By law, at any moment, the union hall could be stormed by the police—federal or military, it didn't matter—to arrest him. Beyond that, there was a risk that Moro, irritated by the defendant's audacity, could order his preventative detention, which could result in tough legal consequences.

A closed-off area inside the union hall was transformed into a crisis room to deal strictly with legal issues. The lawyers started their work with bad news: the Superior Court of Justice had just rejected a motion filed shortly before midnight the previous night, in which Lula's lawyers had argued that by ordering his arrest before his appeals were ruled on, the TRF-4 had disobeyed the position that prevailed in the writ of habeas corpus. It didn't work. The crisis group quickly gained the services of two groups of jurists, Grupo Prerrogativas and the Associação Juízes para a Democracia (AJD). Along with Lula's lawyers, Valeska Teixeira and Cristiano Zanin, other important figures from the legal world were present, including judges Kenarik Boujikian and Magda Biavaschi, and attorneys Wadih Damous, Sigmaringa Seixas, Luiz Eduardo Greenhalgh, Carol Proner, Marco Aurélio de Carvalho, lawyers' union leader Aldimar de Assis, and Rosane Lavigne, Rio de Janeiro State public defender. They decided to set up a rotating group that would stay on duty around the clock to react in case of any abuse of power or arbitrary decision by the court, the prosecutor's office, or the Federal Police. Since nobody knew how long the agony would last, they set up a schedule for the lawyers that required some of them to sleep on the union hall floor among the activists and reporters. Despite considering the arrest warrant arbitrary and unconstitutional, most of the group was against resistance. Under such circumstances, obeying the arrest warrant was not an issue of a better or worse solution; it was the only solution.

Lula periodically interrupted the meetings to ask questions and speak with the lawyers. In one of these moments, he repeated what he had told other groups that day: taking refuge in an embassy was totally out of the question. Fleeing Brazil, he said, would provoke stigma that he was guilty and be mobilized against him by his enemies.

"Two weeks ago, I was with Dilma, Pepe Mujica, and Rafael Correa [ex-presidents, respectively, of Uruguay and Ecuador] in the town of Santana de Livramento in Rio Grande do Sul, near the border with Uruguay," he said. "The Uruguayan town of Rivera started on the other side of the street. Some people said, 'Lula, why don't you pretend you are going to buy a bottle of whiskey, cross the street, and stay there under the protection of Mujica. Or, from there you could go to the Bolivian or Russian embassies.' I said I was too old for that, but old enough to confront my enemies while looking them straight in the eye."

Between one meeting and another, Judge Boujikian gave Lula a talisman: a tiny silver dove of peace that he had received during the Vatican's 2014 World Encounter of Popular Movements, for which he had volunteered as an observer.

"Hold on to this charm, which was blessed by Pope Francis," he said. "In these circumstances it makes more sense for you to have it than me."

It was true. The exit doors were closing. The lawyers were continually asked to solve emergencies that almost always turned out to be false alarms caused by the generalized sense of tension. There was the threat of cutting electricity to the building and dissemenation of fake news that the military riot police had just been ordered to invade the union hall to open a path for the Feds to take Lula by force. During the process of negotiating with the authorities, the lawyers hit a brick wall. Sergio Moro was refusing to answer any phone calls, arguing that as a judge, he couldn't speak with the defense team under any condition.

One year later, when the investigative news site the Intercept exposed a series of Car Wash investigation secrets, the public would learn how dishonest the judge's excuse really was. Although Moro rejected speaking with the defense team, he secretly fraternized with and even coordinated actions with Lula's accusers in the Car Wash prosecution task force for the duration of the investigation and trial.

Without asking anyone for permission, groups of metalworkers closed all the access gates to the building with thick chains, steel cables, and rigid plastic seals, locking everything with thick padlocks and disappearing with the keys. Seeing this happening, the crowd outside yelled, "Lula don't leave! Federal Police don't enter! Lula don't leave! Federal Police don't enter!"

Night had fallen when Lula discreetly tugged on Marcola's arm, taking him to an empty room. He locked the door from the inside and turned off the light, leaving them in darkness. His aide didn't understand what it meant. Speaking low, as if the room was bugged, Lula walked to the window and said, "Marcola, look over here to see why I turned off the lights."

He opened a hole in the plastic blinds with his fingers and pointed to an apartment building called "The Place" on the other side of the street, less than twenty meters away. On the balcony of one of the apartments directly across from them, TV Globo had set up tripods, reflectors, and video cameras with telephoto lenses. Like hunters waiting for their prey, reporters and camera operators had their eyes glued to the union hall's second floor.

Anyone who witnessed that scene would have had a hard time understanding what would make the ex-president of Brazil lock himself in a dark room and gruffly whisper to his aide. With the blinds now closed, Lula asked, "Marcola, are you going to stick by me until the end?"

"Yes, President," he answered. "Of course."

"Okay. Then leave without drawing anyone's attention, pack your bags, and buy a ticket to Curitiba. When you get there, meet with our lawyers Luiz Carlos da Rocha and Manoel Caetano and wait for me."

Marcola became the only person besides Moraes to formally learn what the lawyers and some politicians were suspecting: even though he had passed Moro's deadline to turn himself in, he had decided not to resist arrest. In fact, even some of those who first defended a radical solution were now backing down. If there had been 100,000 or 200,000 people out there, rather than 10,000, as the most optimistic people calculated, perhaps it would have been realistic to consider resistance. The older union workers who had participated in successive strikes had already gotten a taste of the violence of the São Paulo military riot police, the cavalry, and the jaws of the police dogs. Union activists who had come up in the conflicts at the factory gates knew that the riot police would have no real problem breaking up the crowd—even if they injured a lot of people—busting through the doors and opening a path for the Federal Police agents.

The crowd who held vigil around the union hall, however, didn't seem to believe this. Within a few hours, the three streets around the hall were completely blocked off, occupied by tents that were set up wherever anyone could find a patch of ground, filled with people who had decided to stay there until Lula announced what he was going to do. Among the red party and social movement flags, the war cry continued as it had from the beginning, "Don't surrender! Don't surrender! Don't surrender!"

Ever skeptical, a small group of metalworkers discreetely began to prepare for potential resistance and stockpiled the so-called "earth shakers" and "rubber": long-range fireworks to keep helicopters from flying overhead, and old tires that could be set on fire at strategic points around the block to produce thick clouds of black smoke that would make matters more difficult for the police.

Inside the union hall, the meetings continued, always in small groups and in separate rooms. Exhaustion had set in. Even Lula had to force himself not to nod off when people spoke to him. Without abandoning the state of emergency, since the police could arrive at any moment, they continued their plan for the ceremony the next morning, to be led by Dom Angélico Bernardino, bishop emeritus of Blumenau and an old family friend of Lula's. De Souza, Damous, and Sigmaringa would be tasked with returning to the Federal Police headquarters that Saturday to negotiate with Superintendent Rossetti as to how Lula would turn himself in, conveying Lula's decision not to do so at the Federal Police headquarters, as Moro had ordered. If they wanted to arrest him, they would have to go to the union. It was nearly one o'clock in the morning when Lula, surrounded by his security staff, descended to the basement to sleep. Most of the rest of the crowd slept on the floor, while others headed back to São Paulo or arranged nearby hotel rooms.

3

GloboNews network runs a fake story—"Lula Will Resist Arrest!"—and its ratings rise 694 percent

One of the first people to return to the union hall the next morning, at seven o'clock, was MTST leader Guilherme Boulos. Learning he was in the building, Lula invited him for breakfast in the small room adjoining his bedroom in the basement. He told him he had decided to obey the arrest warrant, but that he would not turn himself in at the Federal Police headquarters. They would have to pick him up at the union hall.

"I am innocent, and I would resist if I could, but I am convinced that this is the best decision," Lula said.

Boulos insisted on resistance. "I respect your point of view, President, but I still think the best alternative is to expose your enemies' contradictions. Getúlio Vargas killed himself, João Goulart was exiled.[1] How will you go down in history? What will they do? Are they going to gun down thousands of people in the streets? Will they violently invade the union hall to remove you? All of the international press is outside. This will expose them to worldwide hatred. It will expose Moro's persecution of you. But if this is your decision, I respect it."

After breakfast, Boulos walked down the narrow hallway and, while approaching Lindbergh Farias, who was on his way to meet with Lula, shook his head no. "Forget about it," he said. "There's no way. He's made up his mind."

---

1 Getúlio Vargas was president of Brazil from 1930 to 1945 and from 1951 until his suicide in 1954. João "Jango" Goulart was president of Brazil from 1961 until he was deposed during a military coup on April 1, 1964.

The young senator didn't give up. He sat down next to Lula and made a final attempt to convince him to resist. "President, I know that it's all pretty much been decided, but I ask you to hear me out. You are innocent. You have committed no crime. You haven't done anything wrong, and there is no reason for you to turn yourself in—you are not obligated to do this. The whole nation and the world have their eyes on São Bernardo, and the repercussions are very positive so far. If we flood the streets with people, we can trigger a stalemate and will have a chance of getting your habeas corpus next week."

Lula listened to Lindbergh in silence, stroking his beard. Then he told the senator that he understood and even agreed with his argument, but that he was convinced that resistance could result in a bloodbath.

"I don't want anyone injured. I don't want anyone to get hurt," Lula said. "But I'm not going to get in a car and turn myself in at the police station like Moro is demanding. I refuse. I don't accept it. If they want me, they can come and get me here."

It was at this moment that the former mayor of São Paulo, Fernando Haddad, arrived with his wife, Ana Estela, and their children Frederico and Ana Carolina. Haddad and Lula had known each other since the end of the 1990s, four years before the 2002 elections. Haddad was a little over thirty at the time, a lawyer with a master's degree in economics and a PhD in philosophy. He was frequently invited to meetings of intellectuals at the public policy think tank then known as the Citizenship Institute (which would later change its name to the Lula Institute). The two only became closer, however, in 2004, when then president Lula learned that he was the author of two projects that had become important to his government. First, there were the so-called PPPs (public-private partnerships, created at the request of Planning Minister Guido Mantega). Months later, Education Minister Tarso Genro found a project proposal in the ministry's archives written by his predecessor, Cristovam Buarque, that had never been implemented. Learning that this proposal had been cowritten by Haddad, Genro asked him to expand on the theme, which turned into one of the key programs of the Lula administration: the Programa Universidade para Todos (ProUni; "university for everyone program"), which granted full scholarships at private universities to poor students and ended up putting 2 million Brazilians through college. "This Haddad looks like a toucan," Lula joked during a meeting with Genro and Mantega at the time, referring to the nickname given to supporters of the PSDB party. "He acts like a toucan, but he isn't. He likes poor people; he likes black people—this kid is one of ours."

This admiration was cemented months later when Lula nominated Haddad to be his new minister of education, a position he would hold until halfway through Dilma Rousseff's first term, when he ran and was elected mayor of São Paulo in 2012. Despite losing reelection to João Doria, the four years he spent running Brazil's largest city qualified him, according to PT's leaders, for more ambitious flights. If Lula was going to run for president in 2018 and the party decided on a straight left ticket, he was one of the names being floated as a possible running mate. In the event—unlikely according to PT leadership—that the courts barred bar Lula from running for office, Haddad could be his substitute at the top of the ticket, opening the vice presidency for negotiations with allied parties. Such was the state of limbo in which this "*petista* [PT supporter] with the face of a PSDB member" found himself on that morning when he visited Lula at the union hall.

The only member of Haddad's family who seemed nervous was his wife, Ana Estela. Lula calmly spoke with the ex-mayor and his son, Frederico. Daughter Ana Carolina teared up as she hugged him and he asked her how things were going at the University of São Paulo's polytechnic school, where she had just enrolled in an engineering course.

Looking in the eyes of the ex-president, without smiling, Ana Estela, a dentist and activist, asked her husband, "Should I tell him?"

"I don't know if it is the time," Fernando replied. "He is already worrying about so many things."

His words had no effect on her. Nervously, looking at Lula, she said, "President, I know that you are dealing with a lot of problems today, and I don't want to stress you out even more. I don't even know if I know you well enough to talk about this with you, but I have to tell you. I've been talking about this with Fernando since we woke up this morning and have to tell you, no matter how irrelevant you may think it is."

Lula looked surprised and asked her to continue. Ana Estela said, "I had the same dream all night last night that repeated itself over and over again. Someone or something was telling me that if you turn yourself in today, they will never let you out of prison."

With her eyes focused on Lula, she continued, "Yes. This is it. You may not believe it. I don't even know if I believe it, but the warning was clear. If you turn yourself in today, you will never get out of prison. So, President, I beg you, don't turn yourself in."

Her sincere plea for resistance, in fact, had precedents that Ana Estela didn't reveal to Lula: she had had premonitions in dreams before that had come true. However, she decided not to bring them up then and there.

Although he was impressed with the story, Lula told her, quietly so that passersby couldn't hear, that there was no real prospect of resistance. He had rejected the idea of seeking political asylum in an embassy, as some people had suggested to him, because he considered it to be "a confession of guilt that I reject."

In the basement, they could hear the cries from the street, which hadn't stopped, "Don't surrender! Don't surrender! Don't surrender!"

One of those who still believed he should resist was a man who had suggested he take political asylum two years earlier, and one of his best friends and closest confidants: the attorney Luiz Eduardo Greenhalgh.

On the day after Lula gave his statement to the Federal Police at Congonhas Airport, Greenhalgh went to the Lula Institute, where he cut right to the chase. "First they impeached Dilma," he said. "Now they brought you in by force for questioning. They are laying hands on you. They are going to intervene and arrest you. Do you think, if they've already done all of this to you, they're going to let you run for and win the presidency?"

"What do you think I should do?"

"You have to leave Brazil and seek political asylum."

Calling him by the affectionate nickname that Marisa and his kids used with him, Lula replied, "Mococa, I'm innocent. I'm not going into exile. I'm not leaving the country. This land is more mine than it is theirs."

"Lula," Greenhalgh said, "Perón lived in exile in Spain for nearly twenty years. He returned to Argentina, elected Cámpora; he was elected president, and then he elected Evita . . ."

"My dear, I don't want to leave. I am innocent. They have no reason or ability to arrest me . . ."

"Fine," Greenhalgh said. "Just don't forget that I warned you."

Two years later in the union hall, with his arrest imminent, Lula may not have even remembered Greenhalgh's warning.

In an attempt to compete with the frenetic speed of online news and social media, Brazil's largest media conglomerate, the Globo Organizations (TV Globo, GloboNews cable news network, Radio CBN, and G1) invested heavily in covering the events in São Bernardo, interrupting all its regular programming with live updates. Without citing a source for its information, GloboNews announced live that Lula's advisors were divided and that it was most likely he would resist arrest:

> Two groups have formed there: a political group and a legal group. The political group doesn't want Lula to turn himself in. "If the Federal Police want, they will have to arrest Lula here," says Senator Lindbergh Farias (PT / Rio de Janeiro), who is accompanying the ex-president.

Although, in fact, many people were defending the idea of resisting arrest, the claim that politicians were pitted against lawyers was not true. Aside from Greenhalgh, Senators Lindbergh Farias and Gleisi Hoffmann and one or two other politicians, the rest of the people supporting the idea of resisting arrest were social movement leaders or union directors. Nevertheless, Globo announced a bombshell story that Lula was going to resist arrest. Despite the journalistically vague nature of the story (GloboNews itself would later withdraw it), from a commercial standpoint, Globo had done something unprecedented. According to the Observatório da Televisão, a website that measures ratings, on the day of Lula's imprisonment GloboNews led all other subscription-TV channels in the country, with an audience increase in Brazil's largest fifteen cities of 694 percent over the same day the week before. Among these millions of viewers was judge Sergio Moro in Curitiba, who became annoyed with the "officialization" of resistance made by the GloboNews story. When Moro heard the news, he called the Federal Police and told them that if the idea of resistance moved forward, their order was to either arrest Lula or consider him a fugitive of justice, at which point he would immediately order his preventative detention.

Contrary to what GloboNews announced, Lula had been planning how he would turn himself in to the police from the moment he woke up that morning. After speaking with Haddad, he called for Gleisi Hoffmann, the metalworker Luiz Marinho (ex–union president, ex-mayor of São Bernardo do Campo, and ex-minister in the Lula government), and bank teller Vagner Freitas (president of the

CUT). Someone had to tie the bell around the cat's neck—as the Brazilian saying goes—and they were the chosen ones. As he told them what they had to do, he seemed sombre and worried about what might happen.

"I've already decided I won't turn myself in at the Federal Police headquarters," he said. "But outside, people are still shouting for me to resist. You will have to explain to them that there is no way I can do that."

Lula's decision had been reinforced by something else that happened that morning. Just before midnight the previous night, former Supreme Court chief justice José Paulo Sepúlveda Pertence, who had joined Lula's defense team, filed another preventative writ of habeas corpus in the Supreme Court with Zanin and the other lawyers, arguing that the Fourth Regional Federal Court (TRF-4) had broken the law by ordering an arrest before the appeals were ruled on. Although the defense team had demanded a judicial lottery procedure so that a justice would be randomly selected to rule on the habeas corpus (a right guaranteed in Supreme Court internal procedural guidelines), Chief Justice Cármen Lúcia decided to delegate the case to Justice Edson Fachin, known for his sympathy with Moro's war against Lula. The result was predictable. That Saturday morning, Fachin defined Lula's destiny in about fifty words:

> From this perspective, the complaint doesn't show violation of relevant command, as decided by the full bench in ADCS 43 and 44, which is why, based on article 21§ 1º, RISTF, I deny the complaint. The motion is flawed. Publish it, let it be known, and then file it.
>
> Justice Edson Fachin
>
> Brasília, April 7, 2018

It was apparent that, according to a murky legal jargon incomprehensible to most of the public, Lula's luck had run out.

A semi owned by the teachers' union, whose trailer had been stacked with speakers, was transformed into a stage and parked crosswise to block the street in front of the union hall, from sidewalk to sidewalk. The first speakers were Marinho and Freitas. Both were brief, and, judging from the reaction of the public, they seemed to be delivering a funeral announcement. There was no applause, there were no boos. Nothing.

Of the three chosen by Lula, Senator Hoffmann drew the most attention. Despite her jovial appearance, sporting a red T-shirt and hair tied back in a ponytail, she appeared to be suffering, unhappy with the job she'd been asked to do.

"I was moved by the people who didn't want the president to turn himself in, saying he should stay and that we should resist, and that if the coup mongers wanted to arrest him they would have to go through us," she said. "The last thing I wanted to do that morning was to ask the people to let Lula be arrested. It was hard to say because I wanted to be down there in front of the truck together with the people stopping them from arresting the president."

Even though she was acting against her wishes, Hoffmann climbed up on the truck's roof, above the speakers, and asked the protesters to let Lula do what he had decided to.

"He knows that you want him to resist, but he doesn't want anyone to get hurt," she said. "It's not just his legacy that is at stake here. It's his life. We have to respect it." Once again, no one booed and no one applauded, but some groups in the crowd kept yelling, "Don't surrender! Don't surrender!"

The religious ceremony started shortly after noon. Clad in albs and stoles, Dom Angélico and the five priests who accompanied him gathered around the microphone and started the ceremony. By the prudent decision of the bishop, what was first planned as a mass became a "Celebration of the Word." The difference wasn't just semantic. Unlike a mass, a Celebration of the Word can be administered by any layperson, without the presence of a priest. The bishop was stepping into a minefield. Even though São Bernardo wasn't under the authority of the São Paulo Archdiocese (within the division of ecclesiastical territory, it was part of the Diocese of Santo André), the political influence of the head of the São Paulo Archdiocese, conservative Cardinal Odilo Scherer, spread into neighboring jurisdictions. The care taken by Dom Angélico, however, wouldn't be enough to appease the cardinal, as would later become clear.

Broadcast via livestream, on all Brazilian TV networks, and on many foreign stations, a constellation of names participated in the ceremony that must have made a conservative Catholic like Cardinal Odilo, who flirted with Opus Dei, grind his teeth. Various different tones of red surrounded the white-clad priests and bishop. Along with Lula, ex-president Dilma Rousseff was there with Piauí governor Wellington Silva

(PT) and senators Gleisi Hoffmann, Lindbergh Farias, Jorge Viana (PT/Acre), Humberto Costa (PT/Pernambuco) and Fátima Bezerra (PT/Rio Grande do Norte). MST leader João Pedro Stédile was there with CUT president Vagner Freitas, Manuela d'Ávila—the young Communist from the Communist Party of Brazil (PC do B) who was a precandidate for the presidency from Rio Grande do Sul—Guilherme Boulos, São Paulo alderman Eduardo Suplicy (PT), ex-ministers Celso Amorim, Aloizio Mercadante, and Eleonora Menicucci, ex-mayor Fernando Haddad, and actors Osmar Prado and Ailton Graça, along with intellectuals, academics, and dozens of members of Congress from across the country from PT, PC do B, and PSOL.

The first person to speak was Catholic ex-minister Gilberto Carvalho, who read a letter from Friar Betto, a friend of Lula's who had been with him during his arrest by the military dictatorship police nearly forty years earlier. Next, former president Dilma Rousseff read a prayer to St. Francis. Then, Dom Angélico began the Celebration of the Word. A veteran of forty years of strikes in São Paulo's industrial ABC region, the bishop acknowledged the Metalworkers' Union's role in history.

"From here emerged a metalworker who twice became president of Brazil and left office with an 87 percent approval rating," he said with his arms raised, the sleeves of his cassock looking like two wings. "And with his prestige, he helped elect, and reelect, Brazil's first woman president, Dilma Rousseff, who had never previously been elected to any office."

Repeatedly interrupted by yells from the crowd of "Resistance! Resistance!," the holy man tried to calm them down and prepare them for the inevitable. "I really like to hear this word, 'resistance,' but it's important that the struggle is peaceful and that there is mutual respect. We can yell 'Resist,' but it's our Lula who will have the final word later, and we will welcome it."

Dom Angélico continued, saying he deeply regretted that "many people abroad are alarmed with the speed with which they are sending our Lula to prison." According to the bishop, the difference in Lula's treatment from that of "other people out there" was also shocking. His final prayer had the unmistakable tone of a goodbye.

"Here is a citizen who was already imprisoned, but no prison could hold his heart, his mind or his ideas. May Jesus protect you and serve as a source of strength, my brother and comrade!"

All Dom Angélico's care and prudence wasn't enough to tame the heart of Cardinal Scherer. Within twenty-four hours of the ceremony, the old friend of Lula and the Metalworkers' Union was publicly dressed down in a dry letter of less than a hundred words that was released to the press:

> São Paulo Archdiocese
>
> On the religious act held yesterday in front of the ABC Metalworkers' Union Hall, the São Paulo Archdiocese's Press Secretary would like to clarify that:
>
> 1) it was not a mass but an ecumenical act;
>
> 2) it was done through the personal initiative of those who promoted it;
>
> 3) there was no participation of the National Conference of Bishops of Brazil or the São Paulo Archdiocese;
>
> 4) the act took place outside of the jurisdiction of the Archbishop and the Archdiocese of São Paulo.
>
> The Archbishop of São Paulo regrets the political instrumentalization of a religious act.
>
> São Paulo, April 8, 2018

Finally, the microphone was handed to Lula. Emídio de Souza took advantage of the fact that all eyes were focused on the main speaker to discretely leave the roof of the sound truck. Unable to locate Sigmaringa and Damous in all of the commotion, he decided to go to the Federal Police headquarters by himself, as he later put it, "to fulfill one of the worst, one of the most terrible roles that I had to perform in my life": the negotiation of the details of Lula's imprisonment with the Federal Police. Distrustful of all the comings and goings of the negotiators between the union hall and the Federal Police headquarters in São Paulo since the night before, Luiz Eduardo Greenhalgh realized he'd lost his argument for Lula to resist arrest.

"We're fucked," he muttered when he found out Emidio was on the way to the Federal Police headquarters. "They're going to arrest Lula."

Microphone in hand, while saying his first, "Dear comrades," Lula was interrupted by the shouts of thousands who had come to the streets around the Union Hall.

"Don't surrender! Don't surrender!"

Hearing the chorus of voices, he turned inward on the improvised stage and, seeing Ana Estela Haddad leaning on the access stairway railing, walked up smiling and poked her, reminding her of her dream and her plea to not turn himself in. "You're the one who put them up to this, aren't you?"

Without using notes, Lula spent the first eleven minutes of his fifty-minute speech thanking everyone as best as he could. Only then did he start the real speech. He started off by explaining why he had decided to come to the union hall, which he had helped build and to which, he said, "we owe some of the victories of Brazilian democracy from 1978 on."

"This was my school," he said. "This is where I learned sociology, economics, physics, and chemistry. This is where I learned how to do a lot of politics, because during the time I was president of this union, the factories had 140,000 teachers who taught me how to do things. Any time I had any doubt about anything, I would go to the factory door and ask the workers how to do things right in this country."

Constantly interrupted by screams of, "Don't surrender! Don't surrender!," little by little Lula vigorously and didactically expounded on the adventure of the strikes in the 1970s and '80s; the repression; the salary cuts; the federal interventions in the union; the arrests of him and all the other directors; how his mother, Dona Lindu, died while he was in prison, and the final weakening of the movement that had paralyzed nearly half a million workers in the state. Only then, and constantly interrupted by shouts of "Don't surrender! Don't surrender!," Lula reached the subject that had kept the people in the street in front of the union hall since that Thursday evening: Judge Sergio Moro's arrest warrant.

"Now we are in the same situation we were in back in those days," he said. "Once again we are being tried for crimes we didn't commit. I am the only human being who is being tried over the ownership of an apartment that was never mine. They know Globo lied when they said it was mine. The Federal Police from Operation Car Wash lied that the apartment was mine when they opened the investigation. The public prosecutor's office lied when it filed charges saying that the apartment was mine. I thought that Moro would resolve this, but he also lied by saying that the apartment was mine. And he sentenced me to nine years in prison. This is why I am so full of wrath. At seventy-two, I will not forgive them for giving society the idea that I am a thief."

People in the crowd cried and hugged each other, and the calls for him to resist grew so loud that he had to shout into the microphone to be heard. He insisted that he didn't consider himself to be above the justice system. If he didn't believe in it, he said, "I wouldn't have started a political party. I would have started a revolution." If he were a thief, he said, he wouldn't be demanding that they show the evidence to the public. "I would be in jail with my tail between my legs and my mouth shut, hoping the press wouldn't publish my name." To the contrary, it was exactly toward the press that he reserved his greatest wrath.

"Globo's *Jornal Nacional* has spent over seventy hours of airtime putting me through the grinder! There are thousands of pages of newspaper articles attacking me. Record TV network attacks me more than anyone else. Bandeirantes TV network attacks me the most, as do all the radio stations downstate and across the country. What they don't understand is that the more they attack me, the better my relationship gets with the Brazilian people . . . I don't know if it's possible to issue a fair ruling on someone massacred by the press. Because afterward, the judge will say, 'I can't go against public opinion.' Whoever wants to make decisions based on public opinion should lose the toga and run for Congress! Choose a political party and become a candidate!"

With his light-blue T-shirt soaked in sweat, Lula took a short break to take a sip of mineral water from a plastic bottle and started up again, while the crowd continued its chant, "Don't surrender! Don't surrender!"

The next targets of his ire were the Paraná prosecutor's office, Judge Moro, and the TRF-4 court judges.

"I can't tolerate the idea that a prosecutor would come on TV with a PowerPoint presentation and say the PT is a criminal organization that was created to rob Brazil—and that Lula, as the most important figure in this party, is its boss. And in saying that Lula is the boss, the prosecutor said, 'I don't need proof, I only need my belief.' He should leave his beliefs to himself, his cronies, and his minions—not to me. Not to me!"

As his raspy voice began to crack, he took another sip of water, asked for someone to adjust the sound, and continued, "I am not afraid of them! I've said I'd like to debate Moro about the charges he's made against me. I'd like him to show me any kind of proof. I've already asked the judges in the TRF-4 to do it. I've challenged them to debate me at the university of their choice, in front of any audience they want, for them to prove that I committed any crime!"

Lula explained that he could take any beating when he was the only victim, but that he lost his patience when they began harassing his family.

"It wasn't easy for my family to suffer like this. It wasn't easy for my kids. It wasn't easy for Marisa to take. I want to make it clear that Marisa's early death was caused by the sleazy and immoral way the public prosecutor's office and the press treated her. I'm sure of this . . . Because these people . . . I think these people don't have children of their own. They don't have souls. And they don't understand what it feels like for a mother and father to see their child massacred, when they see him being attacked. That, comrades, is when I decided to lift up my head."

He started a long explanation of his "crimes," based on his government's social inclusion programs like the Bolsa Família welfare program and his social housing program, as he prepared the audience—which continued yelling, "Don't surrender! Don't surrender!"—for the main topic: his arrest.[2] According to Lula, his arrest was a dream project for the TRF-4 judges, Sergio Moro, the Car Wash task force, and Globo TV.

"For them, the coup didn't end with Dilma. It will only end when they block me from running for president this year. They don't want me to return, because, in their minds, poor people shouldn't have rights. Poor people shouldn't be able to eat prime cuts of beef. Poor people shouldn't ride in airplanes. Poor people shouldn't go to college. Their dream is to take a photograph of Lula in jail. I can only imagine *Veja* magazine's lust to put a photo of me in jail on its cover. I can imagine the lust Globo has to run a photograph of me behind bars! They are going to have multiple orgasms!"

As the crowd continued to plead with him, he railed on about the media. "You can't condemn a person in the press before he's had his trial. You may remember, when I went to Curitiba to testify, I told Moro, 'You don't have the power to absolve me, because Globo is demanding that you convict me.' They must know that we are going to regulate the communications industry so people will stop falling victim to their daily campaign of lies."

---

2 Bolsa Família (family grant) and Minha Casa, Minha Vida (my home, my life) are two emblematic federal programs of the Lula governments.

The rising tone of his speech caused the crowd to continue, with more and more vehemence, to demand that he resist. But this wasn't the news that he'd planned for his supporters. Speaking even louder to drown out the sound that was coming from the streets, he was interrupted as soon as he tried to get to the point. "They've ordered my arrest, and I am going to respect the warrant."

"Don't surrender! Don't surrender! Don't surrender! Don't surrender!"

Experienced in the art of dealing with large crowds, he calmly thanked the public for being quiet so that everyone could hear. "Let me tell you something. I'm going to respect their warrant. I'm going to do it because I want to transfer the responsibility. They think everything that happened in this country happened because of me. They ordered my arrest, but they'll learn that the death of a fighter doesn't halt a revolution."

The crowd continued, "Don't surrender! Don't surrender! Don't surrender! Don't surrender!"

The voices blended together as one, but Lula continued in a tone that signaled he was about to say goodbye.

"I am a builder of dreams . . . I dreamed that it would be possible to govern this country by bringing millions and millions of poor people in the economy, into the universities, and creating millions of jobs in this country. I dreamed that it would be possible to lower infant mortality by bringing milk, rice, and beans so that children could eat every day. I dreamed that it would be possible to take students from the periphery and put them in the best universities in the country, so that we don't just have judges and prosecutors from the elite. Soon we will have judges and prosecutors who were born in the Heliópolis favela, in Itaquera, who were born on the periphery. We will have a lot of people with college degrees in the Landless Workers' Movement, the MTST, and the CUT. This is the crime that I committed."

He took another sip of water and continued. "They won't be able to sell Petrobras.[3] We'll make a new constitutional convention. We'll revoke the petroleum law they're making. We won't let them sell the Brazilian Development Bank, we won't let them sell Caixa Econômica and we

3 Petróleo Brasileiro (Petrobras) is a publicly traded company whose majority shareholder is the Brazilian federal government. It is one of the world's largest petroleum companies.

won't let them destroy Banco do Brasil.[4] And we're going to strengthen the family farmers that are responsible for 70 percent of the food we eat in this country. And it's with this belief, comrades, with my head held high like it is now as I am speaking to you, that I will arrive and tell the officer, 'I am at your service.' "

It was nearly one o'clock in the afternoon, and the end had arrived.

"Comrades, I will never be able to pay back the gratitude, the warmth, and respect that you've shown me all these years. And I want to tell you, Guilherme [Boulos] and Manuela [D'Ávila], that I am proud to be a member of a generation that is reaching its end seeing two young people like you vying for the right to be president of the Republic. For this, comrades, a big hug. You can be certain that this neck is never going to bow. My mother made me with a short neck, so it can't be bowed. And it won't because I am leaving with my head held high. I will leave there with my head up because I will prove my innocence. A hug, comrades. Thanks to everyone who has helped. A kiss, dears. Thank you very much."

4 The Brazilian Development Bank (BNDES) and Caixa are state-owned financial institutions.

Demonstration in front of the Federal Supreme Court (STF), where the request for preventive habeas corpus filed by the defense with the aim of avoiding the Lula's arrest was being heard, March 22, 2018. Photo: Jefferson Rudy/Agência Senado. "Manifestação em frente ao Supremo Tribunal Federal (STF), onde ocorre julgamento do pedido de habeas corpus preventivo impetrado pela defesa com o objetivo de evitar a prisão do ex-presidente Luiz Inácio Lula da Silva." © Senado Federal do Brasil. creativecommons.org/licenses/by/2.0.

Presidential precandidates Manuela d'Ávila (PCdoB) and Guilherme Boulos (PSOL) with Lula, center, in a demonstration after violence against the PT caravan's journey through the South, March 28, 2018. "Manuela d'Ávila, Lula e Guilherme Boulos em ato contra a prisão do ex-presidente em Curitiba, no dia do fim da caravana petista pelo Sul." Source: Manuela d'Ávila. creativecommons.org/licenses/by/2.0.

4

Emídio learns that the Federal Police had not one but several spies filming everything that happened inside the union hall

Lula left the stage and went back inside, carried on the shoulders of Moisés Selerges and Paulo Caires, surrounded by a dense crowd that formed the shape of an orange spiral around the former president, drawing the attention of people watching from above. They were members of Brazil's Petroleum Workers Union Federation (FUP) who had come from the city of Paulínia, in upstate São Paulo, and from Rio de Janeiro. All were dressed in the traditional orange jackets they wear at work.

As Lula was finishing his speech, Emídio de Souza arrived at the Federal Police headquarters. Met only by Superintendent Rosseti, the civil mood from the day before had vanished. Rosetti, visibly angry at the hot potato in his hands, asked for news from the ABC region. Souza coolly stated that Lula didn't want to cause any kind of confrontation but that Federal Police couldn't bring any type of TV crew—something that had become common during the Car Wash investigation. Rosetti agreed, and Souza conveyed their terms and conditions for a peaceful arrest. As he spoke, a group of agents working on the operation entered the room and gathered around him. Calmly, but without smiling or bowing, Souza read the list of Lula's terms:

- The arrest will take place in the union's garage, not the main building;
- no filming by the police of the arrest is allowed;
- no handcuffs may be used, nor may they cut the ex-president's hair or shave his beard;

- all cars used in the arrest should be unmarked, with no Federal Police insignia or plates;
- Lula's transport to Curitiba must be made in an unmarked plane;
- the airplane should depart from São Paulo's Campo de Marte private airport and land in the small airfield of Bacacheri, five kilometers from downtown Curitiba, to avoid the hordes of TV crews and journalists waiting in the commercial airports of São Paulo and Curitiba; and
- two of the president's lawyers should travel with him on the entire route between the Union Hall and the Curitiba Federal Police station, including on the small plane that will transport him.

While Rosetti spoke on the phone with Judge Moro in Curitiba and tried to work out logistics with the Federal Aviation Bureau, a police agent struck up a conversation with Souza.

"So, how are things in the union hall?" an agent asked.

Emidio answered with a smile. "Everything is perfectly calm. If our requests are met, the arrest will take place in the most peaceful way imaginable."

A young agent in a blue blazer with glasses and long brown hair that fell past her shoulders named Izabella Mucida—former São Paulo Federal Police intelligence chief—pointed to her computer tablet.

"Perfectly calm?" she said. "It doesn't look very calm to me. That is not what we're seeing here on our live feed."

Shocked, Souza looked at her screen. It was divided into eight frames transmitting live and in color, showing frantic movement on every floor inside the union hall, including the second floor, where Lula was holding his meetings believing he was safe from the cameras. The Federal Police had infiltrated the union hall with several agents, who were using tiny cameras, placed on items like bags, buttons, and badges. It was all really happening, on footage he was watching live in the police chief's office. A summary of the police infiltrators' camera work, he learned, was being periodically shared with Judge Moro in Curitiba.

Chief Rosseti interrupted to explain that two of Lula's demands could not be met. It was too late in the day to take off from Campo do Marte airport, and poor weather had forced the Bacacheri Airport in Curitiba to close.

Souza upped the ante. "You'll have to ban private helicopters around Congonhas and Afonso Pena airports, then. Without this, we have no guarantee that the TV networks won't turn this arrest into a media circus."

While Rosetti made another round of calls to solve the problem, Agent Mucida pointed a finger at one of the tablet windows displaying live images of the garage building where Lula wanted to turn himself in. "Look at the chaos. This area is full of people!"

Souza said he was speaking with the union every five minutes and that the situation was completely under control. The police were impatient and uncomfortable with the race against the clock. They had made a deal that the arrest would take place at five o'clock in the afternoon. Souza told them that after the religious ceremony, which ended late because Lula spoke longer than planned, Lula decided to have a goodbye lunch with his brothers, sons, daughters-in-law, and grandchildren in the union. The police were getting more and more annoyed. After a long phone call with the union director, Souza suggested moving the deadline back to seven o'clock, two hours after originally planned.

Rosetti gave an ultimatum. "The problem of closing airspace over Congonhas and Afonso Pena airports has been solved. You can go back to São Bernardo now. But if our deal isn't met by seven o'clock, we're going to invade the union hall and take Lula by force."

In a navy-blue suit, white shirt, and tie like the rest of his colleagues, Rodrigo Costa—a bearded man of forty, criminal law scholar, and the chief arresting agent—suggested that Souza ride with him to São Bernardo because they didn't know their way through the side streets around the union. In the police headquarters' basement garage, he learned that the convoy was made up of five unmarked black SUVs with vans in the front and rear full of armed agents in camouflage uniforms. As they pulled out onto the street, he saw other unmarked cars of diverse models and colors join the convoy, guided by agents riding with him in the lead car via two-way radio communications.

The procession snaked through the megacity toward the south side, running red lights and passing vehicles on the right. Watching those unmarked cars, without sirens or the removable flashing lights stuck on hoods that Brazilians call "Kojaks," an average bystander might have thought it was a crazy drag race, not a police operation. But the crazy drag race ground to a halt in a traffic jam on the border of the ABC region. As they approached the destination, some vehicles were cut off from the convoy and had to park on the street, as close as possible to the union hall.

A diligent local municipal traffic guard, ticket pad in hand, walked up to fine one of the vans for illegal parking. The tinted window rolled down, and he backed down in surprise when he saw ten uniformed passengers in ninja hoods carrying assault rifles.

Souza and Agent Costa had agreed that the unmarked cars would give cover to the operation by parking wherever they could find a space, and that only two SUVs would enter the enormous closed garage, which belonged to the union but only had one entrance, on João Loto Street—a dead-end alley in the back of the union hall, across the street from the sound truck that had been used for the religious ceremony.

The agent ordered that everything be done as quickly as possible. "If we get stuck for more than a minute trying to get through this chaos," he said, "we'll be recognized, and this will be a problem."

The first part of the arrival went without a hitch. While Souza went upstairs to get Lula on the second floor, agents Rodrigo Costa and Izabella Mucida waited on the ground floor of the garage with a third agent. The rest stationed themselves outside of the building, strategically distributed in parked unmarked cars. All Lula would have to do is walk through the union gate, cross the alley, and enter the garage, and agent Costa could formalize the arrest.

Then, something unexpected happened that caused all the anxiety of the past two days to resurface. Lula was crossing the union parking lot toward the exit when a crowd, learning through word of mouth that he'd left the building and was heading toward João Loto street, ran up to the gate and started pushing the bars, shouting, "Surround him! Surround him! Don't let them take him! Don't surrender! Don't surrender!"

It was now impossible to leave on foot. Someone had the idea of putting Lula in a car and trying to drive through the crowd across the alley to where the agents were waiting. The vehicle chosen was the only one on hand—a silver Toyota Corolla belonging to one of the PT directors.

Dressed in one of his flashy Hawaiian shirts, Moisés Selerges stuck Lula in a rear passenger seat next to a bodyguard. Defense lawyer Cristiano Zanin, wearing a suit and tie as always, got in the front passenger seat. Slowly, the car advanced a few inches before being stopped by the crowd. The standoff continued as the crowd swelled with new arrivals from the front of the building who had heard the news.

"Don't surrender! Don't surrender!" they yelled.

A small group of union directors, Paulo Okamoto, and Lula's armed plainclothes bodyguards Captain Moraes and Sergeant Melo went to the gate in attempt to negotiate with the protesters and convince them to open a path, reiterating that Lula had decided not to resist arrest. They had hardly opened their mouths when their pleas were drowned out by the screams and violent kicks against the gate. "Don't surrender! Don't surrender! Don't surrender!"

Pushed against a narrow wall, photographer Ricardo Stuckert simultaneously shot from two Canon cameras, one pointed at Lula inside the car and the other pointed at the crowd that shook the wall he was leaning on to keep his footing. When the crowd pushed over the heavy, two-meter-tall cast-iron gate, barely missing Okamoto, Moraes decided Lula had to get out of there. Three human chains of metalworkers, arms locked, created a barrier to keep the crowd from entering the union while Lula left the car and returned to the second floor.

At that moment, the commercial airliner on which Marcola was discretely flying landed in Afonso Pena Airport in Curitiba. The hourlong flight had been hell. After boarding in São Paulo with a single item of hand luggage, he saw and waved at PT lawmakers Luizianne Lins (Ceará) and Marco Maia (Rio Grande do Sul), who were on the same flight. Then, he sat down in the first row. The last thing he saw on his phone before the captain ordered all electronic devices turned off was the headline reading "Lula Tries, but Is Unable to Turn Himself In."

After the plane took off, he tried to relax. He had slept only eight hours since Thursday. Losing control of his emotions, he began to weep. He cried during the entire flight, drawing the attention of the flight attendants and other passengers. He went to the bathroom two or three times to wash his face and try to pull himself together.

Back in the union hall, Damous and Zanin decided to call Manoel Caetano, Lula's lawyer in Curitiba. Zanin suggested that he call Moro and ask for an extension to the deadline so that the problem of Lula's exit from the union could be solved. Minutes later, he called back with bad news. "Nothing can be done. I spoke with Moro, and he is adamant. He won't bend an inch and demands that the deadline be met."

It was already well past six o'clock. Agent Costa—who had watched the failed attempt to leave on his tablet—called Lula's chief bodyguard.

"Moraes, we're only going to stay until the time agreed on," he said. "If the arrest isn't made by seven o'clock, we'll abort the operation and only return after the riot police clear out the area."

There was no alternative. Agent Mucida, who was watching everything on her tablet, told Souza, "They pushed the gate over, they keep yelling, and now it looks like they're holding an assembly. You haven't kept your end of the deal. We're calling the riot police."

Souza calmed her down and promised that before seven o'clock—that is, in the next ten minutes—Lula would make it. Then he, Moraes, Okamoto, Selerges, and the ex-president's security team put together the greatest number of people they could find and started setting up a human corridor to open a path for Lula to cut through the crowd in João Loto alley to the garage, where the police agents were looking more and more impatient, on foot.

Surrounded by Moraes, the other bodyguards, Souza, Selerges, and dozens of metalworkers, Lula came down the stairs in a gray suit and navy-blue T-shirt, without a tie. Looking tired, he clutched a bottle of mineral water. He didn't smile but held his head high.

Seeing the lights on the street and making a quick assessment of the situation, Sergeant Elias dos Reis took off his blazer and offered it to Lula. "President, look at all the cameras. Would you like to cover your head?"

Lula refused the act of courtesy. "Thank you, Elias, but I don't want to do that. I am not a bandit who has to hide his face. "

As they neared the gap in the fence where the gate had been pushed over, the group realized neither a human corridor nor a human wall would be enough to get Lula through the crowd of supporters and journalists, which had been worked up into a frenzy. Someone suggested they form a human wedge in front of Lula and his bodyguards and, if necessary, elbow and knee their way across the five-meter-wide alley. As kicks and pushes were exchanged between all parties, Lula was pushed into the crowd, which kept yelling, almost directly into his ear now, "Don't surrender! Don't surrender! Don't surrender!"

The crowd turned aggressive and threw things at the group surrounding Lula. A full plastic water bottle hit Captain Moraes in the face. "Did they hurt you, Moraes?" Lula said. "Did it hurt?"

After a very tense few minutes, the group arrived at the garage gate and met the federal agents. Lula went in with his bodyguards, Selerges, negotiators Souza and Sigmaringa, and defense lawyer Zanin. According to their deal, no TV or internet channel was allowed to record Lula's arrest. The only images recorded of the scene were taken by Stuckert, Lula's photographer. A young police agent in a navy-blue suit, white shirt, and dark tie waited for them. Respectful and polite, he took Lula by the arm to the door of the black SUV, where he met the arrest operation director, Rodrigo Costa, and agent Izabella Mucida.

Moraes and Souza formally delivered the ex-president to the police agents. Lula said goodbye to friends and aides with long hugs. For the first time in the last few hours, he looked relieved and seemed to have regained his sense of humor.

When Souza, his friend for decades, said goodbye, Lula couldn't resist teasing him. "That's it, Emidio," he said, smiling. "Now that you have turned me in to the police, I'll have to go."

Fighting back tears, Souza managed to force a smile. "You son of a bitch, I already feel like shit. You've got a lot of nerve!"

The last one to say goodbye was Captain Moraes, who looked crestfallen as he helped Lula get into the back seat of the SUV.

"Don't worry, President," he said. "We are going to come get you in Curitiba sooner than you think."

Lula sat down between Mucida and another agent. The young agent who had brought the ex-president in from the gate sat in front next to the driver. Five more agents, all armed and dressed in suits and ties, rode in the second SUV. Exiting onto narrow João Loto Street was complicated by members of the crowd who tried to block them from moving forward. As the vehicles moved farther from the union hall, other unmarked federal police cars that had been on standby joined the convoy, which was now making full use of its sirens and Kojaks to disperse protesters and cut down one-way streets in the wrong direction.

As he rode from São Bernardo toward the Federal Police station, Lula saw up close—maybe as never before—the level of hatred that had been stirred up against him and his political party in a segment of society. Tipped off by news broadcast live on all the TV networks, the radio, and the internet, anti-Lula crowds gathered along the noisy convoy's entire route, hurling insults and trying to hurt Lula. From above the viaducts on Anchieta Highway, they shot fireworks at the vehicles and threw sticks, rocks, empty bottles, and whatever else they could find. Glued to the back of the police vehicles and equally targeted by the protesters, Lula's aides rode in a Chevy Omega and a Ford Focus. Attorneys Cristiano Zanin and Sigmaringa Seixas rode in the first car with Moraes and one of the sergeants from the security team. Acting as a member of Lula's defense team, Sig, as he was known, had convinced the Federal Police to allow him to fly to Curitiba along with Lula and Zanin.

Hugo D'Antola, the winding street where the São Paulo Federal Police headquarters is located, was entirely filled with anti-Lula protesters. Contrary to its standard protocol for high-profile cases, the Federal Police had not barricaded the block. Many protesters wore the green and yellow of the Brazilian national football team. Men and women with faces contorted by hatred attacked the vehicles with fireworks, broke their antennas and side-view mirrors, kicked at them, threw rocks, and hit the vehicles with wooden boards. It was clear that if they wanted to move quickly into the parking lot and shake off the aggressors, they would have to run over dozens of people. It was understandable why the crowd's fury put everyone in the convoy on edge. Other than Lula, Zanin, and Sigmaringa, all of the other passengers were armed. If any one of them decided to react, even defensively, the situation could quickly turn tragic. Luck is the only explanation for how, minutes later, they stood safe and sound in the Federal Police building basement.

In an office reserved for this purpose, a doctor gave him a legally required medical checkup. Twenty minutes after arriving in the Federal Police headquarters, Lula was flying toward Congonhas Airport, which had closed its airspace for takeoffs, landings, and flights overhead by private helicopters, in a Bell 412 police helicopter. Zanin, Sig, and a few Federal Police agents joined him on the flight.

An incident at the São Paulo airport nearly ruined the agreement. Unlike his Federal Police colleagues, who were always polite to the Lula and his lawyers, the grumpy agent Jackson Rimac Rosales Alanic, director of the Federal Police Aviation Control Center (COAP), scowled at Zanin and said, "We're going to have to handcuff the president."

It was the first time the agents had ever seen affable Cristiano Zanin raise his voice. "No way! No, sir! If you handcuff him, he's not getting on the plane. You're violating the terms of the arrest warrant, which explicitly bars the use of handcuffs under any circumstance. Handcuffed, the president will not board the plane."

Agent Alanic lost the argument but not his attitude. "I'll bring them with me on the plane, anyway," he growled. "If they're needed, they'll be used."

"This will not be necessary," Zanin dryly replied. "It won't happen."

At 8:45 p.m., Lula prepared to board the flight to Curitiba, on the only unmarked plane available that night: a light-gray single-engine turboprop Cessna Grand Caravan, with registry letters PR-AAC. The Grand Caravan has a fragile appearance but is considered by many pilots to be a "jeep of the air" for its durability and safety. This plane had only registered one incident in twenty years of use by the Federal Police. In 2016, it made a forced landing with a flat tire in Campo Grande, in the central-western state of Mato Grosso do Sul, while it was transporting US$2.4 million in cash that had been confiscated from two passengers in a bus. This PR-AAC had transported other famous passengers, like arrested politicians Delúbio Soares and João Claudio Genu, and the drug gang leader Fernandinho Beira-Mar. Five months after Lula's arrest, the same plane was used to fly the bricklayer Adélio Bispó de Oliveira—accused of stabbing candidate and future President Jair Bolsonaro—from Juiz de Fora, Minas Gerais, in the Southeast, to a maximum-security penitentiary in Mato Grosso do Sul.

The group was divided into two rows that lined the windows inside the cabin, which had the capacity for two pilots and nine passengers—five on the right, four on the left, and a free space for the door hatch. Agent Alanic sat in the first seat on the right, Lula sat in the second, and Sigmaringa Seixas sat behind them. Cristiano Zanin rode in the third seat on the left, separated from Sig by the narrow aisle. A Federal Police agent in boots, camouflage, and balaclava sat across from the passenger door clutching an HK417.

As the plane taxied down the runway, someone listening to the same radio frequency overheard an exchange between the pilot and someone in the control tower that immediately leaked to the social media:

"Take him and never bring him back," said an unidentified voice. Pressured by the media, the Brazilian Air Force confirmed the authenticity of the leak but assured them that the comment was not made by an air traffic control worker. As to whether it was a pilot, the air force remained silent, although it wouldn't make sense for a pilot to say "Take him and never bring him back" to himself.

With a maximum speed of 350 kilometers per hour, the Grand Caravan took an hour and a half to fly from São Paulo to Curitiba. It was ninety minutes of absolute silence: the prisoner, his guests, and the police agents didn't utter a word. The arrival at Afonso Pena Airport went off without a hitch. As in Congonhas, the airspace was closed to private helicopters. Together with his lawyers, and surrounded by a nervous group of federal agents, Lula entered a helicopter and was taken to the Federal Police headquarters building where, according to Moro's orders, he would start serving his time.

As they prepared to land on the rooftop heliport at the Federal Police headquarters, the passengers saw a police battalion violently repressing protesters who had come to support Lula, who were now wedged between them on one side and angry residents of Santa Cândida, the middle-class neighborhood where the building was located, on the other. From the helicopter window, it looked like the Military Police, but they later found out it was the Federal Police. That afternoon, Congressman Dr. Rosinha, president of Paraná's state PT organization, had reached an agreement with Military Police colonel Péricles de Matos. Matos had assured him the Military Police wouldn't interfere with Lula's arrival, but, ultimately, he would not keep this promise. From his helicopter window, Lula could see people being clubbed and lots of blood. It was his last glimpse outside before his incarceration. In response to the state violence, hundreds of activists from different social movements and unions decided to set up camp, creating the "Free Lula Vigil" directly in front of the Federal Police building. They promised they would leave only when the ex-president was released.

As the Grand Caravan took off from Congonhas Airport, PT president Gleisi Hoffmann, Lindbergh Farias, Emidio de Souza, Lula's press attaché José Chrispiniano, photographer Ricardo Stuckert, Journalist Ricardo Amaral, and Otávio Antunes from the Lula Institute boarded a Learjet that had been leased by the PT. They arrived in Curitiba a half hour before the slower Federal Police plane but were still unable to say goodbye to Lula, because the arrest took place so quickly.

If he had come in through the front door of Federal Police headquarters instead of the heliport, Lula would have seen irony materialized in bronze: a one-meter-wide plaque fixed to the marble wall commemorating the date in which he personally inaugurated the building in February 2007. Indeed, Lula was about to be held prisoner in a building not only of his own making but for which he had personally cut the ribbon at its inauguration.

Around forty prisoners were held in the six large cells on the building's first floor. Some were foreign drug traffickers waiting for deportation, like Domenico Pelle of the Calabrian mafia 'Ndrangheta, who was accused of making cocaine deals with members of the Brazilian First Capital Command (PCC) organized crime group. Most of them, however, were accused of involvement in the Car Wash scandal, and a few had given coerced plea-bargain testimonies against Lula. Those imprisoned there included Antonio Palocci, ex-minister in the Lula and Rousseff governments; Renato Duque, ex-director of the Petrobras state petroleum company; businessman Marcelo Odebrecht; José Adelmário Pinheiro Filho, known as "Leo Pinheiro," and Agenor Franklin, both from the OAS engineering company; Gerson Almada, from Engevix; Aldemir Bendine, ex-president of Banco do Brasil and Petrobras state petroleum company; and the businessmen Adir Assad and Jorge and Bruno Luz, who were father and son.[1]

Lula was taken to the second floor, where he was met by agent Igor de Paulo and the thin, pallid, and polite Paraná Federal Police superintendent, Agent Maurício Valeixo. Both officers treated him politely and respectfully. Valeixo introduced him to the federal agent who would bring him to his cell, along with his lawyers Zanin and Sig. Jorge Chastalo Filho, a handsome forty-five-year-old blond man, six feet tall, was coordinator of armed escort operations and warden of the prison at the Federal Police headquarters. Together, the men ascended a flight of stairs—because the elevator only reached the third floor—down a hallway and, finally, arrived at Lula's cell.

According to Brazilian law, some authorities—among them former presidents of the Republic—have the right to do their time in larger cells that are referred to as "staterooms." Lula's "stateroom" was eighty square feet with two barred, opaque glass windows high on the walls, a large single bed, a little bathroom with a plastic curtain, electric shower, sink, and toilet, a table, four chairs, and a bedside table. Built as a dorm room for Federal Police agents traveling through Curitiba, it had never been used as a prison cell before.

1 Odebrecht, OAS, and Engevix, three of the world's largest heavy-construction companies, declared bankruptcy after Car Wash judge Sergio Moro used corruption allegations against a few top executives as justification for paralyzing their activities in 2015, causing hundreds of thousands of job losses.

When the police officer asked Lula to remove his belt, his shoelaces, and the drawstrings of his shorts, he smiled and said, "You can rest assured that I am not going to commit suicide. I still have a lot of things to do for Brazil."

After heartfelt hugs, Zanin and Sig departed. Exhausted from the stress of the previous few days, Lula refused a guard's offer of sandwiches, took off his jacket and shoes, and left his bag packed. As was his habit when he was sleeping for the first time in a new place, Lula kept the lights on. He lay down and covered his eyes with a simple sleep mask, like those given to passengers on overnight flights. This way, he said, if he had to get up in the middle of the night to use the bathroom or get a glass of water, he wouldn't get lost in the dark looking for a light switch or trip over the furniture.

Rather than praying, or cursing anyone, he immediately fell asleep and slumbered peacefully, without the aid of medication. After all, he was certain that, whether by political or legal means, he would be a free man within a week, or ten days at most.

5

After standing up to the neighbors and the Federal Police, the people spend 581 days shouting greetings to Lula. He can't see them from his cell, but he can hear them

Lula was wrong. If he'd known what was coming, instead of sleeping peacefully, he may have had nightmares that first night in his cell inside the Federal Police headquarters in Curitiba. The room where they had stuck him would turn into his home, not for one, as he imagined, but for an interminable eighty-three weeks of seclusion.

The next morning, the night guard gave him a cup of coffee with milk and a piece of bread with butter. The "stateroom" where he had slept had no view of the street, where 1,500 people had spent the night. Most were union members from across the country or members of the Landless Rural Workers' Movement (MST). At a crossroads, 300 meters from the Federal Police building, someone had already painted an enormous circle with the words "Praça Olga Benario" (Olga Benario Square), written in letters large enough to read from the top of a ten-story building. The name honoured the Jewish wife of Brazilian Communist leader Luís Carlos Prestes, who was deported to Nazi Germany during World War II and murdered in a gas chamber in Auschwitz.

The Free Lula Vigil the activists set up that first day became a place where people would visit from around the world. In order to stay there, the activists would ultimately have to contend with successive legal problems with the police and with the neighbors in the upper-middle-class neighborhood of Santa Candida where the Federal Police headquarters was located. During the 581 days Lula would spend in prison, activists at the vigil rotated continuously, without abandoning the location for a single minute. On some days, the size of the group shrunk to a few dozen people, but on special occasions—May Day, Lula's birthday, a ruling on an important appeal, or the visit of a foreign head of state—the crowd would swell to over 2,000.

During the eighty-three weeks Lula was held prisoner, the vigil was visited by dozens of union leaders, businesspeople, economists, movie stars, artists, and musicians from Brazil and abroad, as well as by religious leaders of diverse faiths, personal friends, family members, and politicians from every state in Brazil. Five foreign ex-heads of state visited Lula, including Massimo D'Alema (Italy), Eduardo Duhalde (Argentina), Ernesto Samper (Colombia), and José "Pepe" Mujica (Uruguay). He was visited by future Argentine president Alberto Fernández, who interrupted a difficult campaign season to come to the prison, wearing a red "Free Lula" cap. The former president was visited by two Nobel Peace Prize laureates, Adolfo Pérez Esquivel and Kailash Satyarthi. Foreign politicians Cuauhtémoc Cárdenas (ex-governor of Mexico's Federal District), Jean-Luc Mélenchon (parliamentarian from the left-wing La France Insoumise party and former candidate for the French presidency), Argentinian economist Juan Grabois, an envoy of Pope Francis (who was barred from visiting Lula to give him a rosary blessed by the pope because "it didn't qualify as a religious visit"), French Communist senator Laurence Cohen and German Social Democratic parliamentarian Martin Schulz. Union leaders who came to visit the former president included American Federation of Labor and Congress of Industrial Organizations (AFL-CIO) president Richard Trumka, Spanish union leader Pepe Álvarez (UGT), International Trade Union Confederation (ITUC) general secretary Sharan Burrou, and United Food and Commercial Workers (UFCW) international relations director Stanley Gacek.

Although the Brazilian press published little to nothing about the vigil—even during visits by renowned intellectuals like Noam Chomsky and Hollywood celebrities like Danny Glover—within a few weeks the electrifying activity that developed in front of the barbed wire fence of the Federal Police headquarters transformed the Free Lula Vigil into an object of curiosity that started being included in sightseeing tours for visitors to Curitiba. All of these characteristics contributed to transform the vigil into not simply a protest site against an arbitrary imprisonment but an international space for expressing discontent and protesting against inequality and injustice in Brazil and around the world.

From the cell where he ate his first frugal breakfast that Monday, April 9, 2018, Lula couldn't see any of this; the opaque, barred Venetian windows revealed only a blurry patch of sky and the tops of the araucaria pines over the empty neighboring lot where the vigil would be set up.

That Monday, nine kilometers away in the modest and sombre Petras Hotel, which boasted of an undeserved four stars, PT president Gleisi Hoffmann held a meeting in a rented conference room with the national party directorate and the support group that had been in Curitiba from the moment of Lula's incarceration. When Lula's cell door shut on that first Sunday night, the whole tired and disheartened group went to the Petras together, feeling broken and stressed. Many of them had not slept for three days. Hoffmann took control, saying, "Let's all take showers, eat, and get some sleep so that we can get an early start tomorrow."

The Petras would turn into a command center for the PT, activists, advisors, photographers, security officers, defense attorneys, and lawyers from the progressive Grupo Prerrogativas, all working together to decide what could be done to guarantee Lula's stay in prison would be as short as possible. Two of the people there were from the PT's inner circle, attorneys Luiz Carlos da Rocha, sixty-two, and Manoel Caetano, sixty-five. First cousins, both were children of Northeasterners who were respected among Paraná's legal elite. Rocha, nicknamed "Rochinha," had been a communist from birth, the son of a Communist father who was persecuted by the dictatorship as a member of the Central Committee of the Brazilian Communist Party (PCB). Manoel's political awakening took place in the MST, a social movement that he would never leave, and both ended up joining the Workers' Party. It is a peculiarity of Brazilian culture that a man like Rochinha, despite having political alliances that were viewed as frightening in the conservative state of Paraná, with his Italian doctorate and reputation as a wine connoisseur, could be the owner of a lucrative law firm that worked for large corporations in and out of state. Manoel Caetano had a respected academic career as law professor at Paraná Federal University. More than cousins, they seemed like fraternal twins. And, due to the idiosyncrasies of Paraná culture, they happened to be, or to have had been, friends with Sergio Moro and Supreme Court justice Edson Fachin, who was a big ally of the Car Wash investigation.

Both had been recruited by Roberto Teixeira, a friend of Lula and the father-in-law of Cristiano Zanin. Teixeira had known them for years, and it was because of him that they represented Cristiano and his wife Valeska in Curitiba, a task the two old leftists happily accepted, with one caveat: they would do it pro bono and wouldn't take no for an answer. After all, they said, if they calculated how much it would cost to guarantee Lula a minimally comfortable prison stay, the total would be ridiculously high. As Lula's designated lawyers, they would have the legal right to visit him as much as they wanted, any day of the week, respecting the times stipulated by law, between 8:00 a.m. and 7:00 p.m. (excluding Saturdays, Sundays, and holidays because Lula wasn't in a normal prison but a public building that closed its doors outside of commercial hours).

The first to visit Lula was Manoel Caetano, who only knew him from the news. Seeing that the door was shut, he asked the jailer, Jorge Chastalo Filho, to open it so he could have his first contact with his client. That morning, Lula had eaten breakfast and gone back to bed. Caetano saw him lying in bed in the fetal position, silently shut the door, and told the jailer that he would wait in the hallway until Lula woke up.

When the lawyer came back in, he introduced himself respectfully, and they spoke about the case, prison, and trivialities. Toward the end of the morning, Caetano's partner, Luiz Carlos da Rocha, arrived and introduced himself. As was his habit, Lula asked the two lawyers a lot of questions. He found out that they were what Brazilians called "cousin-brothers" (cousins who had been raised in the same household) and was surprised to learn that Rochinha was born in Buique, a town in the Agreste region of Pernambuco, only sixty kilometers from his birthplace of Caetés.

Rochinha and Caetano's visits were never restricted in any way by the jailers. Lula's prison stay took place under the care of a group that varied in number between eight and ten federal agents from the Operations Department, directed by Jorge Chastalo, who became more popular with the public for his physical appearance than for the fact that he was in charge of the incarceration of an ex-president of the Republic. Intelligent, well informed, and refined, but a man of few words who rarely smiled, Chastalo, at the end of his task when Lula was freed, now at the height of his career, was appointed as a police attaché to the embassy in Lima, Peru, where he lives to this day with his wife and two teenage daughters. In addition to Chastalo, another jailer who Lula grew close to was Paulo Rocha Gonçalves Jr., nicknamed Paulão, a good-natured Afro-Brazilian man who had an imposing physique equal or superior to that of his ruggedly handsome coworker.

Two or three other agents would sit to the right of the door to Lula's cell, in front of a security monitor, whose cameras guaranteed the supervision of any person who wanted to enter the floor where Lula was being held. A small TV located next to the monitor made the job less monotonous—since this monitoring service operated twenty-four hours a day, seven days a week. A door at the end of the hallway opened onto a courtyard with high walls but no roof, a sinister-looking place that gave one the impression of an abandoned kennel. This was normally used as a smoking area where agents would meet for a cigarette. With the arrival of Lula, the approximately three-by-two-meter rectangular space, which had a concrete block in the middle that looked like a water tank, was converted into an area where he could exercise his legal right to a daily sunbath.

Even when he was off duty, Chastalo brought along his two-way radio, which maintained a dedicated line of communication to those worn by the jailers who guarded Lula's cell.

Lula, who had never been exactly sedentary, took advantage of his time in prison to exercise. In addition to rubber resistance bands that he used to work on his pectorals, Rochinha managed to get him a used treadmill, which had to be exchanged for a new one weeks later.

"Rochinha, I think you bought this treadmill in a junkyard," he complained. "I have to brace one of my feet on the floor like I am roller skating to get it to work at all."

Smiling, the lawyer went out and bought a new one; he would never let the PT or Zanin reimburse him for anything. Judging by Lula's boasts to visiting friends, it looked like his workouts were showing results. "I've become a very young man," he would say with a mischievous smile. "In biological terms, I'm seventy-two, but I have the energy of a thirty-year-old and the vigor of a twenty-year-old."

For the Petras Hotel group, one of the first orders of business was to visit the vigil. The neighbors were already annoyed with the crowd of strangers wandering the carefully manicured sidewalks of Santa Cândida. During the first few weeks, they pressured local authorities to issue an eviction order from all public space in the neighborhood—something that, in theory, could have destroyed the vigil. The union members, MST activists, lawyers, and politicians quickly organized a kitty, transforming the problem into a solution that was even better than the original idea. They leased the empty lot directly in front of the Federal Police station and, a few hours after the contract had been signed, around 1,200 people divided tasks to organize it. Experienced at occupations, the MST, within a few hours, had set up a huge tent covering half the lot, a collective kitchen, and a coffee stand. In addition to the lot, "the collective," as they referred to themselves, rented a sizeable house fifty meters from the vigil, with rooms for overnight stays and a garage, which was transformed into a communications center where a group of volunteers recorded the most important images of the day at the vigil and uploaded it all on the internet.

Since they could no longer complain about the physical presence of the activists, the well-heeled residents of Santa Cândida filed a noise complaint with the police, claiming the protestors were singing all night, disturbing the peace. Curitiba mayor Rafael Greca, from the conservative Democratas party, accepted the complaint and issued a fine for municipal noise-law infractions of R$500,000 per day. Two neighborhood residents filed charges that "protesters from the PT, the CUT, and MST" were overrunning the streets where they lived and demanded an end to the "disturbance of the peace," which they defined as "noise all day and parties all night where alcoholic beverages and drugs were consumed."

Ultimately, the vigil ended up striking a deal with the city inspectors and the Military Police. The Municipal Law of Silence would be rigorously respected, respecting the noise limit of forty-five decibels between 10:00 p.m. and 7:00 a.m. However, the protesters refused to budge on something that would become a tradition lasting until the last day of Lula's imprisonment: every day at 9:00 a.m., 2:30 p.m., and 7:00 p.m., the people at the vigil would shout, in unison, thirteen times (representing PT's ballot number), "Good morning, President!," "Good afternoon, President," and "Good night, President!" A few weeks later, the peace deal with the authorities was not enough to prevent a neighbor named Gastão Schefer, a forty-five-year-old Federal Police agent, from kicking and breaking sound system the vigil used during daylight hours to amplify the voices of Lula's supporters. Schefer only escaped a severe beating due to the intervention of the vigil's own volunteer security staff and was himself arrested afterward for disturbing the peace. Schefer went on to run for Congress that year for Jair Bolsonaro's ultraconservative Social Liberty Party (PSL), receiving a modest 4,670 votes, earning him the 111th place in the line of succession—that is, in the event that another 110 PSL congressmen from his state resigned. Transferred by his employer to Caxias do Sul in Rio Grande do Sul state, Gastão Schefer died on August 9, 2021. According to the Federal Police, he committed suicide.

Visits to Lula were regulated through a strict official schedule. Monday afternoons from four to five were reserved for visits from religious leaders. During his time in prison, he was visited by priests, friars, Buddhist monks, evangelical pastors, imams, rabbis, and *pais de santo*.[1] Eventually, due to authorization from Department of Corrections judge Carolina Lebbos, national political leaders were allowed to visit him on Tuesdays. Known for her bad faith toward Lula, Judge Lebbos barred eight lawmakers from the Congressional Human Rights Commission from inspecting the conditions under which he was serving his sentence. Overruled by Supreme Court Justice Fachin, her decision fell back to earth and the members of the commission were eventually allowed to conduct their official visit. Judge Lebbos also barred two personal visits, by journalist Mino Carta and the author of this book—who had scheduled a visit and already traveled together to Curitiba—arguing that Lula was barred from giving interviews to the press. This ruling was made despite the fact that neither of the two men had planned to visit Lula as journalists. Children and grandchildren of the ex-president could visit him on Thursdays from 9:30 to 12:00 and from 1:30 to 4:00. During at least one of these visits, the family was authorized to eat lunch with him.

When family members didn't use all of the visitation time on Thursdays, part of the day was reserved for foreign visitors. It was on Thursday, July 21, after the visit of Uruguayan ex-president José "Pepe" Mujica, that Lula received news that caused a crisis among his defense team. Lula's chief defense lawyer, Cristiano Zanin, had filed yet another writ of habeas corpus with the Supreme Court. Without consulting with either Lula or Zanin, José Paulo Sepúlveda Pertence, also a member of

1 A *pai de santo* (father of the saint), or *babalorixá* in the Yoruba language, is a priest in Afro-Brazilian religions such as candomblé and macumba.

the defense team, had added a clause requesting that Lula be granted the right to wait for his appeals processes to play out in freedom. The way this legal privilege was used by the Car Wash task force, it implied, if granted, that they would put an ankle monitor on the defendant and transfer him to house arrest. Despite being an old friend of Lula's, the respected octogenarian Sepúlveda Pertence apparently didn't know that Lula would have preferred to meet the devil than to accept house arrest and an electronic ankle bracelet. In fact, Lula had made this very clear on April 7, during his speech in front of the union hall in São Bernardo hours before he was arrested.

Even before this, on December 3, 2016, two years and four months before his arrest, Lula had rejected the idea while speaking to a group of friends en route to Fidel Castro's funeral in Santiago de Cuba. During the eight-hour flight, when the conversation turned to Operation Car Wash, one of the ten passengers on the Learjet asked a question that seemed to have been on everyone's minds: "President, if Judge Moro orders your arrest and decides that you can serve your sentence in freedom as long as you wear an ankle monitor, would you accept it?"

Lula's reaction was surprising. His face turned red, like a man possessed, the veins on his neck bulging like he was about to have a heart attack. With the seat belt restricting his movement, Lula beat his fists on the arms of his chair.

"If Moro wants to put an ankle monitor on me, they'll have to cut my foot off first!" he yelled. "And if he gets ten brutes to hold me down and put it on against my will, I'll go to a mechanic on the first corner I see, grab a pair of pliers, and cut it off myself! Do you know why? Because I am innocent! I won't accept house arrest either. Moro can put an ankle bracelet on his mom! I'll never let him put one on me, because I'm innocent!"

Former president Dilma Rousseff, social movement leaders João Pedro Stedile and Guilherme Boulos, and the other passengers watched in silence. The mourning had begun before they even arrived at Fidel's grave, and no one spoke about the subject for the rest of the trip.

The crisis provoked among Lula's defense team by Pertence's request—evidently made with the best intentions—sparked a war of egos that would last months. Many of the big names in legal circles whispered that Zanin, who had yet to reach forty, was a novice without any experience in criminal law. There was more: they almost unanimously gossiped that he was only chosen to defend Lula because he was married to Valeska Teixeira, his law firm partner and the daughter of Roberto Teixeira, who was an old friend of Lula's. Long after the ankle monitor crisis had passed, after the convictions were reversed, even the lawyers who had supported Pertence's initiative (many of them connected to Grupo Prerrogativas) had to admit that, although Zanin had been a novice in criminal law, his tactic of confrontation—always under the guidance of the ex-president—had been the best strategy.

On the morning of Sunday, July 8, 2018, Lula's aids, security team, lawyers, and the PT national directorate frantically called an emergency meeting in the command headquarters at the Petras Hotel. Lula was about to be released, by order of Federal Judge Rodrigo Favreto, who was on weekend duty at the TRF-4 Regional Federal Court in Porto Alegre. The judge had ordered Lula's release in response to a writ of habeas corpus filed by PT congressmen Wadih Damous (Rio de Janeiro), Paulo Pimenta (Rio Grande do Sul), and Paulo Teixeira (São Paulo). The move was so unbelievable that when Lula's advisor Marcola asked him to go to the Federal Police headquarters and pick up Lula, lawyer Manoel Caetano joked, "We're going to the Feds to release the president? Where's my damn machine gun?"

Minutes later, Caetano, Rochinha, Congressman Damous, and the jailer, Paulão, were in Lula's cell with the release order in hand. Congressman Pimenta sat in his car in front of the building's front gate with the engine idling, expecting to race off with Lula the minute he walked out the door. Congressman Paulo Teixeira was on route to Curitiba. When they arrived, Lula looked at the group in disbelief.

Damous broke the news, "President, we are going to get you out of here."

Instead of celebrating, Lula seemed relaxed. Later, he would recall that, seeing a group show up at his cell door at that hour on a Sunday morning, he imagined that they were there to give him the news of the death of his oldest brother, Vavá, who was suffering from terminal cancer.

After hearing the details, he answered them calmly. "You came to get me out, but how much time will I be out for?" Seeing their shocked expressions, he continued. "Don't fool yourselves, my friends. This was an order made by a weekend judge. It'll be reversed on Monday. I can't get in a plane and fly up to São Paulo just for them to say, 'Fly back to Curitiba, you are under arrest again.' "

While Chastalo and Paulão packed Lula's suitcase, certain that he was about to be released, the rest of the group, including Captain Moraes, Lula's chief security officer, went down to the second floor to bring the release order to the superintendent. With Maurício Valeixo off for the weekend, the man in charge was his substitute, Agent Roberval Vicalvi. With this hot potato in his hands, he stalled, offered them coffee, talked, and talked . . . But the group's demand was legitimate. They had a direct order from a judge from a higher court than Sergio Moro—who happened to be on vacation—and there was no room for interpretation, only compliance. Damous, Caetano, and Rochinha stuck to their guns. There was no room for argument, they said; the order was to release the prisoner.

The bewildered Agent Vicalvi tried to stall them. "Yes, yes, this is a prisoner. But this doesn't refer to just any prisoner. It's Lula that he is ordering to release."

Even the jailers Chastalo and Paulão tried to intervene. "Director, jailers have to obey the law. If a judge orders us to release a prisoner, our legal duty is to bring him to the exit turnstile and put him out on the street."

During that nervous moment of "should he stay or should he go," an agent walked in with news. "Dr. Moro called saying that you have to wait before releasing him. He says the decision can't be made by one judge but has to be made by the whole TRF-4 court."

While they were trying to find a solution—and Lula calmly waited in his cell—the TRF-4 judge who delivered the original opinion on Lula's case decided to revoke Judge Favreto's release order. The Car Wash prosecutors, terrified at the possibility of seeing their war trophy slip between their fingers, had mobilized every resource they had. At two o'clock in the afternoon, Judge Favreto declared that the order reversing his decision was unconstitutional and that Lula should be released immediately, under threat of punishment of everyone involved, from the Federal Police superintendent to the jailers responsible for guarding him.

Chastalo went up to Lula's cell. "President, you have to leave now. We can't stay with you here or the rope will be around our necks."

"Damn it," he said. "How long am I going to be out there for?"

"I don't know, but it's now illegal for you to stay here."

"OK. Then I'll go to Dr. Rocha's house and drink some wine, and tomorrow I'll come back, and you won't be blamed for any of this."

As evening set in, TRF-4 chief justice Carlos Eduardo Thompson Flores Lenz ruled that Lula should remain incarcerated, reversing Judge Favreto's order. The ex-president was right: he definitely would not be sleeping in São Paulo that night.

But the coup de grâce was still to come. On August 31, during a ten-hour special session, six of the Superior Electoral Court's seven justices voted to bar Lula's candidacy for the presidency, based on the so-called "clean slate law," removing him from the race.[2] Furthermore, the court ruled, the PT had ten days to replace him, and during this period it was prohibited from holding any campaign rallies or using its free radio and TV airtime to promote Lula—nor could they even do so online.

There was a sense that the favorite to replace him would be former São Paulo mayor Fernando Haddad, currently Lula's vice-presidential running mate. According to the terms given in the majority opinion by Justice Luís Roberto Barroso, the ruling was the final word on the matter and took effect immediately, even if the defense tried to appeal to the Supreme Court.

Lula's hundreds of days in prison were not entirely bitter, though. His tedious daily routine behind bars was occasionally broken by curious and sometimes funny episodes. On July 26, the anniversary of the Cuban Revolution, someone brought him a flash drive with the song "Guantanamera," by renowned Cuban musician Joseíto Fernández, adapted from verses by José Martí. Rochinha and Caetano had replaced the old TV in Lula's cell, not just because of its age but because it was suspected of having a bug or hidden camera in it that could capture conversations and images from the cell. In its place, they installed a modern LCD TV with a USB port. And it was from this TV that the first verses of "Guantanamera" emanated:

---

2 The "clean slate" law of June 10, 2010, makes candidates ineligible for eight years if they have been stripped of their mandate, have resigned to avoid disqualification, or have been convicted by a collegiate court, with the appeal not having suspensive effect. This law was adopted during Lula's second term in office, following a popular initiative referendum that put it on the agenda.

Con los pobres de la tierra
Quiero yo mi suerte echar
El arroyo de la sierra
Me complace más que el mar
Guantanamera, guajira Guantanamera
Guantanamera, guajira Guantanamera[3]

Lula happily sang along and danced in his cell, and was joined by friends, lawyers, and even the jailers—all this in a cell only a few square meters in size.

A similar scene took place on April 25, 2019, on the anniversary of Portugal's Carnation Revolution. Someone brought Lula a flash drive with José Afonso's song "Grândola, Vila Morena," which served as the signal for the soldiers to rise up across the country to depose the fascist Salazarist dictatorship.[4] Before the first notes of the song began, the audio started with the sound of marching military boots hitting the ground. Four years earlier, Lula had been in Lisbon as a special guest for the celebration of the fortieth anniversary of the April 25 Revolution. Hearing it in prison, Lula rose to his feet and stamped his tennis shoes on the ground—*tum tum tum!*—along with the sound of the boots, and sang:

Grândola, vila morena
Terra da fraternidade
O povo é quem mais ordena
Dentro de ti, ó cidade[5]

Behind him, singing and stamping their feet on the ground in single file, marched the jailers, bodyguards, lawyers, and friends who were there

3 "The poor of the land / I want to share their fate / The mountain stream / Pleases me more than the sea / Guantanamera, guajira guantanamera."

4 On April 25, 1974, in Portugal, a movement organized secretly in the lower echelons of the army overthrew the oldest and penultimate explicitly fascist regime in Europe in what is called the Carnation Revolution. During the secret preparations for the coup, it was decided that the signal giving the order to attack would be the broadcast of the song "Grândola, Vila Morena," at 00:20 on Renascença, a Catholic radio station.

5 "Grândola, the brown city / Land of brotherhood / It's the people who rule / in your heart, O city."

for a routine visit. By the time José Afonso reached the song's final verse, everyone was in tears.

On another occasion, during an afternoon reserved for visits from religious leaders, a priest managed to smuggle a holy water flask under his cassock past the prison entrance security checkpoint. The police guards in charge of pat-downs, used to looking for sharp objects and cutting instruments, let him through with the small bottle. During his visit, the priest pulled Lula into a corner in the room, put his hand under the black cassock, and, smiling, gave him the mysterious present, practically whispering in his ear, "President, this is the best cachaça in the Northeast. It was skimmed off the top of the still just for you. Drink it slowly and it can last a few weeks."

Lula acted pleased and thanked him for the present. As soon as the visit ended, he called the jailer. "Chastalo, please, save this bottle in some cabinet or drawer here. Alcoholic drinks are not allowed inside, and this could cause problems for the police guards doing the security checks, for you and for me. But don't throw it out. Save it, and I'll drink it with the people from the vigil when I get out of here."

It wasn't just alcoholic beverages that caused problems for Lula. One afternoon, the two lawyers from Curitiba appeared with a present from Adriana França, Rochinha's wife: a giant French cheese packaged in a round wooden box. The present came with a gift from the manufacturer: a cheese slicer. The cheese made it up into his cell, but the slicer was confiscated by the policewomen patting down female visitors at the security entrance. The Brazilians say that a cat that has been scalded is afraid of cold water, and Lula knew this well. He politely suggested it be shared with the people at the vigil.

"Thank you very much for the gift," he said, "but it was due to a piece of French goat cheese that ex-governor, Sérgio Cabral, lost all of his privileges in Gericinó Penitentiary in Rio. They even canceled his daily sunbath. Please don't take this the wrong way, but I can't take any risks."

The two understood his concern, went downstairs, and gave it to the people at the vigil, to their delight. Manoel Caetano was given the cheese slicer back, and as he was crossing the street with it toward the vigil, he was surprised by shouts and laughter. "Look at this! It was him! It was Dr. Caetano who stabbed the cop, and he's here to show us the weapon! Bravo, Dr. Caetano! This guy here is a real macho man!"

They would soon find out that minutes earlier, 1,000 kilometers away in Juiz de Fora, in the state of Minas Gerais, an anonymous citizen, apparently mentally unwell, had just stabbed far-right candidate, congressman, and ex–Army captain Jair Bolsonaro. According to the polls, Bolsonaro was Lula's main adversary in the elections that would take place that October. Even behind bars, Lula had maintained his decision to run for president when the interim mandate for Michel Temer, who had taken office after the coup against Dilma Rousseff, expired. The most recent public opinion polls, by the Datafolha polling agency, still showed he had a large lead. According to its August 22 poll, Lula led with 39 percent, followed by Bolsonaro (PSL) at 19 percent, Marina Silva (Rede) at 8 percent, Geraldo Alckmin (PSDB) at 6 percent, and Ciro Gomes (PDT) at 5 percent.

One gift that carried no restrictions for Lula was books. Lula gave the impression that he was obsessed with organizing the things around him. The books, recommended by friends or in letters he received in jail, were read, then stacked in a neat pile in a corner behind his wardrobe that grew with a speed that surprised returning visitors. The president declined his right to a sentence reduction for each book read. He wasn't embarrassed to ask his lawyers the meaning of any word or concept, saying things like, "Dr. Rocha, explain something to me: What is the deal with identity politics?"

To spare his friends and visitors from constant questions about what he was reading, he asked for two excellent reference books: a Portuguese dictionary and a thick atlas, to which he could turn to while reading novels, biographies, or academic articles. But the subject that interested him most was the history of popular revolts in Brazil since the arrival of the Portuguese—a subject that was traditionally watered down and sanitized in textbooks.

Sometimes, formal visits revealed big surprises, not just for the people at the Free Lula Vigil but for the population at large. In May 2019, Lula was visited by renowned economist Luiz Carlos Bresser-Pereira, ex-minister in the José Sarney and Fernando Henrique Cardoso governments, which the PT formally opposed.

Two days later, Bresser broke the news on his Facebook page. "This Thursday I visited Lula. He is in great physical and mental shape. His biggest worries right now are the defense of sovereignty and uniting Brazilians to defend Brazil and its people against this 'thing' in office [as then president Jair Bolsonaro was nicknamed by his detractors]. His greatest demand is that his innocence is recognized."

At the end of the paragraph, after a brief summary of national political themes discussed, Bresser-Pereira revealed a secret that had all the trappings of something that had been agreed on in advance with Lula. "Lula is in love, and his first plan when he gets out is to get married."

Lula's relationship had been kept secret for a year and four months. On December 23, 2017, the MST's Florestan Fernandes National School, located in the São Paulo countryside, had held a feijoada feast to inaugurate its new soccer field, named in honor of the late Corinthians soccer team star, Workers' Party member, and personal friend of Lula, "Doctor" Sócrates. The main event was a soccer match between famed musician and writer Chico Buarque and his friends, and Lula's pickup team: an assortment of men and women including MST leader João Pedro Stedile and a dozen artists and activists. The game, refereed by sports journalist Juca Kfouri, ended in a tie, five to five.

It was on that day that Lula met and fell in love with sociologist Rosângela da Silva, fifty, a striking light-brown-skinned woman with long hair and a friendly smile. "Janja," as she was called by friends, was a card-carrying member of the PT who had worked in Curitiba for sixteen years at Itaipu Binational Electric Company, supervising social programs for families that were relocated due to their hydroelectric projects. Ultimately, the marriage plans announced by Bresser-Pereira would have to be moved forward due to Lula's presidential campaign, once all charges against him were reversed and his right to run for office was restored. Making plans to wed as quickly as possible, they would move into a rented house in São Bernardo do Campo as soon as he got out of jail.

Despite the rare moments of joy and humor, Lula had real conundrums to work out from inside his cell in Curitiba. Since he had been barred from running for office by the Superior Electoral Court, the PT had ten short days to either register someone to run in his place or lose the right to run another candidate. Lula had never stated who his preferred replacement was, but he had mentioned three names to a few confidants, which were, in order of preference, Jaques Wagner, from Bahia; the ex-mayor of São Paulo, Fernando Haddad; and PT president and senator Gleisi Hoffmann. Each one had their pros and cons, but they were the only names big enough to face Bolsonaro at the polls, especially after, using his stabbing in Juiz de Fora in all of his political ads, his poll numbers had surged from 19 percent to 31 percent in less than a month.

Senator Jaques Wagner was the first potential replacement summoned to Curitiba, where he joined Lula and a few party leaders for the meeting. Neither Haddad nor Hoffmann had been invited.

After exchanging greetings, Lula cut to the point. "The candidate I'd like to replace me is among us in this cell," he said. Nobody uttered a word. Lula called Wagner by his nickname, "What do you think, Galego? You haven't said a thing. It's you."

With his deep-blue, "sunburnt" eyes and hair that always gave the impression that he had just come out of the shower, the senator looked less like a Carioca who grew up in Bahia than an old fox from the mountains of Minas Gerais.

"President," he said, "you know that it would be an honor to replace you, but I don't think I'm ready to board this flight."

Lula went for the jugular of his old friend. "Galego, you are still far from seventy" (at the time he was sixty-seven). "You were a petroleum platform worker, a union leader, congressman, senator, presidential chief of staff, minister of international relations, minister of labor, of defense . . . Damn it, Galego, is there anyone in Brazil who has your résumé? The only thing left for you to do is be president."

Wagner's ambivalent response made it clear that he wanted to run for reelection as senator, where he could get elected without leaving his home state, and that he wasn't interested in adding an electoral loss of that magnitude to his CV. The battlefield of politics was full of trenches. If Wagner had accepted Lula's offer, he would have certainly faced strong opposition from the base of his own party. He had never hidden the fact that his favored name for vice president was Ciro Gomes—the moody native of Ceará who half the PT wanted to keelhaul.

This left the next choice, economist and university professor Fernando Haddad. Although he had been clobbered in his São Paulo mayoral reelection battle against inexperienced multimillionaire João Doria by 53 percent to 16.7 percent, Haddad was well educated and had enough prestige and charisma to avoid being made into a lame duck.

Whatever misgivings there might have been, it seemed prudent to choose Haddad over Gleisi Hoffmann, who emerged as a lioness in the congressional hearings during the coup against Dilma Rousseff. According to Lula, she had directed the PT in an exemplary manner during some of the worst moments in its history. "You don't change a winning team," he said. In other words, it was best that Hoffmann continued as national president of PT.

After deciding on Haddad, Lula summoned him to Curitiba, where they had a brief conversation in his cell.

"You're going to be our candidate," Lula said.

"Okay. If this is my mission, I accept it."

"I'll draft a letter presenting your name, and we'll announce the decision to the public."

Just as Lula had pushed until the last minute—only giving up after the Superior Electoral Court ruling—he wasn't in a hurry to draft the public announcement. His reticence was understandable, and he only gave up when there was no more time and no legal maneuver left that could keep him in the race. It wasn't an unconscious move; indeed, he talked openly about it. Lula believed that giving up, even under legal duress, could be interpreted as something that he had never accepted and would never accept: acknowledgment of guilt. Remaining a candidate until the end, as he and many of his friends defended, would be one more palpable, objective show of innocence.

"If I drop out, I'll give up on one of my most important defense tactics," he told his lawyer Manoel Caetano. "It would be like signing an electoral death warrant."

The problem was that sustaining this position implied taking the PT out of the game for the first ten days of Brazil's one-month election season, and it was a party that had run the nation for fourteen of its thirty-year existence. It was the world's second-largest left-wing political party, with 1.5 million registered members, trailing only the monumental Chinese Communist Party, with its 95 million.

After Lula's draft passed through several hands and was ready to go public, he decided that, instead of distributing it through the newspapers, blogs, sites, radio, and TV networks, it should be read at the door of the Federal Police headquarters—at the Free Lula Vigil. Everyone agreed, but then the question arose of who would read it. Gleisi? Haddad himself? Some of the party leaders from the Chamber of Deputies or the Senate? Wisely, Lula chose someone who was not part of any of the internal party caucuses, was not planning on running for office, and was certainly, among all those in his circle, one of his oldest and most faithful friends: the lawyer Eduardo Greenhalgh. When asked, "Mococa," as he was nicknamed, told Lula he thought the task should go to Gleisi Hoffmann; after all, she was the party president. Lula put his foot down, said he wasn't going to change his mind, and asked Greenhalgh to go personally to the national party directorate at the Petras Hotel to explain his decision.

With the exception of Gleisi, the reaction couldn't have been worse. Everyone thought that it made no sense for such an important statement to be read by someone who, though a founding member and part of the party's executive directorate, was a relative unknown both nationally and internationally.

Greenhalgh returned to Lula's cell and told him that, as he had feared, the idea had been almost unanimously rejected. Lula put his foot down. "Go back there and tell them that it's my decision and that the conversation is over."

That afternoon of September 11, in front of a crowd of journalists, party activists, and everyone else who happened to be at the vigil that day, Greenhalgh, wearing a brown sport jacket over a red polo shirt and black sweater, stroked his long, gray mustache while Hoffmann made a short introduction. Then, he approached the mic on the small stage they'd set up in front of the police headquarters front gate and began to read. At his side stood ex-president Dilma Rousseff, Haddad and his wife Ana Estela, Hoffmann, Senator Lindbergh Farias, Congressman Paulo Pimenta, and Manuela d'Ávila, the Rio Grande do Sul state parliamentarian from the Communist Party of Brazil. It took Greenhalgh thirteen minutes to read the seven-page letter from Lula to the Brazilian people.

After the applause ended, Greenhalgh handed the microphone to the new candidate for president.

Fernando Haddad spoke for about ten minutes. "I feel the pain of many Brazilians hearing the news that we can't vote for that person who we would like to see walking up the ramp of the Presidential Palace this January 1, to lead our country," he said. "This pain is especially felt by the poor, who know what our governments represented from a historical perspective, a history so cruel and unjust, a history that penalized two-thirds of the Brazilian population so harshly . . . We are going to win this election for Lula, for the PT, for the PC do B, for the social movements, and for Brazil, because Brazil deserves this victory."

The news broke, but by all appearances, the election gods were not poised to smile on the Workers' Party. A poll released the night before by Datafolha showed that if the election were held that day, Bolsonaro would win 24 percent of the vote while only 9 percent would go to Haddad.

Letters from Prison

During his 581 days in prison in Curitiba, Lula received 35,000 letters from admirers across Brazil. Lula himself wrote more than 300 letters to his aide Marcola, which included political advice, schedules, and motivational messages for the struggle for democracy. Marcola wrote 482 letters to Lula, almost always in response to letters he'd received. The former president wrote 500 letters to his girlfriend Janja, and she wrote 500 back—yes, exactly 500 each, not one more or one less. Below are some of the letters Lula wrote. Lula and Janja have chosen not to share their personal letters with the public.

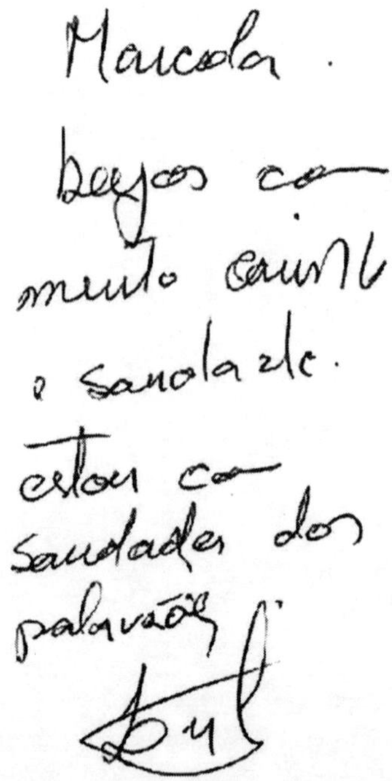
Marcola.
beijos com
muito carinho
e saudade.
estou com
saudades dos
palavrões
Lula

Lula's first letter to his aide Marcola (4/17/2018).

Marcola,
Big hugs, I miss you. I miss the swearing,

Lula

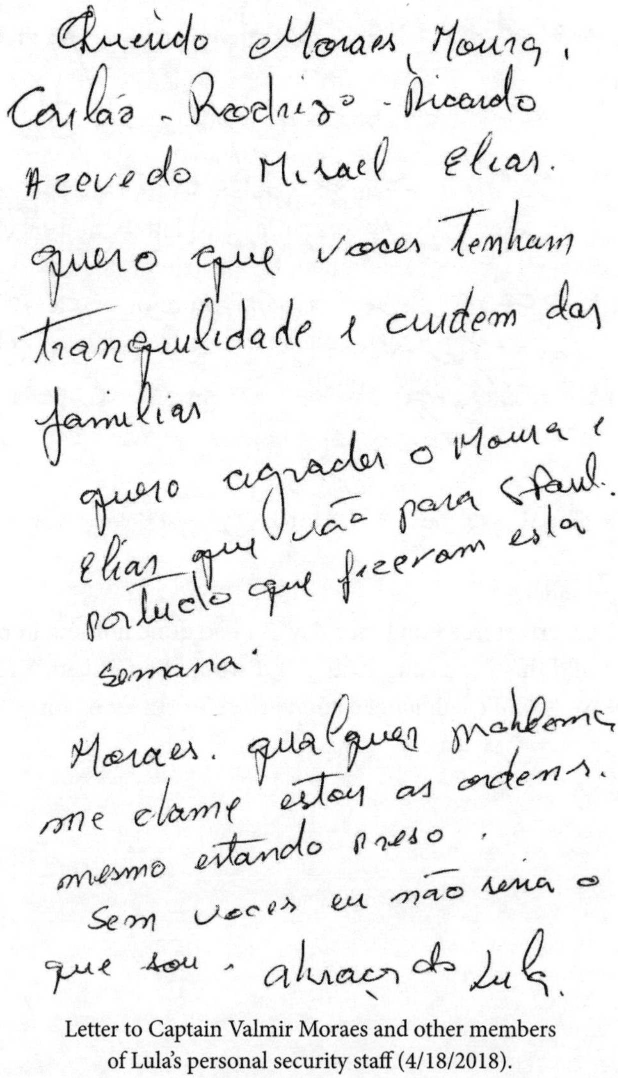

Querido Moraes, Moura,
Carlão - Rodrigo - Ricardo
Azevedo Misael Elias.
quero que vocês tenham
tranquilidade e cuidem das
familias
quero agradecer o Moura e
Elias que vão para S.Paul.
por tudo que fizeram esta
semana.
Moraes. qualquer problema
me chame estou as ordens.
mesmo estando preso.
Sem vocês eu não seria o
que sou. abraço do Lula.

Letter to Captain Valmir Moraes and other members
of Lula's personal security staff (4/18/2018).

Dear Moraes, Moura, Carlão, Rodrigo, Ricardo Azevedo, Misael, and Elias. I want you to be calm and take care of your families. I want to thank you, Moura and Elias, who are going back to São Paulo, for everything you did this week.

Moraes, call me if you have any problems. I am at your service, even in prison. Without you I wouldn't be who I am.

Hugs,
Lula

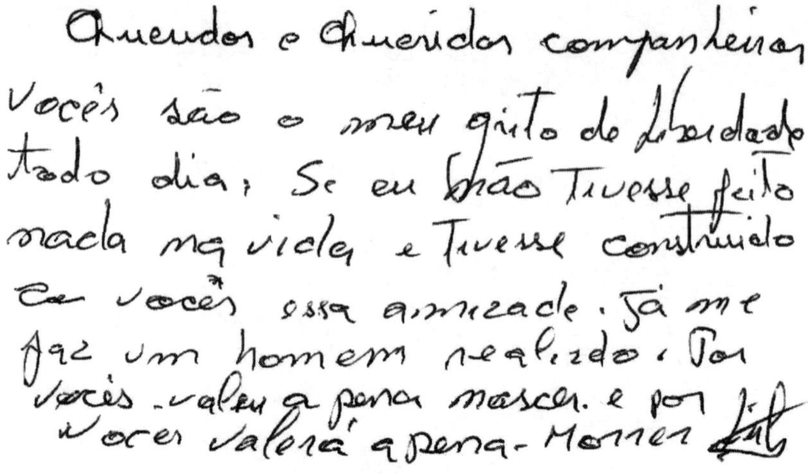
Queridos e Queridas companheiros
Vocês são o meu grito de liberdade
todo dia. Se eu não tivesse feito
nada na vida e tivesse construído
com vocês essa amizade. Já me
faz um homem realizado. Por
vocês valeu a pena nascer. e por
vocês valerá a pena morrer Lula

Letter to the activists at the vigil, read to them by Gleisi Hoffmann (8/1/2018).

Dear comrades,
You are my cry of freedom every day. If I had done nothing in my life except build this friendship with you, I would be fulfilled. You have made it worthwhile being born and you are worth dying for.

Lula

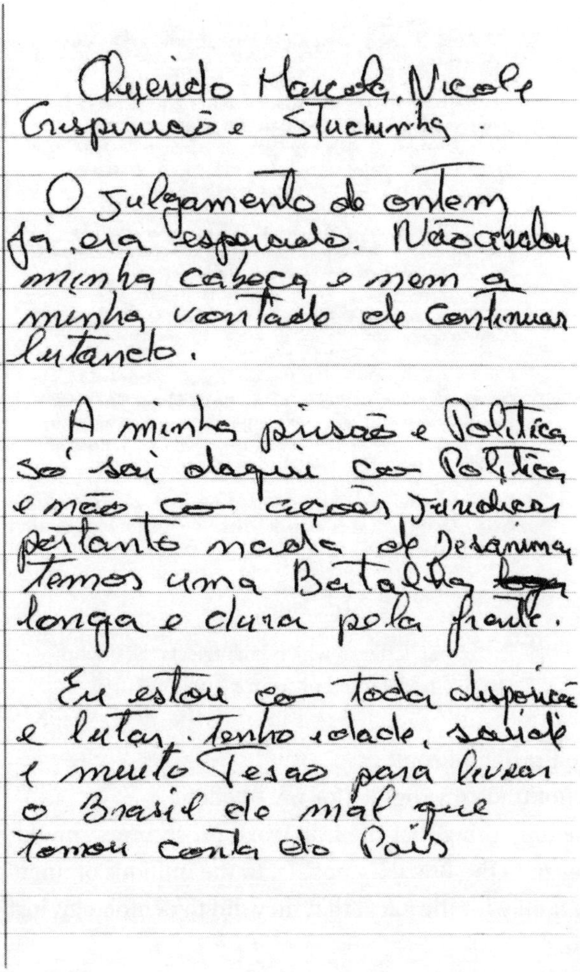

Querido Marcola, Nicole
Crispiniano e Stuckinha.

O julgamento de ontem
já era esperado. Não abalou
minha cabeça e nem a
minha vontade de continuar
lutando.

A minha prisão é Política
só sai daqui com Política
e não com ações jurídicas
portanto nada de desanima
temos uma Batalha ~~longa~~
longa e dura pela frente.

Eu estou com toda disposição
e lutar. Tenho idade, saúde
e muito tesão para livrar
o Brasil do mal que
tomou conta do País

Letter to Marcola, his wife Nicole, José Chrispiniano, and Ricardo Stuckert on the day that the Superior Court of Justice upheld Lula's conviction while decreasing his sentence to eight years and ten months (4/24/2019).

Dear Marcelo, Nicole, Chrispiniano and little Stuckert
Yesterday's ruling was predictable. It hasn't upset me nor lessened my willingness to keep fighting.

My imprisonment is political. I'll only get out of here through politics and not through legal rulings, therefore don't feel bad, we have a long, hard fight ahead of us.

I am fully willing to fight. I am willing, able and full of energy to rid Brazil of the evil that has taken over the country.

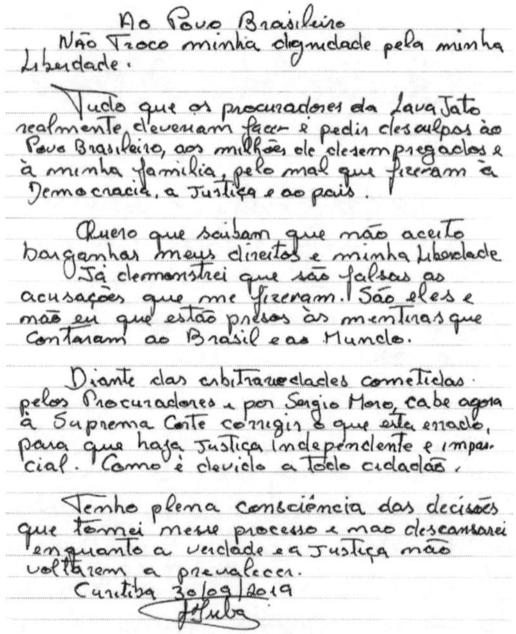

Ao Povo Brasileiro

Não Troco minha dignidade pela minha Liberdade.

Tudo que os procuradores da Lava Jato realmente deveriam fazer é pedir desculpas ao Povo Brasileiro, aos milhões de desempregados e à minha família, pelo mal que fizeram à Democracia, à Justiça e ao país.

Quero que saibam que não aceito barganhas meus direitos e minha Liberdade.

Já demonstrei que são falsas as acusações que me fizeram. São eles e não eu que estão presos às mentiras que contaram ao Brasil e ao Mundo.

Diante das arbitrariedades cometidas pelos Procuradores e por Sergio Moro, cabe agora à Suprema Corte corrigir o que está errado, para que haja Justiça independente e imparcial. Como é devido a todo cidadão.

Tenho plena consciência das decisões que tomei nesse processo e não descansarei enquanto a verdade e a Justiça não voltarem a prevalecer.

Curitiba 30/09/2019

Lula

Open letter in which Lula rejects the offer of transfer to house arrest (09/30/2019).

To the Brazilian People,

I will not trade my dignity for my freedom.

The only thing that the Car Wash prosecutors should really do is apologize to the Brazilian people, to the millions of unemployed and to my family for the harm that they did to democracy, justice and our nation.

I want you to know that I will not accept any bargain over my rights and my freedom. I have already demonstrated that the charges that they made against me are false. It is they and not me who are imprisoned by their own lies to Brazil and the world.

In response to the arbitrary acts committed by the prosecutors and by Sergio Moro, it is now up to the Supreme Court to correct what is wrong, so that we can have independent and impartial judges, which is the right of every citizen.

I have a clear conscience about the decisions that I made in this process and will not rest until truth and justice prevail, once again.

Curitiba 09/30/2019

Lula

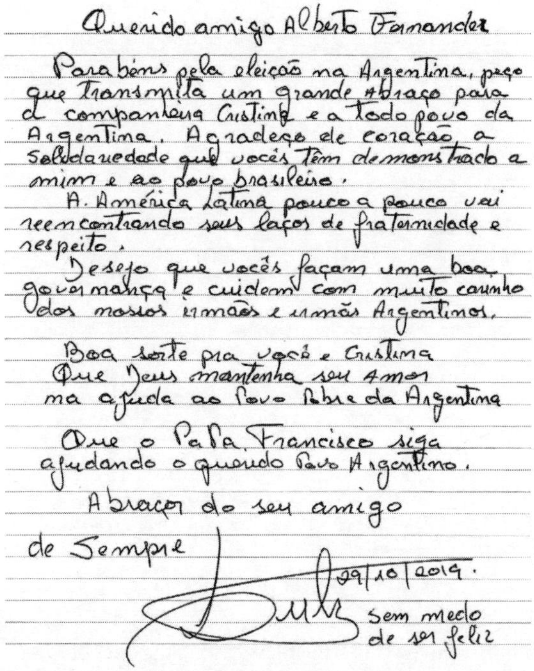

Querido amigo Alberto Fernandez

Parabéns pela eleição na Argentina, peço que transmita um grande abraço para a companheira Cristina e a todo povo da Argentina. Agradeço de coração, a solidariedade que vocês têm demonstrado a mim e ao povo brasileiro.

A América Latina pouco a pouco vai reencontrando seus laços de fraternidade e respeito.

Desejo que vocês façam uma boa governança e cuidem com muito carinho dos nossos irmãos e irmãs Argentinos.

Boa sorte pra você e Cristina
Que Deus mantenha seu amor
na ajuda ao povo pobre da Argentina

Que o Papa Francisco siga ajudando o querido povo Argentino.

Abraços do seu amigo
de sempre

29/10/2019.

Lula

sem medo
de ser feliz

Lula congratulates Alberto Fernández on his election to the presidency of Argentina. Fernández interrupted a difficult campaign in his country to visit Lula in prison (10/29/2019).

Dear friend Alberto Fernández,
Congratulations on your election victory in Argentina. Please give a big hug to comrade Cristina and to all of the people in Argentina. I thank you with all my heart for the solidarity that you have shown me and the Brazilian people.

Little by little, Latin America is rebuilding its ties of fraternity and respect.

I wish you a good government and that you take good care of our Argentinian brothers and sisters.

Good luck to you and Cristina. May God maintain your love of helping the poor people of Argentina.

May Pope Francis continue helping the dear people of Argentina.

A hug from your friend for life,
10/29/2019
Lula
Without fear of being happy

6

A hacker named Red opens the gates to hell, and the Supreme Court buries Moro and the Car Wash investigation. Lula steps out of prison as a presidential candidate

When the first poll results came in following Haddad's replacement of Lula, agony set in among *petistas* and other progressives. Lula had been hitting 40 percent in the polls, nearly double Bolsonaro's numbers. When Haddad first stepped in, he was unable to hit 10 percent while Bolsonaro, capitalizing as much as he could on the stabbing incident in Juiz de Fora, rose in popularity with every poll by Datafolha, Ibope, and the regional polling agencies.[1] The initial scare, however, was short lived. Over the following weeks, the ex-mayor of São Paulo showed that he had drive and passion, and he began to close the gap with Bolsonaro. The distance between him and the ex-captain was still wide, ranging from 10 to 15 percent depending on the polling agency or methodology, but the risk that Bolsonaro would win the election in the first round seemed more and more remote.

The arena of battle, different to what the Brazilian electorate was used to, was no longer TV or the debates but the internet. In the eyes of everyday citizens, the Bolsonaristas seemed to dominate the digital world by a wide advantage over the petistas. With a total lack of scruples or sense of decorum, the campaign made extreme use of so-called fake news—a new name for the old lies, slander, and yellow journalism.

The further the campaign advanced, the greater the similarities became between the methods used by Bolsonaro and those used two

1 On September 6, 2018, Bolsonaro was wounded in the abdomen by a knife attack during a campaign rally in Juiz de Fora, Minas Gerais.

years earlier in the US presidential campaign. In that race, the billionaire Republican Donald Trump had beaten Democrat Hillary Clinton, Barack Obama's former secretary of state. The "news" spread, multiplied in the millions on US social media networks, that Mrs. Clinton had promoted orgies with children when she lived in the White House during her husband's presidency. The reporters who looked for the sources of the information discovered that it had first appeared in a note attributed to a backwoods newspaper that had already gone out of business by the time Bill and Hillary were teenagers. By the time that the story was debunked in the press and by the Democrat campaign, millions of voters had already been poisoned by the fake news. In some of Trump's committee offices, they distributed free T-shirts with an enormous photo of Hillary next to a single word, "bitch." For the more prudish electorate, the word "bitch" was substituted with "wanted by the police."

The heavy artillery fired against Haddad in Brazil seemed like a carbon copy of the strategy successfully used by Trump in the US. Hundreds of thousands of memes were distributed on social media claiming that, as mayor of São Paulo, Haddad had distributed "cock baby bottles" in which the nipples had been substituted with rubber penises, and that, if he were elected, he would distribute them in all of the nation's public preschools. They claimed that if Haddad were elected, a sex education pamphlet would be included in public school curriculum teaching schoolchildren about the best ways to "convert to homosexuality." According to the Bolsonaro campaign, Haddad supported incest and, if he were to become president, he would legalize pedophilia. Millions of posts on social media sites and anonymous blogs displayed a photomontage of Haddad's vice-presidential candidate, the young PC do B leader Manuela D'Ávila, wearing a T-shirt with the phrase "Jesus was a transvestite."

The mystery of the glaring similarity between Trump's and Bolsonaro's campaigns was revealed by "03," the nickname Haddad's opponent gave to one of his sons, Eduardo Bolsonaro, a police clerk and congressman from São Paulo who lived in Rio de Janeiro. At the height of the campaign, 03 published a selfie on his social media accounts from New York with his arm around his new guru, the controversial political strategist Steve Bannon. Several books have been published on him, but journalist Michael Wolff's *Fire and Fury*, on the people behind the

Trump campaign, includes what may be the most accurate profile of Bannon.

Before becoming a nationally known personality, Bannon directed Breitbart News, a right-wing extremist website financed and disseminated by neo-Nazis, white supremacists, antisemites, and radical nationalists. Investigating the site directed by Bannon, Wolff found his fingerprints, among other crimes, on the sale of information from personal Facebook profiles, gathered by the company Cambridge Analytica, to trace voters and digitally influence them to vote for Trump.

It was his performance at Breitbart that led Trump to recruit him for the disputed post of chief strategist for his campaign. Chubby and short, with a sweaty face and messy hair—the only sloppily dressed member of a team that otherwise wore suits from London's Savile Row—Bannon was often humiliated by his boss during meetings. "Steve, I think you should take a shower at least once a week," the future president of the United States used to say.

Trump quickly found out, however, that he was more than just a slob. This became clear when Bannon made a quick proposal to the candidate's staff on the direction Trump should take, telling them that the campaign was headed for failure because they were fooling the American public with the same speeches and promises of any other candidate for the White House.

What Bannon defended as "the truth" revealed itself as an infallible tactic: Why not be honest? Why not tell the Americans what they really think and what values you defend? Why should you be embarrassed to tell the people that we are white supremacists, that we want to build a wall separating the United States from Mexico to block the entrance of starving Hispanics that sneak into our country by the thousands like rats every day to steal the jobs of Yankee workers? Why don't you say, with absolute clarity, that you are against the entry into the US of Muslim families who hide terrorists like those who destroyed the World Trade Center on September 11? Why should the US stay in the North American Free Trade Agreement, "which only sucks our resources without giving us anything back"? Why should we allow cockroaches like Venezuela to threaten American military power? What responsibility does the US have for European colonialism in Africa and Asia, and thus to welcome the hordes of Pakistani, Indian, and North African refugees who knock on our doors? Great Britain, Belgium, and France should take in the children of the people they enslaved—we can't foot the bill for them.

In front of a stupefied audience in that small meeting, Bannon concluded by saying they would have to tell their countrymen that "we want a great America" or lose the election, that there was no other way.

The campaign turned upside down, as instructed by Bannon, launching a barrage of millions upon millions of daily lies across the internet. Although Trump was a billionaire who could bankroll the daily costs of that digital revolution, the Democrats insinuated that it was Russia that was sponsoring this cyberwar. According to the Democratic Party, President Vladimir Putin believed Mrs. Clinton was a warmonger who was infinitely more dangerous than Trump and, if elected, that she would throw international geopolitics out of balance.

Trump began to rise in the opinion polls and started repeating the same theme in all of his public events: the Democrats were preparing to manipulate the elections and put Hillary Clinton in the White House by scamming the convoluted US electoral system—in which a candidate can win the popular vote and still lose the elections. Bannon's strategy worked, and on January 20, 2017, President Barack Obama handed the keys to the White House over to the histrionic and unbalanced Donald Trump.

Two years later, in Brazil, there were suspicions that an unprecedented fake news campaign against Haddad, in favor of Bolsonaro, was monopolizing the online discourse and forcing an apparently uncontrollable rise of the ex-captain in the polls. Haddad resisted with conventional weapons, but the PT and his campaign directors seemed stunned and confused by what was happening. The more that democratic sectors of society denounced the racist, xenophobic, and violent nature of Bolsonaro, the more he rose in the polls. In his online videos, he unequivocally defended rape, referred to residents of the *quilombolas* (villages, founded by escaped slaves, that have similar rights to indigenous reserves in Brazil) as animals who should be weighed using cattle scales, and attacked all supporters of LGBTQIA+ rights. He called all his adversaries "communist pedophiles" and "a scourge that deserves to be machine-gunned down for wanting to transform Brazil into another Cuba or Venezuela."

Filling the entire Batata Square in São Paulo, a huge popular protest called #EleNao (#NotHim) was estimated to have been the largest street protest since the Diretas Já (Direct Elections Now) protests against the military dictatorship in the early 1980s. Led by women and their allies in the anti-Bolsonaro alliance, #EleNao was designed as a people's response to Bolsonaro. However, inexplicably, it had no effect. Bolsonaro continued to rise in the polls.

At end of the night of October 7, 2018, the date of the first round of the election, the top floor of the Pestana Hotel, on the corner of Brigadeiro Luís Antônio and Tutoia Streets in São Paulo's Paraiso neighborhood, where the Haddad campaign operated, looked like a funeral parlor. The Superior Electoral Court had announced the final results from the electronic ballot boxes across Brazil. Bolsonaro received 46.3 percent (nearly 50 million votes), against 29.3 percent for Haddad (a little over 30 million votes). Since no candidate had surpassed 50 percent of the vote, the contest would be decided in the second-round runoff election, which would take place three weeks later.

Eleven days after the first-round election results came in, reporter Patricia Campos Mello, from *Folha de São Paulo* newspaper, published an investigative report revealing what was behind Bolsonaro's vertiginous online campaign. The headline story, entitled "Businessmen Bankroll Campaign against the PT on WhatsApp," was the tip of an enormous iceberg that had been used for a long time by the Bolsonaro family, most notably by "son 02," Rio de Janeiro city councilor Carlos Bolsonaro. Mello had spent four years investigating the use of social media networks around the world, and specifically the use of social media direct messages as an instrument of political propaganda to manipulate public opinion—a tool used mainly by right and far-right populist regimes. Mello identified this as a clear factor in 2014 in India, when Narenda Modi won the parliamentary majority, becoming the first president in the country with a campaign primarily structured using instruments offered publicly on the internet, such as Twitter and WhatsApp.

In 2016, *Folha* sent Mello to the US, where she had previously worked as a correspondent, to cover the presidential election. There, she identified the same methods used by Modi, employed at a stratospherically larger volume. This time, in addition to Twitter and WhatsApp, a new and efficient weapon was being used for identification and invasion of personal data: Facebook.

When she was covering the election, Mello initially assumed that the overwhelming volume of fake news benefiting the Trump campaign had organic origins, from individual supporters acting spontaneously and independently. Soon, however, she realized that the quantity was too large and that there were signs of automation. It was something that required material resources—money—to put into operation. For any garage-level hacker, the tactic was simple: using software, computers emulated the news that the operator wanted to spread across social media platforms. They then connected this software to dozens of computers and started firing shots.

Since it is easy to acquire user profiles on the black market or through phone companies, the client can, for example, say that they want to send a specific message to *x* million people and choose the region or country where they live, their age group, gender, economic class, and so on. As one hacker said, "You can even choose the color of the socks your target is wearing, or discover if they are vegans or cannibals." In this manner, when a Brazilian recipient received a message claiming that Haddad would distribute "cock bottles" or pamphlets inducing children to become homosexuals, it would arrive on their computer amid dozens of offers for real products like T-shirts, package vacations, or toothbrushes—which, in theory, increases the credibility of the fake news.

Something so simple, with relatively low investment and very high return, turned heads in the underworld of the internet and politics. Patricia Mello's investigation unearthed dozens of companies that offered service-provision packages to candidates and political parties in which voters were identified as if they were under microscopes. The key word was "segmentation": information recipients could be divided by income bracket, profession, location, marital status, age group, and whether they lived in a rural or urban area. To make it clear to her readers that this wasn't science fiction, Mello ran in her newspaper article a photo of a budget offered by Croc Services (which was apparently rejected) to Geraldo Alckmin's 2018 presidential campaign for the PSDB party, in which he ran against Jair Bolsonaro. According to Croc's budget, as readers learned, for R$8.7 million, any candidate could send any message they wanted to around 120 million voters.

Although the Workers' Party had some of the greatest internet-technology specialists in Brazil among its members and supporters, and all of the means necessary to confront the Bolsonarista Moloch, it seems to have opted for another tactic. As the October 28 runoff election approached, Haddad's campaign directors—without consulting Lula in his cell in Curitiba—decided to change the direction of their marketing campaign. The first move, undoubtedly reacting to the results of Bolsonaro's continual accusations of communist sympathy leading up to the first round, was to go more conservative in its advertisements—in essence, to de-PT-ize it. Lula did not like this at all. Angered that the change didn't seem to be producing any results, and worried about an imminent loss, Lula wanted to know who was responsible for it. As the old Brazilian expression goes, an ugly child has no father, so the blame ended up falling on the official marketing director of the campaign, advertising executive Sidônio Palmeira, who had run the victorious gubernatorial campaigns of Jaques Wagner and Rui Costa in Bahia. From his cell in Curitiba, Lula issued an order, "Buy him a plane ticket and tell Sidônio to come to Curitiba to talk to me."

Without Gleisi Hoffmann or Haddad knowing a thing about it, a silent battle was being fought over the list of social media handles of Lula's faithful supporters, which numbered around 10 million people. Haddad's marketing team wanted to get their hands on it. While this silent battle didn't make it into the newspapers, it resulted in a standoff between two groups. It's always risky to name names, or "name the bulls," as the Brazilian expression goes, but among Lula's group were, certainly, Paulo Okamoto, Marcola, and Nicole Briones, the press attaché responsible for the president's tweets. The small group, which may have had another two or three names in it, feared that, in possession of the list of Lula's followers, the advertising people working for Haddad could use it to repeat what they were doing on the Haddad campaign: try to crib votes from Bolsonaro by pushing Lula's tweets and statements toward the center. It was a tactic that, in the opinion of Lula's backers, would not take votes away from their rival and would damage Lula's progressive image. Relying on the weight and prestige of Okamoto, who was never a leftist, the small group entered the battle and toed the line, following Okamoto's lead. "Lula's ideas and proposals stay with Lula," he said. "Whoever wants to change course, go ahead. But Lula is Lula."

Small changes were made, and the campaign moved forward. Without anyone knowing or wanting to reveal why, the marketing director did not show up in Curitiba, and nobody could ever personally identify if there was, in fact, a single person in charge. But the fact is that on October 28, 2018, Bolsonaro, the retired captain who had been an obscure lawmaker for three decades in the underworld of the Federal Congress, was announced as the thirty-eighth president of Brazil, with 57.8 million votes.

In addition to all of the mishaps, during the following months Lula would suffer the anguish of losing three people. The first took place on Christmas, with the news of the death of his dear friend of so many years, who rode with him from São Paulo to Curitiba in the Federal Police plane and was with him until the final minute of his last night in freedom: ex-congressman Sigmaringa Seixas was finally defeated by the myelodysplasia—an incurable form of bone marrow cancer—that had caused him so much suffering. The second death was even more dramatic but, as in the case of Sig, had been expected. Genival Inácio da Silva, "Vavá," Lula's older brother, who at seventy-nine was suffering from diabetes that had already caused the amputation of his leg, died of cancer in São Bernardo do Campo on January 29, 2019. Lula's defense team requested that the court authorize him to travel to São Bernardo to bid farewell to the body of his brother. The initial request was denied by Curitiba Department of Corrections judge Carolina Lebbos, based on a request from the Car Wash task force.

In a social media chat app conversation revealed later by the website the *Intercept*, Car Wash prosecutor Carlos Welter said, "I think he should have the right to go."

His DA Office colleague, Januário Paludo, a man with a big, bulging, shaven head, answered with a phrase that should be used as his epitaph: "This rascal just wants to go on a field trip, and Welter shows pity for him."

Lula's defense attorneys appealed to the Supreme Court. Besides being incredibly indecent, the ruling made by Justice Dias Toffoli—then president of the Supreme Court (nominated by Lula)—would belong perfectly, verbatim, in any work of Latin American magical realism:

> I have conceded a writ of habeas corpus to, according to the law, concede the petitioner, Luiz Inácio Lula da Silva, the right to exclusively meet with his family members, today, at a military building in

the region, allowing the possibility of the body to be transported to said military base, according to the family's criteria.

In fluent Portuguese, extracted from the legal jargon, Toffoli proposed a procedural inversion of the tradition of the wake as it occurs in nearly any culture or religion. Instead of enabling the brother to attend the wake, the cadaver would be transported to a military base—in this case, a military building in the region—where Lula could have a few moments with the body of his brother and old companion in the neighborhood soccer games of their amateur team, Capibaribe de São Bernardo. Lula sent an expletive-laden message to the president of the Supreme Court. He would not submit himself to that level of humiliation. Fortunately for Dias Toffoli's legacy, by the time the incomprehensible ruling was published in the Supreme Court's daily bulletin, *Diário da Justica*, Vavá's body was already underground in Pauliceia Cemetery.

But the most devastating blow was still to come. Shortly after noon on Friday, March 1, Lula was surprised to see Jorge Chastalo arrive at his cell to accompany him to his sunbath. On that typically cold and drizzly Curitiba day, what kind of sunbath could it possibly be? Lula didn't know it, but he had been removed from his cell so that he couldn't see the leading TV news story, about a boy's death. He grew nervous when his lawyer Manoel Caetano came in with agent Luciano Flores, the new Curitiba Federal Police superintendent.

"It's Arthur, President," Caetano said.

"Which Arthur?"

"Your grandson Arthur."

"What happened to him?"

"He had a serious health problem and just passed away in Santo André, President."

"What do you mean he died? How? He died of what? Two days ago he was fine, in good health! He died? How did he die? What did he die of?"

The day before, on family visitation day, Sandro Luis, the father of Arthur, a seven-year-old boy and fast friend of his grandfather, hadn't shown up in Curitiba. His family explained the absence, saying that they had stayed in São Paulo's ABC region taking care of the boy, who had a fever. Lula joked at the time, "The lazy guy decided to skip the visit to Curitiba, and he's using Arthur's fever as an excuse. I know how it is."

Now, hearing this, Lula didn't know how to react. He repeated the same phrase over and over, "Arthur, my grandson? How could this be? He was fine two days ago. What could have happened?"

Someone tried to explain that it was a surprise case of meningococcal meningitis—a diagnosis later disproven by the Santo André public health service. Lula was inconsolable.

"But meningitis doesn't kill. He was supposed to come here yesterday." He sat down, sobbing and repeating, "but why him, a seven-year-old boy with his whole life in front of him? It would have been normal if it was me, in my seventies, but a child like Arthur who hadn't even started to live yet?"

The nonsensical rules and demands imposed after the death of his brother Vavá were absent, and Lula had no problem going to Arthur's funeral in the ABC region, where he was transported on a Federal Police plane.

Lula was authorized to leave prison for the burial—a right guaranteed in Article 120 of Brazil's Penal Code. Looking haggard, he arrived at the cemetery, where the wake had taken place the night before, at around eleven o'clock that Saturday morning. Even though he was surrounded by a huge military escort, as if he were a violent felon, the Jardim da Colina Cemetery in São Bernardo was surrounded by armed military and federal police officers who had formed a human wall to prevent the crowd from getting near him. During his arrival and departure, Lula barely had a chance to wave. Throughout the entire ninety minutes in which he stood next to the body, three military helicopters hovered over the location.

This was the first time Lula had stepped outside prison since his arrest. During this period, the only big, surprising political news since Bolsonaro's election was his appointment of Sergio Moro, the judge who had worked diabolically to block Lula from running for president, as his minister of justice. Basking in the glory of years of hero treatment in the media, to many Brazilians Moro was not just another top-level collaborator with the Bolsonaro administration but a proto-prime minister. In exchange for Moro's giving up all of the benefits he had accumulated during his twenty-two years on the bench, President Bolsonaro merged the Ministries of Justice, Public Security, and Comptroller General to create a new super-ministry for the former judge. The icing on the cake was the transferal of jurisdiction over the Council of Financial Activities

(COAF) to Moro's new super-ministry, after removing it from the Ministry of the Economy, which was controlled by "Chicago Boy" economist Paulo Guedes— a former protégé of Milton Friedman who had spent years rendering services to the dictatorship of General Augusto Pinochet in Chile.

Moro's princedom didn't survive halfway into Bolsonaro's term. Following repeated public humiliation by the president, on April 24, 2020, Moro resigned and was no longer a judge or a minister. Like a shipwrecked sailor in a Gabriel García Márquez story, the former strongman of the Republic looked destined to be forgotten forever.

Moro had walked into the lonely trap of his own destiny, but Lula, despite the pain of nearly twenty months in prison in Curitiba, didn't spend a single day without visitors. Just as the activist Roberto Baggio had promised on the day of Lula's arrest, the vigil didn't abandon the front gate of the Federal Police headquarters for a single moment, rain or shine. After making their deal with the mayor's office, there were no more problems there. Even the Federal Police agents across the street had established a peaceful coexistence with the red horde. The episode of the federal agent's destruction of the vigil's sound system seemed forgotten by both sides.

Only the Military Police, under control of right-wing Paraná governor Ratinho Jr.—son of a well-known Bolsonarista national TV host—continued harassing the vigil. Whenever it could, the Military Police would come up with a reason to cause problems at the camp, harassing activists whenever limits of the sidewalks were overstepped by a few inches and filing frivolous noise complaints.

On one of these days, an unidentified tall, thin, and big-nosed Military Police officer arrived with a dozen armed men. "The neighbors went to the police and complained that you are violating the Law of Silence," he yelled. "I have orders from the commander to evacuate the vigil. You have ten minutes to take everything down and get out of here. There will be no 'Good evening, President' tonight."

As he shouted, a middle-aged man with a white beard in a dark suit and tie stepped out of a nylon tent and walked up. Calmly, he said, "Excuse me, sir, do you have a warrant to shut down this vigil or to arrest anyone?"

"I don't need a warrant from anyone!" he yelled. "I am an officer of the Paraná Military Police!"

"I deeply respect your organization, but everyone needs a warrant to do what you are trying to do. These people are standing on rented property and, therefore, you are trespassing on space that legally belongs to them."

"This doesn't make any difference at all. The orders I received are to clear out the area and arrest anyone who resists."

"So, you are saying that you are going to arrest everyone who refuses to leave?"

"This is exactly what you just heard!"

"Okay. You can start by arresting me, because I am not leaving."

"No problem—you will be the first person we arrest."

"Okay, but I'd like to inform you that I am a federal judge. If you want to arrest me, there has to be another judge present."

It came out later that the bearded man was São Paulo Federal Judge Edevaldo Medeiros, forty-seven, who had come to deliver a letter of solidarity to Lula in the name of the Associação Juízes para a Democracia. The police officer, whose name and rank were never determined, lowered his tone, sauntered over to the armed troops that were waiting for him meters behind, sent them away, and quietly followed them.

"Even miracles happen at the vigil," said Manoel Caetano, laughing, as he told the story of Gerson and Renata Arruda from Amazonas. The young couple had been on a cross-country bus trip to Rio Grande do Sul when the driver decided to take a detour in Curitiba to show the passengers the much-talked-about Free Lula Vigil. Married for many years, they had a health problem that no doctor had been able to solve: no matter how hard they tried, Renata couldn't get pregnant. During their short stopover on Professor Sandália Monzon street, where the vigil was located, she sipped coffee and explained her health problem to Neudi, one of the women who led prayers in the camp.

"They say Lula can do anything," she said. "Maybe he can give me luck so I can get pregnant."

They laughed together at the time, and shortly afterward the passengers got on the bus and continued toward Porto Alegre. Three months later, lawyer Manoel Caetano brought an ultrasound image to Lula's cell, which he had just received from an incredulous Renata Arruda. Not only did she become pregnant after visiting the vigil, but the fetus clearly appeared in the ultrasound image making the "L" for Lula sign with his thumb and forefinger.

"President, now Moro's really fucked," Caetano said. "You've started performing miracles."

Worried that the news would spread and that the vigil would become a pilgrimage site, transforming Lula into a new Padre Cícero (the legendary northeastern Brazilian religious leader and politician, 1844–1934), his advisors laughed and kept the story to themselves. No one ever spoke of it again.

On Lula's side, there was no risk that the story would leak. After all, even though there was no law giving them the right to do this, Moro, the Paraná Attorney General's Office, Department of Corrections judge Gabriela Hardt, and the Federal Police had banned Lula from doing interviews. Even professional journalists who tried to arrange social visits with him in prison had their requests zealously rejected by the authorities. This lasted for nearly his entire time behind bars. During late 2018, the attorney Cezar Britto, ex–national president of the Brazilian Order of Lawyers (OAB), decided to fight back. Britto was outraged to see TV and newspapers interviews with jailed international drug-trafficking gang leaders and arms dealers without any objection from the courts. If hardened criminals in maximum-security penitentiaries could speak to the public, why wasn't this right guaranteed to a nonviolent ex-president of the Republic—someone whose voice posed no risk to society?

Furious at this double standard, he sought out journalist Florestan Fernandes Jr., who was the director and anchor of *Voz Ativa*, a weekly TV interview show produced in partnership with the Spanish newspaper *El País*, for which Fernandes also wrote. Britto asked the journalist if he would like to file a request to interview Lula with Department of Corrections judge Gabriela Hardt. Naturally, Fernandes Jr. agreed, expressing enthusiasm. A known foil for Lula and his lawyers, Judge Hardt, as expected, denied the request. Raul Jungmann, minister of justice under the interim presidency of Michel Temer, who took power after the 2016 coup against Dilma Rousseff, also spoke out against the idea of the interview, under the pretext that Lula's interview could disturb the "electoral mood." As it turned out, Britto wasn't the only person with this idea. Around the same time, *Folha de São Paulo* columnist Mônica Bergamo tried to do the same thing, supported by the newspaper's attorney, Luís Francisco Carvalho Filho. Both Britto and Carvalho Filho appealed to the Supreme Court. The justice chosen by lottery to rule on the requests was Ricardo Lewandowski, who authorized the interviews on the condition that the prisoner consented.

Supreme Court president Dias Toffoli and his VP, Luiz Fux, worked so hard to slow down the interview authorization that when it was finally conceded in 2019, Jair Bolsonaro was already president of the Republic. When the news reached the journalistic community that Bergamo and Fernandes Jr. had been authorized to perform the interview, journalists from the website *O Antagonista* and *Crusoé* magazine, detractors of Lula and enthusiastic supporters of Moro and Operation Car Wash, filed their own requests. Lula announced that he would speak with *El País* and *Folha*, but that there was no way that he would grant an interview to Diogo Mainardi, Mário Sabino, or anyone else from *O Antagonista* or *Crusoé*. Federal Police superintendent Luciano Flores authorized them to participate in the interview anyway, alleging that he was defending freedom of the press. On the eve of the day marked for the interview, Mônica Bergamo conducted the following conversation with Superintendent Flores over the WhatsApp social media app:

Bergamo: Hello, Dr. Flores, how are you? I have learned that the Federal Police in Curitiba plan to place other journalists in the room in which *El País* and *Folha* will hold their interview with Lula. However, the Supreme Court ruling clearly states that the interview can only be conducted with the authorization of the interviewee, and he doesn't want to do it with the other journalists. Nobody can force him to do this. I believe that *Folha* and *El País* have their entrance guaranteed, since we have authorization of the both interviewee and the Supreme Court, and we will follow all of the Federal Police guidelines. The other journalists should try to convince the ex-president to let them participate and not attempt to intrude on the interview or force the ex-president to do something he doesn't want to do, that the law does not require him to do.

Flores: Good morning, Monica. You are correct. The president will only be asked questions from the journalists he allows. The others can only accompany the interview without asking questions.

Bergamo: This is an insult to our work as journalists. In practice, everyone will be able to take advantage of our work. I understand, from the Supreme Court ruling, that Lula has the right to only receive those who he wants. The other journalists know this. They are trying to force a collective interview, which has not been authorized by the Supreme Court.

Flores: Come on, this isn't really what we planned. We would never want to insult anyone. To the contrary, we strive to always honor freedom of the press, in a case that involves not just the right to an exclusive interview but the right to free exercise of the profession, freedom of the press, and acts that are not under orders of secrecy.

Bergamo: Dr. Flores, the other journalists are pushing things too far. We all know that a person only gives interviews to people he wants to, and Lula doesn't want to speak to the other journalists. It's his decision, and this is guaranteed by the Supreme Court and by the law.

Flores: Let's do the following: I'll ask my chief of staff to formally summon their lawyers, giving them a copy of my dispatch so that they can submit it for legal analysis in time for it to be overruled. If you prefer, we can reschedule the date of the interview for Friday of next week, so that you will have time to overrule my decision. Does that work for you?

Bergamo: I didn't know that this was your decision. Let's do the following. We understand that only journalists who Lula accepts may be allowed to enter the room. If he accepts a thousand journalists at the same time, we won't and can't make any objection. But we are dealing with an interview and not a public hearing. He can't be forced to do this. I have never heard, in the history of the world, of a specific press outlet accompanied by hundreds of other journalists who can all publish the interview at the same time.

Flores: The problem is that the other journalists who are requesting this have already had access to the decision, despite not wanting to participate on these terms, because they will only be there as observers.

Bergamo: *O Antagonista* has advertised a collective interview on its site for two days. I thought they were lying.

Flores: The problem is that the other journalists who are making this request have already had access to my decision. All the journalists in Brazil will be wanting to do this too.

Bergamo: It's "want," not "be wanting." But Lula has to want this too.

Flores: For sure.

Bergamo: He doesn't. He does not want them to participate, and he can't be forced to let them. He agreed to an interview with two journalists, not to participate in an event with several other observers. It's an interview, not a hearing. Every journalist knows this. You are pushing the Federal Police to make a mistake and trying to derail the interview. But this will not happen, because the law guarantees his right to speak only with who he wants, without an audience.

On the eve of the interview, Chastalo stopped by Lula's cell to make sure everything was in order. He found Lula in the middle of a treadmill session. Seeing on the digital screen that he was running 6.5 kilometers per hour, he leaned against the door and listened to him as he explained his position.

"Chastalo, do you know why I won't speak with *O Antagonista*?" he said. "Because I don't speak to fascists. These guys, especially this Diogo Mainardi, are scoundrels. He is a liar of the most disgusting type I have ever seen. If I have to speak with them, I would rather not give an interview to anyone. The Supreme Court ruled that I only have to give interviews to people I approve of. I am going to talk to Mônica Bergamo and Florestan, from *El País*. Afterward, I am going to think about doing interviews with other outlets. It's me, not the Federal Police, who gets to decide who I will speak to, damn it."

The ex-president interrupted his run for a few minutes, wiping his face, and complained to his jailer that his physical performance that day was worse than normal because the treadmill belt was sticking on one side. Chastalo found a jar of silicone, fixed the problem, and continued listening while Lula resumed his vigorous exercise.

"I'm old, Chastalo. I've lived a lot and never traded my dignity for my freedom. These guys don't know who they arrested and don't know what they are doing, but history will judge them. Yes, they will be remembered, but as the garbage of history. The triplex apartment case, damn it, all started with an article in *O Globo*, which was supplied by a dirty Federal Police agent, who put it into the hands of dirty Dallagnol, and it arrived in the hands of dirty Moro. It finally arrived at the TRF-4 court—a group of cowards who confirmed Moro's ruling without even reading it or analyzing the evidence, damn it!"

The next day, wearing a grey suit jacket, black pants, and a white shirt with no tie, Lula spoke for an hour and fifty minutes to the two journalists. He gave a brief introduction on the injustice committed against him and answered twenty-seven questions from Bergamo and twenty-one from Fernandes. By the end of the next day, the interview had been read by more than 200 million people. On *El País*'s sites alone, 170 million people read and saw Lula tell his story.

Two weeks after the interview, on May 12, 2019, Mother's Day, Lula's story would take another turn—one of, if not the most, important of his life. Without him knowing, in the city of Araraquara, 300 kilometers from São Paulo, a man nicknamed Red was having milk and cookies in the kitchen in the house where he lived with his grandmother. Minutes later, Red set in motion a series of events that would put an end to Lula's ordeal and light a fire under the Car Wash investigation and all of its operatives, from Moro to the ogre Januário Paludo—the Paraná federal prosecutor who considered Lula's wish to help bury his brother as "naughtiness." The tidal wave would also swallow Deltan Dallagnol, the young prosecutor who had promised to end corruption in Brazil while simultaneously running real estate scams, with property sold at negative interest to low-income members of the working class.

The thirty-year-old law student Walter "Red" Delgatti Neto had had a difficult life, ridden with controversy. After his parents separated when he was a child, he moved in with his maternal grandmother.

"In this fight over who stays, who doesn't, as if I were a yo-yo, my mom ended up sending me to my grandmother's house, leaving me at her front door with a suitcase and everything, all my clothes, and I stayed there," he later told a CNN interviewer.

The nickname Red had nothing to do with his ideas but with the color of his red beard and his receding, curly hair. There was nothing political about it; indeed, it's possible that he didn't even know the political significance of his nickname. With no mother or father, he spent his life living in the houses of relatives like his grandmother Otilia Delgatti. After getting involved in financial scams, declaring bankruptcy due to purchases of luxury cars, and facing criminal charges that he had eighty pills in a drawer in his nightstand (which the police swore were amphetamines but that he swears were prescription antidepressants available in any pharmacy), Red appeared to have tried to get his life in order by entering law school at UNAERP, a private university in the city of Ribeirao Preto, less than an hour drive from Araraquara.

To survive, Red made money doing homework for classmates who didn't like to study. He wasn't exactly a hacker, as often depicted in movies and on the news, but he was interested in smartphones and computers and knew more on these subjects than the average person. Eventually, his appetite for knowledge on this new, constantly evolving technology led to his becoming an expert. Capitalizing on vulnerabilities of the Russian communications app Telegram, which enabled its users to solicit an access code over the phone, Red figured out how to access any account in the system.

Red would go to speeches at his university, not necessarily because he was interested in the content, but because his school allowed students to make up for absences by watching any speech or lecture in person or online—regardless of the subject. One day, while making up for a skipped class, Red noticed that one of the speakers that evening was friendly Paraná prosecutor Deltan Dallagnol, leader of the Car Wash task force. Red had read about the investigation, which was in the headlines almost every day, but he became mesmerized listening to Dallagnol talk about corruption, politicians receiving million-dollar bribes, and political parties' embezzlement of funds from the Petrobras state petroleum company. To Red, this attorney from Curitiba didn't seem like a creature from another planet; on the contrary, he identified with Dallagnol's nervous speaking style. It reminded him of himself. Red left the event convinced that those guys in Curitiba were saving Brazil from the crooks.

Every new secret Red learned from the Telegram accounts he had hacked using his computer left him more excited about the mysterious cyber-universe. He spent his nights in a daze in front of the blue light of his computer screen at his grandmother Otilia's house. Soon after seeing Dallagnol speak, he began to hack the accounts of random political celebrities, without paying much attention to their parties. The target might just as soon be center-left Senator Cid Gomes (PDT / Ceará) or Congresswoman Joice Hasselman (PSL / São Paulo), who was at the time a fanatic Bolsonarista. He tried to hack into the account of ex-congressman Jean Wyllys (PSOL / Rio de Janeiro), who was in self-exile in Europe, or former state lawmaker Manuela D'Ávila (PC do B). It was through the hands of the young Manuela, who had been

Fernando Haddad's vice-presidential candidate, that Red was able to transfer to *Intercept* editor Glenn Greenwald data that opened the gates of hell. As he read messages between Curitiba prosecutors and Judge Sergio Moro, Red, who had up to that point been an enthusiastic supporter of Operation Car Wash, began to suspect that the entire operation was a monumental farce designed to destroy Lula's political career. And it looked like it had achieved its goal by imprisoning the former president and barring his candidacy in the election won by Jair Bolsonaro months earlier.

Having lived in Brazil for years, where he met his husband, the future politician David Miranda of PSOL, Glenn Greenwald, a fifty-two-year old former lawyer, had transformed from journalist to celebrity after he won the Pulitzer Prize for leading a team from the British newspaper the *Guardian* in publishing a series of stunning revelations. Their reporting uncovered closely guarded secrets of the National Security Agency (NSA), the most powerful security organ of the US government—which had, in theory been set up to protect telecommunications. Afterward, Greenwald was one of the main characters in Oliver Stone's movie *Snowden*, which dramatized the leaking of those military and global espionage secrets by the former US intelligence agent Edward Snowden (who now lives in exile in Moscow).

In possession of an ocean of information, Greenwald used the Brazilian version of the *Intercept* to slowly publish, drip by drip, what turned out to be the largest secret information leak in the history of Brazil. Nicknamed by readers as "Vaza Jato" (a play on words meaning "Car Wash leaks," from the Portuguese *lava jato* or "car wash"), the process of revealing material captured by Red took place across more than a hundred stages, in the form of articles published in *Intercept Brasil* and other media outlets between June 2019 and March 2021. In a clever strategic move, the *Intercept* shared the dissemination process with prestigious conservative media outlets and with journalists who were considered anti-Lula or anti-PT. In so doing, Greenwald's site succeeded not only in reaching a wider audience but in protecting itself against accusations that it was building a media campaign to disqualify the arguments against the ex-president and his party. Using this tactic, the *Intercept* allied itself with the Bandeirantes TV network, the news website *UOL*, journalist Reinaldo Azevedo, *Folha de São Paulo*, *Veja* magazine, the Brazilian edition of the Spanish newspaper *El País*,

Buzzfeed, and *Agência Publica*—an independent outlet widely considered to be unaffiliated with political parties.

The damage caused by the revelations of the *Intercept* and its partners was enough to bury Operation Car Wash forever, but the Federal Police discovered that Red still had a lot up his sleeve. After arresting the hacker, who spent six months in Papuda penitentiary in Brasília, the Federal Police started an investigation called Operation Spoofing, during which hundreds of times more information than what had been shared with the *Intercept* was seized and delivered to the Supreme Court. Justice Ricardo Lewandowski then shared it with Lula's defense attorney Cristiano Zanin, who, little by little, went public with more secrets of the so-called Republic of Curitiba.

According to the Federal Police, Red had downloaded around seven terabytes—the equivalent of 45 million pages of data—from the Car Wash investigation. The gravity of the information provoked a legal and political earthquake in Brazil. Faced with the scandal caused by the release of leaks by the *Intercept* and Operation Spoofing, two Supreme Court justices turned Brazil upside down. On March 8, 2021, Justice Edson Fachin—in a shocking and unexpected decision—ruled that the Thirteenth Federal District Court of Curitiba, which had been presided over by Moro and received all of the charges related to the Car Wash investigation, had no legal jurisdiction to rule on any of Lula's charges, reversing all of his convictions. With this decision, Lula regained his freedom, had all of his political rights restored, and became eligible to run for office. One day later, Justice Gilmar Mendes decided to act on a motion that had been sitting in a drawer at the Supreme Court since November 2018 and declare ex-judge Sergio Moro a suspect of committing judicial bias in all of the remaining open cases against Lula, rendering them null and void.

In November 2019, the Supreme Court ruled that a defendant could only serve time after all of his appeals had been exhausted. This resulted in the release of hundreds of people, including ex-president Lula. Between the time the release order was issued by the Supreme Court and the moment his cell door opened, however, Lula had one final headache. Gathered together in an enormous room in the Federal Police headquarters, the Paraná Federal Police chief and the commander of the state Military Police attempted to add a clause to Fachin's and Mendes's decision that constituted an additional punishment. Fearing that a festive reception for Lula at the vigil could turn into a political uprising, they demanded that he leave the building by helicopter to Afonso Pena Airport and be immediately transported on an official plane to São Paulo. The resistance to this proposal was unanimous. Defense lawyers, Moraes and his aides, and even the jailers insisted that this would violate the Supreme Court ruling. Even Chastalo, the person ultimately legally responsible for the prisoner's release, refused to comply with the crime the authorities were trying to commit.

"The order determines that the prisoner should be freed," he said. "My responsibility is to open the door of the cell, take him to the ground floor, and open the exit gate. Once this is done, he can go wherever he wants."

The maneuver by the Military Police and the Federal Police superintendent failed.

Together, a group of lawyers and jailors walked up to the cell. Lula signed his release order and grabbed his suitcase, which had been packed by Paulão and Chastalo. Then, to avoid crowds squeezing into the elevators, Chastalo decided to take Lula down the fire escape stairs, which were encased in concrete and attached to the outside of the building. At every fire escape door, as they went down four flights of stairs to street level, hooded, armed federal police agents smiled and said goodbye to the ex-president, who greeted them all one by one by their names or by the cities they came from.

"Paranaguá, take that shit off of your face, young man! I want to see your face. Pollock, thanks for everything! Bye, Fulano, thank you very much! Ciao, Cicrano, go with God and hug your wife for me!"

At each floor, there was another round of goodbyes. Some of the agents tried to hide their tears by lowering their heads. As they reached the bottom, they could hear the chorus rising from the streets as a crowd surrounded the Federal Police building:

"Free Lula! Free Lula! Free Lula!"

A few minutes before 6:00 p.m. on Friday, November 8, 2019, Lula walked through the front door of the Federal Police building as a free man, after spending 581 days in prison. In a black suit with a navy-blue T-shirt, he walked out of the building and was surrounded by dozens of friends, relatives, and security officers. Smiling, he hugged his girlfriend Janja, his daughter Lurian, and his grandson Thiago. At his side, the scene was transmitted live on TV, and an online stream showed his security chief, Captain Valmir Moraes; ex-congressman and attorney Wadih Damous; MST leader

Roberto Baggio, who had been one of the organizers of the vigil; jailer Jorge Chastalo, who kept him company in his cell during his entire imprisonment; Gleisi Hoffmann; attorneys Cristiano Zanin and Valeska Teixeira; Luiz Eduardo Greenhalgh; press attaché José Chrispiniano; lawyers and daily companions Manoel Caetano and Rochinha; Fernando Haddad; Congressman Emídio de Souza; Rio de Janeiro state PT leader Lindbergh Farias; Marcola; Nicole Briones; and the excited photographer Ricardo Stuckert, who seemed to be operating a machine gun, not a camera, as he worked to capture so many emotional images.

Without taking his arm from around Janja, Lula was practically dragged to the small stage set up at the front of the vigil, which was surrounded by hundreds of people. The ex-president spent the first half of his fifteen-minute speech reading a long list of thank-yous to everyone who had shown him solidarity during his imprisonment:

> Every single day, you were the fuel of democracy that I needed to resist the mischief and the immorality that the rotten side of the Brazilian state did to me and Brazilian society, this rotten side of the Federal Police, the rotten side of the District Attorney's Office and the Revenue Service that worked and worked to criminalize the left and Lula. And I can't leave her without thanking you . . .
>
> The deceitful arm of the Federal Police opened an investigation against me. The lying and immoral side of the DA's Office and Moro with the TRF-4 court, these people have to know one thing: they didn't imprison a man. They tried to kill an idea, and you can't kill an idea. An idea doesn't disappear . . .
>
> There is a gang, a group of mafiosos in this country that did this dirty trick to create an image, led by Globo TV network, that the PT needed to be criminalized and that Lula was a bandit. I tell you, if they take Dallagnol, Moro, and some of the Federal Police agents behind the investigation and mix them in a blender, you won't get 10 percent of the honestly represented in this country . . .
>
> I have no grudge with the Federal Police. I have no grudge with the jailers. I don't have a grudge with anyone. I only have the desire to prove that this country could be much better if it had a president that didn't lie as much as Bolsonaro. Thank you for everything, from the bottom of my heart! I will be eternally grateful to you and faithful to your fight! May God bless every man and woman here! . . .

> I want to introduce you to a person I've spoken about but that not everyone here knows. I would like to introduce you to my future comrade. I pulled off the feat, in prison, of getting a girlfriend, and she has even agreed to marry me. She has a lot of courage."

To shouts of, "Kiss! Kiss! Kiss!" Lula dramatically kissed Janja, walked down the stairs of the stage, and, without having to say anything to anyone, stepped onto the street as a candidate for the Brazilian presidency.

Lula spent 581 days in a twenty-five-square-meter cell that was called a "state room," from where it was impossible to see his supporters as they held a vigil outside the police headquarters. These are the only two photos of Lula's cell taken while he was imprisoned there. © Fernando Morais archives.

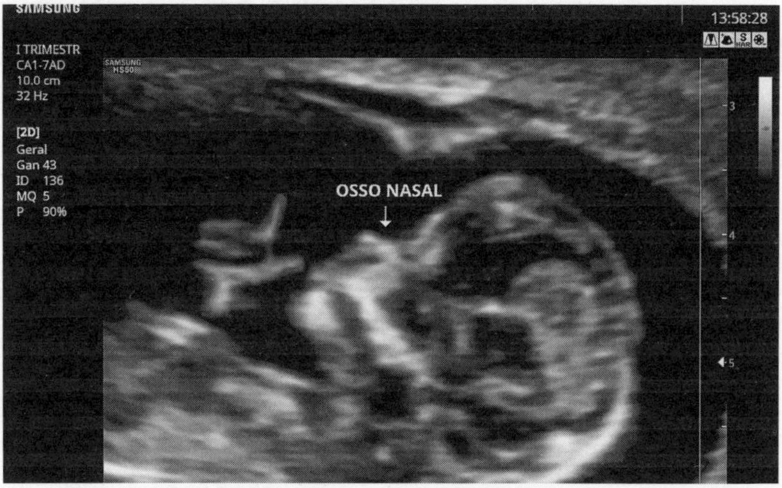

"The miracle" of Curitiba. The ultrasound image shows a baby conceived at the vigil making the "L for Lula" sign in his mother's womb. © Instituto Lula.

7

Jardim Lavinia, April 1980—With the police at the door to arrest him, Lula growls, "I'm sleeping, damn it! They can go fuck themselves!"

The clock had just struck one on the Saturday morning of April 19, 1980, when Congressman Geraldo Siqueira announced that he had drained the last of four bottles of Liebfraumilch (a sweet German wine that was then cheap and very popular in Brazil). The wine had run out at the right moment. Siqueira, who had the long, messy hair of a hippie, looked as sleepy as his other three companions that night: Friar Betto, from the Dominican Order of the Catholic church, and the two hosts, Lula and Marisa. Together with the wine, they had just finished the final round in a marathon of gin rummy that they had started playing in teams after dinner—with Lula and Marisa against Betto and "Geraldinho," as the congressman was known. José Carlos Dias and Airton Soares, political prisoner defense attorneys (the latter of whom was now a federal congressman for the recently formed PT), had visited and left earlier. The long night of cards ended without the friar–congressman team winning a single round against Lula and Marisa, who had a reputation among friends for being unbeatable.

The unusual presence of a holy man and a politician in Lula and Marisa's house at that hour of the morning had an explanation. Two days earlier, at the height of a strike in which 140,000 workers had paralyzed the ABC region, the Metalworkers' Union of São Bernardo do Campo and Diadema, led by Lula, endured a federal intervention that saw all of the directors removed from office. Certain that Lula's arrest was imminent, Betto and Geraldinho had started sharing the one-story, thirty-three-square-meter house in Jardim Lavinia in São Bernardo with the couple who lived there and their youngest son, Sandro, who was a year and nine months old. Geraldinho slept on the living room sofa, and Betto shared a bunk bed with Sandro in a back room. Marisa and Lula slept in the house's only bedroom. During that emergency, the other children—nine-year-old Marcos, from Marisa's first marriage, and five-year-old Fabio—were taken to relatives' houses. Six-year-old Lurian, child of a brief relationship between Lula and a nurse named Miriam Cordeiro, lived with her maternal grandmother, Beatriz, in São Bernardo.

Before dinner, Lula had walked with Congressman Soares to Assunção Hospital, a few blocks from his house, to visit two union workers who had been injured in the strike when riot police attacked a picket line. One had broken his foot trying to escape, while the other had lost part of his right hand from an exploding tear gas grenade. When they arrived back home, they met attorney José Carlos Dias, president of the Justice and Peace Commission, who was worried about Lula's security. The two had known each other since 1975, when Lula had asked Dias for help for his older brother José Ferreira da Silva, "Friar Chico," who had been arrested for belonging to the pro-Moscow Brazilian Communist Party (PCB). Even during that short walk to the hospital, Lula was trailed at close distance by men in civilian clothes in unmarked cars with no license plates.

Lula and Marisa first noticed they were being trailed around the clock earlier that year, by agents who they assumed were from the Federal Police. They were wrong. It turned out that the men worked for army and navy intelligence. Wherever Lula went—the union hall, friends' and relatives' houses, or the local bar for a quick glass of cachaça—they were ever present. Always driving Chevrolet Veraneio vans, the preferred vehicle of security organizations, they made no effort to hide themselves. Even on the weekends, during lunches with friends or family at the Leão de Ouro cantina, as soon as they sat down, Lula would see undercover agents, normally in groups of four or five, sitting at nearby tables. The surveillance operation was so obvious that Soares suggested Marisa cross the street and offer them fresh coffee a few times a day, just to provoke them.

The large numbers of agents trailing Lula, rather than just one or two each shift, also had an explanation. Since they were operating in a hostile region, with ongoing conflicts between the Military Police and striking workers, the agents, despite their weapons and civilian clothing, were afraid of being identified and attacked by the hordes of picketing workers who circulated through the city. It wasn't paranoia; in fact, Lula himself had personally prevented a tragedy. "One day, some comrades appeared at my house suggesting that we get a group of forty or fifty workers together," he later recalled. "They wanted to get a bucket of gasoline, sneak up behind a police car, douse it, and light it on fire with the cops inside. I told them it was crazy and didn't let them do it."

The vigil held by Geraldinho and Friar Betto—who, in addition to being a family friend, was responsible for the Santo André Diocese's Pastoral Operária (Workers' Pastoral)—was the center of a spiderweb that connected union activists, sectors of the Catholic church, journalists, human rights lawyers, intellectuals, and politicians. Some of them were part of the newest Brazilian political movement, the Workers' Party—created two months earlier—of which Lula was the president and most visible figure. The network was set up to be activated by a phone call by Betto or Geraldinho immediately after Lula's arrest. The recipient of the call would pass the information on to another ten people, and each of them would pass it on to another ten, always by phone. The plan required the permanent mobilization of this mesh of people, since all involved had to remain next to a telephone. This was their plan to guarantee that the news of Lula's arrest would reach the national press and foreign correspondents as quickly as possible.

These were not exaggerated concerns. Whether in service of big business or the government, the police had a surfeit of motives to take Lula out of circulation. Nearing its third week, the strike that he led had brought hundreds of thousands of workers to a standstill not just in the Brazilian giants like Villares and in multinationals like Volkswagen, Ford, General Motors, Mercedes-Benz, and Scania but in hundreds of small and mid-sized factories in the greater São Paulo area that built parts for the big car and truck companies.

The workers had won an initial victory when the Regional Labor Court responded to a complaint from the factory owners by declaring itself incompetent to rule on the strike's legality. The size of the strike set off alarms in the federal government. The Navy Intelligence Center (Cenimar) began monitoring it, sending regular updates to the histrionic General Newton "Nini" Cruz, director of the National Information Service (SNI) in Brasília. The reports were ultra-secret, and copies were shared with no one—not even with São Paulo governor Paulo Maluf, the secretary of public security, or the director of the Department of Political and Social Order (DOPS)—the notorious secret police force that had been responsible for the torture and disappearance of hundreds of labor union leaders. In one of these reports, Cenimar warned the SNI about the fact that the strike was spilling out of the ABC and had kicked off in cities upstate like Campinas, Taubaté, Sorocaba and Piracicaba. The red alert light began to flash.

The metalworkers' first victory in the 1980 strike was short-lived, however. The Group of 14 from São Paulo State Industry Federation (FIESP)—a group of twenty-two company union directors from the auto industry—decided to repeat the strategy it had used to confront and defeat the metalworkers a year earlier, during the strike of 1979. Under pressure from the bosses, the Regional Labor Court backpedaled, declaring the strike illegal. With this, FIESP had legal justification to demand that the labor minister, former bank executive Murilo Macedo, order the federal government to intervene against the union. This ruling also gave carte blanche to appointed governor Maluf to use police force to break up picket lines, protests, and marches. As these measures were put in practice, the bosses turned the screw another notch by announcing they were suspending pay to striking workers.

The cord tightened, but despite the pay squeeze, the pressure from the Labor Court, and the threats of intervention and Military Police violence, the workers refused to return to the factories. On the contrary, the strike continued to grow. According to a report from the Group of 14 released by Governor Maluf, the outbreak that had started in São Bernardo had now spread to small and mid-sized factories in cities across the state of São Paulo, including Santos, Sertãozinho, Pindamonhangaba, Guaratinguetá, Piracicaba, São José dos Campos, Santa Barbara d'Oeste, Araraquara, Américo Brasiliense, Ribeirão Preto, Ourinhos, Mococa, Jundiaí, Lorena, and Cruzeiro.

By the government's reckoning, nearly half a million workers in the state of São Paulo had crossed their arms and refused to go to work—a number representing half of the factory workers in the entire country. The striking workers didn't seem to be intimidated by the truculence of blue-eyed Colonel Dalter Dimas Rigonatto, a short, broad-shouldered man with the physique of a buffalo who was the commander of São Paulo's military riot police and its mounted police. By night, the cavalry charges and riot police attacks that sowed terror on the picket lines were countered with rocks, clubs, and burning tires. Hospitalizations in the ABC region doubled with the daily arrival of workers injured in confrontations with the police.

One indidvidual who who played a crucial role in those ongoing strikes in 1980 was a Northeastern migrant from Pernambuco named José "Ratinho" Dilermando, a machinist and union representative in the Ford factory. Short and wiry ("he must weigh two *arrobas*," they used to say, referring to an old unit of measure used for weighing livestock) and uninclined to break a smile, Ratinho was known by journalists and police for his bravery, which seemed inversely proportional to his physical stature.

During one of his many arrests, Ratinho refused to be led to a paddy wagon by a military police officer.

"If you want to arrest me, you will have to get promoted to sergeant," he yelled. "I'm not a bum to be arrested by a private like you!"

He ended up being personally arrested by the violent Colonel Rigonatto, director of the riot police. Ratinho spent most of his time during the strikes at picket lines in the cold predawn hours on Piraporinha Square, where the buses that transported workers to the factories parked. There, it was common to see reporters and cavalry soldiers—mounted on horses that were five feet seven inches (175 cm) tall at the withers—gather around Ratinho to watch him point his bony finger at the police, frown, and repeat his catch phrase: "Brazil will only be fixed when the blood starts lapping against our ankles."

More than the tear gas bombs launched by the police, what caused the most sleepless nights among the workers were their bills at the markets, the butchers, the pharmacies, and the supermarkets. The factories paid their office staff on the fifteenth and thirtieth of the month, while floor workers were paid on the fifth and the twentieth. With their paychecks frozen after three weeks of striking, most strikers' household budgets were already in the red. Their salvation was a support fund created by Santo André Diocese bishop Dom Cláudio Hummes—who, decades later, would come close to being nominated for pope. It was a big help, at that moment, to have an ally like Dom Cláudio.

Born in Montenegro and raised in Rio Grande do Sul, the skinny and soft-spoken Franciscan led the huge diocese of Santo André, which stretched from the smoggy neighborhood of Ipiranga in São Paulo to the jungly fringes of the Atlantic coastal range. In addition to Santo

André, his diocese covered the cities of São Bernardo do Campo, São Caetano do Sul, Mauá, Ribeirão Pires, and Rio Grande da Serra. Collectively known as the ABC region, they had a collective population of 1.6 million across one hundred parishes. Within the dominion of Dom Cláudio was an industrial park responsible for 10 percent of Brazil's GDP and a legion of organized union workers the size of which had not been seen since before the 1964 military coup.

Dom Cláudio's solidarity action was supported by other unions, social movements, political parties, and hundreds of parishes in the huge city of São Paulo. Within days, the enormous parish hall in the diocese headquarters in Santo André was transformed into a donation center that was packed to the seams. In the state legislative assembly, lawmakers' offices overflowed with donations from all over, including other states. At the door of the statuesque marble building on the edge of Ibirapuera Park, trucks lined up to unload sacks of rice, beans, cassava flour, packages of powdered milk, and canned goods packed in cardboard boxes that were forwarded to the unions to supply the thousands of striking workers and their families. Artists and intellectuals held concerts and debates to raise funds, and liberal professionals organized kitties that arrived in Santo André in the form of cash that was converted into medicine, boxes of food staples, and hygiene products.

The strike-fund coordinators organized what promised to be a huge funding source: a concert in São Bernardo do Campo's Vila Euclides Stadium with some of Brazil's most important pop, samba, bossa nova, and tropicalismo musicians. A galaxy of entertainers had signed on that no amount of money or sponsorship could ever have assembled, including Adoniran Barbosa, Chico Buarque, Gal Costa, MBP-4, Gonzaguinha, Alcione, Dominguinhos, Elba Ramalho, Fagner, Francis Hime, Ivan Lins, João Bosco, João do Vale, João Nogueira, Martinho da Vila, Paulinho Nogueira, Sérgio Ricardo, Toquinho, and Ze Kéti. The masters of ceremony were to be the cartoonist Ziraldo and actress Bete Mendes. Scheduled for April 20, the show ended up being pushed back to the following Sunday. With tickets sold for Cr$100 (100 cruzeiros, Brazil's currency at the time), if they were able to put 100,000 people into the stadium, as had already happened in some union assemblies, the most optimistic projections estimated proceeds of an incredible Cr$10 million (around $R2.3 million, or US$460,000 in

2021). The dream, however, would be short lived. Before they could start selling tickets, the Federal Police banned the event. Four days after the date of the canceled event, Agent Sérgio Fleury, founder and director of the São Paulo death squad accused of torturing dozens of political prisoners to death, died in an accident in the town of Ilhabela, on the São Paulo coast. His downfall served as something of a consolation prize to many frustrated organizers and would-be concertgoers.

Refusing to believe that the mountain of donations to the strike fund were merely the result of public solidarity, the military intelligence organizations working to destroy the strike believed there was foreign funding behind it. In a report delivered to the SNI Central Agency in Brasília, the São Paulo division of Cenimar speculated that US$1.5 million (around $5 million in 2021) in clandestine funds had been snuck in from abroad to support the strike. Without confirming the information, the report insinuated that the origin of the funding could be Industriegewerkschaft Metall (IG Metall). Founded in Berlin in the nineteenth century, it was then the largest metalworkers' union in the world, with over 2 million members.

There was, indeed, support from abroad. It didn't come anywhere close to the amount imagined by the navy spooks, however, and its arrival was mainly due to the efforts of two Brazilians. At the outset of the strike, two young men from the countryside, a short thirty-year-old from Paraná and a twenty-year-old gaucho from Rio Grande do Sul, both metalworkers connected to the Catholic Workers' Pastoral, were invited by the Catholic Church to travel to Europe to take courses and complete brief internships in labor unions and social organizations. The goal was to learn how to put a European union tactic into practice in Brazil—something that was already happening informally in the ABC—and create factory commissions, which operated as an extension of the union inside the workplace.

During the last leg of their trip, in Paris, the two Brazilians were given a political task: to deliver a fat envelope to the Santo André Diocese containing a US$20,000 donation from the French Democratic Confederation of Labor, a center made up of hundreds of unions from across France. Although they had never seen so much money in their lives (equivalent to nearly US$70,000 in 2021), they decided to bring it to Brazil like two genuine country folk: by dividing the notes into eight wads and sticking them in their pockets.

Despite its simplicity, the strategy worked. After crossing borders and going through customs, the money arrived intact in the hands of Dom Cláudio Hummes. This unexpected gift to the strike fund was so generous that the bishop called Lula to the diocese headquarters to personally introduce them and to receive the valuable donation from France directly from their hands. Trembling at the privilege of meeting their idol up close, neither of them could dream that, twenty years later, they would both would become cabinet ministers for the bearded, messy-haired man they met that day.

"Lula, this kid is Miguel Rossetto, from São Leopoldo in Rio Grande," said Hummes, "and his colleague is Gilberto Carvalho, from Londrina, Paraná."

Along with the donation from France, vicars from Catholic churches around the world, including the United States, collected donations in their parishes and found ways to get the money to the ABC region. Lula and the union directors knew that the contributions, coming from where they did, together with the surprising success of the food-donation campaign, gave more oxygen to the strike. The longer they could continue, the more power they would have to negotiate with the bosses.

Protected under the mantle of Dom Cláudio, even after they were removed by the government, the union directors continued to meet every day in the church headquarters in Santo André. All of this, however, raised an imminent risk of escalation by the government. If its intervention in the union wasn't enough to cut the ties between Lula and the strikers (even with the union closed, the assemblies continued in Vila Euclides Stadium or in the diocese headquarters), the only move left for the government and the bosses would be to order his arrest. It was this fear that explained why Friar Betto and Congressman Geraldinho packed their suitcases, grabbed their toothbrushes, and moved into his house.

At 1:30 a.m., Geraldinho covered himself with a sheet and lay down on the sofa. Friar Betto silently entered the room shared with Sandro, without turning on the lights, sat in a lotus position, and meditated for a few minutes. He made no special request of God. He simply prayed the regular Our Father and Hail Mary that he always did before going to sleep. Everyone there knew that the night would be short because a new workers' assembly had been called for later that morning, Saturday, in

Vila Euclides Stadium. Lula liked to hold the assemblies in the morning as a trick to ensure that the workers wouldn't arrive in the crowd after a few shots of cachaça or cognac and exaggerate their demands.

As Lula switched off the last light in their house in Jardim Lavinia, twenty kilometers away, on Radial Leste Avenue on the other side of São Paulo, an unmarked Chevrolet Veraneio van with no plates traveling at high speed veered right, causing the driver of a car in the next lane to slam on his brakes. The intercepted car was a black Chevy Opala with black and bronze plates with the insignia AL-92, which identified it as an official vehicle in the service of a São Paulo state congressman. This vehicle belonged to Geraldo Siqueira, Geraldinho, who was sleeping in Lula's house at that moment. Four machine-gun-toting men in civilian clothes stepped out of the van and grabbed the steering wheel from Luis Blefari, a young black man of thirty who worked as the congressman's driver.

As they yanked him out of the car, put a hood over his head, and pulled him into the back seat of the van, one of the men calmed him down. "Nothing is going to happen to you. We know that you are part of Lula's security team, and we're just going to ride with you until he is arrested."

Blefari was not a bodyguard of Lula or anyone else, but the stacks of pro-strike newspapers and pamphlets that he was bringing to the ABC in the car's trunk and back seats were more than enough to cause him a lot of problems in those days. With his head covered with the hood, he spent the entire night trembling with fear, without knowing where he was or where they were taking him. At six o'clock in the morning, they left a relieved Blefari at the same place they had taken him from and gave him his car keys back, without beating him up. The papers and pamphlets were transferred into the kidnappers' vehicle, and he was allowed to go on his way without showing any identification.

At that moment, in São Bernardo, Geraldinho awoke to the clang of hands beating on the front gate. Through a crack in the door, through the thick fog from the coastal range that normally covered the streets of the city during the mornings this time of year, he saw two unmarked vans and a group of men in civilian clothes, all carrying long guns. He gathered his courage, opened the door, and took three steps toward the gate.

With puffy eyes, tangled hair, and a beige suit that was rumpled from his few hours of sleep on the sofa, the congressman walked up to a sizeable middle-aged man with a gray mustache who looked like the leader. "Good morning," he said. "What is it that you want?"

Although they had a small arsenal in their hands, the men looked nervous, glancing around as if they were afraid of confrontation with metalworkers who might wander by on their way from a picket line to the assembly that was about to start.

The mustached man responded sharply. "We are here to arrest Mr. Luiz Inácio da Silva."

Geraldinho asked an insolent, unexpected question. "Do you have an arrest warrant?"

It was daring irony to demand an arrest warrant during a military dictatorship, but the man silently reached into the inner pocket of his leather jacket, pulled out a typewritten sheet of paper, unfolded it, and quickly put it back in his pocket, without giving Geraldinho time to read a single word. It could have been an arrest warrant, or it could have been nothing. In fact, it was a mere police form that had been quickly filled out by someone named "Scribe Nilton," but, under the circumstances, it didn't seem wise to start a legal argument—mainly because it looked like the man's patience was getting short.

"If he doesn't come out right now, we will go in and arrest him," he said.

Geraldinho calmed him down and said he'd wake Lula up, and that he'd be ready for arrest in a few minutes. He ran into the house, woke up Friar Betto, explained what was going on and asked him to wake up Lula. While this was happening, he got on the phone in the living room and called the apartment of a young sociologist and student leader named Beatriz "Bea" Tibiriçá—his cabinet aide. In four words, he performed the task for which he'd been preparing for days: "They are arresting Lula."

In jeans and a striped short-sleeved shirt, Betto softly knocked on the door of the couple's bedroom and realized that the husband and wife were sound asleep. He walked in and poked Lula in the shoulder. "Get up, the men are here to arrest you."

To the his surprise, Lula rolled over and growled, "They can go fuck themselves. I'm sleeping, damn it!"

Worried, Betto insisted. "Lula, the guys are out there! They are yelling that they are going to come in and arrest you!"

He stood up. Barefoot and shirtless, Lula walked out onto the street buttoning his fly. Showing no fear, but in a very bad mood, he struck up a tense conversation with the supposed boss of the group.

"What is it? What do you want?"

"You are under arrest."

"Under arrest for what?"

"We don't know either. They just told us to arrest you."

"Okay," Lula said. "Hold on a minute, because I want to brush my teeth, get dressed, and have a cup of coffee."

He came out a few minutes later with Marisa, Betto, and Geraldinho. They put him into the back seat of the van, where he was guarded by six men: one on each side, two in front, and two more in the baggage compartment, all armed. A few meters down from the house, four more men in civilian clothes sat in a second Veraneio van. Both vehicles pulled out and set off at high speed toward São Paulo.

The same Lula who had spoken rudely to the cops minutes earlier was now very afraid. There was no guarantee that these men were the police, or even members of another government security agency. He couldn't stop thinking about the brutal torture his brother Friar Chico had suffered five years earlier at the hands of DOI-CODI, the official name given to the Brazilian government's torture centers. Nearly forty years on, Lula still vividly remembered that morning. "I started to get scared the moment that I entered the van. I was alone with six armed men. I started to remember people who were assassinated whose bodies had vanished. Damn it, there were no witnesses there! Where were these guys taking me? What if they killed me, then ran over my body and said I was hit by a car?"

Luckily, his macabre thoughts didn't last long. Minutes later, when they drove by Leão de Ouro restaurant, a kilometer from Lula's house, the silence was interrupted as the driver turned on the radio. It was tuned in to *O Pulo do Gato*, a popular morning news and variety program on Rádio Bandeirantes, directed by José Paulo de Andrade. It was Andrade himself who interrupted the programming and came on the air.

"Attention, pay attention!" he said. "The union leader Luiz Inácio da Silva, Lula, has just been arrested. This information is being given by a reliable source: the Metropolitan Curia of São Paulo."

Lula was relieved to learn that Bishop Dom Pedro Evaristo Arns had told the radio journalist that he'd been arrested by the police and not paramilitaries, but it didn't please the armed men sitting next to him.

"This son of a bitch bishop should go fuck himself!" one of them said.

An experienced radio journalist, Andrade added a sense of drama to his scoop, telling his listeners that he was trying to solve a mystery.

"We are trying to find out who ordered the arrest," he said, "but neither Governor Paulo Maluf nor his security secretary, Octávio Gonzaga Júnior, or even DOPS director Agent Romeu Tuma have the answer to this question. What we can say with absolute certainty is that Lula was arrested at six this morning in his house in São Bernardo do Campo."

The "spider's web" had worked. Immediately after getting the phone call from Geraldinho, Bea called Anna Maria Wey, the cardinal's secretary and informal chief of staff at the Metropolitan Curia. Wey gave the news to Dom Paulo. Almost simultaneously, he received a phone call from Santo André from Bishop Dom Cláudio Hummes with the news that Friar Betto had just told him the same thing. (Dom Cláudio was the first person on Friar Betto's list.) José Paulo de Andrade ended his program that morning convinced that the state authorities had tried to confuse the press by feigning ignorance. A source from the Second Army Corps cited in an *Estado de São Paulo* article that day stated, "The Army had nothing to do with this. It was DOPS, the political police, who arrested him."

8

Navy intelligence intercepts communications from the Curia and reveals that Cardinal Arns asked the German Catholic Church to support the ABC Metalworkers' strike fund

Lula was taken to a prison, located inside an early twentieth-century building originally built by the Sorocaba railway company, which was owned by the US billionaire Percival Farquhar. The aesthetically pleasing red-brick building, designed by the celebrated São Paulo architect Ramos de Azevedo, had operated as an office building and railway station until the 1940s, when federal intervenor Ademar de Barros renationalized the company and transformed the enormous four-story building on General Osório Square in downtown São Paulo into a prison. Since then, famous writers and other celebrities had passed through its cells, including author Monteiro Lobato, members of the São Paulo modernist art vanguard (including Oswald de Andrade, Pagu Galvão, and Flávio de Carvalho) and religious leaders like Friar Betto—the same man who was sleeping in Lula's house.

When Lula arrived in the building on April 19, 1980, he realized that he wasn't the only person to have been arrested. All of his colleagues from the union directorate and other union leaders from the region, including his brother Friar Chico, were there too. It wasn't seeing his brother and the other union leaders that rekindled the fear that had overtaken him when he first left his house, however. Paranoia set in when he saw two celebrity attorneys who worked with political prisoners and were directly connected to the Catholic church hierarchy: José Carlos Dias, who had been in his house hours earlier, and Dalmo Dallari.

"My God," he thought, "if they've even arrested Dallari and Dias, it's because there's a coup d'etat going on inside the coup d'etat. We're fucked!" Even the normally smiling and good-humored DOPS director, Agent Romeu Tuma, looked sullen and worried as he received Lula at the building door.

Tuma's apparent confusion and the doubts of journalist José Paulo de Andrade continued. It was only many years later, with the release of part of the dictatorship's secret paperwork, that the public learned that, like Lula, Governor Maluf, his security secretary, and the director of DOPS had only found out about the arrests from the Bandeirantes radio station.

The fierce persistence of the striking workers had brought the crisis from São Paulo to the office of the presidency in the capital, Brasília, the Planalto Palace, where an informal task force was quickly set up. The group was personally led by the president of the Republic, General João Batista Figueiredo, and included three generals from his cabinet: Armed Forces chief Danilo Venturini, National Information Service (SNI) chief Otavio Medeiros, and the presidential chief of staff, Golbery do Couto e Silva. The only lower-ranking officer in the group was ex-major Heitor Aquino Ferreira, the president's personal secretary. Worries of maintaining the secrecy of the operation were so great that even Justice Minister Ibrahim Abi-Ackel was left out of the loop and only learned about it after it had been set up.

"Our goal was to break the back of the ABC union movement," Golbery later told journalist Elio Gaspari. General Figueiredo, who had taken office in 1979, was now free to solve the problem his way, by force.

The mission could not have been put into more adequate hands than those of the silent, bone-thin general Milton Tavares de Souza, known among his colleagues as "Little Skull," who was commander of São Paulo's Second Army Corps. An active leader in right-wing extremist sectors within the military, Little Skull's résumé was the stuff of nightmares. According to a memo from the CIA, Tavares de Sousa reported to Generals Geisel and Figueiredo that he had personally assassinated 104 people considered enemies of the state in just one year. One of his responsibilities was directing the Army Intelligence Center (CIE) which operated all of Brazil's DOI-CODI centers—military dungeons where opponents of the regime were tortured and murdered.

The federal government first lost its patience with Lula and his strikers when the secret service forwarded a report to Brasília made by the

National Association of Automobile Manufacturers (ANFAVEA) summarizing the losses caused by the strike, not only to the auto industry but to the public treasury. According to the study, the strike had already caused losses of around Cr$18.5 billion (around R$4.3 billion in 2021) among the car manufacturers and parts factories, of which Cr$5.7 billion (R$1.3 billion in 2021) would have been paid to the government in taxes. During that period, said the bosses, 64,000 vehicles had not been exported, which increased losses by an additional Cr$52 million (R$806 million in 2021). To the further annoyance of the military leaders, the Foreign Relations Ministry forwarded piles of telegrams every day to the Planalto Palace from the US, Europe, and Japan with complaints by individuals, religious organizations, and labor unions against its repression of the strike and the indifference of the business leaders to their workers' demands.

After the arrests, the government's anger toward the Catholic Church—the institution that the task force identified as the main pillar of the strike—continued to rise. Demonstrating his clumsy way of speaking, President Figueiredo met a half dozen reporters as he left a ceremony in Itamaraty Palace, the headquarters of the Ministry of Foreign Affairs. Visibly angry, he complained that the strike had caused the loss of billions of cruzeiros. He complained about Lula ("He has made some of the most offensive speeches I've ever heard in my life") and denied that the federal government had participated in the arrests. After some back-and-forth with the reporters, he took aim at the church. Taking the ball handed to him by one of the journalists, he delivered the attack in his traditional style, which was brief and insolent.

Reporter: How do you see the role of the church?

Figueiredo: It's bad, very bad. But it's not the church, just certain segments of it. Many bishops have also gotten in touch with me and spoken against the role being taken by the church in São Paulo, saying that they don't agree with it.

Reporter: Even after the letter from the Brazilian National Bishops Conference?

Figueiredo: The Brazilian National Bishops Conference is not the church.

Reporter: So it's only a part of the church that supports the metalworkers?

Figueiredo: The fact is that the church is divided.
Reporter: Are priests leading the strike?
Figueiredo: I don't know if they are leading it or not. But they are giving the impression to the public that they are positioning themselves against the law.
Reporter: And Cardinal Dom Paulo Evaristo Arns?
Figueiredo: I don't know him. I have never had any contact with him, but judging from the information that I have, he is instigating the strike.

Sought out by the journalist hours later, the cardinal appeared perplexed by the president's words and responded with irony. "I don't believe it . . . Maybe this is coming from Colonel Erasmo rather than from the president of the Republic, who I only know from his public statements."

Dom Paulo compared Figueredo with the angry and unbalanced Colonel Erasmo Dias, São Paulo's ex–security secretary.

The cardinal reaffirmed that he had never met with the strikers but believed that the conflict could end if they met three demands:

1) reopening Vila Euclides stadium;
2) freeing all of the prisoners, which would represent "relief from the tension that has swept across the nation from North to South; no one would be hurt, and it would be the cheapest solution for the state";
3) a meeting between representatives of the workers and the companies; but "what we want is a dialogue with dignity, so that the workers can go back to work happy, not humiliated."

The certainty with which Figueiredo pointed his finger at Cardinal Arns as instigator of the strike intrigued the reporters. To speak in that way, he must have had information that they didn't know about.

They were right.

In its sweep to identify the Brazilian sources that fed the "defamation campaign against the country overseas," the SNI had intercepted a telegram sent on the eve of Lula's arrest, written in German and personally signed by Cardinal Dom Paulo Evaristo Arns, to Reverend Paul Bocklet, director of the Commissariat of Katholisches Büro, headquartered in Berlin in what was then West Germany. In the short message, the cardinal asked the Büro to put some pressure on German manufacturing giants Volkswagen and Mercedes-Benz:

> The São Paulo Congregation of Bishops, entirely in solidarity with Bishop Dom Cláudio Hummes, urgently asks the Katholisches Büro to make your influence matter. São Bernardo do Campo metalworkers have been on strike for seventeen days for higher wages, employment guarantees, and the right to union delegates. Volkswagen and Mercedes are refusing to negotiate together with smaller companies and forcing their salary demands downward, denying employment guarantees and the right to union delegates. There has been a standoff for seventeen days without negotiations. Termomecanica, a mid-sized national company, has already negotiated and met nearly all of the demands. Volkswagen and Mercedes have better conditions to meet them. We insist on labor rights, a reopening of negotiations, and that these two companies that are operating in Brazil make a deal.

In addition to holding strong influence over unions and workers' associations throughout Germany, the Katholiches Büro had legal authority to submit legislative proposals to the federal government, Parliament, and state lawmakers through the Episcopal Conference and the German Dioceses' Association. The effect of the telegram was seen days later when workers at the Volkswagon factory in Wolfsburg and the Mercedes factory in Stuttgart threatened to cross their arms and slow down production through a "turtle operation" if the two companies Brazilian affiliates didn't reopen negotiations with the ABC metalworkers' union.

Although President Figueiredo knew about the contents of the telegram, when he spoke to journalists he didn't refer to the document directly; after all, this would require the government to admit that it had committed a crime by spying on Dom Paulo's correspondence. The medium chosen by the military to leak the cardinal's message was the most important newspaper in the country at that time, *O Estado de São Paulo*, which announced its short interview with the president on its front page with, "Figueiredo: Dom Paulo Instigated the Strike." Three days later, the newspaper opened its daily coverage of the strike with an eight-column headline, "Cardinal and Bishop Pressure for Support from Abroad." It couldn't directly say that it had access to a telegram that was illegally intercepted by security agencies, so the article was deliberately vague in places:

> The cardinal-archbishop of São Paulo, Dom Paulo Evaristo Arns, and Santo André Bishop Dom Cláudio Hummes pressured religious organizations so they could force them to support the ABC metalworkers' strike. This pressure was exerted in several ways. One of them was by sending very explicit messages to these organizations, including complaints of supposed maneuvers made by the subsidiaries of foreign companies installed in Brazil and claiming they are trying to obstruct negotiations.
>
> According to our source, the cardinal-archbishop and bishop specifically mentioned Volkswagen Brasil and Mercedes-Benz of Brazil, which refused to accept demands to allow union delegates and provide employment security, two of the items on the list of demands by the ABC Metalworkers union . . .
>
> In messages sent to international organizations, Cardinal Arns and Bishop Hummes said that the negotiations with the workers had to be reestablished and that the German businesses operating in Brazil had to accept the demands.
>
> As a pressure tactic, the religious leaders are accusing the Brazilian subsidiaries of supposedly forcing down wage demands to cause smaller raises. This pressure on foreign organizations was exerted during the third week of the strike.

Instead of responding with an official statement or a press conference, the curia produced its own "interview" with Dom Paulo, made up of his own questions and answers. In it, he rejected the use of the verbs "pressure" and "force," without denying the existence of the telegram:

> Q: What do you have to say about the news, published last Sunday by a São Paulo daily newspaper, claiming that you and Dom Cláudio Hummes "pressured religious organizations abroad to force support for the ABC metalworkers' strike?"
>
> A: The statement is false and malicious. During the last several years, churches in developed nations where corporate headquarters are

located have been very attentive to ethical demands made on these multinational or transnational organizations.

Commenting on suspicions that the telegram had been intercepted by government intelligence services, the cardinal said, "If this is the case, it is a serious violation of the Constitution, which prohibits any kind of communications surveillance."

This was indeed the case. On the same page in which it published the "interview," *O Estado de São Paulo* printed a photocopy of the original telegram, typed in German and signed by hand by Dom Paulo Arns.

What neither the *Estado de São Paulo* nor any other newspaper seemed to have discovered or written about at the time is that the military's original plan was much more ambitious. If the decision had been left to General Little Skull, there would have been 120 people arrested on the nineteenth, among them the leaders of the Brazilian Communist Party (PCB) and the pro-China Communist Party of Brazil (PC do B), union leaders, dozens of state and federal lawmakers, and eleven parish vicars in the ABC region and on São Paulo's west side who had all been identified as strike supporters.

Despite not reaching the numbers dreamed about by "Little Skull," the strategy was kept under such tight secrecy that, to prevent leaks, the arrests were made not by DOPS or the São Paulo police but by hundreds of agents supplied by the Second Army Corps. The DOPS building only served as a jail because the Army itself didn't have enough cells to hold that many prisoners.

Paperwork from the regime that was declassified decades later shows that the only reason the blitzkrieg planned by Little Skull wasn't carried out in full was due to a tactical error, an "operational mistake" that the government itself regretted: the inexplicable arrests of Dalmo Dallari and José Carlos Dias. At the time, arresting strikers seemed natural to the public. But the negative impact caused on public opinion, the press, and even among supporters of the regime by the arrest of the two lawyers forced the government to abort the rest of the operation. No one else was arrested and, by mid-afternoon, Dallari and Dias were released by order from Governor Maluf (the only moment he opened his mouth during the entire crisis). By nightfall, the authorities had started releasing the metalworkers and activists who were not part of the union directorate—among them Friar Chico. The imprisonment of those who remained behind bars was justified by claiming they had broken Brazil's draconian National Security Law of 1969.

The release orders of some prisoners were nothing but a smokescreen. The boot continued to come down on anyone seen showing solidarity with the strike, which continued to grow, despite the commotion of the arrests on the nineteenth.

One week later, new prisoners arrived at DOPS: Bank Tellers Union vice president Luis Gushiken, a short and stocky Japanese Brazilian with a Fu Manchu–style mustache and goatee, and São Paulo chess vice-champion Herbert Carvalho. Feared by the authorities as a social agitator, the Trotskyist Gushiken, himself a chess aficionado, decided to organize a veritable "installation" in solidarity with the strikers on São Paulo's twentieth-century "Wall Street," Antonio Prado Square, known at the time as the heart of Brazil's financial sector. During certain times of the day, it was common for some 20,000 pedestrians to circulate around the block formed by São Bento, Boa Vista, and Quinze de Novembro streets around Antonio Prado Square, most of them being bank workers and customers.

On Monday, April 28, while the banks closed their doors for lunch break, Gushiken set up ten tables and ten chessboards out on the wide sidewalk, along with thirty-two pieces each. He hung a large red banner behind the tables with the painted slogan "Down with the Dictatorship!," and below it, "Challenge São Paulo's Chess Vice-Champion, Who Is Here. The Income from the Matches Will Be Donated to the ABC Metalworkers' Strike Fund."

Moments later, the action had transformed into a public spectacle. The ten challengers sat down at the tables, pulled out their money, and started playing. With big black eyebrows and beard, Carvalho walked between the tables making his moves—always accompanied by a group of onlookers curious to watch a champion react so quickly to ten simultaneous challenges. An ex–chess columnist for *Folha de São Paulo* and *Folha da Tarde*, Carvalho had already had a run-in with the police when he wrote that the chess player Iluska Simonsen, wife of Finance Minister Mário Henrique Simonsen, had used her husband's power to fix championships and prevent the best players from playing against her.

The activity downtown was short-lived. The crowd drew the attention of the police, and soon, a convoy of DOPS squad cars surrounded the area. Officers confiscated the tables, the banner, the rooks, knights, and queens, and dumped them all into a paddy wagon. Along with Gushiken and Carvalho, DOPS arrested anonymous challenger Genesio dos Santos. A Banco do Brasil worker, he was concentrating so hard on his game that he didn't notice the arrival of the police. Cícero Braga, bronze medalist in the 1978 Chess Olympiad, managed to escape by luck. After quickly winning two matches simultaneously, he had just walked away when the police arrived.

The consequences of the "operational mistake" continued. On the same day Lula was arrested, a manifesto protesting against the arrests was reprinted in several newspapers and reached the hands of the foreign correspondents, signed by many of the most important intellectuals, artists, and politicians of the time, including José Carlos Dias (a victim of the police operation), Alceu Amoroso Lima, Alfredo Bosi, Antônio Cândido, Antônio Houaiss, Augusto de Campos, Aurélio Buarque de Hollanda, Barbosa Lima Sobrinho, Boris Fausto, Bruna Lombardi, Caio Prado Jr., César Lattes, Chico de Oliveira, Cláudio Lembo, Cleide Yáconis, Décio de Almeida Prado, Edgard Carone, Edgard da Mata Machado, Evaristo de Moraes Filho, Fábio Konder Comparato, Fernanda Montenegro, Fernando Henrique Cardoso, Fernando Moreira Salles, Flavio Rangel, Florestan Fernandes, Francisco Iglesias, Francisco Weffort, Gianfrancesco Guarnieri, Gofredo da Silva Teles, Haroldo de Campos, Hélio Bicudo, José Aparecido de Oliveira, José Goldemberg, José Gregori, José Honorio Rodrigues, José de Souza Martins, Juca de Oliveira, Lélia Abramo, Lilian Lemmertz, Luiz Carlos Bresser-Pereira, Maria Victoria Benevides, Maurício Tragtenberg, Mino Carta, Paulo Autran, Paulo Francini, Paulo Freire, Paulo José, Paulo Sérgio Pinheiro, Plínio de Arruda Sampaio, Raphael de Almeida Magalhães, Raymundo Faoro, Rogério Cézar de Cerqueira Leite, and Ruth Escobar.

The fiasco of the mega-operation revealed that there were disagreements over the arrests on that Saturday morning that went to the heart of the government itself. A confidential Navy report, addressed to the SNI, made this clear: "The wide range of targets, without specifying exactly what crimes they were accused of, makes it hard to understand the real goal of this operation," it said, "so that, if it can't be considered untimely, at the least, in the eyes of public opinion, it is eroding support for the authorities."

The report ends with the following, discouraging analysis:

> The repercussions from some of these arrests, such as those of the lawyers José Carlos Dias and Dalmo Dallari, is causing more publicity than would have happened otherwise, causing a negative reaction at the heart of public opinion, the clergy, and the opposition politicians. It has caused so much pressure on the Ministry of Justice that it has had to admit to making an "operational mistake."

Six days after the arrests, journalist Antonio Gouveia Jr. discretely published a scoop in *Gazeta Mercantil*. Visually dour but with great prestige because of its wealthy readership, *Gazeta* was a daily business newspaper that also covered politics. Geared toward the "productive classes" and the national industrial and economic elite, it was owned by nine-time Federal Congressman Herbert Levy, one of the owners of Itaú Bank, who was an active member of the Institute of Research and Social Studies (IPÊS), the civil society organization created to support the 1964 military coup. Little by little, starting with friends, the multimillionaire had secretly revealed his curious suspicion that Lula was not a Russophile like his older brother, but an "agent of German trade unionism" that had infiltrated the base in the ABC.

It is possible that the telegram intercepted by Cenimar had strengthened his suspicion, but his theory was primarily based on faulty information—namely, that while most Brazilian union leaders met at an international political summit in Moscow in September 1975, Lula was in Berlin celebrating the birthday of IG Metall, the German metalworkers' union. The truth is that Lula never went to Germany. At the time, he was at a Toyota and Nissan factory workers' summit in Japan, and rushed back to Brazil when he found out that his brother Friar Chico—who actually was a Russophile—had been arrested and was being brutally tortured in the basement of DOI-CODI.

Regardless of its owner's right-wing pedigree, *Gazeta* was known for sheltering a horde of communists from different ideological currents among its editors and reporters. Even its managing editor, Roberto Muller Filho, had been a card-carrying member of the Brazilian Communist Party—like Friar Chico—since his activist youth. In a short article of less than 500 words, *Gazeta* revealed the secret that was being hidden by the President's Office:

DOI-CODI Arrests Were Made without DEOPS' Prior Knowledge[1]
A report that was brought from São Paulo to Brasília Tuesday morning by the president's secretary, Heitor Ferreira, left Governor Paulo Maluf feeling calm enough to speak more openly with the press. Yesterday, at the Bandeirantes Palace, the governor broke the silence that had been imposed on him since the arrests of the union leaders in São Paulo.

The arrests started before sunrise on Saturday and, according to the governor's aides, no one in the state government had any prior knowledge of them. The governor, Security Secretary Otavio Gonzaga Jr., and DEOPS general director Agent Romeu Tuma knew nothing about it. State security staff say that the prisoners were taken to the door of DEOPS before they had learned why. Taken by surprise, with prisoners placed into the state government's police cells, neither Romeu Tuma nor Otavio Gonzaga Jr. or even Paulo Maluf took responsibility for the arrests. Instead, they exercised extreme caution and waited for the situation to develop.

They were just as surprised in Brasília. Awakened before dawn by a phone call from São Paulo, Justice Minister Ibrahim Abi-Ackel said he didn't know who ordered the arrests, saying, "The president doesn't want anyone arrested."

At DEOPS, the night shift workers didn't know what to do with the prisoners, but they soon discovered who had brought them. The arrests were made by agents of DOI-CODI, an organization controlled by Army commander general Milton Tavares. Military authorities managed to solicit the transfer of some of the detainees to the DOI-CODI prison on Tutoia Street, but DEOPS kept them in their unit on General Osório Square until the situation was explained.

That Monday, General Milton Tavares justified the arrests in an interview, and that night he flew to Brasília. On Tuesday morning, Heitor Ferreira landed in São Paulo. He came to confirm the situation

1 "DEOPS/SP," shortened to "DEOPS" in the newspaper headline, was the state branch of the government's political police, DOPS, which fell under the jurisdiction of the governor of São Paulo.

> and compare it with a report from the Second Army Corps that, the week before, had served as the decisive factor for the President's Office to order the intervention against the union leaders.

Four decades later, very active at eighty-five as an English-language book translator and the only survivor of that tiny group of secret holders, President Figueiredo's former personal secretary, retired army major Heitor Ferreira, denied having anything to do with the operation. "As far as I am concerned, the idea is completely crazy," he said. "The part in the article about me is fiction. I never 'went to São Paulo' for anything like that." It's possible that the source mentioned by the reporter had erroneously stuck Héctor Ferreira into the middle of his revelations—but history now shows that he was correct about everything else in the article.

9

After a cruel childhood in abject poverty, Lula receives the key to paradise: a diploma from SENAI technical school

The lathe mechanic and junior foreman Luiz Inácio da Silva, who was arrested that morning by order of the president of the Republic, had an upbringing similar to most of the other hundreds of thousands of his coworkers in the strike. He was a thirty-five-year-old Northeasterner from rural Caetés, three leagues from the town of Garanhuns, in the semi-arid Agreste biome of Pernambuco. He had migrated south on the back of a passenger truck in 1952, when he was seven, with his mom, Eurídice Ferreira de Melo—known as Dona Lindu—and his seven siblings. Lula was the second to last on a stepladder that started with José "Ze Cuia" Inácio, born in 1936; Jaime (1937); Marinete (1938); Genival, or "Vava" (1940); José "Ziza" (1942—yes, there were two brothers named José in the Silva family); Maria, nicknamed "Maria Baixinha" (1943); Lula (1945); and the youngest, Ruth, or "Tiana" (1951). When he grew up, Ziza would go bald from the center of his head outward, which made him look like a clerical tonsure and caused him to end up with a nickname by which he would be known for the rest of his life: Friar Chico.

All Lula remembers of his maternal grandparents are shadows and a vague memory that his grandfather drank a lot. He remembers nothing at all of his paternal grandparents. "I don't remember them, and don't even remember if I had a grandfather and grandmother on that side," he would later say.

Although tragic droughts in the Northeast in the middle of the twentieth century caused the life expectancy in the region to fall to thirty-five, and it was only with great luck that someone would live long enough to see their grandchildren, the truth is that the paternal grandparents that Lula never met, João "Big João" Inácio da Silva and Guilhermina da Silva, beat the curve and died in their eighties.

Lula does have vivid memories of his father, Aristides Inácio da Silva, and they are not good at all. Like three-fourths of the population of the Northeast, Aristides, who was a farmer, was illiterate and "couldn't even read the letter O," according to Lula. He never drank to excess and worked tirelessly, but he behaved erratically toward his family and his wife—more precisely, toward his famil*ies* and his *wives*. In 1945, he left Dona Lindu when she was pregnant with Lula and got on a passenger truck for Santos, a city on the São Paulo coast, secretly bringing his sixteen-year-old girlfriend, Valdomira Ferreira de Góis—Lindu's cousin, nicknamed "Dona Mocinha," with whom he would have ten children, the first of which was in her belly when she snuck onto the back of that truck going south. During a trip back to Pernambuco in 1950, Aristides got Lindu pregnant again with Ruth, "Tiana," who would be born the next year. This was the first time he met Lula, who was already a five-year-old boy. On his return south, Aristides brought his son Jaime, and oldest son Ze Cuia would soon follow.

In 1952, Dona Lindu decided to change her life. She sold her ten-acre farm for Cr$13,000 (R$18,600 in 2021) in a deal that included an adobe shack, a donkey, half a dozen chickens, and a cow that had provided milk to the family. Then she took her remaining belongings and loaded the children who had stayed in Caetés on the back of a truck. After thirteen days and nights of dirt roads, during which the family ate only pressed blocks of brown sugar and cassava flour, they arrived in Santos. With her remaining money, Lindu paid for two taxis to take them to Itapema, a neighborhood in the seaside town of Guarujá—a suburb of Santos, where Aristides was living with Mocinha and their kids.

During the first thirteen months after the arrival of the new migrants, they lived in two separate houses while Aristides supported the women and over a dozen children ranging in age from sixteen-year-old Ze Cunha to a baby of Mocinha's who was still nursing. The family organization conceived by Aristides, however, was not bigamous. From the moment that she learned that her husband had slept with her niece, Lindu never let him touch her again.

The Silva family's eccentricity didn't stop there, or even with the peculiarity of having two brothers with the same first name. Baptized after birth with the name Sebastiana, the youngest child was "a pretty girl who didn't deserve such an ugly name," according to friends her mom made after arriving in São Paulo. Lindu agreed and didn't think twice about it. When she applied for her daughter's first birth certificate, she told the Santos Notary Public that her name was Ruth. All that was left of Lula's sister's original name was the nickname she'd be known by for the rest of her life, "Tiana."

They lived by the port, and Lula's mom enrolled him in Marcílio Dias Public School, three blocks from their home. On weekends, he would join his friends and take the ferry across the channel to Santos, then board a small steam locomotive train back to Guarujá. The fun part was sneaking onto the train and hiding from the conductor by jumping from car to car, then stealing and eating bananas that grew along the sides of the track—which, decades later, would become the Piaçaguera-Guarujá Highway. Later, during the 1970s, Guarujá would become one of the most chic and elegant coastal resort towns in São Paulo, but during Lula's childhood, perhaps due to its inaccessibility, it was a poor hamlet with an inhospitable, nearly deserted beach.

Those day trips across the channel are some of the only good memories Lula has from those hard times. Worse than the vicissitudes of poverty was life with his father, of whom Lula only has the worst memories. The passage of time may have softened and rationalized his anger toward his dad, but it hasn't completely rid Lula of the bitter feelings in his soul. Aristides was a brown-skinned, tall, strong but thin and bony man with low ears and a crooked nose that he passed on to his son. A vain man, even though he worked as a longshoreman, spending his days carrying sacks of coffee in the port, he would go to and from work in a suit and tie. To hide the illiteracy that embarrassed him so much, he would always carry a newspaper folded under his arm. As a nonunion day laborer, he was paid by productivity, for each sack of coffee he loaded. He took advantage of his physical strength to work up to twelve hours straight per day. In the entire port, you could count the number of longshoremen on one hand who were capable of carrying three sixty-kilo sacks of coffee at a time—one on the head and one on each shoulder. This feat made Aristides one of the most sought-after longshoremen by the middlemen who managed the port warehouses.

His main hobby was hunting. Known for his good aim, on weekends Aristides would take off with a group of friends and a little pack of mutts into the Atlantic rainforest of the coastal range with his Flobert, a French .22 calibre single-shot rifle. The armadillos, pacas, peccaries, and occasional deer killed on his hunts would be used to feed his two families and sometimes even as a gift to his warehouse boss. Aristides would use the spare change left over at the end of the month to play the *jogo do bicho*, an illegal but popular Brazilian lottery racket based on animal names instead of numbers. His faith in luck was understandable: it was with *jogo do bicho* winnings that he had been able to visit Dona Lindu in Pernambuco in 1950.

Despite being a violent father, he did everything to make sure that his two families never lacked food. Every Wednesday, rain or shine, the vegetable peddler would pull his cart up to the doors of both houses—located a block apart from each other—to bring them their weekly supply of beans and vegetables, all paid for by Aristides.

But his relationship with and brutal treatment of the children from both marriages was a living hell. It started with dictatorial rules he made for both families: girls were not allowed to go to school, date, or dance. Nobody could go out at night or to the movies on weekends, and no one was allowed to smoke—not even Ze Cuia, who was already eighteen. Corporal punishment in the form of beatings with a sandal or a belt was common among all Brazilian social classes at the time, but the memories that Lula and some of his brothers have of Aristides verge on sadism. This was not a case of a strict father punishing a rebellious son, but one of a torturer and a victim. None of the children behaved poorly or showed signs of delinquency, and none could have been labeled as bad examples. They were well-behaved kids, but even so, they were all, without distinction, treated in an overtly cruel manner by their father. It isn't just the physical punishment that stands out in the children's memory. Lula also recalled seeing acts of pure evil by Aristides on multiple occasions. "My dad would buy regular bread for all of us," he remembers, "but would buy a sweet bun for himself. He would save whatever was left over in a can, and nobody would dare touch it. At night, he would come back and eat the rest of his bun. My two-year-old sister Tiana would see him with the crust of the bun in his hands, cry with hunger, and ask for a piece. He wouldn't budge. He'd sit outside and divide the rest of it with his dogs, indifferent to the hunger and crying of his baby daughter."

Lula couldn't understand what went on in Arestides's head. Why would a worker who was obsessed with providing breakfast, lunch, and dinner, no matter how simple, to his two families treat his children so cruelly? His father's contradictory behavior made him wonder: Was it cultural, the result of a rough upbringing and the hard life in the Northeastern backcountry? Or was Aristides just a monstrous human being with a serious personality disorder?

The beatings would happen for no reason, and sometimes they would even risk the life of his chosen victim. For example, one day the old man got into it with Rubens, the second of his sons with Dona Mocinha, and decided to beat him with a chain. He immobilized the sixteen-year-old boy with one hand, pushing him against the floor while using his right hand to whip his back. When his back started to look like raw meat, Lindu decided to interrupt this family problem (which didn't involve her) and snatched Rubens, who was covered in blood, from the hands of Aristides. Lula, who watched the scene terrified, was certain that if his mom hadn't stepped in, his half brother would have been killed.

More than six decades later, Lula still remembered in minute detail the last time he saw Aristides beat one of his children. His dad had ordered him and his brother Ziza to watch his wooden fishing skiff, which he left tied up on the bank of the Aracaú, one of the many streams that drained into the Santos Estuary, halfway between their house and the air force base. When the tide went out, the little boats, canoes, and skiffs would run aground in the sand, making easy work for the boat thieves that infested the area. The job was simple. They were told to keep an eye on the skiff until the tide came in and the risk of theft disappeared. Although they knew what could happen if they disobeyed their father, the two kids committed the mortal sin of abandoning their job to play soccer. When they returned home, they saw Aristides, with his typical bad breath, waiting for them.

"How is the skiff?"

"We watched it," Ziza lied. "It's there the way you left it. Everything is okay."

Not believing them, their father decided to walk to the stream where he left his shoddy little boat and heard the news from a fisherman. "The tide went out, Aristides, and they stole it."

The old man galloped back to the house, furious, and grabbed the first thing he could reach, a piece of rubber hose. He whipped Ziza's thigh with extreme cruelty, only stopping when the boy peed in his pants and fell to the ground screaming in pain. Then he turned toward Lula who, until then, for unexplained reasons, he had never beaten. Hearing the yelling outside, Lindu ran out and arrived on time to put herself between her ex-husband and her son. The first strike hit his mom across the front of her face. As violent as he was, Aristides had never hit Lindu. That was the first and the last time it ever happened.

Lindu left before dawn the next day and, by that afternoon, had already found a new house to rent—little more than a shack—with her own money, on the same Minas Gerais street where she had lived with Aristides. The move consisted of bringing everyone's clothes, a wooden tub for washing clothes, a knife, and an empty powdered-milk tin that served as the safe where she saved the change from the odd jobs and under-employment of her children. Lindu left her oldest daughter, Marinete, in the old house to tell Aristides that their shared life together had come to an end. The old man didn't believe what he heard and tried to bring her back with a tempting bribe. He had gone to the warehouse and spent everything he had on dried beef, cod, and sweet buns for everyone. His attempt failed. Dona Lindu sent word to him that neither she nor any of his children would ever set foot in that house again. Despite knowing the future ahead was going to be hard, she was proud not to have let her husband abuse her.

After three miserable years in the Baixada Santista (the metropolitan area around the port of Santos), in 1955, when Lula was ten, the strict and tireless Dona Lindu, in search of a better life for her family, dragged her children up the coastal range to the state capital of São Paulo. The move forced Lula to interrupt his studies at Marcílio Dias Public School. Marinete was the only one who decided to stay in Itapema. The small amount of savings Lindu had accumulated from her and her son's labors was only enough to rent a house with one room and a kitchen, behind a bar belonging to one of her uncles on Albino de Moraes Street in Vila Carioca, in Ipiranga. One of the oldest neighborhoods in São Paulo, Ipiranga was full of different kinds of factories, from giant multinationals to tiny workshops. Its borders ended at the region that became known as the ABC, which contains the satellite cities of Santo André, São Bernardo do Campo, São Caetano do Sul, and Diadema.

Sprawled on folding beds, hammocks, cribs, mats, and mattresses, the eight newcomers lived with of one of Lindu's brothers, Odorico; his wife Laura, and their children Leoni, Luiz, and José "Graxa"; a family friend named Severino; and two renters who paid to sleep in a cubicle connected to the house. The Silvas and their guests, a group that sometimes totaled over twenty people, had to share the only bathroom in the building with the bar patrons.

"I know what it's like to live in the back of a bar," Lula says. "We had to use a bathroom where a drunk had just thrown up in the sink, and we'd have to shit on a piece of newspaper. It was that bathroom that we used—me, my mom, and my sisters. I know that life as well as anyone."

There was no shower, and the water was pulled up from a well so that each resident could take a bucket bath. Instead of toilet paper, there was always a stack of old newspapers next to the drain that was used as the toilet.

Decades later, as an elderly man, Lula could still describe the situation in detail. "My mom slept in the bedroom with my two sisters and me. As the youngest son, I could sleep with the girls. Seven or eight people slept on folding beds in the kitchen. The bathroom didn't have a toilet; it was what was known as a "Turkish drain," a squat toilet, like those used in Brazilian prisons. From Monday to Thursday, there wasn't much movement in the bar, and we managed to keep it clean. But when Friday, Saturday, and Sunday rolled around, it turned into a pigsty."

The family's poverty didn't harden Lindu's heart. If someone clapped their hands at the front gate asking for food, she would invite the person in, no matter how shabbily dressed, and ask them to sit down and eat with everyone else—which meant making do with a box or a bench. When Ziza got sick with symptoms of pneumonia, they called a doctor from the Industrial Workers Pension and Social Welfare Institute (IAPI), a housing and social services delivery agency connected to the federal government, and he asked for a chair to examine the patient. However, he was forced to do the examination standing because there weren't any chairs in the house.

The precarious conditions and the nausea of having to share a bathroom with drunks led Lindu to move away from Albino de Morais Street one year after they arrived in São Paulo. Lula, now a preadolescent, had enrolled in Visconde de Itaúna Public School in Ipiranga, where he hoped to at least finish grammar school. Records saved by the school show that during his one year of study there, Lula was better than average in written and spoken Portuguese and in general knowledge, but weak in the other subjects:

> The results of the tests for boys 5th grade group B, under the regency of Professor Selma de Campos on November 19th, 1959. Grades: Written language—45; Arithmetic—25; Reading and oral language—75; General Knowledge—80; Average: 55. Luiz Inácio da Silva. Retained

With these grades, Lula couldn't move forward to the next level of school, *ginásio*, which at the time started at the sixth grade. Years later, when he was in the union, he started a general equivalency course, but he soon learned that it was impossible for him to spend all day directing the union and all night poring over schoolbooks.

He would go to school in well-worn brown denim shorts, the only pants he had, that were held up by multicolored suspenders with one green and one yellow strap, which his mother had made with leftover cloth. Lula made it through the whole school year with three articles of clothing: his brown shorts, a white shirt, and a pair of cotton shorts. From Monday to Friday, he would leave home early for school wearing the brown shorts and the shirt. He would return in the afternoon, hang his clothes over the bed, and put on the other shorts. The next day, those shorts, which also served as his pajamas, would be left in a corner.

His weekly routine didn't vary much. He went to school in the morning, ate lunch, worked half of the afternoon as a delivery boy for a dye company, and spent the rest of the day with his great love, soccer. Sometimes, he would play as a center or full-back, sometimes as a right wing. It was in those neighborhood soccer games that he began to show his first signs of leadership. He was the one who organized the teams, found the ball and the field, and set up neighborhood championship games—which would often end in fistfights. On these occasions, it was Lula who would go to the front to challenge and provoke the adversaries to fight. The bravery he showed came with a family guarantee: anyone who threatened him knew that he had his older brothers to back him up, stocky Vavá and Friar Chico, who had already started lifting weights. The fights would often end in slingshot wars, and he'd get hit by flying objects. Dona Lindu was used to seeing her children arrive at night with a black eye, bloody nose, or other injuries caused by rocks. Two decades later, many of his former antagonists from those childhood battles would stand with Lula on the picket lines and in strikes.

On Saturday and Sunday mornings, he'd go through the neighborhood shining shoes, carrying a wooden box that he had made himself. On Saturdays, he would shine five or six pairs of shoes, and on Sundays, his clientele would nearly double. Unlike the modest salary from the dye company, the money he made from this work wouldn't go to his mother. It had a clear destination: Tarzan movies, Westerns with Roy Rogers, and serial films starring Zorro and Buffalo Bill. When he didn't have enough money for the movies, he would go to a friend's house that had a record player to hear music by Carlos Alberto, Trio Irakitan, Trio Los Panchos, or the unparalleled "king of bolero," Cuban singer Bienvenido Granda. Roberto and Erasmo Carlos, Wanderleia, and the other longhairs of the Jovem Guarda movement would only arrive on the scene a few years later. In those days, television was only for the rich, and it was rare to see a TV in Vila Carioca. Lula himself would only buy his first TV in the 1970s, after he got married.

Lula's material temptations were infinitely smaller than the dream of owning a TV. One of the things he dreamed about was eating an apple. Once a week, on the way home from school, he would stop in front of the fruit stand in the market that sold Argentinian apples wrapped in crepe paper with the origin printed on them: Neuquén, a western-central province. Apples would only start to be cultivated in Brazil ten years later, and they were still considered exotic in those days. Lula knew that all he had to do was reach out his hand and grab one without the vendor seeing him. Even if he was caught, the only risk would be having to give it back. But every time he thought of it, he was haunted by the image of Dona Lindu and would give up. Another object he craved was even more modest than an Argentinian apple: Ping Pong chewing gum, which had just been put on the market in Brazil by the Kibon ice cream company. He would gnash his teeth with envy seeing his friends blow bubbles so enormous they would cover their whole face. The stoicism that kept the teenager from stealing a single piece of gum stemmed not from a fear of being caught but from the shame he would feel if his mother ever found out that he had taken something that didn't belong to him. The only way he could satisfy his craving was to ask his friend Boquita—a big consumer of Ping

Pong—to give him his used gum. He would wrap it in paper, bring it home, wash it, sprinkle it with sugar, and chew until all that was left was a thin, flavourless paste. Ethereal as a shadow, the strict Dona Lindu and her lessons about honesty would follow him wherever he went. One time, Lula walked by an empty truck with its window open and saw a Cr$20 note in the open glove compartment. For a second, he thought about sticking his hand through the window and taking the money. But the mere memory of his mother was stronger than the demon that almost made him give into temptation. The Cr$20 note remained where it was.

In 1960, shortly before he turned fifteen, Lula took his first formal job, with signed work card, as a stock boy at Columbia, a storage and logistics company.[1] His duties included answering the phone and delivering messages and documents for the office staff. It was during this period that a manufacturing plant called the Marte Screw Company, located in Vila Carioca between the districts of Sacomã and Ipiranga, announced it was looking for an apprentice lathe mechanic. He had no idea what a lathe mechanic did, but the job offer came with a seductive promise: there would be a selection process that might potentially lead to enrollment in a technical training course at SENAI, the National Service of Industrial Education. Lula applied, got the job, and, later, wearing patched overalls handed down from his big brother Jaime, became the first of Dona Lindu's children to earn a fixed, monthly minimum wage. In the eyes of the neighborhood, his friends and especially the girls, the overalls were a source of pride. Though nobody could see his signed labor card, the government ID which proved he was gainfully employed, which he kept in his wallet, the overalls were a symbol that their owner had a job and a future.

Lula's first days at Marte Screw Company were a huge disappointment. Even without knowing the difference between a vice and a lathe, he thought that he would arrive at the factory and be immediately put on the production line, making pieces and building machines. It was a letdown to find out that his main work activity was to search the floor for all of the metal shavings and scraps, load them into a box, and throw

1 The Brazilian work card records all the stages in a worker's life: employers, positions held, the dates on which contracts began and ended, salaries, reasons for leaving, union affiliations, and so on.

them in the garbage. It was in fact the role of a janitor, not someone who was supposed to be an apprentice lathe operator. Upset at the end of his first day on the job, he rubbed grease on his hands and his overalls to give the impression to the neighbors on the way back from work that he was working as a metalworker, not a garbage man. Despite his disappointment, he obeyed his orders quickly and with discipline during the eight-hour workday, which included a one-hour lunch break that he almost always spent playing improvised soccer games in the factory courtyard.

Despite being new to the profession and only having a fifth-grade education, the dedication he showed to his job pleased his boss and, within a few months, Lula was chosen to take the entrance exam for SENAI. He passed and, in his own words, "received the key to paradise." Getting into one of the training programs offered by SENAI, a parastatal institute financed with the 2.5 percent of the industrial payroll that trained workers and technicians throughout the country, was everything that a young, unskilled worker could hope for. Due to the partnership between Marte Screw Company and SENAI, he could choose between three courses: general mechanic apprentice, lathe mechanic, or mechanic's assistant. Lula chose the second option, which meant that he would have to spend the next three years working half time at the factory and spending half his day at SENAI. The first two years of the course were taught at its facility in Ipiranga, an enormous two-story building located a few blocks from where, years later, the Lula Institute would be established. The last year of the course was taught in SENAI's Roberto Simonsen Building, with the same schedule of a half day at the factory and a half day of classes. Years later, when he was on the verge of becoming president of the Republic, Lula still got excited talking about it.

"It was paradise! SENAI was the best thing that happened in my life," he recalled. "Why? Because I became the first of my mother's sons to have a profession. I became the first of my mother's sons to make more than minimum wage. I became her first son to have a house. I was her first son to buy a car. I was her first son to have a television. I was her first son to have a refrigerator. All because of this profession of lathe mechanic, because of SENAI. The time I spent at SENAI may have been the most important period in my life—first of all because I was learning a profession, secondly because it was the first time I ever had contact with citizenship. Do you know that feeling you have when you are in a good-quality school and you have a decent breakfast, lunch, and dinner every day? I think that was the first time I ever achieved real citizenship, because, outside of SENAI, life was really hard. At SENAI we had our aprons, we had good food served at the right time of day, we had coffee, we had futsal and basketball. So it was something really special for me."

After the three-year course, Lula proudly received his coveted diploma. Now he was a real professional, card-carrying lathe mechanic. Lula's ambitions were low. He didn't aim to be rich or important. For someone who had been working since he was eight years old, to rise to the level of lathe mechanic was a dream come true. He thought he would start out as a factory worker, save some money, and one day start his own business, either with a taxi or a bar. When he was really dreaming, Lula would imagine himself driving a big truck, "one of those silver Shell trucks, hauling gasoline." In short, he never wanted to be a boss. But he thought the profession he had chosen was already great. It changed his way of thinking and became a source of pride for the rest of his life.

"The work we lathe mechanics did wasn't that simple," he would say many years later as president of the Republic. "We were able to transform a piece of steel into a work of art."

It was during his time at Marte Screw Company that Lula had his first experiences in strikes, but they were weak, without any confrontation. He had yet to develop political consciousness. It would only be years later when he would wake up excited to see the walls of his neighborhood painted with the slogan "General Strike!" Of those early experiences, Lula remembered, "The truth is that it wasn't any great sacrifice to stay home doing nothing."

In those days of disorganized work stoppages, without any central leadership or unified demands, every time a union called a strike, the owners were the first ones to close the doors and send the workers home, fearing that the picketers would start rioting and committing vandalism. Lula joined one of these skirmishes in the early 1960s at a picket line set up in front of Jutificio São Francisco, a burlap bag factory where one of his sisters worked. The guards locked the two- story-high front gate to protect the factory from the picketers, who were threatening to enter by force and drive out the scabs—one of whom was his sister Maria

Baixinha. The gate was so high that they couldn't even see the factory from the street. But the crowd was big—perhaps 500 people. One of the picketers yelled, "Knock down the gate." Minutes later, the crowd pushed over the entire fence, which crashed to the ground with a bang. The picketers invaded the factory, and the scabs, including Lula's sister, were pushed outside and forced to flee through two lines of picketers as they punched and kicked at them.

Young Lula's second strike experience ended dramatically, but he was lucky to have left the scene beforehand. One night, as he was walking down Vemag Street in Vila Carioca, he joined a group of workers who were trying to break into a small sock factory to pull the scabs off of the production line and bring them out to the picket. Suddenly, the owner of the factory appeared in the doorway, brandishing a revolver. Apparently trying to scare the group, he fired a warning shot, but the bullet hit a picketer in the thorax, and he died shortly later in a nearby hospital. Shocked with what he had just done, the businessman raced into the building and ran up the stairs to the second floor, but he wasn't quick enough. Disarmed by the protesters and pushed into a room by the angry mob, the man was thrown out the window, then beaten to death with kicks and punches, dying on the spot. When the trouble started, terrified Lula got out of there as quickly as he could.

At Marte Screw Company, labor conflicts never reached that level of excitement. Whenever a work stoppage was organized, "Mr. Ze," the boss, would take a company van and move his workers to picket lines in front of other nearby factories. Lula's relationship with his boss only deteriorated when he decided to ask for a raise. During his four years there, he had only received the raises determined by collective bargaining. Little by little, he realized that several coworkers who were doing the same job were paid more than he was. When he learned that Vitorio, his neighbor on the bench, produced half of what he did but was paid three times more, he got his nerve up and demanded the same pay.

"A raise?" his boss said, "Don't even think about it. We paid for three years of your studies and have no reason to give you a raise."

"You didn't pay jack shit," Lula said. "SENAI paid for my course, and I want to make as much as everyone else. Either you give me a raise, or I quit."

The boss refused to budge, so Lula left and got a night job at Metalúrgica Independência, a small company owned by a Polish immigrant that was also located in Vila Carioca, which produced combination locks for bank vaults. It was there, during the middle of the night in June 1964, that Lula lost the pinkie finger on his right hand.

"I was doing a lot of overtime. I'd come in at seven at night and leave at six in the morning. I'd work all night and sleep all day. I wouldn't eat dinner there. I'd just bring a snack. Only a few people worked on the night shift—six or seven, tops," he recalled.

One night, a screw in his cross vice broke, and he had to make a new one to replace it. He asked a buddy at the nearest bench to help him out.

"I don't even remember his name, but when I started putting the screw into the vice, he nodded off. It was around two or three in the morning. This buddy, visibly exhausted, messed up and released the vice handle. He closed it at the moment that I was sticking my hand in to change the screw. I tried to pull my hand out, but it crushed my finger. Man did that hurt!"

With his hand immobilized by the accident, Lula spent the rest of the night in an emergency room waiting for a doctor to show up.

"They took me to a hospital there in Vila Carioca," he said. "I think the doctor could have saved half of the finger, from the joint down, but he thought it was easier to rip the whole thing off than to do surgery. He decided to amputate. I know a lot of people who had the same kind of accident, and they didn't have to rip off the whole finger. I think it was a little presumptuous. Or maybe it was easier for him to amputate than to perform surgery. In any event, I spent two days in the hospital. They removed my finger with a local anaesthetic, and I went home. I spent fifteen days recovering, then I went back to work."

Lula didn't know that every finger lost in a work accident had a different standard settlement value associated with it, but he took advantage of his fifteen days off to learn about his rights. "A lawyer came knocking on our door. I went to his office and signed all the paperwork. When I received the settlement of around 300 cruzeiros, or cruzados, I saw that he'd charged me 20 percent."

Seeing what had happened, Lula began to cry. "How could I tell my mom that I had lost part of the money? I ran to the union hall, explained what happened to a lawyer, and he called my case lawyer and said, 'Don't charge this boy. He's just a kid. He just lost his finger. Imagine you, losing your finger and having to pay for the legal fees.' I went back to his office, and he was pissed off and gave me a dirty look, but he gave me my money."

For the first few months after the accident, Lula was deeply ashamed. He developed a complex and tried to keep his hand in his pocket as much as possible. He was embarrassed to take the bus, worried that people would see he was missing a finger. As time passed, however, he stopped worrying about it. Soon, it only bothered him when he tried to cup his hands under the faucet to wash his face and the water would run down his wrist. Finally, he started joking about it. "They could have left a tip for me to scratch my ear with," he would say.

Lula ended up receiving a Cr$351,000 settlement for his mutilation on the job. It's difficult to know exactly how much this value would be worth today, since consumer price index indicators from this period show values that, in today's currency, range from R$3,500 to R$16,300. Although Lula may not be able to calculate exactly how much it would be worth today, he hasn't forgotten what he did with the money. "I used part of the money to make a down payment on a lot in Vila Livieiro, near Sacomã, which I ended up selling later," he said. "I also upgraded my mom's kitchen with a cabinet, a table, and four Formica chairs that were in style at the time. There were 40,000 cruzeiros left over. I saved half of it and lent the other half to my big brother Jaime."

Despite the accident, Lula stayed at the factory for a few more months. Then, he quit and was unemployed for a short time until he was hired as a lathe mechanic at Fris Moldu Car, a mid-sized factory in Ipiranga that made steel body parts for the auto industry. It was there, in December 1965, that he received his first annual thirteenth paycheck—a new benefit that gave workers an extra monthly paycheck as an annual bonus. The benefit of an extra holiday-season paycheck had first been suggested in 1962, during the government of João Goulart. Goulart was deposed in the 1964 coup, but the military dictatorship decided to roll out the benefit anyway, starting in 1965. The check's arrival was a surprise, and to celebrate the unexpected arrival of this money, Lula went on the first bender of his life. During a long night with a group of work buddies, with innumerable plates of olives and mortadella, they downed several four-liter bottles of the popular red wine from Rio Grande do Sul, Sangue de Boi. The next day, still feeling the buzz from the night before, Lula bought himself the first present of his life: a secondhand bicycle so beat up that it ended up giving him more problems than it was worth.

Lula's new job was short lived. Less than a year in, the boss ordered him to start working overtime on Saturdays and Sundays. One Friday night, he let his brothers and a group of friends talk him into spending the weekend with them on the beach in Santos, using the money that the boss had given him to buy lunch during his overtime shifts. That Monday morning, the boss came up to him and said, "Where were you?"

Burnt like a shrimp by the coastal sun, Lula was too embarrassed to lie. "I went to Santos with my friends."

"Okay, then," the boss said. "Hit the road—you're fired."

Lula's parents: Aristedes at thirty; Dona Lindu in 1959. Source: Lula da Silva family archive.

Lula and his sister Maria. Source: Lula da Silva family archive.

The family at the beach, from left to right: Dona Lindu, Tiana (holding the wooden fish), Lula, Aristedes, Zé Graxa (on the Lambreta), and Maria. Source: Lula da Silva family archive.

The ABC soccer team: Lula (third from left in front row) would play either center back or right midfielder. Vavá (farthest right in back row) would play as goalkeeper and also acted as manager and organizer of tournaments. Friar Chico (farthest left in front row) would either play or help coach the team. Source: Lula da Silva family archive.

Lula (second from left) with a group of classmates from SENAI, in Ipiranga, 1964. Source: Lula da Silva family archive.

Lula wearing a tie for the first time in his life, 1964. That evening, he received the "key to paradise": his diploma from SENAI. Now he has a job: he is a lathe mechanic. Source: Lula da Silva family archive.

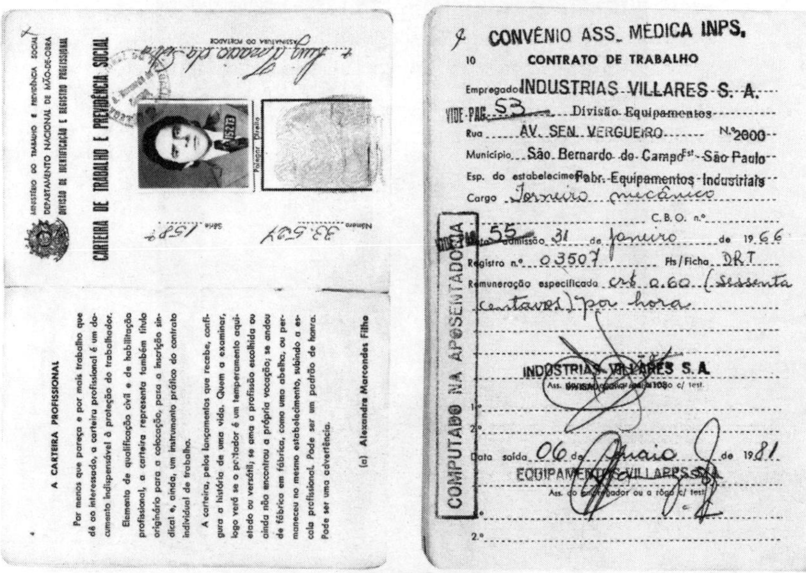

CONVÊNIO ASS. MEDICA INPS.

CONTRATO DE TRABALHO

Empregado INDUSTRIAS VILLARES S. A.

Divisão Equipamentos

Rua AV. SEN. VERGUEIRO N.º 2000

Município São Bernardo do Campo Est. São Paulo

Esp. do estabelecimento Fabr. Equipamentos Industriais

Cargo Torneiro mecânico

Data admissão 31 de Janeiro de 1966

Registro n.º 03507 Fls/Ficha DRT

Remuneração especificada cr$ 0.60 (sessenta centavos) por hora

COMPUTADO NA APOSENTADORIA

INDUSTRIAS VILLARES S.A.

Data saída 06 de Maio de 1981

Lula's "work card," a document all workers held indicating position, salary, union dues, and contributions to unemployment insurance. His card indicates that he was admitted to the factory as a lathe mechanic in January 1966 with an hourly wage of Cr$0.60, and also that he was fired in May 1981 (in retaliation for his activity during the strikes of 1980, and despite his title of union delegate). Source: Lula da Silva family archive.

Lula (with his shirt open) with the best friends of his youth: Lambari, who would become his brother-in-law, and Olavo, who managed to arrange a posh Aero-Willys for the groom to drive the bride, Lourdes, to the church. Source: Lula da Silva family archive.

Lula and Friar Chico at the time when he still had hair. A weightlifter, Chico crossed his arms in photos to show off his biceps and triceps. Source: Lula da Silva family archive.

10

Lula's fiancée makes an ultimatum: "You have to choose between the union and marriage. You can't have both"

Lula would soon find out that there couldn't have been a worse time for him to be unemployed. The contractionary economic policy of the dictatorship that took power in April 1964, following a military coup against President João Goulart, had damaged the labor market, and "Help Wanted" signs started disappearing from the factory doors.

A military coup? To Lula, it had been a Democratic Revolution—with capital letters, as it was described in the newspapers—that had freed the country from communism and corruption. Neither he nor any of his colleagues from Metalúrgica Independência, where he had worked at the time that the military took power, had any doubts about this. Unlike his communist brother, Lula was very proud to see the armed forces take on the task of fixing Brazil. His understanding of what was happening in the country didn't go much beyond the basics—in fact, it was mostly based on things he heard at work and while drinking beer with his friends.

"When the coup came, I didn't have the slightest idea of what it meant," he recalled. "I was eighteen or nineteen, and what we heard during our half-hour lunch breaks at the factory was that people were very optimistic because 'the army would solve the problem'—without knowing exactly what the 'problem' was. The armed forces had an impressive amount of credibility with the workers."

Uninterested in politics, Lula would open the *Diário da Noite* newspaper and go straight to the soccer section to read news about his beloved team, the Corinthians. The level of his alienation was shown by the fact that, although he supported the military, he had silent admiration for two ex-governors, Leonel Brizola and Miguel Arraes—sworn enemies of the new regime who had been forced into exile.

"The problem," as Lula soon found out, was the lack of jobs. Whoever was at fault, layoffs were spinning out of control in most factories in Brazil. In the 1960s, the country still wasn't regularly measuring its unemployment rate, but a stroll through the ABC region provided ample evidence that the economy was recoiling in plain sight. The Silvas were living in a little house in the São Caetano do Sul neighborhood of Vila São José that Lula's brother Jaime had bought with bingo winnings. The first house the family owned since leaving Caetés, it was from there that Lula left every morning at six, Monday to Friday, to walk ten to twenty kilometers knocking on factory doors in search of a job. On days when the pilgrimage was especially long, he'd sit on a park bench and take his shoes off to relax, but it was often hard to put them back on because his feet had swollen so much. He spent months painfully balancing on the tightrope of unemployment. Without money for transportation, a beer at the end of the day, or even a cigarette, at twenty Lula was, once again, subjected to the humiliation of having to smoke cigarette butts picked off the ground. He didn't have a job and didn't have anyone to borrow money from, since his brother Friar Chico and sister Maria Baixinha were also unemployed, and his youngest sister Tiana's boyfriend wouldn't let her get a job. Desperate, he overcame his embarrassment and borrowed small amounts of money from friends who were a little better off. Even his habit of reading the newspaper changed. He switched from the soccer newspapers to *Diário Popular* and started by leafing through the ever-shrinking jobs section in the classifieds. Only afterward would he read the news about the Corinthians. On the smoggy streets of the ABC, he met with nothing but frustration. Dulcora had no openings; Fontoura had no openings; Mercedes had no openings; Karmann-Ghia had no openings. It looked like there wasn't a single job opening in the largest industrial zone in Latin America.

"I would get home at two or three in the afternoon completely exhausted, without having eaten lunch or even smoking a cigarette," he remembered. "One time I arrived at the Mercedes-Benz factory at six a.m. and saw a huge line. The guy said, 'Wait here, because we are going to need you. We are going to hire people today.' And we waited. They started interviewing us at two. I was disgracefully hungry, without a cruzeiro in my pocket, and I had a strong craving for a cigarette. Seeing those big cigarette butts on the ground, my eyes started twitching with an urge to grab them, but I held off. Finally, the guy took all of our labor cards and went inside the building. Half an hour later, he came out and said, 'We don't have any more openings. We aren't going to take anyone else.' Holy shit! I still had to walk back home to Vila São José from the Mercedes factory. I had shoes that I don't know who had given me, that were hard, made from that kind of hard leather that they used to call crocodile leather, and my feet had swollen up. I took them off at the Mercedes factory, and I wasn't able to get them back on. I walked home barefoot. When I got home, that son of a bitch Friar Chico called me a bum because I wasn't able to get a job. There I was, dead tired at four in the afternoon. I hit him in the face with one of my shoes!"

With his hope fading, as 1964 turned into 1965, he saw a help-wanted ad in the classifieds for lathe mechanic in Villares, a giant factory in São Caetano do Sul. Lula went to the factory and repeated the ritual he had completed dozens of times since he was fired from Fris Moldu Car: he filled out a form with his personal information and work history, left xerox copies of his diploma from SENAI and his labor card, took a test, and left, this time with an invitation to come back two days later to find out the result. Numbed by so many fruitless journeys from factory to factory, he went in and out of the test room with his tail between his legs. After all, he'd been wandering around the ABC looking for a job for eight months without any success, without a fixed job offer or even a temporary gig or offer to cover someone's vacation—nothing. To his surprise, he was asked to return. Before dawn that day, Lula arrived at the factory door, raising his arms to the sky when he heard a human resources worker ask for his labor card. He'd passed the test and, therefore, was hired. This was no garage workshop, but Villares's main factory, where over a thousand metalworkers were employed. Lula would spend eighteen years at Villares. It would be the last factory he ever worked at.

Used to small factories where the owner was the boss, accountant, and HR director, and sometimes even worked alongside his staff, where the modest machinery was manually operated, on January 29, 1966, his first day on the job, Lula's eyes bulged at the sight of that world that built earth excavators, overhead cranes, subway cars, and giant diesel ship engines. Each ship engine was as big as a three-story building, and when they were tested they made all the windows in the neighborhood shake. Owned by the traditional Dumont Villares family—who had given the world the most famous of all Brazilians, aviation pioneer Alberto Santos-Dumont—years later, Villares would open a factory in Araraquara, 270 kilometers from São Paulo, with the capacity to produce 300 locomotives per year.

Employment at a big, modern factory like Villares that paid well and on time was the gate to paradise. More than ever, Lula felt like an artist. Every day, he would transform a shapeless block of steel into a shaft bearing that looked more like a sculpture, a piece that would help propel a transatlantic ship with the capacity to transport 2,000 tons of cargo (years later, visiting the factory, Lula would see machines capable of producing not one, but over 200 of those pieces per day).

It would take time, however, for Lula to enjoy the fruits of his labor. Settling the countless small debts he'd accrued during his bitter period of unemployment ate up all of his pay during this first few months on the job. No son of Dona Lindu could have bad credit. Even after he'd paid back all his debts, he wasn't able to burn through his salary buying whatever he wanted. As always, his mother had an unusual method of organizing the always-tight household budget. It was a primitive system, but it would influence Lula for the rest of his life, even after he had become a globally recognized political leader.

At the end of each month, she would put all of her children's earnings, regardless of whether they were from formal employment or odd jobs, into a box. No one could touch any of the envelopes they had brought back from the factories. Then, she would redistribute the money. First, she would pay off all of the household expenses—dry goods, butcher, bakery, corner store, pharmacy, water, electricity, and gas. If any money was left over, which wasn't always the case, the balance was divided among the children. The distribution criteria that Dona Lindu used always left someone grumbling: the amount paid out didn't depend on the amount paid in but on each child's needs. Many years later, as president of the Republic, Lula spoke candidly about how inspiration for his government's policies for reducing social inequality didn't come from a panel of people with PhDs and postdoctorates in economics; they were based on how his mom had managed the income of a poor family. As much as people have tried to attribute it to Marx's "from each according to their ability, to each according to their needs," the truth is that it was rooted in the unique household arithmetic of Dona Lindu, who had never learned how to read or write.

Lindu's method was simple: if one of the children was dating, they would receive extra money to buy a new outfit, even if they hadn't contributed to the family coffers that month. The boys who smoked (Lula's sisters were nonsmokers) would get a little extra change for cigarettes, and those who liked to drink would get a little extra for a *rabo de galo* ("rooster tail"—a cachaça-vermouth cocktail) or a rum and coke on Saturday. Whoever worked farther away would get a little extra money for public transportation. This system would inevitably leave one of the children who had put their whole salary into Dona Lindu's box not getting anything back, or a bit of money given to one who hadn't contributed a penny that month. Nevertheless, protest was unheard of, since none of the children would dare confront their strict mother.

Not much of a spender, Lula didn't have any reason to complain about his mom's accounting. His only love, playing soccer, didn't cost a dime. For a game playing center forward for his neighborhood team, Bangu da Vila Carioca, he would give up anything—even his girlfriend. Indeed, it was on account of soccer that his first relationship, with a young Japanese Brazilian woman named Mitiko, came to an end.

"She was a beautiful Japanese girl," Lula recalled, smiling, "but I was a soccer fanatic, and, between a girlfriend and soccer, I preferred playing soccer. So our relationship didn't last very long."

On top of his love for soccer, Lula was shy. A big talker when he was with his friends at the factory or on the soccer field, Lula would freeze up whenever he tried to talk to a girl. He would only get up his courage and shake his bashfulness to ask a girl to dance after a few generous shots of Palhinha or São João da Barra cognac, the cheapest brands (the money allocated by his mother wasn't enough to drink Dreher, which was popular but expensive, despite being just as mediocre as the others). His friends from those days who confirm his short romance with the "Japanese girl" add a spicy detail: it wasn't one girl but two, the cousins Mitiko and Sumiko. And they swear that he dated them both at the same time, without either one knowing of his adventures with the other.

Lula entered adulthood at a moment when a new innovation in the pharmaceutical industry was changing not only the concept of birth control but customs around the world: the contraceptive pill. Treated by most of the world's religions as a mere means of reproduction, the practice of sex for pleasure would be liberated by the Pill. Until then, nearly ten out of ten Brazilian teenage boys lost their virginity in the arms of sex workers. A boy having his first sexual relationship with his own girlfriend was rare. This was also because virginity was one of the virtues demanded for a woman to achieve a good marriage. The sexual revolution caused by the Pill became so widespread that it evolved into the most celebrated slogan against the Vietnam War: "Make Love, Not War." It was thanks to this invention, developed by biologist Gregory Pincus in the United States, that Lula had one of his earliest sexual experiences at age sixteen, not in a brothel but with a girl from the neighborhood with whom he had been flirting—though the fleeting romance did not develop further.

In a conversation with friends, years later, when he was running for president, Lula confessed that he had also had an early experience with a sex worker in Boca do Lixo, São Paulo's red-light district. "I went to the red-light district for the first time when I was sixteen. They recommended I go to a club called 'The Famous 69,' on Andradas Street, but it was totally depraved. I lost my virginity with a woman who must have been seventy years old."

Lula fell in love for the first time when he was eighteen. The object of his affection was Maria de Lourdes, a beautiful, slender woman from Minas Gerais with dark skin, a tapered nose, long hair that fell over her shoulders, delicate eyebrows, and dark-brown eyes. Lourdes, who was born in the city of Montes Claros, in northern Minas Gerais, came from a similar background as Lula. Both had traveled to São Paulo on the backs of passenger trucks with their respective families in 1952. In addition to being neighbors, she was the sister of factory worker Jacinto Ribeiro, "Lambari," whom Lula would never forget.

"Lambari wasn't just a cachaça-drinking buddy. He was my best friend," Lula remembered. "When times were tough, if he had two cigarettes in his pocket, he'd come to my house and give me one. If he had ten cents in his pocket, five were for me and five were for him. When I was unemployed, Lambari did everything he could to help me."

Lourdes was seventeen and worked as a loom operator at Damatex, a factory that produced carpets and rugs in the São Paulo district of Sacomã—the place where, years later, Heliópolis, São Paulo's largest favela, would spring up. Though he realized his feelings for his friend's sister went beyond mere friendship, Lula was overcome by his insidious shyness. He simply couldn't figure out what to say to her, how to say it, and when to say it. Realizing that he wouldn't be able to get out of his bind alone, he decided to ask for help. Lula struck up an awkward conversation with Lambari, stuttering and addressing him by his formal name:

"Jacinto . . . I like Lourdes . . ."

"That's great, man."

"But I don't know how or what I should do . . ."

"There is only one way: go over there and talk to her."

"But I am embarrassed. I don't know . . . What will your parents say?"

"There is no problem at all, bro. Go up to her and talk to her."

He decided to wait for the next neighborhood party to ask Lourdes to dance and lay his cards on the table. The night of the dance arrived, but Lula's courage didn't. With the help of a shot of Palhinha cognac, however, he began to get his nerve up. Hearing the chords of the first *seleção*—the name given to the thirty minutes of each side of an album—Lula made his way across the hall and asked Lourdes to dance. They made small talk but, by the time the first selection had ended, he hadn't been able to pronounce the word "date." Taking advantage of the break, he went to the bar, ordered another shot of cognac, and asked her to dance again for the next selection. They danced and danced and talked about all kinds of things, except dating. Nothing. It was only during the fourth selection, which corresponded with the fourth shot of cognac, that he blurted it out. He asked Lourdes to go out with him, she agreed, and, within months, they were engaged with the approval of their parents and wedding bands on their right ring fingers.

It was during the two years of his engagement with Lourdes that destiny carried Lula from the factory floor to the path he would take for the rest of his life: the labor movement. The most important figure in this metamorphosis was, without a doubt, his older brother, whose baldness had put an end to his family nickname, Ziza, and was now known as Friar Chico. Lula's nicknames at the time were "Bahian," a pejorative that some people in the Southeast used to refer to Northeasterners in general, or "Taturana," which was slang for marijuana at the time.

The latter nickname started with a rumor from a coworker at the factory who said that Lula's red eyes were a clear sign that he, in addition to drinking cachaça, smoked a joint before punching in every day. "And it's not dirt weed either," he said. "Lula smokes the good stuff, he smokes *taturana*, the strongest weed there is." It wasn't true; in fact, the red eyes were caused by allergies. Lula never tried any drugs, but the nickname stuck for a few years.

After a few months at Villares, Lula suggested that Friar Chico apply for a welding position that had opened at the factory. Unemployed, his brother was a lathe mechanic by training but had also worked as a truck driver's assistant and welder. Although Villares wouldn't normally allow two brothers to work at the same factory, they had different last names (Lula's is Inácio da Silva and his brother's is Ferreira de Melo). He was cleared by the HR department, and Friar Chico got the job. Since Lula worked nights and his big brother was hired for the day shift, the two rarely bumped into each other at work. In contrast to his skinny little brother, Friar Chico was muscular, politicized, and had been going to union meetings since the 1964 coup.

The big brother's insistent but discrete attempts to get Lula interested in union life had so far been fruitless. Their conversations on the subject, whether at home or over a glass of cachaça in the bar, were always the same.

"You need to pay a visit to the union. Come to an assembly."

"No way," Lula would say, "that place is full of crooks."

"Go, at least to see what it is like. If you don't like it, don't come back."

"I'm not going. I've seen those 'Wanted' notices about terrorists the police are looking for, and I see a lot of them are from unions."

"No, Lula. You're wrong. These are good people. There aren't any crooks there. Those people on the 'Wanted' posters are good people too. They are the people who are trying to overthrow the military dictatorship."

Friar Chico ended up suffering from one of the many waves of unemployment provoked by the government's political economy and got laid off by Villares. However, Lula was lucky enough to survive the round of layoffs, and Friar Chico didn't stay unemployed for long. Shortly after leaving Villares, he got hired as a lathe mechanic at Carraço, a mid-sized factory in São Caetano do Sul which produced steel hoods for jeeps that were manufactured in Brazil by the American company Willys Overland, and for the small DKW-Vemag sedan, which was manufactured by a German company.

In late 1968, the São Bernardo do Campo Metalworkers' Union

started setting up elections to renew the executive board, which were scheduled for the beginning of the following year. Due to an agreement between the leaders of the labor sector, there would only be one ticket. President Afonso Monteiro would turn over the presidency to Paulo Vidal, a metalworker and longtime activist from the union, and new names would be incorporated into the future directorate. Despite unanimous support for Friar Chico for one of the positions on the directorate, the factory where he worked already had a representative on the ticket. It didn't make sense for a mid-sized factory like Carraço to have two people on the directorate of the union while the giant Villares, with 1,000 workers on its payroll, wouldn't even have one.

This was when Friar Chico made a passing suggestion that would forever change the destiny of Lula and Brazil. "My younger brother is a lathe mechanic in Villares. But I'm not sure if I would want to get involved with the union."

"Friar Chico was an activist," Lula recalled years later. "That guy who would go to the union, that guy who had breakfast and lunch at the union hall. Everyone else in my family was anti-union. We thought what a lot of workers still think today: that it was full of thieves, that the directors were all thieves, that everyone was crooked, and that my brother was a fool to go to the union hall. This was the motive of constant arguments . . . We would have a family meeting, or we'd be there drinking cachaça, and he'd start up with, 'The union says this . . .' Whenever he started, we'd all turn against him. Everyone would give him a hard time because we didn't want to hear him talking about it again."

Just as Friar Chico had feared, Lula didn't want anything to do with it. Speaking sincerely, Lula said he was afraid to get involved in a world that he and most of his friends associated with subversion, prison, and torture. Friar Chico insisted that there was no clandestine organization behind the movement—which was true—and Lula ended up asking for a few days to think about it.

The first person Lula told about the invitation was his fiancée. Although she didn't have much understanding or interest in politics, she didn't like the idea. Like Lula, Lourdes thought that it was a dangerous adventure. All you had to do was look at what the newspapers and TVs were saying about jailed union leaders. Their conversation was inconclusive, and they only returned to the subject a few days later, the next time they met. If she had her doubts before, now she seemed to be armed with a strong opinion.

"Lula, I mentioned at the factory that you'd been invited to join the union board."

Smiling, he wanted to know how the people at Damatex had responded to the idea. But she cut him off. "The boss said that you shouldn't get involved in this. The people said that being a union director, man—it will turn you into a communist! They'll arrest you and you'll never find another job for the rest of your life!"

Before he had a chance to open his mouth, she continued. "There's more. If you accept the invitation, there's not going to be a wedding. You have to choose: if you prefer the union, I'll wait for three years until your term runs out and you leave office, and then we can get married."

The problem was that, between the two times they had talked about it, Friar Chico had already managed to drag his brother to a conversation with the union leaders. They had met with President Afonso Monteiro, who was about to leave office, and board members Paulo Vidal, leader of the new ticket, and Mario Ladeia. Lula's conversation with Vidal and Ladeia had been cordial, but he had gotten a bad impression of the president.

"That Monteiro paid less attention to me than that ragged little street dog they use as the union mascot," he told his friends.

This factor didn't keep the meeting from ending on a high note, however. The four men eventually decided that Lula would enter the ticket as a substitute director—a solution that solved the problem with Lourdes and ensured that their wedding could go ahead as planned. After all, he wasn't going to be a director, just a substitute. But there was a downside for Lula: without being an active director, he lost the right to paid leave during his term and the legal right to one-year guaranteed employment after the end of his mandate.

Lula managed to convince Lourdes with the idea of becoming a substitute, and they immediately set their wedding date. With their forms in hand, they chose the last Sunday in the "brides' month" of May, the twenty-fifth. For the next few months, time seemed to fly by. Along with all of the boring tasks that precede weddings—bureaucratic paperwork, furnishing a house, scheduling the time at the church, organizing a modest party—he had to take part in all the rituals leading up to the union elections. Even though there was zero risk of losing, since he would be running unopposed on the sole ticket, the candidates for directors and substitutes had to go to the factory doors, distribute pamphlets, shake hands, and introduce themselves to the voters. Most of all, they had to guarantee that people came out on election day, since voting in union elections was not obligatory.

For Lula, his engagement to Lourdes represented a commitment, but it didn't change anything in the day-to-day routine of house–factory–house from Monday to Friday, dances on Saturday and Sundays at Lourdes's home under the watchful eye of his future mother-in-law, Dona Herminia. It was nearly always the same group: Lula, his friends Toninho and Zezinho, the Japanese Brazilian couple Olavo and Kiva, future brother-in-law Lambari (who was trying to make a move on Tiana, Lula's youngest sister), and, of course, the bride. The repertoire on the record player also didn't change much: if it wasn't Ray Coniff or Roberto Carlos, it was Carlos Alberto, the "king of bolero." The atmosphere was familial, with meat pies, soft drinks, and no alcohol.

The weekly routine was only interrupted on Saturday, April 19, when Paulo Vidal's group took over the union board. At the time, the headquarters was as modest as the inauguration ceremony, which was followed by a cocktail party in a gymnasium owned by the municipal government's Public Workers' Association. A predictable and unimportant news story, Vidal's victory wasn't covered by the big newspapers. That week, papers like *Estadão*, *Folha*, *O Globo*, and *Jornal do Brasil* focused on France's senate reform referendum, along with the attempt by Palestinian leader Yasser Arafat to appease Lebanon by convincing the diverse internal currents of the Palestinian Liberation Organization to support the social democratic Fatah movement. It was the start of Lula's long journey that would bring him to the presidency of the Republic, but the event was scarcely covered even in the *Diário do Grande ABC*, the main newspaper in the region and a reference in coverage of labor news. The paper ran a three-paragraph article on the bottom corner of a back page with no photos. Lula's name appears lost at the bottom of the article, nineteenth in a list of twenty-five board members and substitutes that had taken office.

The peaceful mood of that Saturday night was far removed from the atmosphere of violence and repression that prevailed in Brazil outside the union. Wielding the cutlass of Institutional Act 5—the "coup within the coup" that dissolved Congress and initiated a violent clampdown against so-called political enemies, imposed by the dictatorship in December of the previous year—President Marechal Costa e Silva had already purged ninety-four politicians from several political parties, canceling their mandates and suspending their political rights for ten years. To ensure that a Supreme Court majority would sanction the regime's discretionary measures, Costa e Silva forced Justices Antônio Carlos Lafayette de Andrade and Antônio Gonçalves de Oliveira into retirement and reduced the number of Supreme Court Justices from sixteen to eleven. The unions didn't escape the purge. On the contrary, the first target of the military after taking power had been the labor movement. The government had already intervened in 483 unions, 49 federations, and 4 confederations since 1964. The organizations were dismantled, and the main leaders were imprisoned, forced into exile, or had gone underground as fugitives. Even so, to protect itself from eventual criticism, three weeks before the election of Lula's ticket in São Bernardo, Costa e Silva had issued an institutional act ordering that "crimes against national security" would no longer be judged by the Supreme Court but by the military courts. The workers that celebrated the inauguration of Paulo Vidal may not have known this, but among the "crimes against national security" stipulated in Costa e Silva's act were strikes, a number of which were about to kick off across the ABC region.

Lula's mind, however, was focused on other things. On Friday, May 23, one month after his debut in union life, he and Lourdes got permission from their respective bosses to leave work early and get legally married at a notary public's office in São Bernardo. The quick ritual, presided over by a justice of the peace, was only accompanied by four witnesses, as required by law. Nevertheless, the bride and groom were very elegant. Her braided hair emanating from a bun, Lourdes wore a dark cloak and Lula, with his mustache shaved and hair neatly trimmed and slicked back, wore a brand-new gray, four-button suit, a white starched shirt, and a gray tie. Just to ensure that the day didn't go by without any commemoration, they got together a half dozen friends and went to the bride's house for a few beers and appetizers. At the end of the night, when all had said goodbye, Lula stayed, sure that he would sleep there that night with Lourdes, starting his honeymoon. After all, they were husband and wife now. His boldness was vetoed on the spot by Dona Herminia: they could sleep together only after the church wedding.

He pulled out the marriage certificate and tried to argue his case.

"We are already married on paper—look at this!" But Dona Lindu's agreement with his mother-in-law ended the discussion. Until the union was consecrated by a religious wedding, each would sleep in their own house.

That Sunday afternoon, as the sky began to darken, Lourdes arrived at Our Lady of Mercês Church in Sacomã in a sparkling gray Aero-Willys—at the time the most elegant car produced in Brazil—that had been arranged by a friend from the factory. Dressed in white, the bride had her head covered by a veil embroidered with tiny silk flowers that ended in a long tulle train. Lula wore another new suit—navy blue with a silver tie and, as in the civil wedding, had his hair meticulously slicked back.

The wedding photos from the civil and religious ceremonies give the impression that the bride and groom were nervous. The only smile noticeable—a discreet one—is Lula's, captured at the moment that he solemnly extends his hand to receive Lourdes at the door of the car in front of the church, from where they would depart to celebrate in Dona Lindu's house on Jabaquara Street, in the neighborhood of Vila Pauliceia. The mothers of the bride and groom took care to supply the party with meat pies, sandwiches, french fries, and cake. The beverages were provided by the groom. Lula remembers money being so tight that he had to calculate how many children were coming and buy a bottled guarana soft drink for each of them.

After the party, the bride and groom took the night bus to Poços de Caldas, a hot springs resort town in southern Minas Gerais, for a six-day honeymoon. The groom traveled in the worst seat on the bus, next to the bathroom door. As they left the house and headed to the bus station, their goodbye was long and tearful. At twenty-three, it was the first time in his life that he would spend this much time away from his family. Arriving in Poços, they took the traditional newlywed tour. They threw coins in the lovers' fountain, rode around town in a horse and carriage, and fed pieces of bread to the swans from a replica of a Venetian gondola they rented from the country club. One week later, they started their married life in a little one-room house on Jabaquara Street, in the same neighborhood they lived in when before marrying, which they had purchased with a loan from the National Housing Bank, a state-owned company that gave long-term loans to prospective homeowners.

Thanks to the power of several shots of cheap brandy, Lula got his nerve up and invited Lourdes to dance; months later they got married (in 1969)—without his having to abandon union life, as she initially demanded. Their honeymoon took place in a paradise in Minas Gerais called Poços de Caldas, where the PT would later be founded. Source: Lula da Silva family archive.

11

"I know, doctor, my baby was born dead." "Be strong, Mr. Lula, because the news is worse: Your wife, Lourdes, has died too"

A visible metamorphosis was taking place in Lula's life. Despite his initial reluctance, he had ended up liking the labor movement and the constant excitement at the union. He wasn't yet thinking of making a career out of it, but, little by little, he had become a regular at the assemblies that used to bore him. As time passed, he became a rare presence at the beer-drinking parties, barbecues, and even the weekend soccer games for his neighborhood team, Bangu. All his free time was dedicated to the union. Lula didn't need catechism or theories from his communist brother to discover the importance of the union in the daily life of the workers. Rather, he figured this out by himself through observation. The union's role was not just to provide social assistance, such as the health insurance that spared the members from the travails of the public health system. More than a shelter, in his eyes, the union had begun to feel like a home, a kind of protective sentinel for the workers. It was a place where he felt safe.

The presidency of Paulo Vidal—who was neither a man of the left nor a sellout—led to an era in which the union emerged from a lethargy that had taken hold under previous administrations. One of the first things done by the new team was to cut the umbilical cord that connected the union to the São Paulo State Federation of Metalworkers, presided over by Argeu Egídio dos Santos, considered to be a yellow union federation by the more combative leaders. Without having to go through Argeu, the ABC metalworkers looked for shortcuts and grey areas in the law and managed to work around obstacles in the labor court. They started negotiating their salary campaigns directly with the automobile factory bosses. The union increased its base and registered thousands of new members, with discreet support from the Catholic Church's Basic Ecclesial Communities, which went on to be consolidated internationally in Puebla, Mexico, in January 1979, during the Third Conference of the Latin American Episcopalial Council, in the presence of Pope John Paul II. By the end of Vidal's first term in 1972, the proportion of union workers had risen from 20 percent to 50 percent of the employed labor force in the ABC region. The union's power to pressure the bosses and the government grew commensurately.

Although he occupied a job that was formally irrelevant—as substitute director of the financial board—Lula began to actively participate in union life. He closely followed the legal campaign in support of workers, challenging their contract termination, and became a big supporter of vocational training programs. In many of these courses, the worker would start the course as a factory-floor grunt, at the lowest position in the hierarchy, and finish in the toolmaking department, at the top of the profession, with the lathe mechanics, foremen, and maintenance mechanics. Above this were only the supervisors and the inspectors. In an academic thesis published in the journal *Anuário Unesco / Metodista da Comunicação*, Professor Antônio de Andrade explains the change that happened after Vidal's group was elected:

> The new union leadership invested heavily in support of the workers on solving basic problems that were essentially related to day-to-day complaints. The union was strengthened through membership campaigns that were promoted inside the factories, giving rise to a new generation of workers interested in participating in politics and the union structure. An immediate consequence of these transformations was the permanent promotion of gatherings, courses, speeches, and congresses with the goal of consciousness raising so that workers would discuss their complaints, work through problems, and come up with plans of action to resolve them.

In a short time, the union completely changed its face. Along with the vocational courses and recreational activities, the directors set up seminars on political issues and rudimentary economics for its associates, and even a diploma-equivalency program created by the government. Enabling people to earn credit for three years of high school in one year of intensive study, the course would enable them to take university entrance exams. Lula had a talent for being conciliatory and respectful toward opponents in arguments and negotiations, and this made him stand out among union leaders not only in the ABC, but in the entire industrial region. His way of treating adversaries and bosses, despite his gruff appearance, wasn't a natural gift that stood out from the outset of his union life—to the contrary.

Although, years later, he would become known as an excellent speaker who magnetized large crowds, the twenty-three-year-old lathe mechanic with colorful shirts and a black mustache shook with fear at the mere thought of speaking into a microphone.

"I was so shy that whenever they called my name in an assembly, I would turn red," he would later say.

Whenever they passed him the microphone in a meeting or an assembly, he would begin to nervously sweat. In order to overcome his fear, he secretly created what he would call the "Lula method of public speaking." He would cut photographs of anonymous people out of old newspapers and magazines, paste them one by one to the walls of his room, lock the door, and start practicing. Whoever saw him loudly reciting incendiary speeches for an audience of ghost impressions on yellowed pieces of old newspaper would have certainly thought they were looking at a man with mental health issues. (He later told the German magazine *Der Spiegel* that when he felt lonely during his time in prison in Curitiba, in 2018, he'd glue photos to the wall and "talk" to them.)

Life was good. In conversations with friends and family members, he would tell detailed stories about the art of making parts that would help move transatlantic ships. His union activity was stimulating, and the work in Villares filled him with pride; the honeymoon seemed to never end.

Together, his and Lourdes's income enabled them to realize a dream they'd shared since the first days they started dating: to have a baby. That October, six months after their wedding, Lourdes told her husband that she was pregnant.

Continuing to work at the factory, Lourdes experienced no complications with the pregnancy. With regular examinations through the union's efficient medical services, the couple bought clothes for the baby, whose birth was expected in mid-July 1971. But on Friday, June 4, Lourdes grew pale, complained of sharp pain in her abdomen, and her skin took on a dull and yellowish appearance. Lula made an appointment with the union doctor, but Lourdes thought it was an overreaction and didn't go. That Saturday, when he arrived home from work for lunch, he was worried to find out she'd skipped a second appointment, with the excuse that she had to work overtime to help with the household expenses. "She'd work extra hours just to make another twenty bucks," Lula recalled.

Rushed to Modelo Hospital emergency room, on the border of the ABC and São Paulo (which had a health plan for workers from Villares), Lourdes was diagnosed with jaundice provoked by the underdevelopment of the fetus's liver—a dysfunction that, according to the doctors and nurses, would probably disappear within a week. Their explanation did not convince Lula, who was worried about Lourdes's increasing pain. Lula thought it would be better and safer if Lourdes stayed in the hospital that night.

The next day, he received the news that his wife had lost the baby. He rushed to the hospital, and when he tearfully arrived, the doctor said, "Mr. Luiz, you are going to have to be strong. I have some horrible news to give you."

Wiping the tears from his face, between hiccups, he said, "I know, doctor. Lourdes lost the baby. Our little boy died in his mom's belly."

The doctor grabbed him by the arms. "No, Mr. Luiz, it's much worse than that. Your wife has also died."

Still clutching the package with the little clothes he had bought to bury his baby in, Lula collapsed into the arms of his friends who had brought him there.

The grief of irreparable loss left him in a zombie-like state. He would round the corner to avoid seeing friends' relatives; any image, scene, or fragment of music that reminded him of Lourdes was enough to send his soul into a deep freeze. He tried to live alone, but the melancholy was so great that he ended up moving back in with his mother. Soccer, movies, beer-drinking parties—nothing seemed to pull him out of the hole. He couldn't begin to imagine finding a new girlfriend. During the following months, whenever he noticed a woman glance at him with interest, he would lower his head and change course.

Life began coming back in bits and pieces. Lula ended up returning to his old love, soccer, and, on weekends, he started playing again on Náutico do Capibaribe, a team that he had founded with his brother Vavá when they still lived in Vila Carioca. The name may have sounded strange to people from São Paulo, but it was familiar to boys like them from Pernambuco. The Capibaribe is a winding river that flows through Lula's home state, dividing the capital city of Recife into islands, giving rise to the lofty nickname "the Venice of the Americas." With red uniforms, just like the original Náutico team from Recife, which, although not top level, never caused embarrassment for anyone, the Silvas were starters in three positions. Lula was the right midfielder, and Friar Chico played center-back. The atrophy of his right hand didn't slow down team captain Vavá, who was a good goalkeeper. Vavá had lost the movement of three fingers while saving the life of a coworker. His workmate's hair had gotten tangled up in an electric loom and started pulling his head down toward the gears. Vavá instinctively stopped the machine with his hand, saving his friend at the cost of a mutilation he would carry for the rest of his life.

Soccer, the factory, conversations on weekends, and the intense union work pulled him, little by little, out of the cesspool in which widowhood had buried him. Even women, which the tragic death of Lourdes had made him forget about, started to interest him again. However, the time that he had previously dedicated to homelife began to be occupied by the place where he spent most of his energy—the union. Despite its modest size, the union hall became a meeting place for friends for courses, debates on salaries and politics, and friendly conversations at the end of the workday. Even as an obscure substitute, one of the lowest names in the hierarchy, Lula's tireless work during those three years made him a natural candidate for the 1972 elections, with unanimous support for the position of first secretary—the most important post in the organization after president. There were already people on the ticket who would join him in the marathon of strikes and confrontations with the bosses from that point forward: Rubens "Rubão" Teodoro da Silva, Nelson Campanholo, Antenor Biolcatti, Devanir Ribeiro, and Djalma Bom. In addition to being an active and brave union man, the mustachioed Djalma was as talented an interpreter of boleros as the greatest TV and radio stars of the time.

During the final days of 1971, Lula was approached by a group of workers from Ford Brasil, a company that had just entered the big leagues after taking over Willys Overland of Brazil, which, among other things, built the Jeep. The group made him a seductive offer: in February, there would be elections to renew the union directorate, and Lula's prestige had grown beyond the limits of the first secretariat. The people from Ford suggested that he break from Paulo Vidal and accept their nomination as president on an opposition ticket that was being set up inside the Ford/Willys plant. The icing on the cake was explained at the end: the ticket would have the official support of the Brazilian Communist Party (PCB) and, therefore, of all of the workers connected to the party, among them his brother Friar Chico. Although, at the time, he worked in São Caetano do Sul, the disciplined Friar Chico openly campaigned for the blue opposition ticket, against the green ticket led by Vidal. Detecting the unmistakable scent of betrayal in the air, Lula refused.

He had made the right choice. When they tallied the results, the Vidal/Lula ticket had 4,814 votes, against 3,389 for the opposition ticket led by Luciano Garcia Galache from Ford/Willys.

Released from his duties at Villares in accordance with labor laws, Lula now had his own office and permanent support from two first-class lawyers: Maurício Soares, who would later become a congressman and three-time mayor of São Bernardo, and the journalist and poet Possidônio Sampaio, who seemed to have one foot in the PCB. Afterward, the labor lawyer Almir Pazzianotto Pinto joined the team, who, after the return to democracy, would become minister of labor and then president of the Superior Labor Court.

The first secretary was a kind of union mayor. All of the retirement-pension and severance-pay processes passed through Lula's hands, along with retirement applications based on time of service or disability claims, and the management of all of the insurance and government services for the labor sector. Even the city permit requests by workers to build an extra room or second floor on their houses would move faster if they were made by the union. But one of the biggest campaign promises of the newly elected directorate was the construction of a new union hall, an enormous building that would replace the three-room house from which they operated at the time. It was a campaign promise that, contrary to the kinds of things politicians and union sellouts always promised, would be delivered before the next elections.

Since Paulo Vidal was not able to meet all of his scheduled demands as president, Lula soon began to travel around Brazil representing the union in congresses and debates with workers from other labor sectors, revealing what the press would dub the "new Brazilian unionism." What, exactly, was so new about it? The best source on the earthquake in labor relations in the ABC is probably the diminutive six-page newspaper the union started publishing sporadically. At the time, it was hard to distribute newspapers at the doors of the factories. The union was only able to do so during wage campaigns, their own assemblies on things like financial reporting and budget revisions, and elections, which happened every three years.

Edited by veteran journalist Antônio Carlos Félix Nunes—who had also been a member of the PCB—the *Tribuna Metalúrgica* was more than a mere information bulletin on benefits and social programs. Daring and funny, the little newspaper was founded to debunk the legal precept that unions were organizations that collaborated with the government. The *Tribuna* bypassed traditional obstacles—the workers' confederations and their directors in their expensive suits, the repressive labor legislation, and the iron hand with which the dictatorship treated the issue of pay raises—and put workers face to face with the bosses. It published the average salaries that were paid in the region covered by the union, factory by factory, and compared them with another table that was regularly updated to show price fluctuations of twenty-eight staple food products. In one issue, the newspaper pointed its finger at one of the giant multinationals: "Silent when asked to grant pay adjustments to its workers above those recommended by the government, Mercedes-Benz increased the salaries of its management board by 50 percent and its directors by 121 percent."

The character who would give these pinpricks to the bosses was "João Ferrador," created by Félix Nunes and drawn by Laerte, a young cartoonist who was connected to the union movement and who, although only twenty, was already a member of the PCB, acting under the code name of "Maurício." Decades later, after becoming one of the most famous cartoonists in Brazil, Laerte would scandalize some old friends from the party when she came out as transgender. The cartoonist's first famous character, João Ferrador, became a symbol of the strikes that rose up in the ABC during the following years. Always good humored, João

Ferrador would appear in the morning pamphlets distributed at the doors of the factories saying, "I'm not okay today!"

The numbers, calculations, and percentages adopted by the union and published in the *Tribuna* came from the Interunion Department of Statistics and Socioeconomic Studies (DIESSE). When Lula began using these numbers, the organization was directed by a sworn enemy of the military, chemical worker Marcelo Gato of the Santos Metalworkers' Union, who was a member of the regional directorate of the PCB. Elected federal congressman for the Brazilian Democratic Movement (MDB), Gato was forced out of office by President Geisel in 1976.

There was a conspiracy theory going around that the fact that so many communists had gravitated around the unions—including the Stalinist and pro-Soviet PCB—proved that the party participated formally or organically in the new directorate. This rumor took wings when it came out that Lula, the most visible and popular figure in the union, was the brother of Friar Chico, a well-known figure in the PCB. However, nothing could have been farther from the truth.

It's hard to figure out who first discovered Lula's talent for captivating a crowd—the dictatorship or the PCB. The oldest police report that mentions him—when he was still known only as Luiz Inácio da Silva—comes from this period in the union. His name appears buried in a Department of Political and Social Order (DOPS) report on several unknown supporters of a strike without any further details. It isn't even a full report—just an event summary.

It was also during this time that the PCB, which had already flirted with him for some time via Friar Chico, decided to pounce. Although he acted as an advisor to his little brother, Friar Chico never insisted on recruiting him to the oldest political party in the country, then led by Luís Carlos Prestes. To reel in such a promising catch, the PCB designated a "black hood"—jargon used to identify high-level party directors—with an extensive record of service: captain and merchant marine commander Emilio Bonfante Demaria, known within the party as codename "Ivo." Fired after the 1964 coup for leading a national sailors' strike, this middle-aged man, who had been in the party since he was seventeen, was sent from Rio de Janeiro to the ABC with the task of enlisting Lula.

Set up by Friar Chico, the meeting took place on Matriz Square in São Bernardo. Sitting side by side on a park bench in the public garden, as if they didn't know each other, Demaria pretended to read a sports newspaper while, in whispers, he tried to convince the metalworker to enlist in the party. Lula became annoyed with what he called a "scene from a cheap movie," cut the conversation short, went home, and chewed out his brother.

"Chico, anytime you want me to talk with anyone, send them to look for me in the union hall," he said. "I don't have anything to hide from anyone, and I don't need to act ridiculous in public. I say everything on the street that I say in the union hall. I don't have clandestine conversations."

Demaria and Friar Chico met months later, in early 1975, in the basement of the Information Operations Detachment–Center of Internal Information (DOI-CODI), as prisoners were being tortured after a raid against the party. Lula's care to avoid involvment in clandestine organizations was the result of a well-thought-out decision: only political independence would enable him to be able to hit hard at the government and the bosses. He never adopted an attitude or made any declarations that were anti-communist, nor would he ever try to convince his brother to stop his militancy in the PCB. To the contrary, he never objected to the fact that at least two of his colleagues in the union directorate were affiliated with the party. Whenever, however, he discovered that one of the miniscule organizations of the extreme left had planted someone as a "worker" in one of the factories in the ABC, he would loudly expose the infiltrator, sometimes with irony.

"I was able to tell the difference between a worker and a university student just by grabbing their hand," he remembered, laughing, many years later. "Any hand that was really smooth would make me suspicious."

Lula didn't want to get involved in conversations with the party or any other clandestine organization. The main focus of his worries was the same as that of most residents of the ABC: wages. Ever since the country's unions first began to organize at the beginning of the twentieth century—some with inspiration from communist and anarchist immigrants from Italy—Brazilians had almost always placed the same issue at the center of their demands: to guarantee purchasing power from the wages paid by the bosses. The arguments that broke out those days in all of the workers' associations always returned to the same subject: prices were rising faster than salaries, and this continually decreased the workers' quality of life. The only numbers companies used for their inflation adjustments were those provided by the government, and the workers didn't have any way to fight back.

This mistrust of official data lasted until the start of the Juscelino Kubitschek administration in 1956, when São Paulo's unions joined together to form DIESSE. The main purpose of the organization was to produce studies that enabled workers to better challenge suspicious government data with real numbers. The government manipulation didn't stop, but it became harder and harder for it to fool the unions.

Long considered to have some of the highest salaries among the working class, the ABC metalworkers found their neck in a noose. The once-coveted salaries in the region were being pulverized. When a coalition of Arab states increased gas prices by 400 percent to punish US support for Israel in the 1973 Yom Kippur War, the so-called "Brazilian miracle" went down the drain, and inflation surged. Published in the *Tribuna Metalúrgica*, studies by DIESSE tracked changes in the prices of the staple foods most consumed by the population. Confirmed by the numbers published in the paper, the price for some products, like pasta and beans, had risen by over 170 percent, generating a real raise in inflation of 37.8 percent per year—more than double the 15.7 percent official number that had been invented by the government to suppress salaries.

The auto industry tycoons argued that the data published by the *Tribuna* was false. The "DIESSE lie," however, became truth when the World Bank decided to investigate the numbers from previous years and verified what the workers had been complaining about for a long time: the real numbers corresponded with Marcelo Gato's reports. Led by the technical director of DIESSE, Walter Barelli, a group of economists and academics (including Octavio Ianni, Lenina Pomeranz, Azis Simão, José de Souza Rodrigues, and Annez Andraus Troyano) discovered, during archival research in Brazil's Federal Institute of Geography and Statistics (IBGE), that Finance Minister Delfim Netto, "the wizard of the miracle," had forged official numbers to shortchange the workers.

"We were lucky enough to discover, in the basement of the Labor Ministry in Brasília, publications in which the IBGE had manipulated the numbers," said Barelli. "It was a Franciscan work—not Franciscan but Benedictine. Annez Andraus Troyano and I ended up finding out everything. It was being done by a group working for Delfim. And that is how the fight began."

Adopting an unknown method and using data that had become secret since the dictatorship's Institutional Act 5, the forgery, pure and simple, of the price indices was based on a magic formula to hide the real inflation numbers. The government's trickery, based on a phrase attributed to Delfim Netto ("If you can't defeat inflation, defeat the index that measures inflation"), prompted the unions to resuscitate a word that had fallen into disuse: "replacement." It involved no complicated economic theory, nor anything cooked up in Moscow, but simple arithmetic: 37.8 – 15.7 = 22.1. Corrected annually, the difference was converted into 34.1 percent—the amount that the bosses ended up owing the workers as replacement for the losses caused by the government's fraud. Lula picked up the replacement ball and would only drop it during the strikes in 1980, when he managed to include the theme in negotiations with the bosses. Because it took place before the fraud had come to light, 1972 marked the last wage campaign by the ABC Metalworkers' Union that doesn't mention the word "replacement" in its list of demands.

The tactic was not unanimously supported, however, and the issue divided the labor sector. Lula and his workers from the ABC, who didn't trust the court system during the dictatorship, argued that the debt had to be compensated for in the strikes and on the podiums, with a knife to the throat of the bosses. Their opinion was not shared by Joaquim dos Santos Andrade, president of Brazil's largest union, the Metalworkers of São Paulo and Mogi das Cruzes. Known at the time as a sellout who ate out of the hands of the bosses—although this later proved to be incorrect—"Joaquinzão" preferred a path that was less confrontational and less obtrusive: a court battle. Scowling from behind his walrus mustache, Joaquinzão could be whatever they said about him, but he wasn't a man who would lose a battle–it was no accident that he had been reelected union president for twenty-one straight years. In December 1977, the federal courts ruled in favor of the São Paulo union, ordering the companies to reimburse the metalworkers for 34.1 percent, while the ABC workers only managed to make up the difference in successive rounds of post-strike negotiations. It was inspiration from the DIESSE investigation that caused the University of São Paulo's Institute of Economic Research (FIPE) to change its research methodology and indicators.

Still mourning the loss of his family, Lula continued to fight for replacement and the right to free negotiation between bosses and employees. It was during this time that Maurício Soares, the union lawyer (and future mayor of São Bernardo), attracted him to a religious movement that was very popular at the time: the Catholic Church's apostolic Cursillo movement. Founded in Spain during the 1940s to prepare young Christians for pilgrimages to Santiago de Compostela, the Cursillo had taken on its own personality and spread around the world as a Christian evangelical movement. At the time, it was a lifeline for Lula.

"I felt so sluggish that I grabbed onto that new movement to survive," he later recalled. "Before and after lunch and dinner, I would pray and at bedtime I would softly sing a Christian hymn, nearly silently."

Discovering that Lula was beginning to act like a fundamentalist, Friar Chico called his brother into a corner.

"Lula, you are becoming a fanatic, man," he said. "I come home, and you are kneeling by the bed. I come back later and there you are on your knees. It looks like you are praying after every fart! Stop this. Find something to do. Play soccer, get a girlfriend."

Little by little, Lula began to feel like he was a victim of a kind of brainwashing. Instead of being a good Christian, he was turning into a kind of devotee, a communion-wafer-junky who didn't think about life anymore, only the Cursillo movement. On top of that, by comparing the pilgrimages with the real lives of the preachers who were hypnotizing them in weekly sermons posing as good Christians, he discovered that they were "nothing but con artists."

"They spent all their time calling everyone 'corrupt Pharisees,' " he said, "but I found out that one of them was the owner of a metal frame factory that was a veritable pigsty, and that he treated his employees like slaves. Another was a social security inspector who used to extort shop owners who didn't collect enough taxes. I got out of there."

Friar Chico was right: it was better to date, as Lula has admitted in numerous interviews and stories.

"Before I got married, I wasn't much of a dater," he said. "I got nervous trying to talk to women. But I learned how to do it after I was widowed. It was only after going through that long period of grief that I got good at dating."

Yes, union life was important, and soccer with friends on weekends was great, but what he was really interested in was women. Not in any specific woman, but in many women.

The stories from this Don Juan period of his life could have been simply excluded from this book, without affecting the history of Brazilian unionism in any way. However, it happens that, in addition to children and hassles, intimacy can produce more than family gossip. In Lula's case, an episode happened during this phase of amorous adventures that, years later, would transform into one of the biggest scandals of his political career.

As if he wanted to compensate for all of the delays caused by his shyness and grief, the insecure boy from before was transformed into a ladies' man. A conservative tally, based on the dozens of times that journalists and researchers have since looked into the subject, reveals that during this time, he had four steady girlfriends: Nair, Tereza, Mirian, and Marisa. Mirian Cordeiro, twenty-four, was a friend of Lula's little sister, Maria Baixinha, who worked as a nurse in a clinic that had a partnership with the union. But the winds seemed to blow in favor of Marisa, who fell for Lula's reckless flirting.

Even though he had a girlfriend, he still, half-jokingly, half by casting his net, asked a friend who received visitors from the union at a desk on the ground floor to let him know whenever a pretty single woman arrived. He had become uninterested in Nair and Tereza and was mad at Mirian Cordeiro when destiny heeded his request, and the woman appeared: Marisa Letícia Rocco Casa, twenty-three, an employee at Senator Robert Kennedy Public School. Pretty, with elegant features, blonde hair, and blue eyes, descendant of immigrants from the Lombardy region of Italy, she had something in common with Lula: widowhood. Her husband had died when she was four months pregnant. A cab driver, he had been brutally robbed and murdered by a passenger who had strangled him with a steel wire. Born in February 1971, the baby was named after the deceased father, Marcos Cláudio. By a cruel twist of fate, Marisa's father-in-law Cândido, who was also a cab driver, was later shot to death in the same Volkswagen cab that his son had worked in.

In those days, São Paulo and its surrounding suburbs were hit with successive waves of different types of crimes. There was a period when pairs of teenagers would join up to rob elderly pedestrians. One would push the victim, leaving them confused, while the other would take their wallet, purse, or necklace. There was a time when the fashion among criminals was to take advantage of cars stopped at traffic lights to rip the watches off the drivers who dangled their left hands out the windows. Marisa's husband and father-in-law were murdered during a criminal fad of assaulting cabbies, mainly at night under the cover of darkness, when the amount of money from the day's fares was usually higher.

The problem of assaults and murders of cabbies became so serious in greater São Paulo that *Jornal da Tarde*, the afternoon paper founded by Mino Carta (and later run by Murilo Felisberto, from Minas Gerais) and the Mesquita family, owners of the Estadão news agency, decided to cover the issue. A creative, sophisticated daily paper with neat themes, photos and stories inspired by the New Journalism school of the US, it wouldn't be enough for *JT*, as it was known at the time, to give conventional coverage to a crime that was terrorizing the population, especially the cabbies. On at least two occasions, *JT* covered the issue in its own way: not as a conventional crime story but in a more humane, film-like manner, having reporters experience firsthand the fear of driving a taxi on the streets of São Paulo. The first story was by reporter Armando Salem, who rented a taxi from Paulinho, a car wash worker and cabbie based out of a stand on Honduras Street in front of the Paulistano Club, in the wealthy Jardim América neighborhood. It was a white VW Beetle with no front passenger seat (it was illegal for "junior taxis" like Beetles to carry more than two passengers). The arrangement was that the newspaper would pay the cab owner a day's rental fee (Salem also donated his fares from the day's rides). Another unmarked vehicle owned by the newspaper trailed Salem's Beetle to take pictures and, if necessary, help him in an emergency. At seventy-eight, after working at *JT*, *Veja*, and many other publications, Salem still remembered the story.

"The story I wrote was divided in two parts. The first was about the fear that the rides that I was afraid would end in assault, which luckily didn't happen. The other was a kind of chronicle of a cabbie describing the travails he went through during an average workday. The article ran on the last page of *Jornal da Tarde*, which was an important page. The front-page headline on the article featured a photo of a Capelinha taxi meter, with the numbers showing the value of the fare replaced with letters spelling the word 'Danger.' "

The second story on the adventure of being a cabbie in São Paulo was penned by Miguel Jorge, a stout man from Ponte Nova, Minas Gerais, with an arabesque mustache. The newspaper rented an Aero-Willys sedan—a luxury car like the one used for Lula and Lourdes's wedding—that belonged to one of the cabbies who worked out of a stand in front of the chicest hotel in the city, the Jaraguá, located next door to the offices of *Estadão* and *JT*. Like Salem, "Miguelão," as he was called by his colleagues, wasn't assaulted but wrote a beautiful story about life in the megalopolis.

"I didn't work at night," he said, "and rode around during the morning and afternoon, around six hours per day. It was a story about the hard life of cab drivers, who had to pay their daily fee to the taxi company before making anything for themselves. It was a tough life."

After winning awards as a reporter for *JT*, Miguel moved to *Estadão*, where he became editor in chief. After a few years, he was invited to be vice president of Autolatina (an ultimately fruitless merger between Volkswagen and Ford Brazil), a job that he would hold while working for Volkswagen and at Santander Bank. During Lula's entire second mandate (2007–11), Miguel served as minister of development, industry and foreign commerce.

At the time he was courting the widow Marisa, Lula had been dating Mirian Cordeiro for over a year. The scheme that he had set up with his friend at the front desk had worked. As determined by law, Marisa was required to visit any union periodically to get a "proof of life" document stamped that enabled her to withdraw the pension left by her husband for her and her son, as well as her brother João Paulinho, who was retired due to disability from alcoholism. In order to not lose sight of her, Lula delayed Marisa whenever he could, inventing bureaucratic obstacles and missing rubber stamps. It looked like he was really in love with her, as he has always sworn, but he wouldn't open his mouth about his relationship with Mirian Cordeiro. In July 1973, when he was already planning on leaving Mirian—"we were single, each living in our own houses"—to marry Marisa, he found out that she was pregnant with his baby. At least in his mind, the idea of getting married to Mirian was short lived. He thought about it and, since he was already in love with Marisa, decided there was no way he was going to do it.

Many years later, while he was in the midst of a campaign for president, Mirian accused Lula publicly, in front of the cameras of a national

TV program, of trying to bribe her to have an abortion and threatening not to recognize the child as his (DNA tests for recognizing paternity would only come out ten years later). Lula has always denied this. He admits that he thought about it but decided to support the pregnancy, which he hid from Marisa for one month. The truth is that on May 23, 1974, the wedding day of Lula and Marisa, the baby who was the subject of the controversy was already two months old. It was chubby baby Lurian—a name made in the popular Brazilian tradition of combining the first names of the two parents.

When he lost Lourdes and his son, Lula had sold the house he had purchased in 1969 and moved back under the always-welcoming roof of his mother. He only left Dona Lindu's house after his marriage with Marisa. The two spent a few months renting until they found what they thought was a good deal. A friend who was a toolmaker at the Ford factory transferred the debt from his mortgage of Cr$48,000 (around R$41,000 in 2021) so he could buy a house in Jardim Lavinia. It had two bedrooms, a living room, a kitchen, and bathroom, but measured only thirty-three square meters. However small, the house was nicely finished, with a front yard big enough for a modest garden and maybe even Lula's light-blue Volkswagen TL sedan. He continued paying monthly payments on it to the public National Housing Bank, which had financed the property.

The paperwork had been worked out and the down payment of Cr$48,000 had reached the former owner's account when, while getting ready to move into the new home with Marisa, Lula discovered a big problem: the entire thirty-three square meters had been occupied by over a dozen people from several families. It was true—their new house was being squatted in by a group of homeless people who had brought their few, shabby belongings with them. There were adults, elderly people, and children everywhere. Lula tried to solve the problem by talking to them. He beckoned to the man who appeared to be their leader and explained that he was the new owner of the house, and it would have to be vacated. The man didn't budge.

"The house was abandoned and empty," the man said. "Now it's ours."

"No, I bought this house, and I have the paperwork to prove it."

The man didn't listen, saying there were elderly people living there and that his wife was pregnant. "You can show me any paperwork you want, but nobody is leaving here," he said.

Lula tried to explain that he wasn't a real estate investor or a slumlord. "You're squatting in the only house that I own, and I have to move here immediately. You haven't occupied a vacant house owned by Caixa or Bradesco Bank or the National Housing Bank, but the house of a worker who only has this place to live in."

Nothing worked. The man said they were going to stay put. The news of the occupation spread through the neighborhood, and soon a group of Lula's friends and relatives—among them the muscular brothers Vava and Friar Chico—offered to solve the problem physically by going there and removing them by force. Marisa was against the idea and suggested that she ask for help from César, the Military Police officer who was dating her sister Joana. This didn't work either. The new residents had resolved not to leave the house. César called on a tough sergeant from his precinct, who appeared armed and in uniform at the house on Maria Azevedo Florence street and said he didn't want to hear a word from the invaders. "I'm coming back in fifteen minutes, and I'm going to take everything in this house and throw it onto the street and light it on fire, including the people," he said.

The threat worked. One of the occupants arranged a vehicle, and minutes later it left filled with people and belongings. In exchange for being kicked out in such a manner, the homeless people had defecated in every room and smeared feces all over the walls and the floor. Before they could move in, Lula and Marisa had to paint the whole house and remove everything that still smelled like revenge.

Union life was important for Lula in facing the tragedy of early widowerhood. In the photo above, Lula (far right), as substitute director, he was already part of the union's leadership with the president, Paulo Vidal (holding the microphone), 1969. Source: Lula da Silva family archive.

Lula remarries, 1974. Marisa (left) appeared at the union one day, and months later the two became husband and wife. Source: Lula da Silva family archive.

12

During his first visit to a foreign country, Lula rushes home from Tokyo: his brother is being tortured in a DOI-CODI prison

Despite the economic disaster, the rising unemployment in the ABC and more and more ferocious political repression, 1975 started off well for Lula. Marisa was pregnant with their first child, job stability in Villares was guaranteed, and, in February, there would be elections for the new union directorate. The leadership was still deciding who would lead the ticket. The construction of the new building, the struggle for breaking the union's ties with the state, and the changes implemented during the 1972–75 term had given so much prestige to the directorate that no other political group dared to put up a rival ticket. Furthermore, as an alternative to keeping Vidal on as president, three other possible names came up: Rubens "Rubão" Teodoro, Nelson Campanholo, and Antenor Biolcatte. Another term for Vidal could have caused legal problems, since Molins, the packaging factory where he worked, had moved to the nearby city of Mauá—a part of greater São Paulo that, technically speaking, was outside of the union's territory, which, at the time, only covered the cities of São Bernardo and Diadema. Rubão, Campanholo, and Biolcatti refused the invitations to lead the ticket and suggested a fourth name—Lula—with Vidal switching to the office of general secretary. There was no risk of attributing the move to any sort of hostility against Vidal, since he knew that the office reserved for him was nicknamed the "mayor of the union."

Even before his name was suggested, Lula had begun to believe Vidal was becoming decadent, particularly following an event that had happened a few months earlier. The union had started holding psychodrama sessions, which were facilitated by Maria "Lurdinha" Lourdes, Walter Barelli's wife. In these workshops, leaders were encouraged to dramatically act out their feelings about family and professional relationships. In an interview given at the union's history center years later, Lula told the story of a psychodrama session that he believed had revealed Vidal's true face.

"On this day the questions were: 'What do you think the role of union president is? How do you see the presidency of the union?' What importance does this have for you?' Paulo Vidal was the first one to answer. He told the whole directorate to crouch down with their hands on their knees and stood up and stretched out his arms like he was above everyone. Then it was my turn. Maybe because I didn't know what to do, I asked everyone to hold hands. We all stood together holding hands, hugging each other. That was what the union meant to me: the union belonged to the workers, and the role of the president was to be one of them. Whoever thought they were above everyone else was a disgrace. That was the beginning of the end for Paulo Vidal."

At the time, Lula and Marisa were celebrating the arrival of their first son, Fabio Luís, who would become known as "Lulinha" (little Lula), on March 3. When he was invited to lead the ticket, Lula decided to ask his brother Friar Chico for advice, as he was an old fox in union negotiations and had served as vice president of the regional union office in São Caetano. There was no sign that his brother would oppose the idea since, unlike what had happened in 1972, this time the PCB supported the single ticket. Lula was thrilled with the idea of becoming president, but, to his surprise, his brother was against the idea. Leading a base of 100,000 workers, warned Friar Chico, would make him a target of scrutiny of the state, the Labor Court, and the bosses.

"Get out of this, man," he said. "Stay in the directorate, but in a secondary position, who knows, even as general secretary. The president is a very public figure. You will be forced to stand off against the bosses and the press. There's the anti-strike law, this law, that law. Mind your own business. If you accept the presidency, you're going to get screwed."

Lula paid no attention to his brother. The ticket was set up by the end of that afternoon, with Lula at the head, Vidal as general secretary, and Rubão, Campanholo, and Biolcatti (who, like Vidal and Lula, were already in the current directorate) as executive directors. Behind the scenes, what first looked like was going to be a *lulista* victory took on a new configuration. Vidal planned to keep calling the shots, while the star of the so-called "new unionism" would have a symbolic role, like the queen of England.

Lula, who was no sucker, smelled a rat. "Vidal thought he was going to keep running things," he said years later.

There were so many people at the inauguration ceremony that even the huge room in the new building couldn't hold them, and it had to be transferred to the old Vera Cruz movie studio. The main authority, Governor Paulo Egídio, estimated that there were over 30,000 people there, but a more realistic figure is that there were at most 10,000—which in itself was a huge crowd for a mere change of union leadership. Nevertheless, a photo of the inauguration lent weight to the intrigue around the outgoing president: the person who appears at the center of the ceremony is Vidal, next to the appointed state governor, Egídio, who oversaw the proceedings. Despite being the star of the night, Lula was pushed to the edge of the table, next to the communist Marcelo Gato from DIESSE. But not even his arrival at the top of his union career was enough to scare off his old shyness, which led Gato to hold the microphone so that Lula, with shaking hands, could make his inauguration speech.

"It was the only written speech I ever made in my union career," he said. "I improvised all the others."

In an extensive testimony to the Getúlio Vargas Foundation History Center (CPDOC), many years later, Paulo Egídio revealed that he decided to go to Lula's inauguration ceremony because he believed he was a positive alternative to the communist union leaders who "opposed the yellow unionism of the Getúlio Vargas years." Despite this, when President Geisel read in the newspapers that the governor he had nominated had gone to the ceremony in São Bernardo, he called him on the phone and, according to Egídio, held the following short conversation:

"Paulo, what was going on in your mind when you decided to go to the inauguration of a worker at the metalworkers' union?"

The governor answered that the ceremony in the ABC had a special meaning, since Lula's election represented a tough blow against the communists. "My political gesture was this. It was this that I wanted to register."

The president seemed surprised. "I didn't know that he had defeated the communists."

Egídio stood by his argument and took advantage of the moment to take a jab at Geisel: "You should ask your intel staff to update their information a little more on this subject."

The early days of the presidency proved challenging for Lula. As time passed, he figured out the trick Vidal was using to push him to the sidelines. As was the tradition, the assemblies, which were becoming more and more common, were opened by the general secretary, who was responsible for the legal formality of reading of the minutes of the previous assembly. Vidal would read the minutes and keep the microphone.

"He would open the assembly, speak for two hours on all of the subjects that interested the workers, and then conclude saying, 'Now I'll pass the microphone to our president,' " Lula said. "Since I no longer had anything to talk about, I would just say, 'I declare this assembly over,' and go back to my room without saying a word. It was mediocre."

It was clear that the ties between the old and new president were beginning to fray.

Patiently, Lula silently tolerated Vidal's behavior and tried to take as much advantage as he could of his position. Little by little, he discovered that the irrelevance of the union movement as a political force was due not only to legal binds or to a few sellout directors who acted as peacemakers in the conflicts between the bosses and the workers. To the general surprise of everyone, he decided to exercise his mandate, not in the carpeted, air-conditioned rooms of the union hall but in the streets.

"All the people saw up to then was the worker who left the assembly line, became a union director, and transformed into a minor boss," he said. "It was a beautiful office with wheeled chairs swiveling here and there, but nobody even thought of going door to door to the factories, face to face with the workers. They used to do a lot of union organizing without the workers. My office became a place where people came to talk about their problems. In fact, we talked about everything there, from soccer to women. There were no secrets. There was always a bottle of cachaça on the table, and we would drink, talk, and argue."

These were accurate observations, but what the workers were most interested in was job guarantees and, primarily, wages that covered inflation losses. Lula's chosen weapon to reignite the effervescence of the workers wasn't new and came not from a random union agitator but from the respected economist Walter Barelli from DIESSE: the wage scam set up by Finance Minister Delfim Netto, who had manipulated the inflation data from 1973.

"We are not going to file charges," said the new union president. "We are going to recuperate the 34.1 percent."

Leading the campaign for recuperation—a strategy that was disliked by Paulo Vidal—Lula crossed the border of the ABC and traveled through Brazil, starting a national movement for recuperating the wage losses and spreading the proposals for the new unionism that was taking hold in São Bernardo and the ABC.

On September 24, Lula left for Japan. His first trip abroad would be marked by bad omens. He was participating in an international union conference organized by the Toyota and Nissan factories in Tokyo. The event sponsored by the two manufacturers had no specific objective, nor was it a training course. It was simply a meeting for metalworkers from dozens of countries to exchange ideas. Only two other union leaders from Brazil participated in the event, São Paulo Metalworkers' Federation president Argeu Egídio dos Santos, and Minas Gerais Metalworkers Federation president, Jorge Noman Neto, both of whom had reputations as sellouts among the younger union workers.

When he boarded the airplane at Congonhas Airport (Cumbica, in Guarulhos, would not be built for another decade), Lula left a country that was being swept by a new series of raids by the dictatorship's security organizations. With all of the guerrilla groups and armed resistance organizations decimated, the military's hunt turned toward the PCB—which had been against all forms of armed struggle, urban and rural, since the 1964 coup. Using medieval torture methods from the slavery era that had been adopted to repress the armed guerrilla organizations, the persecution of the communists reached its climax with the murder of the young journalist Vladimir Herzog, on October 25, and produced another deep military crisis in January when the same DOI-CODI that killed Herzog killed a factor worker named Manoel Fiel Filho.

Lula's trip was cut short before it had even begun. During a refueling stop in Mexico, the Brazilian delegation had to leave the aircraft. Lula had contracted a strong throat infection during the flight that had left him voiceless, unable to utter a word. After four days stuck in a hotel bed receiving medical treatment, he continued on the trip with his two colleagues, landing in the Japanese capital after the conference was already in full swing. With his throat still sore and swollen, Lula was still unable to talk, only to listen.

The Brazilians had barely been there for a week when Lula received a call from São Paulo. On the other side of the planet, Sebastião de Paula Coelho, lawyer for the Metalworkers' Federation (who, from 1979 to 1982, would serve as labor secretary for governor Paulo Maluf) gave Lula the bad news.

"Your brother Friar Chico was arrested by the military, together with dozens of other journalists and union leaders accused of being communists," he said. "It would be better for you to stay there, for your own safety. Things are not looking good here in Brazil."

Friar Chico hadn't been arrested; he'd been kidnapped. On Wednesday, October 1, when Lula was preparing to leave Mexico for Japan, his communist brother had taken office as vice president of the São Caetano do Sul Metalworkers' Union. The following Saturday, October 4, he met with a friend in a bar next to the union, and during his walk home he bumped into his wife, Ivene, who was on the way to pick up their son from his grandmother's house nearby. "Chico," she said, "some men came to the house asking about someone named Antônio Bernardino."

Experienced and knowing that the political situation was getting heavy, Friar Chico assumed it was the police. Minutes later, after he entered his house, an unmarked Veraneio van parked in front of their door, and a group of armed men got out and took him by force. One of them put a black hood over his head and threw him into the vehicle. The van took off at high speed and only stopped when it arrived in hell: the Thirty-Sixth District police station on 921 Tutoia Street, in São Paulo's Paraiso neighborhood, the location of the military dictatorship's cruelest torture chamber, DOI-CODI.

In Tokyo, Lula rejected Coelho's suggestion. "Shit, what am I going to do in Japan?" he said. "I don't speak English or Japanese. I don't like Japanese food. I don't understand fuck all here! I'm coming back to Brazil to look for my brother. If they arrest me, fuck it!"

He immediately left the conference, purchased a ticket on a flight with layovers in Washington, DC, and New York, and returned to Brazil. When his Boeing 707 landed in Congonhas on Friday, October 17, a group of journalists and lawyer friends were waiting for him, but there didn't seem to be any police. Exhausted from jet lag from the twenty-five-hour journey and twelve-hour time difference, Lula went home to rest. He spent the weekend as if nothing was happening. On Saturday, he honored a social commitment, attending the wedding of Marisa's sister Joana. Maintaining a routine before going out looking for his brother—no one had yet figured out where was being held—was a way of figuring out whether state security agents were tailing him.

Early on Monday morning, Lula joined a group of friends and relatives who had been searching high and low for signs of Friar Chico since his kidnapping on the fourth. Terrified by the possibility that her husband was dead—the list of so-called political disappearances had already surpassed one hundred—Ivene had visited hospitals and morgues across São Paulo and the ABC. The dictatorship buried prisoners who died during torture in common graves—as they did with deceased street dwellers—in cemeteries like the one in the Perus District, on the north side of São Paulo, leaving no sign of burial. Tirelessly, between one search and another, she stood in front of the door of DOPS. She spent hours standing on the pavement inquiring about her husband to the police officers, detectives, and bureaucrats who came in and out of the frightening red-brick building. Nothing.

Lula, searching boldly and intensively for any trace of Friar Chico, got his nerve up to knock on the door of the Second Army Corps, an ugly and modern concrete building in front of São Paulo's Ibirapuera Park. Accompanied by Vavá, his oldest brother, he hoped, however unlikely, that he would be able to meet with the commanding officer, General Ednardo D'Ávila Melo. Melo, sixty-four, a Rio de Janeiro native, was connected to the hard-line, right-wing extremist group within the armed forces. During the Costa e Silva government, he had worked as a military attaché in Washington, DC, and as director of the Federal Information and Counter-Information Service (SFICI). As Commander of the Second Corps, Melo was responsible for the São Paulo division of DOI-CODI, considered the stronghold of the military dictatorship. After waiting for hours, Lula and Vavá were met by an unidentified official who said he didn't know anything about Friar Chico but took advantage of the moment to interrogate them about possible connections between them and their brother with "subversion and terrorism." He ended the meeting without providing any information about their prisoner. By the time that Lula and Vavá left the Second Army Corps, Friar Chico had been tortured nonstop for fifteen days inside DOI-CODI.

When he first arrived at the military unit, Chico had been photographed, identified, and given a jumpsuit without a belt—a practice adopted in prisons to prevent suicides.

"The jumpsuit stank," he later recalled. "It had certainly been used by other prisoners before me and hadn't been washed for a long time."

Thrown into a cell full of journalists, workers, and liberal professionals accused of having connections with the PCB, Friar Chico learned from fellow prisoners that he had arrived in the most brutal reception room for martyrs that Brazil had ever known.

During his two weeks in DOI-CODI, he wasn't hung upside down, arms and legs bound to the "parrot's perch"—the most notorious torture device used in the dungeons of the military dictatorship. Instead, he spent his days and nights tied to a torture device even worse: the "dragon's chair." His torturers stripped him naked and tied his hands and feet to a chair whose seat, back, and armrests were made of metal. Electric wires protruding from a point on the chair were connected to the *maricota*, a hand-cranked electricity generator. As the torturer increased and decreased voltage according to the speed of the crank, Friar Chico's body shuddered and his teeth ground uncontrollably, like a man suffering an epilepsy attack, causing his teeth to cut into his tongue. To increase the intensity of the shock and the pain, they would dump buckets of water on him and force salt into his mouth.

Friar Chico only left the dragon's chair for interrogations, during which the torturers insisted on a ridiculous idea: they wanted him to confess that Lula's participation in the union conference in Japan was a smokescreen for the real purpose of his trip: to deliver clandestine communications for the general secretary of the Brazilian Communist Party, Luís Carlos Prestes. Friar Chico told the military officers that he didn't even know that his brother had left Brazil—which was the truth. He repeatedly explained that Lula had no relations whatsoever with the PCB. To the contrary, many times in debates and interviews, he would explain the political differences Lula had with the party and its leader. If the political arguments weren't enough, there was another one: geography. If Lula was in Tokyo, he was 7,500 kilometers from Moscow, capital of the Soviet Union, where the exiled Prestes, the highest leader of the PCB and "knight of hope" lived. When none of this worked, Friar Chico, reduced to a human rag doll, was brought back to the dragon's chair. To prevent his screams from being heard outside the cell, the torturers turned a radio to maximum volume, nearly always tuned to the Rádio Record station. After losing consciousness from the violence of the shocks, Chico would come to hearing Zé Béttio's program of *sertanejo*, the biggest musical phenomenon of the 1970s. Every two or three days, a man would come into the cell to examine him, take his blood pressure, and measure his heart rate. This seemed to be a doctor who was evaluating whether he was able to sustain more torture or if it was time to slow the pace of the horror.

After fifteen days of torture, they handed him back the clothes he had been wearing when they kidnapped him, and he was transferred to DOPS. For people leaving DOI-CODI, DOPS was a relief. Not that torture didn't also take place in that big building on General Osório Square, but everyone on the left knew what hell DOI-CODI was—or what the DOI-CODIs *were*, since São Paulo's torture dungeon had inspired the army to create branches in many of the largest cities in Brazil, like Brasília, Rio de Janeiro, and Recife.

After the fruitless search at the Second Army Corps, Lula decided to pay a visit to DOPS. "In those days," he said, "anyone going to DOPS looking for a political prisoner was either a lawyer or insane." He wasn't either of those things, but he was persistent and managed to get in the building and speak with the night shift director, Domingos Campanella, where he ended up in a conversation straight out of the theater of the absurd.

"Doctor, regarding my brother who is in prison, can you tell me if he's here?"

"What's your brother's name?"

"José Ferreira da Silva."

The officer grabbed the phone and, according to Lula, pretended to talk to a jailer. "Is that communist son of a bitch down there? Oh, he's in the Soviet Union taking a class? Okay, thanks."

He hung up the phone and turned to Lula. "You can you see how democratic this country is, right, Mr. Luiz? Your brother, a communist who wants to destroy the military regime, is in jail, and you, democratically, are here getting information about him. Can you imagine someone in Russia having this kind of freedom?"

"Dr. Campanella, I thank you, but can you tell me if Osvaldo Cavignato, the economist from our union, is also in prison?"

Cavignato had been kidnapped by DOI-CODU on the eve of his flight to Japan. The two had been talking in Lula's office when two strangers came in with an odd message. "Mr. Osvaldo, your father is having a health emergency. It's bad, and we have come to take you to see him." He left the building, got into a Veraneio van, and never came back. Hearing Lula ask about Cavignato in DOPS, officer Campanella rolled his eyes.

"This Osvaldo is here too. Mr. Luiz, you know that every economist is a communist. They are a band of sons of bitches! Look here, this Osvaldo who you are looking for spent two years in Moscow! He took a class there on how to sow communism here in Brazil. And you still have a friendly relationship with this person? You have to cut it off! You are a good man!"

Still disorientated from the torture he suffered in DOI-CODI, Friar Chico didn't know how many days he spent in DOPS, where he met more prisoners who were either affiliated with PCB or accused of having ties with the party. On the morning of October 23, Ivene repeated her daily ritual of standing on the pavement in front of DOPS. Desperate to find out if her husband was in jail, she repeated the same question to everyone who went in and out of the building, "Do you know if there is a prisoner there named José Ferreira da Silva, known as Friar Chico?"

Suddenly, for the first time in eighteen days, a man stopped in front of her. "Ivene," he said, "what are you doing here in front of the door of DOPS?"

It wasn't a good Samaritan put there by the hand of providence, but a police officer who was her mom's cousin, who worked as a jailor at DOPS at the time. Surprised to see a relative, she said, for the *nth* time, "I'm looking for Friar Chico, my husband, and nobody is telling me anything."

The cop whispered, "Act like nothing is happening. Wait around the corner, and I'll go down there and check for you."

Minutes later, he was back with good news. "Yes. Friar Chico is in jail here, but they are going to transfer him soon to the Hipódromo Prison. Now get out of here and go get a lawyer."

Hours later, Friar Chico himself appeared on the same pavement, with one of his hands handcuffed to a big blond man with blue eyes and messy hair. It was the attorney José Roberto Fanganiello Melhem, from the São Paulo PCB directorate. The two were waiting for a "cage"—a prison truck to transfer them to Hipódromo Prison in the Bras neighborhood, where common criminals were detained as they waited for their trials, which had an annex for political prisoners.

The improved treatment of Friar Chico, Melhem, and another dozen prisoners who had passed through DOI-CODI was not a sign that the communist hunting season had ended. The day after they were transferred to Hipódromo Prison, two DOI-CODI agents appeared at the small publishing house Swdalc, in a building on Paulista Avenue, in search of a young journalist who worked there. The three company owners, Samuel Wainer, Domingo Alzugaray, and Luis Carta (younger brother of the famous Brazilian journalist Mino Carta), served coffee to the officers and spoke politely with them, stalling so that the man they were looking for could escape. Meanwhile, the young journalist grabbed his things, galloped down fifteen flights of stairs, and made it out of the building. That night, the agents knocked on the door of Vladimir Herzog, TV Cultura's director of journalism. On Saturday morning, Vlado, as he was known by his friends, was murdered during a torture session. To simulate suicide, the DOI-CODI officers photographed his body with belt wrapped around his neck, hanging from a gate a little over a meter high. It was there that a battle began between two factions at the heart of the military dictatorship—the right against the far right.

The news that Friar Chico was in Hipódromo Prison, safe from torture and with the right to family visits, calmed everyone down. Compared to his time in DOI-CODI, the atmosphere in Hipódromo was so relaxed that the political prisoners decided to have an end-of-year party on the fifteenth, when each one could receive a limited number of visitors from family and friends. On Friday the fourteenth, Ivene was in her kitchen, making trays of meat pies for her husband and his friends' party when the journalist Mino Carta and union lawyer Almir Pazzianotto came to her door asking about Friar Chico. The three were speaking in the living room when they heard a noise outside. Ivene nearly fainted when the door opened and her husband walked in.

The brutal annihilation of the left gave the impression to society that the military hard line, commanded from the shadows by General Sylvio Frota, minister of the army, was winning the internal struggle led by President Geisel and his succubus, General Golbery do Couto e Silva, who had promised the nation that there would be a "long, gradual and safe" political opening, after which they would hand over all power to the civilians. The reaction to the assassination of Herzog forced Geisel to put the brakes on the hand of repression. This time, the death wasn't of an armed guerrilla with a police record full of bombing attempts, but of a respectable journalist. Serious and respected by his colleagues and bosses, Herzog had an important job as director of journalism at TV Cultura, a public company controlled by the São Paulo state government. Furthermore, he had been nominated for that job by the state secretary of culture, the bibliophile and wealthy industrialist José Mindlin.

As news of Herzog's death broke, a mixture of fear, panic, and paranoia swept over everyone who had ever been seen as a critic of the military regime. The left and progressive sectors of society were afraid that the group connected to Minister Sylvio Frota was preparing a path to depose Geisel and start a "Jakarta operation," referring to the massacre perpetrated ten years earlier in Indonesia when the dictator Suharto ordered the murder of half a million communists, dissidents, intellectuals, religious leaders, and pacifists. Since Vlado and Mindlin were Jewish, the crime against the journalist released ancestral ghosts into the influential São Paulo Jewish community, composed of tens of thousands of people.

Mindlin himself, who was in the United States at the time, recognized the threat. "Some journalists who were arrested," he said, "told me later that they had been interrogated about my alleged connection with the Communist Party, which I never had."

The next Friday, exactly one week after Herzog's death, São Paulo Journalists' Union president Audálio Dantas announced an ecumenical mass in Se Cathedral that would be led by Cardinal Paulo Evaristo Arns, São Paulista Israelite Congregation president Rabbi Henry Sobel, and Presbyterian pastor Jaime Wright. In order to make it harder for the population to get there, the Department of Transportation blocked all of the streets that led to the cathedral, as well as suspended bus lines and banned parking in the area. However, it didn't work. An estimated crowd of 8,000 to 10,000 people packed the cathedral, and thousands more spilled out onto the street, filling up the entire square.

As the crowd streamed into the cathedral, Dom Paulo, Pastor Wright, Rabbi Sobel, and Audálio planned the ceremony and worked out their speaking order in the sacristy. The four were unanimous in their fear that afterward, the crowd would take to the streets and march against the dictatorship, and that there could be a violent confrontation with the police. At the same moment, ten kilometers from stuffy Se Cathedral, President Ernesto Geisel gave General Ednardo D'Ávila Melo, commander of the Second Army Corps, a humiliating dressing down in front of a surprised Governor Paulo Egídio.

Geisel had arrived in São Paulo the previous morning, accompanied by his wife Lucy, their daughter Amalia, who was a historian, and General Hugo Abreu, minister of the Armed Forces. He was met by in the official wing of Congonhas Airport by the governor and by the state military hierarchy—led by General Ednardo—and went to the inauguration of a new Social Service of Commerce (SESC) complex near Billings Reservoir, where he had lunch, went to the state government headquarters at Bandeirantes Palace, shared an intimate dinner with the governor, and slept in the governmental palace's residential wing. Hugo Abreu kept him updated the entire time about the movement in the city—nobody risked making a prediction about what would happen afterward—and, at eight o'clock the next morning, he visited a research center at the Federal Government's Paulista Medical School. At nine, he made an official visit to the Thirteenth São Paulo Art Biennial with curator Ciccillo Matarazzo. It was supposed to be a seventy-minute visit, according to presidential protocol, but Geisel, accompanied by rural historian Orlando Villas-Bôas and indigenous leader Yawalapiti Aritana, ended up spending two hours at an installation organized by the FUNAI (National Indigenous Peoples' Foundation) together with representatives from the 2.6-million-hectare Xingu reserve, located in the state of Mato Grosso.

At one o'clock that afternoon, he joined Governor Egídio in the palace stateroom, where the guests sat at an enormous table divided between the olive-green of military uniforms and the navy-blue tropical wool of the businessmen who participated at the meeting, which had been organized by the governor. After the meeting, as everyone got up to leave, the president ordered General Ednardo to stay. Geisel said goodbye to everyone and walked with Egídio to the palace library, in the residential wing, where they spoke for a few minutes. The coffee was still hot in their cups when an aide told them that General Ednardo was waiting in the hallway and Geisel invited him in. In the library, General

Ednardo stood with his cap under his arm. As Egídio politely got up to leave them alone, the president stuck his palm out in a halting motion.

"No, Paulo," he said, "sit down. You should stay here."

The president acted like he wanted witnesses. Furiously pointing his finger in the air, he went for the jugular of Second Army Corps commander, calling him not by his rank but by his first name,

"Ednardo, you've known me for many years. I do not allow or accept what is happening in your area here in São Paulo. And you'd better be careful because I am going to take measures! Listen closely, because I am giving you an order: nobody can be arrested in Second Army territory without it first being reported to Golbery or Figueiredo in SNI, or to me personally. Any political arrest can only take place after we know about it first. No political prisoner can be taken to any army barracks unless these conditions are met. Are you listening to me? Do you understand this?"

Lowering his head, the general responded with, "Yes sir, president. Yes sir, president."

Geisel dryly added, "You can leave now."

Geisel, acting like nothing unusual had happened, left with Governor Egídio to finish his official agenda. With the governor at his side, along with Hugo Abreu, his wife, and daughter, they visited the University of São Paulo School of Public Health, went to Congonhas airport and, at 5:10 p.m., returned to Brasília on the presidential Boeing. Within a few hours, news that the president had chewed General Ednardo out in front of the governor had reached all of the army bases in São Paulo. That night a DOI-CODI policeman left a prisoner alone in a room saying, "Be careful what you do, okay? If another body appears here, they are going to shut us down."

The operation continued for another eighty-three days. At first, Geisel's roars didn't seem to discourage General Ednardo. On January 16, the DOI-CODI directorate ordered a group of agents to invade the Metal Arte factory in Mooca, on São Paulo's east side, and made one more arrest. The victim this time was Manoel Fiel Filho, a press operator from Alagoas suspected of being an activist from the PCB and of distributing the *Voz Operária* newspaper, a clandestine tabloid produced by the party. At ten o'clock the night of Saturday the seventeenth, an unmarked Dodge Dart slowly drove up to the door of Fiel's house in the east side neighborhood of Vila Guarani. From inside the luxury car, an unidentified man threw a light-blue plastic trash bag onto the sidewalk and yelled, "Manoel committed suicide. Here are his clothes."

According to DOI-CODI's official statement, Fiel had killed himself, not using a belt, as they claimed Herzog had, but by strangling himself with his own socks. Above and beyond the absurd story that someone could strangle himself with a pair of socks, the prisoners who saw Fiel arrive at DOI said that he had been wearing flip-flops at the time.

As evening set in that Sunday, the governor still hadn't heard anything about the incident. That night, General Golbery called him from Brasília to give him the news of Fiel's murder. The next day, General Geisel signed an order firing General Ednardo D'Ávila Melo and nominating General Dilermando Gomes Monteiro—a man whose name had already been cited as a possible minister of the army—in his place. To prevent a leadership vacuum caused by the humiliation imposed on Ednardo, the military's right-wing extremist faction nominated a man of confidence, General Ariel Pacca da Fonseca, as acting commander until Dilermando officially took office.

The reaction of the military in São Paulo was negligible, limited to a formality intelligible only to the small group who had witnessed Ednardo's symbolic decapitation. The Armed Forces official procedure during a transfer of power is that the outgoing official repeats a standard phrase: "I hereby transfer command to . . ." General Ednardo remained silent, but Pacca didn't let it go, turned to his fired colleague and said, "I hereby assume the command of the Second Army Corps, in substitution of General Ednardo D'Ávila Melo. Allow me, General, to accompany you to your car."

At Rio de Janeiro's Laguna Palace next to the Maracanã soccer stadium, the de facto headquarters of the army's right-wing extremist faction (the "Tigers" as Geisel's group called them), General Sylvio Frota and his chief of staff, the diminutive Brigadier General Augusto Heleno—who would, many years later, become the minister of the Institutional Security Office during the Bolsonaro administration—were clearly scared. When he learned he was being transferred to the post of army director of education and research, in Brasília, General Ednardo understood that, in military jargon, he was being sent to the kennel. The chief of the largest and most powerful unit of the army would now be battalion commander of rubber stamps and ink blotters. He asked to be transferred to the reserves, and his request was immediately granted.

No one else appeared strangled by belts or pairs of socks on Tutóia Street, but the death machine would only definitively shut down after the so-called "massacre of Lapa," which took place on December 16, 1976, while Geisel was still president. The Brazilian army held a raid on the Central Committee of the Communist Party of Brazil (PC do B)—a dissident Maoist group that had broken off from the PCB in the 1950s—that was meeting in a house on Pio XI Street, in São Paulo's Lapa neighborhood. The action resulted in the deaths of three of the party's Central Commitee. Pedro Pomar and Angelo Arroyo were murdered on the spot, while a third director, João Batista Franco Drummond, who had been arrested hours earlier, was tortured to death in a cell in the DOI-CODI.

The result of Geisel's war with General Frota would only end for good on October 12, 1977, when the president fired him from his position of minister of the army. In the years that followed the murders of Herzog and Fiel Filho, Geisel enjoyed fame as a moderate. His reactions to the deaths of Vlado and Manoel, and to the firings of Ednardo and Frota, contributed to a softening his image in the eyes of history as a representative of civilization against the barbarism of the Brazilian army's years of lead. This aura of a good man didn't last long. In May 2018, Getúlio Vargas Foundation researcher Matias Spektor uncovered a 1974 document from the CIA that was crystal clear:

"On April 1, President Geisel told General Figueiredo that the policies should continue, but that they should be very careful to guarantee that only dangerous subversives would be executed."

Two decades after his death, the memory of Geisel fell into the common grave of the "Tigers," along with the brutal murderers who challenged his authority.

13

After years denigrating the political class, Lula starts building the foundation for the Workers' Party

For Lula and the other activists from the ABC—even those who, like him, were not communists—the threats of imprisonment and repression seemed to end after Geisel performed his house cleaning in the army. But he still had to take care of a big headache that had bothered him since he took office as union president. The problem was Paulo Vidal, the general secretary who was still acting like he ran everything.

Vidal got on Lula's nerves in September, when Ford announced forced vacations for 235 workers on the Maverick production line, alleging that they were going to reduce production of the model and downgrade its engine from six to four cylinders. Without consulting with Lula, who was against the factory's decision, Vidal struck a deal with the directors and accepted their proposal without waiting to run it by the union. Lula made it clear at the next assembly that he didn't agree with the move and waited for the right moment to get back at Vidal.

In September 1976, after his labor sector's biennial convention, Lula took a wage campaign to the streets and picked a fight with the Metalworkers' Federation, led by the "sellout" Argeu, his colleague from the ill-fated trip to Japan. After a tough faceoff, Lula and union comrades took their case to Superior Labor Court, and it recognized, for the first time in Brazil, that the Metalworkers' Federation represented not labor unions but only unaffiliated workers. This court decision meant that the unions now had sufficent autonomy to negotiate their own deals, without depending on the approval from the federation. Until then, the unions had been required to officially request authorization from the federation to represent them in, among other things, wage disputes. Lula took advantage of the opening to blow the door wide open. The ABC Metalworkers' Union immediately secured work stability guarantees for ABC Metalworkers' Union members who were pregnant and for minors who were old enough to enlist in the military (those aged eighteen to twenty-one), and pay compensation for people who had to miss work due to school exams. It wasn't a revolution, but they were objective gains on issues that workers had been complaining about for a long time. Most importantly, over the long term, this would free them from the guardianship of the federation.

Shortly thereafter, Lula chose the right moment to put Paulo Vidal in checkmate. Once again, the battleground was Ford. The company cited the economic crisis to justify proposing forced vacations for its workers. Accustomed to cordial negotiations with Paulo Vidal, they gave him all the details, and he not only agreed to them but went public with the news at a press conference. Lula stepped in and said that the proposal would only be valid if it was approved in a union assembly. The directors of Ford cleverly pretended to accept the demand, with one condition: that the assembly would take place inside the factory. Vidal gave a newspaper interview announcing that the union accepted the counterproposal. Lula announced to another journalist that real assemblies could only take place inside a union hall, and that this would be the case with Ford. The next day, two newspapers ran contradictory stories. Since he was sure he would get seven or eight of the nine members' votes of the union executive board, Lula held a meeting with them and announced a mortal blow against his predecessor.

"Starting today," he said, "only the president is authorized to give interviews and make public statements on issues related to our labor sector. When he is absent, Vice President Rubão, Rubens Teodoro de Arruda, can speak in his place. In the absence of the president and vice president, the general secretary can speak in their place. We can't tolerate a situation in which each person gives a different interview on the same subject. It will make it look like we are divided."

The communists who orbited around the union said that Lula had finally taken the hard line of "democratic centralism." Lula remembers that meeting as the moment he gained his political independence. But the last nail in Vidal's coffin was hammered in months later, when the

MDB, one of the two legal political parties in the country (along with the National Renewal Alliance [ARENA], the official party of the dictatorship), convinced him to run for São Bernardo's city council. Vidal realized they were sidelining him, but it had its advantages. It was an honorable way out, not a luxury funeral. In the previous elections, in 1974, the MDB had delivered a historic blow to the dictatorship by electing sixteen out of twenty-two senators and winning 44 percent of the seats in Congress. Political analysts wrote that the elections that year put a big question mark on the military regime. The deal ended up working out for Vidal: he won the third-highest number of votes in the citywide election, entering City Council behind fellow MDB candidate and future mayor Aron Galante and ARENA's Walter Demarchi, who was a well-known politician and member of one of the most traditional elite families of the ABC region.

Free from the shadow of Vidal, Lula could finally put the new unionism into practice. It started with a change in the annual May Day celebration. Instead of celebrating May 1 with fairs and recreational activities, he started the celebration a month earlier, with film screenings and theater performances, followed by debates and discussions on the themes of the exhibitions. Joined by guest speakers, the union hosted debates on labor rights and other issues of interest to workers. An audience was guaranteed by the students enrolled in the diploma-equivalency courses Lula had created three years earlier, who passed through the auditorium every day on the way to and from their classes. In contrast to similar courses that multiplied by the hundreds across the country, in which the majority of the students were only interested in getting a certificate that would enable them to enroll in university—the so-called "pay-pass" courses—the union's course had an additional requirement: to obtain a certificate of attendance, the student had to take a forty-five-minute daily class on politics and labor unionism.

On June 1, President Geisel arrived in São Paulo to inaugurate a Ford tractor factory in São Bernardo do Campo. The presence of a president who was famous as a nationalist at the inauguration of a factory owned by a multinational corporation was explained by the relevance of the project. Built on a 70,000-square-meter lot, the 16,500-square-meter factory represented an investment of US$41 million (around R$1 billion in 2021), with the capacity to produce 20,000 tractors per year. The generally somber Ernesto Geisel showed up smiling, surrounded by authorities including Industry and Commerce Minister Severo Gomes, Agriculture Minister Alysson Paolinelli, Governor Paulo Egídio, General Dilermando Gomes Monteiro, US Ambassador John Hugh Crimmins, several businessmen, and a horde of armed bodyguards who jostled with each other to take care of so many important visitors.

Geisel supporters would later say that the president was also celebrating something that few people might have known at the time. Before leaving Brasília, he had instructed his chief of staff to tell the Civita family, owners of Abril publishing company, that starting the next day, the censor would be suspended from intervening in *Veja* magazine—the last mainstream press outlet still forced to operate with an in-house military censor. The daring and indomitable independent "dwarf" press"—like *Movimento, Pasquim*, and *Opinião*—would continue to operate under the watchful eye of the military.

Lost among the guests, like a fish out of water, Lula squeezed through the crowd to reach the president. He left the union with a promise to his directors to personally deliver to Geisel an official letter of demands and complaints from the ABC Metalworkers' Union. When he saw that he wouldn't be able to break through the security barrier, he yelled out to Governor Egídio.

"Governor, I have come to deliver a document to President Geisel, but I can't get near him. There are too many people throwing elbows."

Egídio said, "Come with me."

He grabbed Lula by the arm, opened a path, and walked up to Geisel. "President, this here is the most important union leader in the country. I was at his inauguration, and there were 30,000 people there. He has a letter for you."

According to Lula, Geisel didn't even open the envelope. He put it next to another one (which he also didn't open) that he'd received from the US ambassador—a personal letter from Henry Ford II, owner of Ford since 1945—and handed them to an assistant. When Lula returned to the union hall, he explained what had happened to his colleagues.

"I don't know if he is going to read it," he said, "but I delivered it. I did my part."

Even if Geisel didn't read it, Lula thought it would be worth it if he made the pages of *Jornal do Brasil* the next day. It didn't happen—no front-page story, nor any mention of his name whatsoever. The only, anonymous mention of his quick encounter with Geisel made the last paragraph of a June 2 article on the visit to São Bernardo:

> The letter delivered by the metalworkers of São Paulo to President Geisel requests, in addition to raising the minimum wage, revision of the salaries for the different qualified job categories affiliated with the union. They also requested changes in collective hiring and reforms of the labor card.

Geisel's enthusiasm for the inauguration of a tractor factory looked more like an injection of adrenaline into a moribund economy. The damage caused by the oil crisis, even in rich countries, had been brutal in nations with fragile economies like Brazil. The price of a barrel of oil had risen from a little over US$10 in 1973 to US$110 in 1979. To artificially control inflation during the years of the "economic miracle," Petrobras had subsidized gasoline and diesel prices, and this now forced the government to painfully shift into reverse. To address structural problems, it created the national ethanol program, Proálcool, to produce biofuel for automobiles and invested heavily, in partnership with the government of Paraguay, in the construction of Itaipu hydroelectric dam, the world's second largest. The decision to start a nuclear reactor program in Angra dos Reis, with a projected budget of US$8.4 billion, triggered a battle to the death between the Westinghouse Corporation and its German competitor Siemens-KWU, which would end up with the winning bid.

Most of the official propaganda designed to convince the population that the dictatorship was overcoming foreign dependency in the energy sector failed to convince the public. On the one hand, there was the story told in the interminable and well-funded advertisements on TV, in newspapers, and magazines. On the other, there was the daily struggle of the Brazilian people, whose lives were getting more and more difficult and expensive. In addition to the stratospheric prices, the fuel consumed at the pump was subjected to strict regulation: sale of gasoline was banned on weekends, and the speed limit, including on freeways, was reduced from 120 to 80 kilometers per hour. Frequent panics over rumors of fuel price hikes caused huge lines at gas stations across the country.

Another factor further aggravated the economic crisis: the proverbial

Brazilian megalomania. One of the best examples of this tradition happened the year before Geisel visited the Ford tractor factory, in mid-1975, when he met with Lula's boss, Paulo Villares, owner of the megacorp that had factories spread throughout the state of São Paulo. In addition to building the gigantic ship engines that shook the house windows in the ABC, Villares Metals led the market in steel tools, high-speed steel, stainless steel bars, special steel alloys, and large forged-carbon steel components, and it was one of the world's largest producers of steel valves. It also produced subway cars for internal use and export. The company also had a characteristic that would brighten the eyes of a generation of nationalist military officers, of which Geisel was one of the prime specimens: the company was entirely Brazilian.

The meeting between Geisel and Paulo Villares took place during the inauguration of Jabaquara subway station in São Paulo. The president called the industrialist over for one of his typical short and objective conversations.

"Besides subway cars, can you build locomotives?"

"No, President," Villares said. "We make a lot of things, but we don't build locomotives."

"Why not?"

"For lack of a market. International competition is huge. The locomotives used in Brazil, for example, are mostly imported, nearly all from the American company General Motors. Beyond a market, we would need financing to compete with these multinational giants. We aren't complaining. Villares plans to invest a lot on this in the future and, who knows . . ."

"But . . . how much financing are you talking about?"

"I would say . . . something like . . . ten million dollars."

"What?"

Villares thought the president's shocked look would end the conversation then and there, but Geisel continued.

"Only ten million? Why so little?"

According to the book that commemorated the company's eightieth anniversary in 1999, Villares was surprised at the president's reaction and said, "Well, President, in the capital goods industry, which involves numbers and risks that are so great, you can't invest without being sure about the market. You practically only invest after you have the orders placed."

Without thinking twice, Geisel said, "What if I guarantee that you will have the orders? In this case would you be willing to invest a lot more?"

Villares responded immediately, "Without a doubt, President."

Geisel called Marcos Pereira Viana, president of the Brazilian Development Bank (BNDE, later renamed with an *S* at the end for "social"), asked him to have an urgent meeting with Villares and ended the meeting with a handshake and a promise of US$100 million—ten times the initial value Villares thought he would need to finance the new production line. As a counterpart to the loan, the federal government promised to buy at least one hundred locomotives a year from the future factory. The investment begun with the US$100 million promised by Geisel grew to $450 million, ultimately reaching $650 million—not bad for a company that had opened the conversation estimating it would need $10 million! And the promise of delivering locomotives made tripled: once the factory was built in the city of Araraquara, the government said it would increase its purchase guarantee from 100 to 300 locomotives per year.

In time, the dynamics of capitalism and Brazil's political instability revealed that the handshake had not resulted in a successful locomotive factory. First of all, to build the locomotives, the project needed a specialized steel foundry that would have had to be one of the five largest of its kind in the world. Secondly, the money promised by the National Economic Development Bank (BNDE) wasn't really national. It depended on foreign loans that had to be approved by the Brazilian government. This led Paulo Villares to butt heads with the powerful American politician and then president of the World Bank, Robert McNamara (the same man who, as defense secretary under President Lyndon B. Johnson, ordered Vietnam to be lit on fire). The story of the adventures of Villares versus the BNDE and the World Bank merits a book in itself, but it wouldn't have a happy ending. The government changed hands, and Geisel's second National Development Plan, created to stimulate the production of basic inputs, capital goods, food, and energy, ended up buried in a file cabinet deep inside the bureaucracy. Of the 300 locomotives per year that Villares prepared to manufacture, the government ended up ordering only 70 total. In thirty years of successful businesses, Paulo Villares suffered his first major defeat, giving up on the locomotive business and selling his factory in Araraquara.

The money pit that Geisel's failed project opened in Villares may have been a well-intentioned failure, but it didn't affect Lula's life. Villares's ABC factory continued its normal level of production, and workers' wages remained intact. Protected from the losses the government had caused Villares, Lula dedicated his energy to two projects: the old struggle for wage recuperation caused by Finance Minister Delfim Netto's fraud, and continuing to improve the relations between the union and its base. His approach was grounded not in grand theories but in wearing out the soles of their shoes at the factory doors. It was during one of the union directors' campaigns at the door of Brastemp, the Brazilian subsidiary of American appliance giant Whirlpool, that a young worker with Asian features who was speaking with a production-line coworker as he arrived for work one morning noticed a bearded man handing out leaflets. Although it was still before dawn, the machinist Paulo Okamoto recognized a person who he'd seen in newspaper photos and television interviews.

"Shit, isn't that Lula, the union president?" he said. His coworker confirmed, and Okamoto said, "Why is a famous guy like this here at the door of our factory handing out leaflets this early in the morning? Let me go over there and see what this guy has to say."

The surprise wasn't just on account of who was handing out the leaflets, but the content of what was being disseminated. Lula believed that this was a great improvement in union communications. Instead of incomprehensible graphs with statistics about company profit and labor costs, which readers would quickly skim then toss out, the union began publishing daily bulletins with two pages of comics. The authors of the stories were the union directors, supported by the experienced activist Antônio Carlos Félix Nunes. And the artists were Laerte, the creator of "João Ferrador," and the cartoonist from Minas Gerais, Henrique de Souza Filho, Henfil, who was nationally famous and had even had work published on the cartoon pages of the *New York Times*.

But it wasn't just the *calungas*, as Henfil called the comic strips that seduced young Okamoto at the door of the Brastemp factory. The son of a Brazilian woman and a second-generation Japanese immigrant who had been orphaned at fourteen, he managed to take vocational courses at SENAI to become a machinist toolmaker. Disciplined and focused, with plans to become an engineer, he studied for an industrial technical degree at night while working at the Volkswagen factory during the day. Despite being a minor who only received half of the minimum wage, he would wake up at four o'clock in the morning to arrive at the factory by six. When he turned eighteen and was legally allowed to work night shifts, Volkswagen asked him to work a rotating schedule—fifteen days and fifteen nights. The proposal would ruin his studies. It was the union that told him that, with his résumé, he didn't have to submit to the regime imposed by Volkswagen. On the contrary, he could get a better job. The new job, which paid better than Volkswagen, would be at Brastemp, at the gate of which he would first meet the bearded man handing out leaflets. That encounter would be the start of a lifelong friendship between the two men. Okamoto would go on to join Lula at the PT (where he became president of the São Paulo State party apparatus), at CUT, at the Lula Institute, and in the federal government. Discreet and uninterested about being in the spotlight or the news, the only job he accepted after Lula became president was a third-tier position as president of SEBRAE—a support service for micro and small businesses—and then only because his friend refused to take no for an answer.

In terms of material gains, 1977 was feeble and mediocre. Lula fought the battle for 34.1 percent recuperation until August but ended up losing. Politically, however, it was the foundation for the so-called Carbonari years of 1978 and 1979. The sector had decided to cut its ties with the middlemen—the government and the labor courts—and workers' unity was solidifying little by little, factory by factory. It happened in Volkswagen, Scania, and Ford, and in the factories with smaller staff numbers and greater power to pressure the bosses. Instead of dealing with the union bureaucracy inherited from the Vargas era, Lula began holding discreet meetings with the heavyweights in Brazil's economic sector like Cláudio Bardella, Paulo Francini, Einar Kok, and José Mindlin—the same Mindlin the torturers in DOI-CODI had forced Vladimir Herzog to denounce as a communist. In accordance with the language of the time, Lula was becoming a "pop" personality.

Bogged down on one side by the far-right faction in the military, Geisel trudged ahead with his project of "slow, gradual, and safe opening" as society began to organize into people's movements against the dictatorship, demanding direct elections at all levels of government and "broad, general, and unrestricted amnesty." The man who carefully rocked the cradle of democracy was Petrônio Portela, Senate president, from the state of Piauí and man of confidence to the generals who supported the opening, Geisel and his successor João Figueiredo. If Geisel had suffered obstacles in his vague project to democratize Brazil, Lula also had to gnaw on bones from the other side. When the talented and slippery Senator Petrônio Portela, nicknamed the "civilian star of the military dictatorship," invited oppositionists to informal meetings—without making any commitment to guarantee opening anything—he naturally included Lula. The union leader accepted, as long as he could bring a list of demands, but he faced obstacles among his own allies. He was surrounded by all kinds of internal political currents within the union, and each one supported a different position. Lula understood the political milieu that surrounded him.

"I had friends connected to the Catholic Church, and there were people connected to Ação Popular [a political group, originally connected to the Catholic Church, that would later divide, leading to the Marxist-Leninist APML], and some organizations that I knew nothing about," he said. "Alemãozinho, for example, was from one organization, Osmarzinho was from another, and Wagner Lino was from the Communist Party. There was always someone voicing opposition in every meeting and assembly."

Anxiously awaited by all of the press that covered the congressional beat, Lula's meeting with Senator Portela drew attention because, in contrast with the Senate president's navy-blue suit, Lula spent the whole meeting with a denim sport coat draped over his arm, contrasting with his black pants. After the closed-door meeting ended, journalist Hélio Doyle from *Veja* magazine—who, despite having been the director of the Ala Vermelha communist guerrilla organization that fought the dictatorship, was a trusted confidante of Portela—left to eat at the Maloca Querida restaurant with the union leaders who had accompanied Lula, among them Jacó Bittar, Olívio Dutra, João Paulo Vasconcellos, and Arnaldo Gonçalves. With the exception of Gonçalves, a PCB activist, everyone there would go on to help found the Workers' Party in 1980. Doyle's curiosity was not so much about what would happen in the Senate (he said he would find out later after talking to Portela), but with the tacky denim jacket Lula carried on his arm during the entire meeting, which he only put on once. However, contrary to apperances, this was not a case of a poorly dressed worker facing the starched shirts of the regime.

"When we were taking off for Brasília," he said, "they told me that it was impossible to enter Congress without a jacket and tie. Someone leant me a jacket, but when I arrived, I found out it didn't fit. It was too short and tight. I draped it over my arm to save embarrassment."

Due to the success of his meeting with the civilian boss of Geisel's coalition, Lula returned to Brasília several times over the following months. Every time he went, he made a frightening observation that went on to haunt him: Of the 430 members of Congress at the time (364 federal congressmen and 66 senators), there were only 2 from the working class—both from São Paulo. The only 2 Lula could identify were, first, Aurélio Peres, a toolmaker from the Caloi bicycle factory who had a degree in philosophy and was active in the Catholic Church's Basic Ecclesial Communities Workers' Pastoral Ministry. Arrested and tortured by DOI-CODI in 1974, he had gone on to lead the cost-of-living movement in São Paulo. The other was Benedito Marcílio, a metalworker from Santo André who had been elected, along with Peres, to represent the MDB.

Lula's surprise at almost-nonexistent representation of the working class in Congress would lead to a significant transformation in his political life. He was known for saying—in interviews and assemblies alike—that he didn't like politics and didn't "like people who like politics." And he held the same opinion for everyone who wasn't from the working class.

The line that circulated in the ABC and the political movements that was attributed to Lula was short and abrupt: "The place for students is in the schools. For priests, it's in the churches. If someone wants to create a party for workers, he has to wear overalls."

A veritable frenzy took hold in the left when the news hit the campuses of the University of São Paulo, the Pontifical Catholic University, and the federal universities that Lula was flirting with the idea of engaging with conventional politics. It was the students who bothered him the most.

"This guy showed up at the union wanting to help out," Lula recalled, laughing, "and before I asked about his profession, I looked at the palms of his hands. There was no mistake about it: smooth palms with no calluses—he had to be a Trotskyist!"

Lula's insistence in referring to Trotskyists as "infiltrators" in the group that would go on to found the PT had less to do with the real political importance of the group than it did its indisputable capacity to make noise. The effervescent Brazilian student movement was full of followers of Lev Davidovich Bronstein—also known as Trotsky—the founder of the USSR's Red Army who Stalin had pursued across the planet, and who had died in exile in Mexico in 1940 following a blow to the head by an ice axe, wielded by the Spanish communist Ramón Mercader del Río under orders from his Soviet boss. Of the dozens of Trotskyist groups that existed in Brazilian politics, at least three had some level of representation among students and intellectuals: the Lambertists (followers of the current created by the French leader Pierre Lambert), the Posadists (who followed Argentine Juan Posadas), and the mandelistas (who followed the teachings of the Belgian Ernest Mandel). There were others—many others—but those three were the most popular. Years later, President Fernando Henrique Cardoso revealed that he had once been labeled as a Trotskyist for being photographed "performing the courtesy of carrying Ernest Mandel's wife's suitcase" in the Mexico City airport.

Decades later, Lula still laughed remembering the time when he had near-unanimous support from the mainstream media. "The newspapers and TV stations loved it when I used to say, 'I don't like politics, and I don't like people who practice politics.' The press adored it. Finally, a pure worker! Finally, someone who doesn't want to take power! Finally, someone who isn't connected to the Communist Party! It was veritable idol worship."

The newspapers didn't know that he couldn't stop thinking about his visit to Petrônio Portela and the shock he felt seeing so few people from the working class in Congress. The idea of creating a party just for workers, without bosses or political professionals, remained on his mind. The final years of the 1970s in Brazil were so effervescent that Lula had no time to dedicate himself to anything else. Along with thinking about setting up a party, he led strike after strike. In an interview with Altino Dantas, he said there wasn't a single week that went by during that period without a strike.

"We would hold two or three strikes per week," he said. "There would be strikes for any reason. Everything went crazy. The directorate would stick its head into anything that looked good. Bosses would yell, workers would stop. In 1978, the union decided to join this fight. The core of the issue started right there: no union director is producing results anymore, so let's go into the factories and do unionism. Mercedes-Benz tried to fire two directors because of this. We put out a bulletin telling the workers that the company wanted to fire two of our coworkers because they were representing their sector. If they fire them today, tomorrow everyone will stop working. Mercedes backed down."

For years—most of all after the threats of Institutional Act 5, which still hung over everyone's heads—talking about a strike was a mortal sin. Lula remembered that in 1974, when he was still the union's first secretary, a group of Ford workers approached him suggesting shutting down the toolmaking department. Insecure, he called on a more experienced member of the directorate to take part in the decision.

His colleague's comments were terrifying. "We aren't allowed to go on strike. Whoever does it is arrested and tortured. They'll tie you to a chair, leaving your anus open, and stick a broken bottle up it to burn your intestines. Then they'll stick a live rat in there."

Faced with that level of terrorism, only a lunatic would risk crossing his arms inside a factory. The most optimistic said that the government's punishment for striking was prison. Lula said, "After 1978, we changed our tone."

"Look, there isn't a jail big enough to fit everyone," he said. "If one person tries to strike by himself, he'll be torn up. But if everyone goes on strike, they have no way to screw us."

It sounded like a campaign speech, but the new unionism had stifled the fear that had suffocated the workers in the ABC region for so many years. The greatest proof of this, beyond mere rhetoric, took place in April and May of 1978 when two workers—yes, only two, Gilson Correia de Menezes and Severino Alves da Silva—decided to take on the hundred-year-old Swedish industry Saab-Scania, world leader in manufacturing heavy trucks, buses, industrial motors, and ship engines. Officially, inflation that year was 39.9 percent, but the raise given by the company was exactly that, not 1 percent more. Members of the directorate of a union that had never held a strike—and that had taken power only eighteen days earlier—Gilson and Severino spent their days inside the factory stopping machine after machine and repeating the same refrain to their coworkers.

"We are asking for a 3 percent real raise, above the official 39.9 percent. If they won't give us the 3 percent, we are going to stop. You understand, right, damn it? It's 3 percent or we are shutting this factory down!"

The appeals made by the two young leaders ended up reaching the ears not only of the workers but of the director of Scania Brazil, Inge Lunnerdal, who summoned both for a private conversation in which, after a lot of negotiation, he gave into their demand as long as it wasn't presented to the ABC like a defeat for the company.

On the next payday, May 10, paychecks arrived without the promised extra 3 percent. The news traveling through the factory was that Lunnerdal had been chewed out by the Regional Labor Court delegate. If the company gave this tiny raise above the official 39.9 percent, Scania would incur heavy fines and punishment from the government. The next day, Gilson and Severino went to the union to explain what had happened to Lula.

"Comrades, we are going to shut down Scania tomorrow."

The proposal seemed so delirious to Lula at first that he didn't take it seriously.

"We made a deal that they would pay everyone 3 percent over inflation," they said. "The checks came out today, and they only increased by 39.9 percent. We are tired of telling them that either they pay us the 3 percent or we shut it down. So we are going to stop working tomorrow."

They stopped. To the surprise of Lula and regional labor delegate Vinicius Ferraz Torres, Gilson and Severino, practically single-handedly, stopped 3,000 workers at Scania. The labor delegate made a veiled threat. "You'd better go back to work. The country needs high productivity."

The reaction of one of the workers made the delegate's head spin: "We are not going back to work. And anyone who tries to cause problems is going to get hurt."

Despite being labeled by the press as "new unionism," the movement was emerging on the factory floors, not inside the union hall. From nine to eleven in the morning, one or two directors stayed at the union in case of any emergency, along with the bureaucrats who managed the benefit system. The real activity was taking place at the doors of the factories or inside the company offices. Lunch break, which lasted sixty to ninety minutes depending on the factory, was used for mini-assemblies. If a larger group of workers assembled, the directors would stand on tables and make speeches. The tactic proliferated, gaining force until the bosses were no longer able to control the uprising. If any boss barred a union director from speaking in his section, he would end up in a fight.

"It was getting uncontrollable," Lula remembered. "If things continued that way, we would have taken control of the factories within a year. We were gaining power; everyone was gaining freedom of action inside the factories."

This wasn't just happening in the small, local factories but also in the giants, like Mercedes and Scania. A production line would suddenly be paralyzed, and a union director would stand up on a bench and speak in the middle of the section. Work in the section would come to a halt for ten or fifteen minutes, and people would listen to the union leader and receive a cartoon bulletin drawn by Henfil or Laerte, after which the machines would come back on. These weren't strikes or slowdowns but spaces for complaints about salaries, work conditions, and rights that the companies refused to grant. The slogan of the day was, "The director belongs in the factory, not the union hall."

Following the celebrated strikes in 1968 in Contagem, Minas Gerais, and in Osasco, São Paulo—led by twenty-year-old metalworker José Ibrahim, who was connected to the armed revolutionary group the People's Revolutionary Vanguard (VPR)—in which 400 workers were arrested, the commotion at the factory gates had practically disappeared.

Lula remembers leading his first picket line in 1978 at Resil, an auto-parts factory in Diadema that only employed women and had approximately 500 workers. Believing they didn't have the experience or courage to confront their bosses—many were young women barely over the age of sixteen—the owners of Resil repressed salaries and ignored labor laws without any fear of reaction. When the union called the strike, they encouraged participation by saying it was serving snack boxes in the meeting room (the absence of a snack bar or cafeteria inside the factory was one of the workers' complaints).

Taking advantage of the employment crisis that had swept through the ABC, the factory owners landed what they imagined would be a knockout blow: they advertised across the region that the factory was hiring women to take the place of the strikers, with salaries even lower than what it had been paying. Upon learning of Resil's chicanery, Lula called an assembly proposing that the union block off the entrances to keep the scabs from getting in to restart the production line. To avoid using the word "picket," which was associated with conflict, he suggested that the strikers form a human chain in support of dignified working conditions and fair wages. On the eve of the action, a group encircled the factory and identified all of the points where people could enter and leave. By five o'clock in the morning, each entrance point to the factory was blocked off by hundreds of workers—not in an threatening manner, nor even standing, but sitting on the ground with arms locked.

At six thirty, black-and-white DOPS vehicles began to show up. Armed policeman approached saying, "Get up and open a path. If you don't, we're calling in the riot police."

To the general shock of everyone, mainly the police, the strikers weren't intimidated. Without standing up, one young woman said, "You can call the riot police or anyone you want, but we aren't leaving."

Some of them tried to charm the police officers, saying things like, "Heck, you seem like such a nice guy. Do you really have the nerve to hurt us?"

Among the most energetic strikers, Lula identified an activist from the Socialist Convergence (SC), one of the many Trotskyist groups that operated in the ABC. "Get out of here, because you are only going to cause problems," he said. "If the police arrest you, they are going to say that SC organized the strike."

At seven o'clock, an unmarked car tried to push through the chain. The women didn't budge, and the passenger said, "I am the owner of this factory. I have to go inside."

One of the workers said, "Not even the owner is going to get in today. Either you give us what we want, or even the owner doesn't get in."

After a lot of confusion, shouting, and kicking at the car, the man realized it would be better to negotiate. He invited Lula and Djalma Bom into the factory, where they stayed for hours and only left when they had a proposal for negotiations that, as a starting point, required the factory to pay all the workers' back wages, which were already weeks late.

It wasn't just the expansion of strikes and work stoppages that left a bitter taste in the mouth of the dictatorship in 1978. Starting in 1975, amnesty committees had multiplied around the country. Founded by the social worker Teresinha Zerbini—the wife of General Euryale de Jesus Zerbini, who was fired after the 1964 coup—the movement gained force during the municipal elections of 1976. The Brazilian Committee for Amnesty (CBA), led by the young political prisoner defense attorney Luiz Eduardo Greenhalgh, had headquarters in dozens of state capitals across the country and large cities abroad where exiled Brazilians lived, and it was active in unions and the student movement. The CBA's activities reached an apex in 1978 when, to the dismay of the dictatorship—especially President Geisel—US first lady Rosalynn Carter got involved, becoming its unofficial godmother. The few government officials who acknowledged the issue were objective. In the unlikely event that some form of amnesty would be approved, they said, they would only allow the return of the "subversives" who lived in exile or who were in jail. Prosecution of government agents, torturers, and those accused of violence against political prisoners was out of the question.

There was still a painful thorn in the side of the military. The 1978 elections were coming. The governors would be chosen indirectly, by state assemblies (the majority of which were dominated by people connected to the regime), and of every three senators, one would not be elected but nominated by the president of the Republic. They were called "bionic senators"—a trick that was part of the "April Package" of 1977, composed of amendments that General Geisel inserted into the 1967 Constitution to try to prevent the electoral trainwrecks that had humiliated the dictatorship in 1974 and 1976.

The final results—at the time there was no electronic voting, and votes were registered by pen and counted, one by one, by hand—may not have shown conclusively that the dictatorship had come to an end, but they certainly gave signs that it was in its death throes. The most visible example that the regime was falling apart was in São Paulo. In the most important and populous state in the nation, the military regime, despite the deck being stacked in its favor, managed to lose the indirect race for governor, which was decided by members of state legislature, where the military's own official political party, ARENA, held a clear majority over the run-down, constrained opposition party, the MDB. Although the dictatorship's candidate was the banker Laudo Natel, ex-governor and ex–vice governor of the state, the winner was the millionaire Paulo Maluf, ex-president of the Caixa Econômica federal mortgage bank and ex-mayor of São Paulo—unelected positions to which he had been appointed at the time.

The favorite for the only Senate seat available was the austere André Franco Montoro, who had started his political career in 1950 as a São Paulo city councilor (in the same legislature with former president Jânio Quadros). Historically a Christian Democrat, he was elected a state congressman in 1954 and thrice as a federal congressman (in 1958, 1962, and 1966). During the brief period of parliamentarism in Brazil, he was minister of labor and retirement pensions in the cabinet of Prime Minister Tancredo Neves (from September 8, 1961, to July 12, 1962). He affiliated with the MDB immediately after the 1964 coup, and his main rival in the 1978 elections was the respected lawyer, dean of Mackenzie University and professor Cláudio Lembo. Lembo's trajectory and political integrity made him look like a fish out of water as representative of São Paulo's ARENA party apparatus, which defended the military dictatorship.

But it was the third senatorial candidate who created the biggest buzz. The military government had created a legal maneuver, dubbed a "subticket," that allowed up to three candidates from the same party to run for a single seat in the Senate. The winner would get the seat, and the second-place candidate would automatically become the winner's substitute. It was an awkward policy that created the odd title of "subsenator," or "vice senator." The MDB set up a subticket to cater to the left and nominated the prestigious social scientist Fernando Henrique Cardoso, a professor at the Sorbonne who had been fired from the University of São Paulo by the dictatorship, to run along with its primary candidate, Montoro. Although he was as much of a newcomer to electoral contests as Lembo, the respected and charming academic had joined other intellectuals who had been persecuted by the military regime in founding the Brazilian Center of Analysis and Planning (CEBRAP), a think tank that united well-known progressive academics from different political currents, many of them veterans of a young collective reading group of Marx's *Capital* from the late 1950s. Target of organizations on the far right, in 1976 CEBRAP's headquarters was bombed by the Brazilian Anti-Communist Alliance (AAB). Cardoso preferred to avoid new problems by keeping a prudent distance from guerrilla organizations. FHC, as he was later nicknamed, illustrated this in an interview in *Folha* in which he told the story of a young communist from Minas Gerais, Vinícius Caldeira Brant, who had been released from prison and was looking for a job.

"I said, 'Look, I'll arrange something for you,' " Cardoso said. " 'I only have one question: Are you connected to any armed organization?' Because if he did, there was no way I could hire him in CEBRAP."

FHC's candidacy for the MDB caused arguments that went to the heart of the party. For one, he appeared to have a total lack of political savvy, as he himself recognizes in his autobiography:

> In the beginning, my campaign was a comedy of errors. My first speeches literally put the audiences to sleep, because I looked like a sociology professor teaching a class. Since I lived in Europe, I was seen as an intellectual snob who was disconnected from Brazilian reality. The fact that I cited French and English authors in my speeches didn't help. In one particularly disastrous stage of my campaign, when asked what I thought about the landless workers' movements in Brazil, I answered with a lecture about the land distribution in England in the sixteenth century.[1]

There was also bad blood with Montoro. With plans to become a candidate for governor and—why not?—president of the Republic when the dictatorship ended, he wanted to be the party's only candidate, in an election that promised the highest voter turnout in state history. But the left caucus within the MDB held its ground, and Montoro ended up as the primary candidate, with FHC on the subticket. The great success of Cardoso's campaign was a parody, made by singer-songwriter Chico Buarque, of the carnival song "Acorda, Maria Bonita," written by legendary outlaw Volta Seca, which had become a hit in 1967 when it was recorded by Ari Cordovil. Cardoso's campaign events and marches would open and end with the popular and provocative verse, which translate:

> The people don't want any more bosses
> The people don't want more directors
> The people have taken the floor
> Fernando Henrique for senator

Suddenly, it looked like Fernando Henrique had a chance of winning the election. He was polling in second place, ahead of Cláudio Lembo from ARENA. Montoro's supporters took their revenge with good humor and composed another parody of the same song:

1 Fernando Henrique Cardoso, *Um intelectual na politica: Memórias*, São Paulo: Cia das Letras, 2019.

The people don't want any more lockers
The people don't want any more deans
The people are already on the floor
Fernando Henrique is just a professor

FHC's campaign was a novelty, not just because of Chico Buarque's jingle or his colorful and noisy group of celebrity supporters, like Bruna Lombardi, Eva Wilma, Carlos Zara, and Gianfrancesco Guarnieri, who muddied their shoes when they joined the candidate on stage at rallies and in marches. The big surprise was when FHC showed up handing out leaflets at factory doors in the ABC, guided by the same bearded man who, months earlier, publicly ridiculed politicians and politics—the man who was famous for saying, "I don't like politics, I don't like politicians, and I don't like people who like politics." Indeed, it was Lula, the man with the sonorous voice who had previously ridiculed political candidates, who was working the vote among the crowds of workers he drew to the factory doors and picket lines in the ABC.

The story of of this historic 1978 alliance has many versions, nearly all of them contradictory. Voting had already started when news broke that that Lula and Cardoso had been introduced by a renowned sociologist and former director of the Northeast Development Bank (SUDENE) during the João Goulart administration, Francisco "Chico" Oliveira, who worked with FHC at CEBRAP.

As the results came in, aside from the appointed, bionic senator (the unknown lawyer Antônio Osvaldo do Amaral Furlan), the results revealed that the military had, as Northeasterners used to say, been "whipped with an armadillo tail." Montoro was elected with 64 percent of the vote against 18 percent by FHC and 17 percent by Lembo. With strong ties to São Paulo's civilian right, Paulo Maluf crushed military candidate Laudo Natel in the indirect governor's race. The results were similar in the congressional race. Of São Paulo's fifty-five seats in federal Congress, ARENA was only able to win eighteen, against MDB's thirty-seven. The distribution of seats in the state legislature was even more humiliating for the regime, which elected twenty-six lawmakers, less than half of the fifty-three elected by the MDB.

14

While Lula faces the police and the bosses in the ABC, Brizola tries to rebuild the Brazilian Labor Party and is blocked by General Golbery

According to the Gregorian calendar, 1979 officially began on January 1, the date planned for a transition of power in Brazil. It wouldn't be for another ten weeks, however, until General Ernesto Geisel would finally vacate the presidency of the Republic and move with his wife and daughter to the hilltop town of Teresópolis, in the state of Rio de Janeiro. His family was happy to leave. Brazil's official presidential palace, the Alvorada, was beautiful and elegant and had won architectural awards, but, like many presidents, Geisel complained about it. He said that the smell of grease from the kitchen would spread through the whole house. (Thirty-seven years later, during his interim presidency, Michel Temer would only spend a week with his family in the palace. "I couldn't sleep in the Alvorada, from the first night I got there," said the successor to Dilma Rousseff. "The energy wasn't good.")

On the night of March 15, Alvorada's newest resident, João Batista de Oliveira Figueiredo and his wife, Dona Dulce, decided to move into the Granja do Torto, a secondary official residence often reserved for a top cabinet minister. As governor, Paulo Maluf nominated his sad former rival, Laudo Natel, to the board of Bradesco Bank in Osasco. In Congress, the MDB had fallen short of a majority by only 5 percent but had managed to cram the House with members of its left caucus, the so-called "Autênticos"—as the press referred to lawmakers who didn't accept the role of controlled opposition consented to by the military.

On a rainy Saturday, March 10, 900 kilometers from Brasília, metalworkers in the ABC were oblivious to the political changes that were causing the hotel lobbies in the capital to buzz with excitement. There in São Bernardo, led by Lula, a crowd of workers raised their hands in the union hall courtyard to approve, in a first vote, the decision to shut down the industrial zone responsible for 10 percent of Brazil's GDP. The 21 percent difference between what the union demanded and what the bosses offered seemed insignificant compared to the size of the uprising. The proposal of the bosses was a 57 percent raise. The union workers demanded 78 percent. From a distance, it might seem like a lot of fuss over a relatively small amount of money, but to have some notion of what these numbers meant, it's important to remember that the data later released by the Institute for Applied Economic Research (IPEA) shows that Brazil's GINI coefficient had risen to 0.593, making it one of the most economically unequal countries in the world.[1] Since the metalworkers prepared for what Lula called a "climate of war," the best thing was to enable the greatest number of members possible to vote on the decision. That Tuesday, he announced that a full assembly would take place on the following Sunday.

The number of people who pledged to show up at the assembly was so great that the union had to ask São Bernardo mayor Tito Costa, the taciturn lawyer from the progressive wing of MDB, for use of Marechal Costa e Silva stadium, popularly known as "Vila Euclides," which had a capacity of 60,000 on its field and in its stands. In March 1979, the request to use a stadium that held 60,000 people would have seemed like insanity—or an expression of the union leaders' unshakeable confidence.

As he arrived at Vila Euclides Stadium, with messy hair and red eyes from insomnia, Lula remembered a premonition he had had on Saturday, November 19, 1978. He had been with his friends Janjão and Alemão at a soccer game between his beloved Corinthians and Guarani at Morumbi Stadium. It had been a lucky day: Corinthians had beaten Guarani three to two, and the opening goal had been scored by its biggest star, the tall and thin Sócrates Brasileiro Sampaio de Souza Vieira de Olivera. (One of the last great players who still smoked cigarettes, he had finished his doctorate in medicine before becoming a full-time professional soccer

1 The IPEA, a federal public foundation linked to the Ministry of Planning and Budget, provides technical support for the government's policies.

player. The "Doctor" was also a fierce enemy of the military dictatorship.) Looking out over the sea of soccer fans in the stands—Morumbi held more than 60,000—Lula had told his union friends, "Fucking hell! The day that we manage to hold an assembly with half the number of people here, we're going to turn Brazil upside down."

And this is exactly what the lathe mechanic saw when he walked into Vila Euclides Stadium that morning: the crowd of union workers covered the grass and the stands. People had climbed up trees and posts and were sitting on walls. The crowd spilled out into the neighboring streets, which were teaming with metalworkers. Was it 30,000, 40,000 people? Everyone made up their own estimate. Lula and his comrades from the union hadn't expected that large of a crowd. There was no stage, shade, or security, or even a modest mic and sound system. They had to improvise. A stage was easy to set up—the union dragged four plastic tables into the middle of the field, the kind that are common to see in all the bars in Brazil. But for Lula to be heard without a sound system, their improvisation was more primitive: each sentence he yelled was repeated by the nearest group of people, who passed it on to the next group, one after another, in circles, until his words had echoed by second, third, and fourth repetition to the edges of the stadium: "Companheiras e companheiros . . . Companheiras e companheiros . . . We're here to decide if we are going to face the bosses . . . Once again, they want to take a bite out of our wages, but this time we're not going to take this shit! The bosses can't handle fifteen days of strikes!"

His words were repeated through the crowd until thousands of men and women lifted their hands, illustrating the diverse ethnic and racial makeup of the crowd, to approve that at midnight that Tuesday, two days before the presidential inauguration in Brasília, the ABC would be shut down.

But would it really happen? Lula watched the clock in the union hall until eleven thirty that night. Some of them trembled as the countdown to midnight began. "We looked like children waiting for Santa Claus on Christmas Eve," Lula later said. But it also looked like the countdown to a rocket launch.

At the stroke of midnight, the first messenger arrived. "Schuler shut down!" Then came another: "Perkins shut down!" Then the big news arrived: "Volkswagen shut down!"

Even the Volkswagen factory, which had never been even partially shut down in its history, was forced to turn off its machines.

"Mercedes-Benz shut down! Ford shut down! Metagal shut down! Brastemp shut down!"

Lula remembers that after shutting off the machines, each shift went straight to the union hall.

"Crowds were arriving the whole night. We held assemblies from midnight until noon the next day. The workers arrived, filled the hall, and held assemblies. We would free up one group and the next would arrive. The union was packed."

Then the strike began to spread. Workers shut off the machines and walked off their shifts in industrial cities across the state. They were also now being supported by artists and intellectuals, and the discrete but powerful Catholic Basic Ecclesial Communities. Little by little, the masses of metalworkers in São Bernardo contaminated the other industrial centers, like the Paraíba Valley and the corridor from Campinas to Alta Araraquarense. Suddenly, hundreds of thousands of workers across the state had walked out and refused to go back to work.

There were several motives for the decision to strike that year. Both the outgoing government and the one replacing it were speaking about a political "opening up" with an end to political repression. The success of a series of small surprise strikes that spread through the ABC in 1978 encouraged the union to keep moving forward. The second petroleum crisis, triggered by the political uprising in Iran that deposed Shah Reza Pahlevi, brought stagnation to the international economy. Between 1978 and 1979, Brazil's annual inflation rate jumped from 40.8 percent to 77.2 percent. The foreign debt rose from US$32 billion to US$43.5 billion in 1978, hitting US$50 billion by the end of 1979. Reeling from a succession of electoral losses by ARENA, one might imagine the dictatorship would think twice before repressing the unions, which had mobilized thousands and thousands of workers. But that turned out not to be the case.

A small group of politicians, intellectuals, and religious leaders maintained a rotating presence at the unions in São Bernardo and neighboring cities to try to ensure political and personal security for the leaders. They thought that their presence would limit the use of excessive force—or at least that they would witness any such violence against Lula and his comrades. In addition to the suits and ties, which not all of them wore, they believed their official, black cars with the insignia of São Paulo's state legislature would serve as a sign of authority. On Thursday the twenty-second, the night shift included Substitute Senator Fernando Henrique Cardoso and Congressman Antônio Rezk, who was connected to the PCB, Geraldo "Geraldinho" Siqueira from the MDB, and the author of this book.

The group had dinner on "chicken road," a strip of restaurants on Maria Servidei Demarchi Avenue that all specialized in the same meal, chicken with strips of deep-fried polenta—a dish that drew hundreds of tourists to the ABC. The subject of conversation, naturally, was politics. Each one offered his opinion, the majority expressing worry about what would happen in the coming days. The one person at the table who didn't share in the pessimism was FHC—elegant, as always, in a tweed sports coat with suede-patched elbows. Despite his brief experience in Brazil's political life, the alliance in the elections of 1978 had brought him close to many of the metalworkers, especially Lula, for whom he'd publicly declared his respect.

In his memoir, *The Accidental President of Brazil*, FHC tells a story in which he confuses two different moments, some of which took place at that dinner in 1979 and others in 1980. In addition to not mentioning two of the people who were there that night (Siqueira and Rezk), the ex-president leaves out his own opinion. According to the other people who were there, including Lula, FHC calmed everyone down with an analysis of the political conjuncture that held that Figueiredo, in his honeymoon as president and the political "opening up," would not risk confrontation with the ABC metalworkers. We could all relax, he said, finish our dinners, and go home—which he was the first to do. The story sounds a lot different in the following passage from his book (Fernando Henrique Cardoso with Brian Winter, New York: PublicAffairs, 2006):

> On the radio, we heard that the military had used its powers to intervene in the union and expel Lula from its ranks. Shortly thereafter, he was thrown in jail.
>
> The military probably did not plan on locking Lula up for very long. The authorities merely hoped to scare him and then let him go. But tragedy does not respect such clumsy intentions; while Lula was still languishing in jail, his mother passed away. He was permitted to go to the funeral, although a police escort accompanied him. I also attended, along with several of our friends and colleagues. Lula was

> kept isolated from the rest of us, surrounded by a phalanx of policemen, and he looked utterly numb and defeated. It was as if this was one tragedy too much. He couldn't cry anymore.

After dinner, Fernando Henrique returned to São Paulo. Lula went back to the union hall, accompanied only by the two lawmakers who had eaten chicken and polenta with him. They played a few games of gin rummy and drank a bottle of cachaça infused with *cambuci* (a sweet, acidic fruit). In the middle of the night, contrary to FHC's political evaluation, the military riot police opened a path with their billy clubs, so that they could hand control over the union executive board to federal intervenors nominated by Labor Minister Murilo Macedo—Guaraci Horta (in São Bernardo), Afredo Garcez (in Santo André), and Antônio Donato (in São Caetano do Sul), all employees of his ministry. Facing heavy, physical resistance from the union members, the intervenors were only able to be formally sworn in, after a lot of beatings, at eleven o'clock the next morning. Lula, contra what FHC wrote, wasn't arrested that night, and his mom, Dona Lindu, would only pass away in May 1980.

Now a talented negotiator, at the same time that he managed the strike, Lula tried to negotiate with the bosses without backing off on the demands—and without the Regional Labor Police sticking its nose into the talks. While the assemblies continued, he sought to work out a solution with the bosses that would bypass the intermediation of the Labor Court.

In an interview with former political prisoner Altino Dantas, Lula said, "The first proposal that we refused, of 60 percent, was made at Murilo Macedo's vacation home in Atibaia. We brought down the hammer but said that maybe an assembly would approve of it."

The prospect of making a deal excited Murilo Macedo, who called Teobaldo de Nigris, president of the São Paulo State Industry Federation (FIESP), Alberto Villares, who was one of Lula's bosses, and some of the other members of FIESP's Group of 14, among them the moderate Paulo Francini. According to the interview he gave to Dantas, Lula knew that no deal deal of any kind would be reached without the approval of the workers.

"I thought the only way to get out of this situation was to say I had an assembly to go to and leave," he said. "I left our attorney there to sign the deal. The bosses celebrated, opened bottles of champagne, and sang victory songs. Murilo Macedo called Simonsen and Figueiredo to celebrate. On arriving in Brasília, Murilo heard on the radio, 'The assembly in São Bernardo do Campo has just decided that it will not accept the deal.' "

Despite the decree of intervention and the removal of the directors, the strike continued. Lula joked that he was the only fired union leader who continued working normally. At his request, Bishop Cláudio Hummes authorized the use of the parish house at the diocese headquarters in São Bernardo de Campo, and the workers started meeting there. It was from there that Lula called a new assembly in Vila Euclides, which drew a crowd of 60,000 to 70,000 metalworkers. It had only been a few days since the union had gone under government intervention, and there was nothing to negotiate, since neither side would budge. Even Alemãozinho and Djalma, stars of the movement, were silenced by the boos of the crowd. The respected union attorney Maurício Soares wasn't able to utter a single word. It was then that Lula had the gall to suggest something that would at least help put off the final decision: he proposed to the assembly that they give him a vote of confidence for a forty-five-day truce, during which, without interrupting the uprising, they would return to work.

"May nobody dare to doubt the capacity of the workers' fight ever again."

The truce was accepted, and, during it, the deposed union directors continued mobilizing workers in the diocese headquarters, in the neighborhoods, and at the doors of the factories. On May 1, a crowd appeared at a May Day celebration in Vila Euclides Stadium. Even the Military Police, who normally undercount these kinds of events, estimated that there were around 150,000 people in and surrounding the outside of the stadium. On Tuesday, May 7, 5,000 people packed Vera Cruz Pavilion for a show directed by Mário Masetti, from the artists' union, with a group of the most popular MPB (música popular brasileira), *forró*, and samba musicians of the era: Elis Regina, João Bosco, Belchior, Gonzaguinha, Jards Macalé, Beth Carvalho, Dominguinhos, and Fagner. The take of Cr$500,000 (around R$55,000 in 2021) was donated to the strike fund. The icing on the cake was union director Djalma Bom, who, introduced by Lula, sang an acapella version of the popular romantic song "Rosa" by Pixinguinha.

You are divine and gracious
Majestic statue of love
Sculpted by God
And formed with passion

The strike ended on May 12, the twentieth anniversary of the founding of the union. The next day, 60,000 workers in Vila Euclides, 3,000 in Santo André, and a more modest 500 in São Caetano voted on the peace deal signed between the deposed directors from the three unions and FIESP's Group of 14. The deal approved by the metalworkers guaranteed a 63 percent raise for workers who earned between one and three times the minimum wage. For those who hadn't received a raise in 1978, the indices were 63 percent for workers making between one and three times the minimum wage, and 57 percent for those who earned between three and six times the minimum wage. On May 18, the intervention was suspended and the elected directors were reinstated. Lula's enemies spread rumors through the factories that he had sold out the category for a 3 percent difference over the offer from the bosses. Yes, 63 percent was nearly nothing compared to the 78 percent the more active agitators had dreamed about, but the move consolidated the independence of the movement. It wasn't a spectacular victory, but nobody came out of the strike with their tail between their legs.

Without winning or losing, the political uprising continued. It wasn't just the union workers of the ABC who kept meeting and conspiring, but workers in many regions across Brazil. Wage issues, the "new unionism" (or "authentic unionism") and workers' freedom of organization and expression were the main topics of discussion in the meetings. But, parallel to this, they talked about three other issues that had swept across Brazil and the union movement in the preceding months: the decree of amnesty for people who were punished by the dictatorship, the proposal to create a union federation, and another issue that was taking hold: the formation of new political parties, which would be inevitable when the dictatorship ended, along with the creation of a workers' party.

Although the strict military laws only allowed two political parties—the official opposition party, the Brazilian Democratic Movement (MDB), and the official government party, National Renewal Alliance (ARENA)—in the real world, things were a little different. The MDB had slowly transformed into a big-tent party that sheltered several

Communist organizations, including the Brazilian Communist Party (PCB), created in 1922 and directed by Luís Carlos Prestes, which faithfully followed Soviet political line; and the Communist Party of Brazil (PC do B), which split from the PCB in 1958 after the Khrushchev Report, and went through a Maoist phase until, during the 1970s, it aligned with Albania and its leader, Enver Hoxha. Also among the Marxist currents within the MDB was the October 8 Revolutionary Movement (MR-8, named for the day of Che Guevara's assassination), an armed organization that broke from the PCB in 1964 and was originally known as the Communist Dissidence of Rio de Janeiro (DI-RJ) and the Communist Dissidence of Guanabara (DI-GB).

Aside from a few exceptions, the Communists didn't exercise any decision-making power within the MDB, a political milieu that brought together liberal professionals, businessmen, industrialists, academics of the most varied sort, and opportunist professional politicians. The party included people working side by side with former political enemies who wouldn't even have spoken to each other before the dictatorship. The traditional good nature of people in Rio de Janeiro ensured that the MDB managed to join "the cetaceans of the National Democratic Union" on the same ticket with the "pachyderms of the PSD," parties that fought against each other tooth and nail during the Getúlio Vargas administration.

The vision of the party that Lula and his comrades dreamed of creating, however, had no place in any of the internal factions or caucuses inside the big tent of the MDB. The union activists toyed around with several different names for the new party. Lula may not remember one of them—the Party of the Working Class—but he will certainly never forget the date: July 15, 1978, the day on which he was interrupted during a congress in which he was participating by a phone call from São Bernardo do Campo telling him that Sandro Luís, his second son with Marisa, had just been born.

Ten years later, Lula told the story of that congress in a long interview conducted with Friar Betto.

"It was at that petroleum workers' congress in the Hotel Bahia in Salvador that the idea first arose to form a front to battle the military dictatorship."

Among the illustrious people who participated in that encounter were two stars of national politics, and both seemed committed to the ideas that Lula was talking about. One was Almino Afonso, a former minister to President João Goulart, who was deposed in the 1964 coup. The other was Substitute Senator Fernando Henrique Cardoso. Apparently, however, the party that they had in mind was not the same as the one Lula was thinking about.

"I gave an interview saying that their front was too broad for our liking," said Lula. "I said that what we needed to do was not to found a broad front but a party of the working class. The first idea for this started at that Congress, on July 15, 1978."

It was also on this day that Lula realized that the idea of a new party—which, naturally, would only come into existence after the laws changed to allow their founding—whetted the appetite of some groups that were already politically organized.

"We had plans to print a little newspaper to talk about the project of a party just for workers," he said. "But the people from the Convergence showed up and tried to steamroll over us and produce the paper themselves."

But it wasn't just the Trotskyists from the Socialist Convergence that began to gravitate around the movement that rose out of the strikes in the ABC. Although President Figueiredo would sign the Amnesty Law on June 27, 1979—without punishing any torturers or other criminals who had been at the service of the dictatorship—many exiles had already started discreetly returning to the country. Others returned without making any secrets about it. Almino Afonso, for example, landed at Congonhas Airport in August 1976, three years before amnesty came into effect. Despite his name being high on the list of people fired after the 1964 coup—in other words, he was a big fish—Almino was welcomed by lawyers, friends, and allies, spent a few hours detained in a room in the airport, was personally interrogated by DOPS director Romeu Tuma, and then was immediately released. But there were other adversaries of the regime whose clandestine return could have been considered a veritable act of insolence.

Among these was a sworn enemy of the military, the journalist Franklin Martins, one of the kidnappers of US Ambassador to Brazil Charles Burke Elbrick, in September 1969. Franklin entered Brazil undercover in 1976 to participate in a conference of the MR-8, of which he was one of the leaders, and spent three months in Brazil without being discovered by the police—even though he stood out due to the undisguisable physical feature of being over two meters tall. After the Congress, he traveled to Europe and, unsatisfied, returned to Brazil in March 1977, remaining underground until amnesty was announced two years later.

Another illustrious persecuted person to return to Brazil before the amnesty decree was the anthropologist Darcy Ribeiro, recognized universally as one of the nation's most respected intellectuals. While working at the University of San Marcos, in Peru—the oldest university in the Americas—in December 1974 he was diagnosed with incurable lung cancer. His influential Brazilian friends appealed to Ernesto Geisel for Darcy to fulfill his last wish: to die in Brazil. However, his tumor was removed by surgery in Rio de Janeiro, and, six months later he was cured. Known for his caustic humor, he later said, laughing, "Since I refused to die, the dictatorship sent me back to Lima."

In 1976, Darcy returned definitively to Brazil, establishing himself in Rio de Janeiro. He died in Brasília in 1997.

The truth is that amnesty put an end to the diasporic spread of thousands of Brazilians across the planet—estimates of which, though vague, hover around 10,000 people, adults, and children. For many, the prospect of return gave birth to the dream of rebuilding their lives, which had been previously been foreclosed upon by the arbitrary actions of the military. Workers, bosses, civilians, military officers, union activists, actors, musicians, intellectuals, journalists, religious faithful, scientists, and political activists of the most varied ideologies, each carried the dream of becoming Brazilian again in their eyes and hearts, and to live once again in a democratic, civilized nation.

Lula was eighteen and knew nearly nothing about politics when João Goulart was replaced by three generals who gave themselves the pompous title "supreme commanders of the revolution": General Artur da Costa e Silva, Vice Admiral Augusto Hammann Rademaker Grünewald, and Brigadier General Francisco de Assis Correia de Melo, called "Crazy Melo" by his friends. The first official order signed by the trio was popularly known as the "big list"—a selection of 100 people considered the most dangerous enemies of the new regime. Number one on the list, published in the *Diário Oficial* (the official journal of the federal government of Brazil) nine days after the coup, was Luís Carlos Prestes, general secretary of the PCB, once known as the "knight of hope." Name number 100, closing the list, was fake—the name of an agent infiltrator who collected and passed on names and information to the military, helping them identify and capture enemies: the ex-navy corporal José Anselmo do Santos, or simply "Corporal Anselmo." Once masked, now he became a recipient of amnesty to bear false witness against his colleagues.

Fifteen years after the disaster of 1964, ten out of ten amnesty beneficiaries returned to Brazil with plans to do exactly what they were doing before exile: politics. Just as Almino Afonso, Franklin Martins, and Darcy Ribeiro didn't wait for the Figueiredo's order to return, heaps of pre-1964 political luminaries and activists had already set up political organizations abroad, before even setting foot in Brazil. Along with those who took up arms to fight the regime, like Franklin and many others, the most dazzling stars of national politics from the democratic period had scattered around the world. Prestes moved to Moscow; Miguel Arraes divided his time between Paris and Algiers; the peasant leader Francisco Julião moved to Mexico; Almino Afonso spent a short time in Yugoslavia before moving with his family to several different countries in Latin America; and Darcy Ribeiro worked all over Latin America as a professor and anthropologist.

Reviled by the Brazilian military, Leonel Brizola lived in Uruguay for thirteen years, until 1977, when he was deported by the dictator Aparicio Méndez for "breaking the rules that regulate the right to asylum." Through initiatives of Brazilians who were living in the United States, and with support from Senator Ted Kennedy, he obtained a permanent residency visa for the US, where he lived for four months. The fear of an assassination attempt against Brizola led President Carter to authorize two CIA agents to accompany him undercover on the Aerolíneas Argentinas flight from Buenos Aires to New York. The operation was authorized and undertaken despite the fact that both Carter and Kennedy knew that Brizola, while governor of Rio Grande do Sul, had expropriated the US mega-corps ITT and Bond & Share. Furthermore, from the top ranks of the Jango administration, the "centaur of the Pampas," as his admirers used to call him, was one of the few political leaders who supported the idea of armed resistance in 1964 during the coup against his brother-in-law Goulart.

By the end of 1970, a considerable number of the Brazilian political leaders who were spread across the world had moved to Chile after the presidential victory of socialist Salvador Allende in the September 4 elections. Although many of them had planned to settle permanently in the country—several Brazilians became part of the Allende government—the bloody coup executed by General Augusto Pinochet three years after the socialist victory had scattered the Brazilian community of exiles around the world once again.

The explosion that had scattered so many people across the five continents had ended when it was least expected—in a country that had suffered from the longest authoritarian regime of the twentieth century, the dictatorship of António de Oliveira Salazar, who had ruled with an iron fist over Portugal for nearly fifty years. In the early morning of April 25, 1975, to the sound of the song "Grandola, Vila Morena," by José Afonso, the streets of the country had been taken by the Carnation Revolution, a military movement formed primarily by young captains. With very few exceptions, in a short time, Brazilian exiles from the four corners of the earth all came to Portugal.

In January 1978, Brizola left the old, elegant Hotel Roosevelt in New York, flew to Lisbon, and checked into the Hotel Florida with his wife Neusa. It was a modern four-star hotel where a crowd of Brazilians were already waiting for him, led by the illustrious host of the exiles, the socialist Mário Soares, prime minister of Portugal and one of the main representatives of social democracy in the Socialist International. Brizola set up a base of operations in the Hotel Florida, where he plotted to resuscitate the Brazilian Labor Party (PTB), which had been founded in May 1945 by Getúlio Vargas, during the final days of the Estado Novo regime.

And it was at Prime Minister Soares's side that, during the weekend of June 15–17, Brizola packed the rooms of the Portuguese Socialist Party headquarters to celebrate the meeting of Labor in Brazil with Labor in exile: the christening of the new PTB inspired by Vargas, Goulart, and Brizola. Among the crowd of over 1,000 were former armed guerrillas Carlos Minc, Chizuo Osava, and Alfredo Sirkis (the leader of the kidnapping of the German ambassador to Brazil, Ehrenfried von Holleben), peasant leader Francisco Julião, Herbert de Souza (Betinho, Henfil's brother), and the academics Theotônio dos Santos, Darcy Ribeiro, and José Almino de Alencar, son of Miguel Arraes.

After the Portuguese celebration, Brizola embarked on a lengthy tour of Europe that ended in Hamburg, Germany, during a meeting of the Socialist International, where he was presented as "the most modern and irrefutable representative of Brazilian labor." Afterward, he was seen at the side of some of the most celebrated and respected leaders of social democracy, like Willy Brandt, chancellor of West Germany and president of the International, François Mitterrand of France, Olof Palme of Sweden, and the young Spaniard Felipe González, who, until a few years earlier, had suffered under the dictatorship of the late Generalissimo Francisco Franco.

The number of Brazilians who relocated to Portugal was so great that Brizola frequently had to resort to trickery to dispel the curiosity and gossip of journalists, and to escape the gaze of military intelligence agents stationed in Brazil's consulates and embassies. One way to do this was to schedule meetings in Madrid, which were set up by Brazilian journalist Eric Nepomuceno, a discrete *brizolista* who worked as a correspondent for *Veja* magazine on the Iberian Peninsula. The journalist remembers mediating meetings between Brizola and González, then leader of the moderate wing of the Spanish Socialist Workers' Party (PSOE), with two Brazilians who lived in São Paulo, Almino Afonso and the future governor of São Paulo, Franco Montoro (both of the MDB).

Neither amnesty nor the end of the two-party system—approved months later in November 1979—proved enough to end the rancor that the dictatorship directed toward Brizola. Convinced that his dream was to restart the PTB—an acronym that reminded the public of its creator, Getúlio Vargas—the military swung into action. The plan was made by General Golbery do Couto e Silva, who handpicked the person who would carry it out: ex-congresswoman Ivete Vargas, great-niece of Getúlio and a sworn enemy of Brizola. Even though her mandate had been dissolved by Institutional Act 5, Ivete did not hesitate to assist the military and had the Superior Electoral Court register the acronym PTB in her name—leaving the ex-governor the consolation of founding his party with the acronym PDT (Democratic Labor Party), the organization through which he planned to recreate *varguista* laborism.

15

Lula brings together workers, politicians, intellectuals, and leftist activists to create the Workers' Party. Two months later, he is arrested

Thousands of kilometers from Europe and 680 kilometers from Brasília—the route that the tireless Leonel Brizola traveled during his struggle to restart his labor party—Lula came to placid Poços de Caldas, in southern Minas Gerais, to lay the first brick for his political cathedral: the Workers' Party. Officially started on September 11, 1982, when the Superior Electoral Court legally recognized it as a political party, the traditional narrative holds that the PT was born in the auditorium of Sion Catholic High School, in São Paulo's Higienópolis neighborhood, on February 10, 1980, where the famous photo with Lula, intellectuals Sérgio Buarque de Holanda, Mário Pedrosa, and Antônio Cândido, actress Lélia Abramo, and revolutionary Apolônio de Carvalho was taken. But only union members were present on the day the party was really founded, July 7, 1979, in the imposing neoclassical halls of the Hotel Palace, the elegant establishment founded in Poços de Caldas during the 1930s. During the seven months between the Poços de Caldas event and the ceremony at Sion High School, however, the most brilliant luminaries of the Brazilian left engaged with the party with a level of enthusiasm that hadn't been seen in a long time. It is also true that, to the discomfort of the more radical currents, Joaquim "Joaquinzão" dos Santos Andrade, considered by many to be the most over-the-hill symbol of union sellouts, was among the party founders.

Without anyone knowing until they arrived in Poços de Caldas,

Lula and his allies from the ABC had spent months talking about creating a political party with true working-class roots. First there was Lula's shock at the near-total absence of anyone from the working class in Congress. The idea that there were only two people from the working class among nearly 500 senators and congressmen bothered Lula, and it became a recurring theme at all of the debates, meetings, and congresses in which he participated. Whenever he was invited to talk about salaries, inflation, or unemployment, he would beat around the bush until finally reaching his main point: one of the reasons Brazilians were so poor was the working class's nearly nonexistent participation in the spaces where the laws governing the country were made.

The transformation of Lula from a person who "hated politics and whoever likes politics," which started at the 1978 Petroleum Workers' Congress in Bahia, resurfaced in January 1979 in the upstate town of Lins during São Paulo's Ninth State Congress of Metalworkers, Mechanics, and Electrical Workers. Although it wasn't an industrial center, the town was chosen because of its mayor, the engineer Waldemar Casadei, was a representative of the "authentic" group within the MDB. In addition to returning to the subject of creating a workers' party, the Lins conference gave the press and the public access to information that had previously circulated only behind the scenes, in the unions. Contrary to what was imagined, the so-called sellout Joaquinzão, with the walrus mustache and sideburns of a bolero singer, was on Lula's side. Judging by the reaction of Arnaldo Gonçalves, president of the Santos Metalworkers' Union and a respected director of the PCB, the Communists didn't want to hear anything about it. Furthermore, Casadei's enthusiasm for the idea showed that the MDB's "Autêntico" group was a door that the future party could certainly knock on. It was no accident that the only two members of the working class in Congress were members of the MDB from São Paulo—the metalworkers Aurélio Peres, connected to PC do B, and Benedito Marcílio, president of the Santo André Metalworkers' Union.

The coincidence of the proposals and the affinity with the "authentic" group prompted Lula, before setting up the meeting in Poços de Caldas, to float the idea of starting a new party with left sectors within conventional politics. On the weekend before the meeting in Poços, he and another dozen metalworkers set up what would be known as "the

Pampas meeting," named after São Bernardo do Campo's Pampas Hotel, on June 2 and 3.

The hotel's brutalist cylindrical concrete building buzzed with excitement. As Lula later said, it was time for the jaguar to go to the watering hole—a popular expression meaning that the time had come to settle accounts. With the foundations of the new party solidifying among the workers during the meetings in Bahia and Lins (which would consolidate in Poços de Caldas), the Pampas meeting was called to measure left-wing parliamentarians' interest in the project.

The meeting was originally planned to be closed to the public so that internal arguments wouldn't be exposed. However, when work began on that Saturday morning, Lula and the union leaders who had decided to create the party realized that there were nearly 200 people in the auditorium, all under the watchful eye of reporters from four of the largest national newspapers of the time, São Paulo's *Folha* and *Estadão*, and Rio's *Jornal do Brasil* and *O Globo*. All of the internal currents that would go on to make up the PT were there: union activists, intellectuals, representatives of the Catholic Church, and former exiles, many of whom had belonged to armed resistance groups and the MDB. This, in theory, would be one of the innovations that the party would bring to politics—something inconceivable up to then in Brazilian and even in foreign leftist parties: allowing the participation of groups with their own political ideologies and agendas and with formal representation in the directorate and executive committees, always based on proportionality of representation.

The troubles started with the official opposition MDB, known by everyone as a giant grab bag that mixed together at least three groups: the "Autênticos," representing the left wing of the party; the "moderates," who presented themselves as adversaries of the dictatorship but avoided any kind of radicalization; and the "adherents," who were viewed as military-regime fifth-column infiltrators embedded in the opposition party. People from all three factions were there that weekend in São Bernardo, and they had come from all over Brazil. These people ranged from the "authentic" Alceu Collares (a staunch *brizolista* from Rio Grande do Sul who was opposed the idea of creating a new party) to the "moderate" Jarbas Vasconcelos, from Pernambuco. There were politicians from São Paulo there who had already decided to join the PT, like Airton Soares and Bete Mendes. Another "authentic" politician from São Paulo, Alberto Goldman, connected to the still-illegal PCB, was so radically opposed to the creation of the party that, although he was invited, he didn't even show up. To make this fandango even more confusing, there were "authentics" who opposed the idea of creating the PT because they believed that the new party would rip apart the broad front set up by the MDB, and that this would benefit and increase the life expectancy of the military dictatorship. Political stars like Fernando Henrique Cardoso and Almino Afonso, who supported the idea that a new party should have the characteristics of a socialist front, didn't hide their disagreement with the direction the meeting was going.

All of this took place in the presence of dozens of union leaders who treated creation of the PT as something that was already in the bag, like Petroleum Workers' Union leader Jacó Bittar; Osasco Metalworkers' Union president Henos "Saúva" Amorina, and his vice president, the firebrand José Pedro "Sarrafo" da Silva, who had one foot on the factory floor and other in the "Worker Priests" group of the Catholic Church's Basic Ecclesial Communities; Olívio Dutra, president of the Porto Alegre Bank Tellers' Union; and São Paulo Leather Workers' Union leader Paulo de Mattos Skromov.

There was an impression among the artists and intellectuals there that their support for creating the Workers' Party was nearly unanimous. Although Professor Sérgio Buarque de Holanda has gone down in history as the first intellectual to support the creation of the PT, the truth is that the first person from the academic world to join the party was art critic Mário Pedrosa. First affiliated with the Brazilian Communist Party in 1926, his passage through the Workers' Party was to be short lived. Accused of being a Trotskyist, Pedroso had been kicked out of the PCB in 1931, bringing with him, to what would become the Fourth International, three other luminaries of Brazilian Marxism: Lívio Xavier, Fúlvio Abramo, and Aristides Lobo.

Half a century later, now recognized as one of the most refined intellectuals of the country, Pedrosa didn't just endorse the creation of the PT but became a propagandist for what he considered to be "something that has never existed in Brazil, workers building their own party." Fascinated by the prospect of something so revolutionary, he worked to recruit other intellectuals. His first target was an old comrade from the Democratic Left (*Esquerda Democrática*, ED) and the Socialist Party of the 1940s, Professor Antônio Cândido de Mello e Souza, renowned for his vast, critical body of work, including *Formação da literatura brasileira: Momentos decisivos* and *Os parceiros do Rio Bonito*.

Cândido was reluctant, saying that he didn't want anything more to do with political parties. Furthermore, he added, he had heard rumors that Lula was going to make public restrictions on the participation of intellectuals and students and complained that "these people just want to manipulate and use us." Pedroso didn't back down from these points.

"Cândido, since Lenin, political parties have always been created by intellectuals," Pedrosa said. "For the first time, someone, Lula in this case, wants to join both workers and intellectuals. The party will need people like us, at least as sympathizers."

Although he wasn't able to convince Antônio Cândido, Pedrosa's arguments immersed him once again in what he considered, at sixty, to be "the annoyance of partisan politics." A few weeks later, Cândido and his wife Gilda decided to visit an old friend, the Polish doctor Febus Gikovate. Like Pedrosa, Gikovate was a former comrade from the Democratic Left and had been an activist in the Revolutionary Socialist Party (Partido Socialista Revolucionário, PSR), a Trotskyist group led by journalist Hermínio Sacchetta that had included, among other luminaries, the sociologist Florestan Fernandes and legendary modernist artist Patrícia "Pagu" Galvão. Suffering from cancer, Gikovate was hospitalized in Santa Casa de Misericórdia, whose medical school he had worked at as a professor. Before entering his room, Cândido and Gilda spoke quickly with Febus's wife, who complained about her husband's suffering.

"See if you can try to cheer him up," she said. "He is very depressed about his illness."

Without knowing what to do, Antônio Cândido whispered to Gilda, "I know this isn't right, but I am going to make up a lie to try to raise his spirits."

The couple entered the room smiling, and Antônio Cândido said, "Boss! I didn't come here just to visit you. I'm here to perform a political task. It's a delicate mission."

Febus's eyes lit up. "What is it?"

"The workers of the ABC are trying to found a party, and they've invited us to participate in their meetings. I don't know if I am going to go, because I don't want to participate in party politics anymore."

Gikovate's expression grew serious. "These workers are trying to do what we wanted to do when we were their age but never succeeded at: they are founding a party. It is our obligation to join it."

Lying in his hospital bed, the old Trotskyist wiped the smile from his old friend's face. "I can't go because of my health. But I am asking you to go to represent me. Tell them that I can't join the party, or even go to any meeting, because I am going somewhere else."

Antônio Cândido became emotional. "Febus, don't say that . . ."

"No, Cândido. I am dying. The end is near. I hope that I can hold out a little more, and your company is comforting. But go to this meeting and sign your membership form as if it were mine."

Three decades later, remembering that episode, Cândido said, "Febus died the next day. That is when I told myself that I had to join this new party. That is what caused me to join the PT. I joined knowing that the PT wasn't a socialist party, and I am a socialist. I think that the PT has a workers' energy that gets confused with the real interests of the people."

Due to the importance of symbolism, the PT chose a historic revolutionary fighter, Apolônio de Carvalho, hero of the French Resistance and the Internationalist Brigades that fought against Franco in the Spanish Civil War, instead of a famous intellectual, as its first official member. But intellectuals of the caliber of Antônio Cândido, Sérgio Buarque, and Mário Pedrosa became magnets, over time attracting leftists of the stature of Hélio Pellegrino, Chico de Oliveira, Bete Mendes, Florestan Fernandes, Francisco Weffort, José Álvaro Moisés, Lélia Abramo, Maria Victoria Benevides, Paul Singer, Paulo Freire, Marilena Chaui, Perseu Abramo, and Vinícius Caldeira Brant, among many others.

On Sunday night, when Lula finally closed the meeting in the Pampas Palace Hotel, it marked the end of a long and tortuous gestation period. Then he left the politicians, artists, and activists behind in São Bernardo de Campo and drove 300 kilometers to Poços de Caldas to oversee the birth of the Workers' Party.

On February 10, 1980, the PT was formally introduced to the Brazilian people at Sion High School auditorium in São Paulo. Demonstrating his impressive knack for keeping multiple balls in the air, while he was setting up the party, Lula simultaneously prepared another strike in the ABC. He'd been under surveillance by agents of repression from the start of the year, and in the early morning hours of April 19, at the height of the strike, he would be abruptly pulled out of his house and locked inside DOPS, together with his comrades from the union directorate.

16

In the middle of the night, a polite man in a tie interrogates Lula in a cubicle in DOPS, sent by a general codenamed "the chief"

Regardless of whether President Figueiredo, General Golbery, and General Caveirinha thought that Lula's arrest that morning in São Bernardo would break the backbone of the ABC movement, or at least stop the 1980 strike, they had just tried to put out a fire with kerosene. Lula had been planning for possible arrest from the start of that year, and it was a risk that grew with the announcement of the creation of the PT and the start of the strike. This is why Friar Betto and Congressman Geraldo Siqueira were sleeping over at his house, and why they witnessed the arrival of the cops. And this is why the other union leaders had spent months asking themselves things like, "If Lula is arrested, who will lead the strike? Should Devanir take over? And if Devanir is arrested, will it be Alemãozinho? Or Osmarzinho? And what if everyone is arrested?"

Among the directorate, the atmosphere of trepidation remained. Beginning at six o'clock that same morning, and continuing over the days that followed, Djalma de Souza Bom, Devanir Ribeiro, Gilson Menezes, Enilson "Alemãozinho" Simões de Moura, José Maria de Almeida, Severino Alves da Silva, Rubens "Rubão" Teodoro de Arruda, Expedito Soares Batista, José Venâncio de Souza, and João Batista dos Santos were all kidnapped and taken to DOPS. The only ones who managed to escape were Osmar "Osmarzinho" Santos de Mendonça and Juraci Batista Magalhães. Considered fugitives, they were found and arrested by the hand of repression, three weeks after the first arrests.

However, due to the threat that the government would arrest the entire directorate, Lula and his comrades had set up a huge logistical organization for the strike made up of hundreds of metalworkers—a battalion of the anonymous, unknown to the eyes of the police, that was divided in cells of ten to fifteen members. So it was that, despite all of the arrests, the strike continued and the assemblies moved ahead as planned in Vila Euclides Stadium or in the São Bernardo Diocese headquarters.

The fear that had taken hold during the first hours after the arrests abated somewhat that afternoon, with the release of the two "notable" prisoners, attorneys Dalmo Dallari and José Carlos Dias, along with workers who had no relationship with the strike, like Friar Chico, Lula's brother. Everyone trusted the protective cloak of the church, above and beyond Cardinal Paulo Evaristo Arns and Santo André Bishop Cláudio Hummes. Along with the hundreds of priests associated with the Basic Ecclesial Communities, the striking workers knew they had the support and protection of several members of the church hierarchy, including the bishops Hélder Câmara, Waldir Calheiros, José Maria Pires (an Afro-Brazilian nicknamed 'Dom Pelé"), Moacyr Grechi, Cândido Padín, Marcelo Carvalheira, Pedro Casaldáliga, and Mauro Morelli.

One apparently subtle detail, however, still worried the prisoners: there were two divisions of DOPS. The Political Order division, directed by agent Silvio Pereira Machado, handled the so called "subversive crimes," which were considered minor, such as participating in protests and marches against the regime, in which the majority of the cases led to short detentions and addition of the arrestees' names to their files. The Social Order division, feared by all, was led by the infamous and evil-looking Edsel Magnotti, who handled the so-called "major crimes" that the dictatorship considered terrorism. According to the official report of the National Truth Commission that was set up by President Dilma Rousseff in 2011 to document human rights violations committed by the military dictatorship, Magnotti had participated in cases of "illegal detention, torture, and execution" of, among others, Carlos Marighella, Alexandre Vannucchi Leme, Antônio Pinheiro Salles, Flávio Molina Carvalho, Edgard de Aquino Duarte, and Antônio Carlos Bicalho Lana.

It was not surprising, therefore, that the arrested metalworkers were fearful when they learned that Magnotti would be responsible for their imprisonment, and that they were being accused of violating the National Security Law. The fear intensified at the end of that day when

Magnotti ordered that no one would be able to communicate with the prisoners for ten days.

Minutes after their arrests, Friar Betto and Geraldinho gave the news to Luiz Eduardo Greenhalgh, who Lula had recently hired as the union's attorney. Greenhalgh went to the Second Army's auditing division, near Paulista Avenue in downtown São Paulo, to try to get authorization to visit the defendants, but the building was closed for the weekend. Armed with a letter of attorney, he returned to DOPS. He insisted to Romeu Tuma that the ban on communications didn't extend to defense lawyers and managed, in near secrecy, to speak with Lula and a few other union leaders. While inside, he was surprised to meet Alagoas senator Teotônio Vilela, who had also managed to bypass the communications ban to get the green light from Tuma to quietly get into to the building. A wealthy sugar refinery owner, Teotônio was first elected as a member of ARENA (the official political party during the dictatorship) but, little by little, became opposed to the regime, joined the MDB, and, while battling cancer, became a symbol of the fight for redemocratization in Brazil—to the point that he was paid tribute in a song by Milton Nascimento and Fernando Brant called "Menestrel das Alagoas," which was transformed into a hymn against the dictatorship. The senator was the brother of the conservative cardinal Avelar Brandão Vilela, who was not part of the team of bishops defending the activists from the ABC. During the fight for amnesty, Teotônio Vilela began regularly visiting political prisoners, mainly in São Paulo and Rio, the cities where most of them were incarcerated.

It had scarcely been twenty-four hours since the imposition of the ban on communication with prisoners when it was broken again that Sunday, due to influence from the Catholic Church. Bishop Cláudio Hummes managed to convince Tuma to authorize Lula's wife Marisa to see her husband, as long as she made the promise—which she kept—to not tell anyone from the press about the visit. The couple's three children—Fabio, Marcos, and Sandro—stayed home in the care of Friar Betto, Geraldinho, Greenhalgh, and their uncle Friar Chico. The goal of the lawyer, the senator, and Marisa's brief and discreet visits to DOPS was to bring some comfort and security to the prisoners and to verify that nobody was being tortured. While Marisa met with her husband, the driver of an unmarked car left a letter from Villares to Lula at the house warning him that the strike was illegal, telling him they would dock workers' pay from days when production was stopped and insinuating that disobeying the law could lead to just-cause dismissal—all of which ended up happening.

During a religious ceremony in Se Cathedral on Monday, April 21, Dom Paulo Evaristo pleaded with the government to free the prisoners. His words were repeated by Dom Cláudio Hummes in a mass held in Bonfim Church in Santo André for 1,500 striking metalworkers. Bishop Hummes said that the Catholic Church was on the side of the strikers and asked for the release of the union leaders. In a surprising editorial, the conservative *Estadão* newspaper criticized the government for the arrests, saying the act would not help end the strike and that it damaged the credibility of the redemocratization project that was underway.

Although they had been one of the civic pillars of the 1964 coup, the Mesquita family and its newspapers, *Estadão* and *Jornal da Tarde*, had broken with the military on December 13, 1968, the day that Institutional Act 5 was decreed. From that point forward, until 1976, the two newspapers had been forced to operate with in-house military censors.

On Tuesday, Greenhalgh filed a writ of habeas corpus at the Second Army Corps auditing division, and it was immediately rejected by a military judge. The union leaders at DOPS were submitted to medical exams, which didn't reveal any health problems. Later that morning, the prisoners' wives tried to visit their husbands, but Magnotti denied the request. He had been officially nominated as the leader of the investigation, according to Article 36 of the National Security law, which prohibited "inciting the paralysis of public services or essential activities." Later the same day, Magnotti himself interrogated Lula, reading each question off of a sheet of paper. Officially, it was reported that the questions had been written by Romeu Tuma and given to Magnotti, but it was suspected that they had been sent directly from General Golbery's cabinet in Brasília.

Lula was interrogated for longer than any of the other union leaders, for over four hours. From the afternoon until six thirty, the operational director of the Federal Police DOPS, Agent Marco Antônio Veronezzi, observed silently from a distance. He had been given special orders to listen to each of the jailed union leaders without formally interrogating them. After each interrogation, Veronezzi sent a copy of the transcripts to the Federal Police's Intelligence Department, ordering them to send it to Brasília. Years later, as a constituent congressman, Lula was introduced to Veronezzi by Tuma, and said he remembered him. "I saw him sitting there in DOPS," he said. "I didn't know who he was, but I knew that it wasn't good for me."

A summary of Lula's extensive interrogation (in all, it was over 11,000 words) reveals the interest that the authorities—Figueiredo? Golbery? Caveirinha? Tuma?—had in listening to the man who had who set fire to the ABC:

> The accused appeared at 14:10 on the twenty second day of April in the year of nineteen and eighty, in the city of São Paulo-SP, in the Division of Social Order, where he encountered Mr. Bel. Edsel Magnotti, Chief Agent, and I, the signatory of this document, as his scribe, and answered the questions from the authority as follows:
>
> What is your name? Luiz Inácio da Silva, nickname "Lula"
>
> What is your nationality? Brazilian
>
> Where were you born? Garanhuns, Pernambuco
>
> What is your marital status? Married
>
> What is your age? 34 (06.10.45)
>
> Who are your parents? Aristides Inácio da Silva and Eurídice Ferreira de Melo
>
> Where do you live? 273 Maria Azevedo Florence Street, São Bernardo do Campo
>
> What is your profession? Junior Foreman
>
> Where do you work? Indústria Villares—S. Bernardo do Campo
>
> Do you know how to read and write? Yes
>
> . . .
>
> Are you under the influence of alcoholic beverages or other toxic substances? No
>
> Are you married, divorced, or widowed? Married
>
> Is your married life harmonious? It is harmonious
>
> . . .
>
> Have you ever committed a crime when you were drunk or suffering from strong emotions? I declare that I have never committed a crime.
>
> Have you ever been sued? No
>
> Do you regret committing the crime that you are accused of now, or do you think the action was premeditated and you have achieved your goal? I declare that I have never committed a crime.
>
> . . .

The interrogated party states that: he exercised his first mandate as president of the entity, remained at the job until 1978, when he was reelected for the three-year period of 1978–1981; . . . that the interrogated party, despite invitations to attend congresses and make speeches abroad in countries like Belgium, Sweden, Germany, and others, did not accept the invitations because he thought that the problems of the Brazilian workers have to be resolved here and not abroad, although he made one trip to Japan, in terms of participating in Congresses abroad . . . The interrogated party has made a few speeches about the political organizing of the workers and the need to create a Workers' Party . . .

That, on a professional level, he has met a few dozen people, like Otavio Frias, from *Folha de S. Paulo*, one of the owners of *Jornal da Tarde*, Rui Mesquita, and the owner of *Istoé* magazine, Mino Carta [as well as] some of the owners of *Jornal do Brasil* whose names he does not remember . . .

That he has met dozens of businessmen including Dilson Funaro . . . Cláudio Bardella, Luis Eulálio Bueno Vidigal, Mário Garneiro, Mauro Marcondes, Einar Kok, Paulo Villares, Carlos Villares, José Mindlin, and Paulo Francini, among others.

That the interrogated party has had little contact with intellectuals, because they imagine that the workers don't think and always want to dictate rules to the workers; that he has met and had contact with some of them, like Fernando Henrique Cardoso, Francisco Welford [*sic*], José Álvaro Moisés, Francisco de Oliveira, Leôncio Martins, all of these individuals having published in books or newspapers about unionism, and others that he doesn't remember at the moment.

That he has had contact with several governmental leaders, such as ex-minister Petrônio Portela, ex–labor minister Dr. Arnaldo da Costa Prieto, ex–planning minister João Paulo dos Reis Veloso, ex–finance minister Mário Henrique Simonsen, Industry and Commerce Minister Calmon de Sá, current labor minister Dr. Murilo Macedo, Planning Minister Dr. Antônio Delfim Netto, and with various foreign personalities like German chancellor Helmut Schmidt, Spanish prime minister Adolfo Suárez, and also with several congressmen and senators, among them: Jarbas Passarinho, Magalhães Pinto, Francelino Pereira, Nelson Marchezan, Franco Montoro, Orestes Quércia, Airton Soares, Eduardo Suplicy, Geraldo Siqueira, Sérgio dos Santos, Nabi Abi Chedid, Cláudio Lembo, Paulo Egídio Martins, Laudo Natel, Almir Pazzianoto Pinto, Irma Passoni, Leonel Brizola, Francisco

Julião, Miguel Arraes, Olavo Setúbal, and others who he didn't remember at the time, recalling that he has also met twice with former Brazilian president Ernesto Geisel.

That he clarifies that he doesn't accept invitations to participate in clandestine organizations, for which reason the interrogated party has made many enemies in this area; that he doesn't deny participating in protests against attitudes taken by the government, but not the men, because the interrogated party thinks the problem is the economic model and not the individual people; that he participated in protests against the extinction of the MDB, even though he was against the positions of the MDB; that he has always supported freedom for political parties and after the government opened the possibility of a multi-party system, it (MDB) continues to defend the two-party system.

That he explained that he has received visits from union leaders from the following countries: Germany, Italy, France, Sweden, the Netherlands, Japan, and the US, but that he hasn't maintained good relations with the foreign unions, because the interrogated party has serious differences of opinion with the foreign unions. One of the reasons is that these foreign unions think it's good when the companies from their countries export products to Brazil, taking away our jobs. But if the opposite process happens, in other words if Brazil exports goods to their countries, they hold strikes without caring about Brazilian workers, and they know that the privileges that they have conquered were conceded at the cost of their companies' exploitation of the Brazilian people.

That he further explains that when they started the 1980 salary campaign, every worker was thinking of the revenge imposed by the owners after the 1979 strike, when they deducted the strike days from their pay, and the layoffs of a great number of workers. That he thinks that they are making a modest demand of 15 percent over the consumer price index, taking into consideration two things: first, the 34.1 percent prejudice they suffered in 1972 and 1973, and having received 19 percent raises in two years, there was only 15 percent left to demand . . .

That the interrogated party had no expression after seeing our Glorious Army fly jets low over the heads of 100,000 workers, trying to scare them, and there could have been a tragedy; that he had never witnessed a scene like that, believing that it was done to scare them; . . . that it is important to understand that when the labor sector doesn't want it, there is no union leader in the world who can hold a strike. That we can't forget the strikes of 1978, which happened inside the factories without the participation of the directorate, and other cases in which union leaders attempted to end strikes and the labor category did not obey them . . .

[About] what organizations have given support to the strike movement since before and even after the decree of illegality, specifying the type of support, he responded: he has received thousands of telegrams of support from innumerable organizations in countries like Italy, France, Sweden, Germany, Portugal, and the United States; that, in terms of the contributions . . . he only knows of food donations . . . When asked if there had been any financial contributions and, if so, where this fund was located, he said he didn't know anything about it. Asked if the Catholic Church had participated in supporting the strike and in what manner . . . he responded that the church, in addition to giving moral support, had served as a location for receiving food donations, and that there is no influence of the church on the strike . . .

Asked if when the rumor of possible government intervention in the union arose, a leadership council of 16 people was created in case the entire directorate was arrested and who are these people, he said there is a commission of 475 people who elected a leadership of 16 people in case the entire directorate was arrested, and that he didn't know the names of the people in charge, only that Enilson [Moura] and Osmar Mendonca were part of it . . .

On reading to the interrogated party the news story from Eldorado Radio on 4/11/1980, which aired at 13:00 hours, in which the reporter said that Lula had ordered intensification of the pickets on buses to remove people who were planning on going to work, he answered that he had never used the word "picket," and never ordered anyone to remove anyone from a bus, because his argument is based on convincing people peacefully in the bars, parks, etc., to avoid any kind of friction; that the interrogated party really told an assembly that Cardinal Dom Paulo Evaristo Arns had given integral support to the union campaign in statements made to one of the television stations . . .

> When asked about when he made statements referring to the Labor Court judges Henrique Victor, Afonso Teixeira Filho, and Antônio Pereira Magaldi as "sons of bitches" several times, he responded that when he made statements related to the decree banning the strike, he recalls using strong language referring to the judges, remembering that the businessmen also use the expression "son of a bitch," and that he was sure that a document that was distributed to the workers in an assembly used this "strong" language against the three judges . . .
>
> Asked if he knows Friar Betto . . . he answered that he knows him and that he is currently in the interrogated party's house, and that he is sure that Friar Betto was designated by Dom Cláudio Hummes and by the Workers' Pastoral to coordinate the distribution of food to the workers; that Friar Betto was in the house of the interrogated party because he had spent the night in his house to keep company with his wife and mother-in-law and was certainly still there and that he was there on the day he was arrested. Nothing else was asked about this subject.

Despite the arrest of all of the leaders, the strike continued. One week later, despite the continuing order not to communicate, Lula was able to get a brief message into the hands of Greenhalgh and Congressman Airton Soares, who had already announced he was joining PT, that was read by Nelson Campanholo at the assembly on Saturday, April 26, at the São Bernardo Diocese headquarters. Due to pressure from the government, Vila Euclides Stadium had been closed for protests. Although it was delivered in a coded manner, Lula's message was for the strike to continue.

"We are in prison, but we are okay," Campanholo read from the little piece of paper that had been given to him. "Here in prison, we hope that the metalworkers will continue what they've started."

The crowd had started yelling, "The strike continues!" when a Military Police cavalry division appeared, beating a path through the crowd with billy clubs so that Colonel Rigonatto could enter with his riot police.

While the billy clubs were flying on the streets of São Bernardo, Cardinal Ivo Lorscheiter, president of the National Conference of Brazilian Bishops (CNBB) quietly met with General Golbery in Brasília, requesting that he free the prisoners as a gesture of goodwill that would help end the strike. At the same time, President Figueiredo tightened the political screws, blaming the church—specifically Cardinal Arns—for the fact that the strike was continuing.

It was a cloudy night, on the tenth day of their incarceration, when Greenhalgh received a phone call from DOPS director Romeu Tuma, asking for him to come to the brick building on Osório Square. Worried about what could be going on, Greenhalgh hurried over and went up to Tuma's office on the fourth floor. The agent received him with the expression of a man who had few friends and, without saying good evening, went straight to the point:

"Dr. Luiz, let me tell you one thing. You asked us to guarantee a daily sunbath for the prisoners, right?"

"Yes, I did."

"And I authorized these sunbaths, right? And you asked me to authorize soccer for them in the backyard, right?"

"Yes, and you did it."

"And you asked for a radio for them, and I authorized it, right?"

"Yes, sir."

"You asked for a TV so they could see the Corinthians game, and I had them set my own TV up in the cell, right?"

"Yes, sir."

"You asked me to buy a bunch of tennis shoes for them to play soccer, and I bought them, right?"

"Yes, Dr. Tuma . . ."

"That's right. I gave the prisoners everything that you asked for, Dr. Luiz, and look at how they thanked me."

Tuma set a petition on the table, signed by all of the detectives and jailors in DOPS, asking for a raise.

"Look at this, Dr. Luiz. Look at this!" he said. "I treat them well and Lula messes with my workers' heads? This has never happened here before. They want to do union organizing here? Damn it! Lula wants to turn DOPS into a union? Next time you speak with them, tell them they have to stop this business or their privileges are going to end."

Lula may have been messing with the heads of the police on the issue of wages, but he wasn't doing it with politics. Two days before the conversation between Tuma and Greenhalgh, the police had arrested dozens of people who appeared in Vila Euclides Stadium to see a concert, whose goal was to mobilize resources for the strike fund, that had been canceled by order of the Federal Police. With a ticket price of Cr$100, musicians that had confirmed included Chico Buarque, Gonzaguinha, Ivan Lins, Gal Costa, Alcione, Martinho da Vila, MBP-4, Fagner, João Bosco, Sérgio Ricardo, Zé Kéti, and Adoniran Barbosa.

There was one surprise after another. During the second week of their incarceration, Lula had a puzzling experience that would only be explained thirty years later. Around three o'clock in the morning, a jailor tiptoed into the cell where all of the ABC prisoners slept and whispered in his ear, "Get dressed and come with me without making any noise. Dr. Tuma wants to speak with you."

Half asleep and not understanding what was going on, he put on a shirt, trousers, and shoes and left the cell with the police guard. They went up to the fourth floor alone in the elevator, to the chief agent's office. Adding to the confusion, the police guard didn't enter Tuma's office but led Lula to a storage room under the staircase, filled with stacks of old newspapers. The room's single light bulb flickered, adding tension to the moment. Waiting there were Tuma and a stranger—a middle-aged man in a suit and tie, who looked like an executive without a briefcase.

Tuma spoke first. "Lula, this man has come from Brasília to speak to you. I will leave you two alone. I'll be waiting outside if you need to talk to me about anything."

Terrified to be in front of this strange person at that hour of the morning in that dreary room, Lula was sure he was going to be tortured. To his relief and shock, the man turned out to be polite, speaking softly and treating him with respect, calling him "Mr. Lula." The mysterious visitor suggested that he sit on a pile of newspapers and started what turned out to be a civilized conversation. It was an interrogation, but the man didn't raise his voice or make any sort of threat. He wanted to know about things that were already in all of the newspapers: Why had Lula called the strike? What did he think about the government and the political opening? What did he plan to do with the PT? And he hinted, in a veiled manner, that if he called an end to the strike, he and the other imprisoned union leaders would be released.

Relieved to not be face-to-face with a torturer, Lula answered all of the questions with his regular frankness and, as always, said that the strike would only stop when the demands of the workers were met by the bosses. As mysteriously as he had arrived, the enigmatic stranger left, and Lula was led back to the cell from which he was taken.

On the walk back to his cell, he asked Tuma what was going on. "I don't know what to say," he replied. "I only know that he was sent here from Brasília by someone called 'the chief.' I don't know anyone with that nickname."

Thirty years later, hospitalized with serious cardiovascular problems that would lead to his death, Romeu Tuma, then senator for PTB, received a visit in Sírio Libanês Hospital in São Paulo from the journalist Mino Carta, who had hired his son, neurologist Rogério Tuma, to write a weekly column for his news magazine *CartaCapital*. During the visit, they spoke about the time the strikers were jailed, and Carta asked about the identity of the "chief" who sent someone to interview Lula during that remote early morning of 1980. Tuma immediately revealed the mystery. "It was General Golbery do Couto e Silva, President Figueiredo's chief of staff."

The government seemed to be playing hot and cold. Thirteen days after the arrests, the Federal Police revoked its ban on events in Vila Euclides Stadium in time for the planned May Day celebration. Without the presence of the Military Police calvary, riot police, or helicopters hovering overhead, more than 150,000 people showed up for the event. On the next day, however, the Superior Military Court in Brasília unanimously rejected a writ of habeas corpus submitted by Greenhalgh for the release of Lula and the other prisoners. Then, violence exploded again in São Bernardo. A strikers' march was broken up with billy clubs, tear gas bombs, and cavalry charges. Journalists registered seventy union activists injured and forty arrests.

Days later, Tuma held a closed-door meeting with the detectives Armando Panichi Filho and Osvaldo Machado de Oliveira, giving them a secret task: don't let the newspapers find out, but take Lula to São Bernardo do Campo to visit his mother Dona Lindu, who was in what appeared to be the terminal stages of uterine cancer.

"We have to figure out a way for Lula to visit his mother before she dies," Tuma said. "I'll take full responsibility for it."

Panichi and Oliveira took Lula out of his cell before dawn and left from the building's basement, placing the prisoner in the back seat of a Chevrolet Chevette coupe with civilian plates. After driving through Dom Petro Park in downtown São Paulo's Glicério neighborhood, Lula explained to the police officers—both armed with revolvers—the route to the little house where Dona Lindu lived.

The car stopped at the door, and Panichi said, "Keep your head down and enter quickly so no one recognizes you. You can go alone. We won't go with you."

During the more than two hours he spent at his mother's side, Lula tried to comfort her, saying that he was being treated well by the police and that he hoped she would get better soon. The sun was already high in the sky when the brown Chevette returned to the underground garage door of DOPS and the prisoner was put back in his cell.

On the twenty-first day of their imprisonment, a Friday, lawyer Luiz Eduardo Greenhalgh left the DOPS building after a visit with the prisoners and, meeting the group of reporters gathered on the pavement, said, "My clients have announced they are starting a hunger strike."

At first, support for the hunger strike was not unanimous among the prisoners, starting with Lula, who was, on principle, against that mode of protest.

"I thought that it was pretty harsh to damage your own body to complain about something," he said, "but I ended up going along with it because I understood that, as a prisoner, you don't have many ways to protest anything."

Despite his initial reluctance, the prisoners asked Lula to give the news to Agent Romeu Tuma, who was not happy with it. "Tuma was pissed off and said he was going to take away our radio, cut off our soccer games, sunbathing, and access to newspapers," Lula said. "He didn't end up doing any of this, but he was angry at our decision."

Three days later, while Greenhalgh was visiting his clients, Lula told him, "You guys have to figure out a way to end this. We are all dying of hunger. Djalma has an ulcer—he can't go without eating."

Lula himself was busted by one of his friends when the latter found a few pieces of taffy hidden under his pillow. By the end of the day, to the relief of everyone, they voted to respect a request from Bishop Cláudio Hummes, who, "in the name of God" asked the prisoners to end the hunger strike. Revealing a previously unknown sense of humor, Tuma sent Detective Armando to the Greek restaurant Acropolis, on Graça Street in Bom Retiro, and delivered the prisoners a plate of fried calamari—called *lula* in Portuguese. In fact, Tuma was celebrating the news from the ABC: after forty-one days, the workers had voted in an assembly to end the strike, which concluded without any gains.

For Lula, the bad news was followed by worse news. At eleven o'clock the next morning on May 12, word arrived at Dops that Dona Lindu had died. Once again, Tuma called on his detectives, Armando Panichi and Osvaldo Machado de Oliveira, this time to escort Lula to two funerary commitments. The first would be that evening—the wake at Beneficência Portuguesa Hospital in São Caetano do Sul, where Dona Lindu was being treated when she died.

Her death wasn't unexpected. Lula knew that his mother was in very poor health and that the cancer had metastisized in the body of the sixty-four-year-old woman. But he had lost the person who was, and would continue to be, forever the most influential figure in his life. He had no doubt that all of his best characteristics, like determination, his notion of decency, and his capacity to overcome obstacles were clearly inherited from his mother. Even after he was elected president of the Republic, Lula would never tire of repeating that everything in his character had come from his mother.

Arriving at the wake, he spent fifty minutes in tears, alongside his wife Marisa, next to the body. On the way back to DOPS, he complained of a bad toothache, and the policemen stopped at a dentist's office to remove the molar.

The second task for the two detectives started at nine o'clock the following morning: to take Lula to Dona Lindu's burial in Vila Pauliceia Cemetery, on Julio de Mesquita Street in São Bernardo do Campo, a ceremony that almost transformed into a political protest, causing Detective Panichi some distress.

"It was just the two of us and, under instructions from Tuma, we were unarmed," Panichi recalled. "And the number of people, for the love of God! It was a huge crowd—at least 3,000 people. He was almost unable to walk. The crowd yelled, 'Free Lula!' I stayed within a meter of him the whole time. It was really hard to leave. If I hadn't grabbed his son Fabio and pushed him in through our car window, I think he would have been crushed. We left with Lula, his woman, and their boy. We tried to leave the cemetery from the back, but the gate was closed. The only way out was through the front gate, almost running people over."

Although the strike had come to an end after being targeted by the National Security Law, Lula and his comrades remained in prison. On the fourteenth, an illustrious visitor, Leonel Brizola, who had returned to Brazil months earlier, was barred from entering DOPS, since the no-visitors order remained in place—a rule that would be ignored by Tuma two days later when he allowed Cardinal Arns to visit. Everyone stayed in DOPS until May 20, when Greenhalgh was informed by the military court that the arrests had been revoked. Panichi received the order to drive Lula to a point near his house in São Bernardo in an unmarked beige Veraneio van, where a large crowd of workers, politicians, and lawyers was waiting for him. When he arrived home, he hugged his wife and kids, went into the backyard, and made a meaningful symbolic gesture: he opened the cage of Anu, a black bird he had been keeping as a pet for several years, setting the creature free.

Once the happiness of Lula's release had passed, the problems began to appear. All of the prisoners had been fired for job abandonment. Along with the material consequences of unemployment, the firings, on top of their removal from the union directorate, had brought another problem: without active employment in the sector stamped on their labor cards, they were out of the union. In one of the meetings of the former directorate, someone had an idea for solving that problem: they would set up their own small business to hire them all, enabling them to gain the right to return, at least as base-level workers, to the ABC Metalworkers' Union. This is how the May 12 metalworking shop came about. It was named after the founding date of the ABC Metalworkers' Union, May 12, 1959, which coincidentally also marked the starting date of the 1978 Scania strike, the union's first since the 1964 military coup.

Registered and set up in the backyard of metalworker Paulo Dias's house in São Bernardo's Batistini neighborhood, the metalworking shop faced its first obstacle as soon as it opened for business: it needed to raise money to buy raw materials and equipment like saws and compact lathes that would enable them to produce window frames, sink handles, window bars, and gates for gardens and entrances to houses. The good relations that Lula and the other fired directors had with foreign unions solved half of the money problem thanks to a donation from IF Metall, the Swedish metalworkers' union. But the contributions from abroad were not enough to get the business—which hired the entire fired directorate and would remain in operation until 1988—up and running. Someone came up with the idea to go to a longtime friend of the ABC union movement: the singer-songwriter Chico Buarque. Buarque covered the remainder needed for the shop to begin operations. When Buarque's donation appeared in the shop's bank account, Lula called him up to thank him and explained the legal ramifications of his donation. "Chico, now you are a factory boss—you can run for president of FIESP."

17

Clobbered in the polls, Lula sinks into depression and decides to abandon politics. He travels to Cuba, listens to Fidel, and returns to Brazil to win a congressional seat with the most votes in history

On the afternoon of July 19, 1980, two months after his release from prison, Lula found himself in the scalding heat at the airport in Managua, Nicaragua, waiting for the arrival of President Fidel Castro, whose plane would land in a few minutes. It was the first anniversary of the victory of the Sandinista National Liberation Front, which had buried the dictatorship of Anastasio Somoza, heir to a family dynasty that had dominated the country with an iron fist, through torture and pillage, since the 1930s. Lula was standing next to Friar Betto, Nicaraguan foreign minister and warrior priest Miguel d'Escoto and Army General Humberto Ortega Saavedra, thirty-three, the ex-guerrilla and brother of President Daniel Ortega who was now chief of the Sandinista People's Army.

Fidel had left Havana that morning aboard an enormous Soviet-built, four-prop Ilyushin IL-62 airliner, accompanied by a small delegation made up of Commander Manuel Piñeiro Losada, known as "Red Beard," his personal doctor Chommy Barruecos, ten bodyguards, and a journalist who hitched a ride (who happens to be the author of this book). The presence of the discreet Red Beard in the committee was not an accident. Chief of the Department of the Americas for the Central Committee of the Cuban Communist Party, Piñeiro was responsible for shipping weapons, advisors, and resources to the Sandinista Revolution. It was the first time Fidel had ever set foot in Nicaragua, and he had chosen to be there in person for the celebration. Along with its contribution to the Sandinista guerrilla struggle, the Cuban Revolution had plenty of reasons to take part in its neighbors' celebration: it was in Somoza's Nicaragua that the CIA trained some of the mercenaries who had tried and failed to invade Cuba in the disastrous Bay of Pigs affair of April 1961. On that occasion, Somoza had personally come out to send off the mercenary army and to make a special request.

"After you take power, I don't want you to bring me a single penny from Cuba," he said. "All I want is a hair from the beard of Fidel Castro's corpse."

Lula had left Brazil facing charges of breaking the National Security Law for planning the strikes that year, which would later cost him and his arrested colleagues three-and-a-half-year jail sentences. The fact that his case was still before the judge required him to request authorization to leave the country from military judge Nelson da Silva Machado Guimarães, who ordered DOPS to return Lula's passport and issue him an exit visa (during the dictatorship, all Brazilians were required to have an "exit visa" to leave the country). Despite everything, he did not want to lose the privilege of meeting the mythological idol to a generation of young people around the world, the bearded Fidel Castro who dared to install a Communist regime a little more than 100 kilometers from the United States. When the plane landed, Chancellor D'Escoto introduced Lula to Fidel, kicking off a friendship that would last until the death of the Cuban leader in 2016, and whose funeral Lula would attend. That night, after a long conversation about protocol, Fidel invited Lula to visit Cuba. It was a trip that would happen only a few years later and that would end up having a decisive influence on his political destiny.

Returning to Brazil, Lula had a big problem on his hands: his trial in the military court. Although some of the biggest names in the legal profession vied to defend him, including renowned legal scholar Heleno Fragoso, Lula opted to leave things in the hands of Greenhalgh, who was only thirty-two and had little of the professional experience that one would hope for in such a difficult and consequential case. The choice of a rookie, as opposed to top personalities from the field of law, would repeat itself decades later in the Car Wash investigation, when Lula decided to turn over his defense to young Cristiano Zanin and his wife, Valeska Teixeira, daughter of his old friend Roberto Teixeira, rather than to high-profile names who offered to help—among them ex-ministers of the Supreme Court. In both cases, Lula's intuition turned out to be correct.

After the festivities in Managua ended, Lula returned to São Bernardo do Campo and within a few days was already meeting with Petroleum Workers' Union leader Jacó Bittar in the capital of Acre, Rio Branco, for a public rally launching the PT in that state. Afterward, the two traveled 200 kilometers to the town of Brasiléia along with the rubber tapper and environmentalist Chico Mendes, who ended up joining the PT and, nine years later, would be shot to death by cattle ranchers' hired guns. The group arrived at eight o'clock at night in the little town of Brasiléia on the Bolivian border and went directly to a public protest over the assassination, weeks earlier, of Wilson de Souza Pinheiro, president of the town's Rural Workers' Union. The stage hummed with excitement. According to information from the Federal Police, who had undercover agents spread through the crowd, when Lula, Jacó, and Chico Mendes appeared, "approximately thirty people" had already spoken, "some of them extremely agitated and clamouring for justice."

The temperature rose even more when they gave the microphone to Jacó, who said, "Our land will not go to the foreigners. It won't go to the capitalists. Our land belongs to the people, and the people will have to conquer it with sweat, with blood, or whatever the cost may be."

Riled up by the applause, Bittar hit harder. "We know perfectly well that the workers know how to answer the assassination of Wilson de Souza Pinheiro."

When Lula took over the mic to close the rally, he raised the stakes. "The people who murdered Wilson must have eyes here," he said, "so it will be good for them to hear the following message: the Brazilian working class is tired of promises, it's tired of going hungry, it's tired of running, and it's tired of dying."

The public kept on cheering, and Lula continued. It was then that he gave the bosses the "message" that would cause him to be accused of violating the National Security Law for the second time in two months.

"Bosses are no good in São Paulo, they are no good in Brasília, they are no good in Rio de Janeiro, they are no good anywhere in the world," he declared. "The boss just wants the blood, the sweat and the death of the worker . . . But it's time for the jaguar to go to the watering hole!"

To the authorities from the military courts, the time for the jaguar to drink water came the day after the speeches, when the alleged murderer of Wilson Pinheiro, Nilo Sérgio "Nilão" de Oliveira, foreman from a farm in Brasiléia, was ambushed and lynched by thirty men armed with revolvers, scythes, axes, shotguns, and rifles. According to the police, all of the aggressors were affiliated with the town's Rural Workers' Union. Lula, Jacó, and three other speakers from that night were accused of ordering the crime, in violation of the National Security Law. In a complaint filed by the president of the Acre Agriculture Federation, Lula, Jacó, and the other five were accused of making an "apology for crimes of revenge and hatred, and inciting the workers at the rally to subvert the socio-political order and commit violence between the social classes, achieving their criminal intent, which culminated in the death of the farmer Nilo Sérgio de Oliveira."

Months later, the military prosecutor from the Northern region, headquartered in Manaus, filed charges against Lula, Jacó, and the other five, blaming them for the death of Nilão. In response, the National Confederation of Agricultural Workers (CONTAG) hired Heleno Fragoso to defend the accused members of their organization. The task of defending Lula and Jacó was delegated to Greenhalgh, who invited a friend to travel with him to Manaus to watch the trial—José Paulo Sepúlveda Pertence, a 43-year-old lawyer from Brasília who would later become a justice and then president of the Federal Supreme Court.

Greenhalgh's defense argument was like something out of a magical realist story by Gabriel García Márquez. The young lawyer from São Paulo started a thorough, detailed investigation with the workers from Brasiléia in search of an answer to a crucial question: How had they concluded that Nilão was responsible for the execution of Wilson Pinheiro? All of the answers pointed to a local belief held by the farmers, prospectors, and workers in the region, which was summarized by one of the witnesses.

"Doctor, before we buried Wilson Pinheiro, we put a coin under his tongue. We tied up the deceased's face with a cloth so that his mouth couldn't open and the coin couldn't fall out. Everyone here knows that this method never fails. If the guy was murdered, you put a coin under his tongue and tie his mouth shut, and the murderer always returns to the scene of the crime."

Oblivious of the stupefied look on Greenhalgh's face, the rural worker continued with absolute confidence.

"We buried Wilson, everyone left, but we left a lookout hidden in a corner of the cemetery. When no one else was left there, who came and spent a long time looking at the grave? Nilão. He showed up and spent a half hour there in silence, staring at the place where Wilson was buried. We didn't need to see anything else. It was him."

Greenhalgh spent over twelve hours—long into the night—making his defense argument in the Military Auditing Court in Manaus. He argued that Nilão's death was not the result of Lula and Jacó's speeches but of a popular folk belief that everyone there—judges, prosecutors, and the public—knew very well. Since the case had drawn a lot of attention—mainly because Lula was the defendant—there were politicians and celebrities in the audience in solidarity with the PT, like the actress Dina Sfat, who kept Marisa and Lula company as their eyes remained glued on Greenhalgh. He started with a long speech about the relationship between superstition and reality. He spoke of the symbolism of the month of August, black cats, passing under ladders, of crossing fingers, and Friday the 13th—until he reached the subject of the coin under the tongue. Enervated by the heat and physical exhaustion at the end of that interminable oral argument, Greenhalgh went to bed victoriously that night. Lula and Jacó were absolved. The ruling by the Manaus Military Court was a relief to the labor activists and Lula's supporters, but everyone knew there was still a major hurdle before them: the trial of the strike leaders, which was scheduled for February 1981.

As judgment day approached, this time at the Second Army Corps Court in São Paulo, a high-risk move by Greenhalgh forced the military court to show its cards. The trial started on Wednesday, February 25. Five days earlier, on Friday the twentieth, he went to the Army Auditing Court to get passes for the defendants' families to watch the trial. The court was located in a two-story building on Brigadeiro Luis Antônio Street, near the corner with Paulista Avenue, and its gallery barely held forty people. As was commonplace in some public buildings on Fridays during that era, when Greenhalgh arrived that Friday morning, the building was nearly deserted. Greenhalgh went from room to room looking for the clerk responsible for the passes with no luck. Then, while walking past a closed door, he heard a typewriter. He opened the door, walked in, and saw an army sergeant typing on a sheet of paper with the Second Army Corps Auditing Court letterhead. He discretely looked over his shoulder and witnessed a legal barbarity: five days before the trial, the defendants' sentences were already being typed up! All Judge Nelson da Silva Machado Guimarães would have to do would be to read the pre-prepared sentences, regardless of the defense arguments. Not believing what he was seeing, Greenhalgh began to read aloud what was being typed:

> As stipulated in art. 36, clause IIa of Law 6620/78, the defendants are condemned to the following prison sentences: Luiz Inácio da Silva, 3 years and 6 months; Enilson Simões de Moura, 3 years and 6 months; Djalma de Souza Bom, 3 years . . .

Before he could read the whole list of the defendants and their sentences, the sergeant nervously ripped the page out of the typewriter and set it face down on the desk.

"Damn it, doctor," he said. "You aren't going to mention this, right? Doctor, if this goes public, I'll be fucked . . ."

Greenhalgh galloped down the stairs of the building—which, years later, would be transformed into a museum called the Memorial for the Fight for Justice—gathered the defendants and the lawyers Idibal Pivetta, Airton Soares, and Iberê Bandeira de Melo, who were working on the defense team with him, and made a daring proposal: in addition to going public with the revelation, they should boycott the trial as a form of protest, to expose the kangaroo court process the dictatorship had set up to condemn Lula and his union colleagues.

The legal establishment reacted with shock, arguing that the idea was absurd, confrontational, and could result in immediate arrest of all of the defendants for being in contempt of court—even though it was a military dictatorship court. Despite the warnings, Greenhalgh moved forward. In an article published in *Jornal da Tarde*, attorney Hélio Bicudo, who was famous for confronting the death squads, hit Greenhalgh hard. "This is irresponsible," he wrote. "A lawyer had to face the most adversarial situations. This is why he is a lawyer. If he won't do this, who will?"

On trial day, Judge Nelson Guimarães waited for the reglementary deadline and, since neither the defendants nor their lawyers appeared, nominated public defender Paulo Rui de Godói, who asked for an hour to read the judicial records. At six o'clock that night the judge issued a decision convicting everyone in absentia. Exactly as Greenhalgh had denounced to the press days earlier, Lula, Djalma Bom, and Rubens Teodoro de Arruda were each sentenced to three years and six months in prison. Juraci Batista Magalhães, José Maria de Almeida, Manuel Anísio Gomes, Gilson Menezes, and Osmar "Osmarzinho" Mendonça were each sentenced to two and a half years, while Wagner Lino Alves and Nelson Campanholo were sentenced to two years each. The defendants' first appeal was rejected, but, after a lot of back-and-forth between the São Paulo Military Auditing Court and the Superior Military Court in Brasília, all of the sentences were ultimately reversed.

After the federal intervention in the ABC Metalworkers' Union came to a close that year, Lula decided not to run for office. He recommended a relatively unknown for the job, the Ford toolmaker Jair Meneguelli. A lot of people were curious about what Lula would do next. Now that he had created the PT, would he trade union activity for the life of a politician? Friar Betto wrote a letter to Lula, shortly before the election of Meneguelli, asking him what everyone seemed to want know:

> The people are wondering about certain questions: What do you plan to do in politics? Why are you getting into politics? Why did you create a political party? Will you go back to being a simple worker? Do you want to be governor? I think you have an excellent opportunity to give the people your answers on the day that you pass the union presidency to our comrades from ticket 1 (I know they will win).

Those who wondered what Lula would do with his life were left in the dark. The only hint about his future was provided in two sentences lost in the middle of an interview in *O Estado de São Paulo* where he said, "I don't have a project for the future. My destiny is tied to my labor sector."

Without losing sight of setting up the PT across the country, his main focus seemed to be on union organizing. He campaigned for Meneguelli, but the task that took up most of his time was creating a central union federation that would unite manual laborers with other unionized workers in the country, including doctors, teachers, journalists, engineers, and other professions.

In the intervals between trips across Brazil, he worked on broadening the labor movement's international horizons with several international trips. Since he didn't speak any foreign languages, he traveled with University of São Paulo professors Francisco Weffort and José

Álvaro Moisés, the latter of whom had already been nominated as the PT's international relations secretary. These trips always fell under the vigilant eyes of the Military Police authorities, as shown in the following report, laced with cryptic military acronyms, that DOPS director Romeu Tuma sent to the Second Army Corps Intelligence Service, the National Intelligence Service (SNI), the Fourth Regional Aerial Command Center, the São Paulo Navy Command Center, and the Federal Police:

> Complementing message n. 220/DOPS, the following is the travel route of Luiz Inácio da Silva, aka "Lula," José Álvaro Moisés, Francisco V. Fortes, and Jacob Bittar PT PT
>
> Brazil—Rome—Ateh 22.01;
> Bonn—Ateh 28.01;
> Paris—Ateh 31.01;
> Geneva—2 and 3 of February;
> Brussels—04 and 05/February;
> Amsterdam—05, 06, 07 February;
> London—08, 09, 10 February;
>
> The night of the tenth they will go to New York, staying on the 11, 12 and 13 vg, at which point they should return to São Paulo in the evening.
>
> Romeu Tuma
> Pol. Agt. Chief of DOPS

On one of these international trips Lula acquired two new gadgets. He bought a super 8 film camera for the PT (VHS hadn't yet taken off in Brazil) to use in its campaigns to establish party organizations across the country. He also bought a portable decibel meter for the union so its inspectors could come into the factories and measure ambient noise to verify that it complied with legal guidelines. There is still an old campaign film produced with Lula's little camera in the PT's archives department that was filmed in the jungle town of Camata, on the banks of the Tocantins River, 280 kilometers southeast of Belém, Pará.

The creation of a central union federation took a lot more work than he had originally imagined. For the first time since the old General Labor Command (CGT), which had been destroyed by the dictatorship in 1964, someone was trying to unite all of the unions in the country. The need for a central federation was shown by the number of workers who met in the São Paulo coastal city of Praia Grande in August 1981: 5,247 delegates who had been elected by 1,126 different labor unions, from every state in Brazil. Along with the delegates, union leaders came from around the world, including Hans-Jürgen Kruger from West Germany, Jacques Chérèque from France, Luis Carlos Luster from Venezuela, Álvaro Rana from Portugal, Galvão Branco from Angola, and Juan Ponce from Argentina, who was the leader of the Global Solidarity Network. Transporting, lodging, and feeding this crowd for the three-day meeting cost Cr$3 million (around R$276,000 in 2021), funds which were raised through union contributions, car raffles, and donations. A back-of-the-envelope calculation reveals that 12 million workers were represented at the event, which was dubbed the National Conference of the Working Class (CONCLAT).

Despite the exemplary planning, the number of different political currents and factions participating in the event prevented them from reaching an agreement to create a single central federation, with two powerful groups facing off against each other. One of them, led by union activists connected to the PCB, including Santos metalworker Arnaldo Gonçalves, supported a cooperative and centralized institution. The other, led by Lula, fought for a bottom-up, central federation that would be open to all of the different political currents. In the end, contrary to what Lula had planned, CONCLAT gave birth to two union federations. One became the Unified Workers' Central (CUT), which was umbilically connected to the PT. The second became Força Sindical (FS). Jair Meneguelli became the first president of the CUT, and Luiz Antônio de Medeiros, an ex-militant from the PCB who was flirting with so-called "Eurocommunism" and had renounced the USSR, became the first president of FS.

Lula's successive legal victories, the arrival of amnesty—as flawed as it was—and the creation of two new central union federations were all signs that the days of the military dictatorship were numbered. As opposition leader Ulysses Guimarães said, they were now facing a "toothless, vegetarian lion." But the biggest victory toward democratization appeared on the pages of the *Diário Oficial* on January 19, 1982. With the ratification of Law 6978, General Figueiredo announced that free and secret elections for governors, vice governors, mayors, vice mayors, and city councilors would take place on November 15. The last direct elections for governors had taken place sixteen years earlier, in 1965, when the military dictatorship candidates were defeated in some of Brazil's largest states, including Minas Gerais, Santa Catarina, Mato Grosso, and Rio de Janeiro. The only thing that was missing in the struggle to return to real democracy and bury the authoritarian debris of the military dictatorship was a direct election for the presidency of the Republic, which would only take place seven years later, in 1989, one year after the National Constituent Assembly, which established Brazil as a political democracy and ratified the new constitution.

The direct election of state governors was a major step forward. In São Paulo, the Workers' Party put all of its chips on the candidacy of Lula, who was believed to be unbeatable. Since votes were still manually written on paper ballots, the first measure taken by the PT was to change his official name from Luiz Inácio da Silva to Luiz Inácio Lula da Silva—which would prevent ballots that had only the name "Lula" on them from being thrown out. Adding his nickname to his proper name meant that Marisa and their four children's last names all became "Lula da Silva" too. Nevertheless, this wasn't the campaign's only obstacle. The biggest challenge was the total lack of resources compared to the other candidates. Even in its birthplace of São Paulo, the PT lacked local committees or local candidates in 300 of the state's 571 counties. While the competitors traveled to their campaign rallies in chartered planes, Lula was left at the mercy of commercial flight schedules that didn't always meet the needs of the campaign, or else had to travel by car (which ended up happening most of the time). Lula's national fame meant that he frequently had to interrupt his campaign to support other candidates for governor, senator, and congressman in nearly all of Brazil's twenty-six states—always relying on commercial flights.

Everything was improvised. Marisa took a free silk-screening class offered by the São Bernardo do Campo city government and set up a workshop that she ran by herself, in their house, while taking care of three small children. During the campaign, she managed to single-handedly print 22,000 T-shirts with the PT star logo and the names of Lula for governor, lawyer Hélio Bicudo for vice governor, and Jacó Bittar for Senate. Most of Lula's trips around the state—some more than 600 kilometers—were made by car. Lula would sit in the passenger seat of a VW Beetle lent by one of his friends, and, when night fell, a second campaign car that trailed them would turn on its high beams so he could work on his next campaign speech. When there was no event organized at the destination, Lula would stand on the rear bumper of the VW Beetle and, megaphone in hand, ride slowly around the town making speeches while inviting passersby to join the PT.

One example of the dictatorship's authoritarian debris was the Falcão Law, named in homage to its author, Geisel's justice minister Armando Falcão. According to the law, electoral campaign TV commercials were only allowed to show a photo of the candidate while, off camera, an announcer was required to read a telegraph-like, official summary of the candidate's biography. Since the PT's strategy was based on courting votes from the working class, after the brief biography of each candidate, the announcer would say, "a Brazilian just like you." The problem was many of the PT's candidates were former guerrilla resistance fighters who had been jailed by the dictatorship.

Years later, Lula laughed about it. "Our campaign ads sounded like police rap sheets. Our candidates looked like a bunch of escaped convicts. I remember Athos, from Goiás: 'Athos Magno. Hijacked a plane.' And Altino: 'Altino Dantas, son of a general, sentenced to ninety-six years of prison.' And José Genoino was arrested while fighting as a guerrilla in Araguaia. Tortured and sentenced to I don't know how many years in prison.' And at the end of it all a voice would say, 'A Brazilian, just like you.' "

He didn't spare his own commercial from the criticism. "My ad went like this: 'Luiz Inácio Lula da Silva—ex–shoeshine boy, ex-metalworker, ex–union director, ex–political prisoner—a Brazilian just like you!' Nobody wanted to be like me, damn it! The voters wanted to be like Eduardo Suplicy, who was rich, handsome, and had a bachelor's degree in economics and a graduate degree from overseas!" Eduardo Suplicy was a founding member of the PT who later became a senator.

Without money to hire polling agencies, Lula measured his popularity by the number of people who came out to his rallies. Reporters commented that he was drawing larger and larger crowds, mainly in mid-sized and large cities where there were factories, workers, universities, and students. Lula and the PT seemed to have opened a big lead among young people, and his chance of victory was beginning to look plausible. The crowds that packed the squares and auditoriums for Lula's rallies were growing so large that it started to worry his competitors, and they began to play dirty. The kinds of lies that would later become known as "fake news" were spread across the state. They said Lula had become rich as a union leader and that his house in São Bernardo was just a facade to trick fools; he really lived in a mansion in the posh São Paulo neighborhood of Morumbi, they said. The fact that he was seen one weekend in the house of Congressman Airton Soares, in Guarujá, transformed him into the owner of yet another mansion, now on the São Paulo seaside—"in the same condominium as ex-president Jânio [Quadros]," they lied. PT was forced to publish a note of clarification:

> The story of the mansion in Morumbi didn't stick, because Lula lives in Jardim Lavinia, at 273 Maria Azevedo Street. Now they are making up a story about a vacation house in Guarujá. Over the last ten years, the only vacation Lula had was the thirty-one days he spent in jail at DOPS. We challenge the people accusing Lula to show their faces and give the address of this supposed house in Guarujá and show Lula's deed to it.

Despite all of its challenges, the campaign continued to pick up steam and gained important endorsements. From Paris, the Bahian novelist Jorge Amado, Brazil's most popular writer, announced that, if he lived in São Paulo, he would vote for Lula. Stars of the Corinthians soccer team like left-back Wladimir and center-forward Casagrande, golden boot of the São Paulo championship that year, didn't just endorse Lula—they organized a membership campaign for PT.

As election day approached, two episodes gave Lula's the feeling that the election was in the bag. The first was a debate promoted by *Folha de São Paulo* newspaper and Bandeirantes TV network, the only one in which all of the candidates participated: Lula, Senator Franco Montoro (PMDB), ex-president Jânio Quadros (PTB), ex–São Paulo mayor Reynaldo de Barros (PDS), and congressman and former basketball player Roger Ferreira (PDT). A poll released by the respected Gallup

Institute, published in all the newspapers the next day, declared Lula as the overwhelming winner of the debate.

But the event that really made Lula think he would be the next São Paulo governor was a rally on Charles Miller Square in front of Pacaembu Stadium. According to conservative estimates, Lula drew over 100,000 to the square and surrounding streets. The size of the crowd worried Montoro and his supporters who, despite bringing famous musicians like Milton Nascimento and Chico Buarque on stage at campaign rallies, were unable to draw half the crowds that came out to see Lula.

When Lula arrived home the night before the elections, his wife Marisa greeted him with a worried expression. She showed him an early edition of *Folha de São Paulo* that ran the front-page story on the results of a new poll. The huge eight-column headline "Governor Montoro" appear above a photo of the smiling senator and the poll numbers: "Montoro, 44.8 percent, Reynaldo 26.5 percent, Lula 12.2 percent, Jânio 11.7 percent, Rogê Ferreira 1.7 percent." Lula laughed and threw the paper in the air saying, "This bourgeois rag doesn't mean a thing, damn it! I've already won this election!"

When the votes came in the next evening, they showed that Folha's poll really was wrong. Lula didn't end up in third, but in fourth, after Montoro, Reynaldo, and Jânio, beating only last-place finisher Rogê Ferreira, who won less than 1 percent of the vote. Lula felt like the world had collapsed on him.

Four decades later, Lula still remembers the deep depression that set in that night.

"It hurt. It hurt a lot. I became desperate. I lost my way. I was only sure of one thing: I was done with politics. I felt nothing but deep emptiness for a long time. Along with the crushing defeat, the union had a different president. I would wake up in the morning with nothing to do, and it made me feel desperate."

Lula's electoral hangover seemed like it would ever end; in fact, it lasted over two years. In 1985, Lula traveled to a conference hosted by President Fidel Castro in Cuba on poor countries' foreign debt to international financial organizations. Days earlier, the comandante had spoken with Jamil Haddad, substitute senator from Rio de Janeiro for the PSB. He asked about Lula, and the answer was depressing. "Politically, Lula is finished," Haddad said. "He is an odd man out."

Learning that the ex–union leader was in Havana, Fidel met him and told him what Haddad had said. The Cuban president patiently listened to Lula's complaints and his frustration at the humiliating loss.

Once Lula had finished getting it all off of his chest, Castro said, "Listen, Lula: never since humanity invented the vote and invented elections, no worker . . . I repeat, no worker, no member of the working class, in any place in the world . . . has ever gotten a million votes like you did. If you will allow someone older and more experienced than you to give his opinion, listen to what I have to say: you don't have the right to abandon politics. You don't have the right to do this to the working class."

Fidel's words spent months echoing in Lula's mind. One year later, in 1986, he decided to follow the comandante's advice and run for the position of congressman in the elections for Brazil's new National Assembly. Lula was elected with 651,763 votes. At the time, it was more votes than any parliamentary candidate had ever received in the history of Brazil.

Luiz Eduardo Greenhalgh (behind bench with black mustache) defended PT and peasant leaders in the Manaus Military Court against charges of ordering the murder of a farm foreman. Seated in front are the defendants: Acre peasant leaders João Maia da Silva Filho and José Francisco da Silva, Chico Mendes, Lula, and Jacó Bittar. Source: Luiz Eduardo Greenhalgh.

After losing the gubernatorial race, Lula returned to Cuba with Marisa and Greenhalgh and re-encountered Fidel Castro. The Cuban leader had learned that Lula's poor election result had caused him to give up on politics and dedicate himself entirely to the union movement. Source: Luiz Eduardo Greenhalgh.

Epilogue

This book is being published twenty years late, thankfully. When Lula won the elections for president of the Republic in 2002, I looked up his press secretary, my old friend Ricardo Kotscho. My pretentious project idea was inspired by *A Thousand Days*, the intimate look at the interrupted mandate of John Kennedy, written by his friend, consultant, and ghostwriter Arthur M. Schlesinger Jr. I was not exactly a friend, and I had never been a consultant, much less a ghostwriter, to Lula—and I didn't have the talent and experience of Schlesinger. Nevertheless, I dreamed of writing about what was happening behind the scenes during the government of the first working-class president of Brazil. I believed factors in my favor for gaining access for the project included my involvement in the ABC strikes and the fact that I was not a member of the Workers' Party (PT), which would remove the risk of producing a book that might be framed as a puff piece. To the contrary, I had publicly positioned myself against the creation of the Workers' Party, being one of those who believed that it had contributed to rupture in the political front that the Brazilian Democratic Movement (MDB) had put together during the struggle against the dictatorship. In the first round of the 1989 presidential elections, I worked on the campaign and voted for Ulysses Guimarães of the MDB. In the second round, I voted for Lula.[1]

1 The election was won by Fernando Collor (who advocated economic liberalism) with 53.03 percent of the vote, while Lula came second with 46.97 percent.

With his usual good humor, Kotscho told me that I was 185th in the line of journalists who had asked him to do the exact same thing. I gave up on the idea. When Lula was reelected in 2006, I tried again, and this time it was Lula himself who talked me out of doing it. Without the vocation for what ex-president Itamar Franco called living like a "palace bedbug," I only met him three times during his eight years in office. The first was in the Planalto Palace with actress Camila Morgado, in July 2004, for a debate that First Lady Marisa organized after the showing of the film *Olga* for all of the women who worked in the Office of the President. *Olga* was adapted from my book (*Olga*, Companhia de Bolso, 2008) about the Brazilian communist leader Olga Gutmann Benário Prestes, who was deported to Germany and executed in Auschwitz concentration camp. The second time I met Lula was in a year whose precise number escapes me, when I lent my house for Lula, Leonel Brizola, José Dirceu, and Carlos Lupi to secretly meet in to try to sort out a frustrated alliance between the PT and the Democratic Labor Party (PDT). The third time I was with Lula during his presidency was in November 2008, when I interviewed him as a freelancer for the monthly magazine *Nosso Caminho*, which was edited by renowned architect Oscar Niemeyer. With my voice recorder on, and to the shock of his communications minister, Franklin Martins, who accompanied the interview, Lula gave me a national scoop, announcing for the first time that Dilma Rousseff would be PT's candidate for president in 2010.

In July 2011, I was on vacation in Europe with my granddaughter Clarisse when my cell phone rang. It was the journalist Ottoni Fernandes Jr., who had been the executive secretary of the minister of communications under Franklin Martins. Dryly, as always, he cut directly to the point. "Ex-president Lula wants to have coffee with you tomorrow morning. Can you make it?"

I explained that I wasn't in Brazil, but that if it was something really urgent, I could get on a plane that night and arrive in São Paulo the next morning. He told me it wasn't urgent and that, when I got back, he would set up the meeting. Lula had decided that someone should write a book—not exactly a biography, but a story that would cover the period from his debut in politics in 1980, with the creation of the PT, until the moment he transferred the presidential sash to Dilma Rousseff.

Many people believe that Lula only decided that someone should write a book about his political life after he became conscious of his mortality, with the discovery that he had throat cancer. It's not true. Our deal was made in late July. It was only in October, when I met with Kotscho and the journalist Audálio Dantas at a book fair in Maceió, Alagoas, that we learned, on TV, that the former president was hospitalized in Sírio-Libanês Hospital in São Paulo for treatment of the tumor. At that point, I had already recorded several hours of interviews with him. I later recorded a single interview with him during his treatment, which was registered by his official photographer Ricardo Stuckert, with Lula bald and a chemotherapy needle jabbing into his shoulder. The illness, especially because it affected his larynx and, consequently, his speech, pushed our work back from October to July 2012, when I witnessed his triumphant return at a monumental rally in Fortaleza, Ceará. The massive crowd that accompanied, on foot, the open pickup truck that took him from the airport to Ferreira Square in the city's downtown—seven or eight kilometers—chanted a refrain that I had never heard before that reminded me of stories I had read about Getúlio Vargas.

"Dad is back! Dad is back! Dad is back!"

The deal with my editor Luiz Schwarcz went smoothly. Companhia das Letras, which had published nearly all of my books, celebrated the deal with its new partner, the British company Penguin. Lula made no objection when I told him that he wouldn't get an advance reading. The first copy from the printer would be his, but he would receive it simultaneously with thousands of other readers throughout Brazil.

After a short time, I learned that the best place to record interviews with the ex-president was on airplanes. From that point forward, I began to travel with him, mainly on international trips when we could spend hours talking aboard the Learjets that were put at his disposal by the governments, companies, and institutions that had invited him for speeches around the globe. Without telephones, secretaries, or the lines of politicians who would interrupt our work at the Lula Institute, I could enjoy the company of the main character in my book for hours and hours. When space wasn't available on the jets that had been offered to him, I would take a commercial flight, paid for by my publishing company, and meet him and join his caravans in the middle of his trips. On one round trip to New Delhi that had layovers in Johannesburg, Luanda, Maputo, and Addis Ababa, I was able to record twenty-three hours of interviews going out and another twenty-three on the return flight, thanks to the enormous advantage that Lula didn't sleep much on flights. It was these trips that led me to confront then judge Sergio Moro, who accused Lula of faking speeches abroad in exchange for bribes from companies and governments. I was called as a witness because I had traveled to four continents with him. Excluding Oceania, I traveled around the world with Lula.

When Dilma Rousseff's second term started to unravel due to a parliamentary coup, I became a privileged witness to the crisis. I was able to follow closely, at the former president's side, everything that was set up by sectors of the media, the attorney general, the judiciary, and the Federal Police in the operation that would lead to the impeachment of President Dilma Rousseff and the arrest of the central character in this book.

It was then that, with the experience of nearly half a century as a reporter, I realized that I couldn't write the book that I had proposed to my editor and Lula. Publishing what we had originally planned and ignoring the crisis that brought Jair Bolsonaro to power would be a betrayal of what I had learned during my time in the editing rooms of the newspapers and magazines where I spent years of my professional career. I proposed to Lula and Companhia de Letras that the story should incorporate everything that I had had the opportunity to see and hear. The character and my editor agreed, and I proceeded to accompany Lula through everything that happened until after his release.

The book that you have in your hands tells the story of what seemed most relevant to Lula's political life up to November 8, 2019, when the ex-president, by decision of the Federal Supreme Court, had his charges reversed and gained his freedom—and afterward, ex-judge Sergio Moro had his actions during the Car Wash investigation ruled as suspect by the same court. In the second volume, which I started writing today, I will recount what happened behind the scenes in Lula's three electoral losses (one to Fernando Collor and two to Fernando Henrique Cardoso), the successes and the setbacks of his two presidential terms, and everything that I saw and heard during Dilma Rousseff's two terms in office and the crisis into which Brazil sunk in 2013.

Everything written in this book is my exclusive responsibility. But it would be unfair to say that I made *Lula* by myself. It wouldn't have been possible to reach the final page without the help of many people. I have to thank the Cuban and Brazilian doctors who saved me from the bad case of COVID-19 that I caught on the way to the island while accompanying Lula and his team for the start of filming of the movie that American director Oliver Stone was making about the ex-president. Some people deserve special mention, like Alcides Moreno, the journalist and social scientist who managed to organize the mountain of data that I accumulated in ten years of work. A former contributor to my blog, *Nocaute*, which I edited between 2016 and 2020, Moreno didn't just set up an excellent database but read everything I wrote firsthand, giving advice and making essential suggestions on the clarity and precision of this book. It would also be unfair for me not to thank Friar Betto (my "brother in Castro," as my late mother put it). In addition to giving me a substantial interview, Betto regaled me with a package of cassette tapes with dozens and dozens of previously unreleased recordings he made with Lula during the 1980s on three occasions: one on a farm in the São Paulo countryside, one at Cajamar Institute, and one at the musician Chico Buarque de Holanda's house in Rio de Janeiro. I would also like to equally acknowledge the generosity of the journalist Luiza Villaméa, who shared two excellent exclusive interviews she carried out with Federal Police agent Marco Antônio Veronezzi and DOPS agent Armando Panichi Filho, both speaking about Lula. Last but not least, I would like to give a hug of thanks to the couple Nicole Briones and Marco Aurélio "Marcola" Santana Ribeiro for their round-the-clock help from behind the scenes.

In addition to them, I have to thank the biblical patience of my editors, Luiz Schwarz and Otavio Marques de Costa. To my relief, after receiving the manuscript of this book, Luiz said, "The long wait was worth it." It would be unfair to forget the sweet iron hand of Lucila Lombardi, editorial multitasker—without her, this book wouldn't be in your hands right now, beautiful, revised, dated, and signed. I would like to thank all of the people I interviewed for this book about Lula and will do it below. Many of these interviews will only appear in volume 2, for which I undertook another extensive round of interviews, but I made a point of including them here.

Since the termites of COVID ate fragments of my memory, I am probably forgetting a name or two, for which I apologize in advance, but the following people merit my eternal gratitude: Abelardo Blanco, Ademir Medici, Alberto Villas, Alexandre Padilha, Aline Piva, Aloizio Mercadante, André Felix, Anna Dieguez, Angela Ziroldo, Cacá D'Arcadia,

Camilo Vannuchi, Carolina Maria Ruy, Celso Antônio Bandeira de Mello, Cinthia Fanin, Clarisse Cecconi, Cláudia Troiano, Cláudio Guedes, Cláudio Kahns, Dainis Karepovs, Dayton Lopes Rigoto, Didu Motta Carvalho, Edinho Silva, Edmundo Leite, Edson Moura, Eduardo Barbabela, Elenita Barbosa, Elias Reis, Eric Nepomuceno, Érico Melo, Ernesto Abdalla Filho, Evaldo Novelini, Everaldo de Oliveira Andrade, Fábio Pannunzio, Fausto Augusto Junior, Fernando Alves, Fernando Mitre, Firmina Firmeza, Gabriel Manzano Filho, Helena Gasparian, Hélio Bacha, Hélio de Almeida, Iraci Silva Dantas, João Domingos Cavallaro Junior, João Feres Júnior, João Palma Júnior, João Pedro Stédile, João Vieira, José Chrispiniano Junior, José Gaspar Ferraz de Campos, José Silvestre Oliveira, Juca Kfouri, Júlio Moreno, Julius Weinberg, Laerte, Larissa da Silva, Lena Wormans, Luciana Franzolin, Luis Nassif, Marcio Pochmann, Marco Antônio Rodrigues Barbosa, Marco Aurélio Costa, Mariângela Araújo, Marilia Cajaíba, Marina Maluf, Mario Prata, Maximilien Arvelaiz, Milton Cavalo, Misael Melo, Mônica Dallari, Neudicleia de Oliveira, Orlando Brito, Paulo Tadeu Silva D'Arcadia, Percival de Souza, Regina Perpétua Cruz, Ricardo Amaral, Ricardo Carvalho, Ricardo Messias de Azevedo, Ricardo Schwab Schirmer, Ricardo Silva dos Santos, Ricardo Stuckert, Roberto Baggio, Rogério dos Santos, Rosângela da Silva, Rosilene Alves de Souza Guedes, Sérgio Antunes, Sérgio Gomes, Ubiratan de Paula Santos, Vladimir Sacchetta, Weida Zancanar e Xixo Wilson Ramos Filho.

Interviewees:
Ana Estela Haddad, Antônio Cândido de Mello e Souza, Antonio Palocci, Antônio Delfim Netto, Ariovaldo Moreira, Armando Panichi Filho, Armando Salem, Carla Jiménez, César Borges, Clara Ant, Cristiano Zanin, Dilma Rousseff, Edevaldo Medeiros, Eike Batista, Emídio de Souza, Emílio Odebrecht, Eric Hobsbawm, Fábio Lula, Fernando Haddad, Florestan Fernandes Jr., Franklin Martins, Frei Betto, Geraldo Siqueira Filho, Gilberto Carvalho, Gleisi Hoffmann, Guilherme Boulos, Heitor Aquino Ferreira, Hélio Doyle, Jacó Bittar, Jorge Chastallo, José Álvaro Moisés, José Dirceu, José Eduardo Cardozo, José "Friar Chico" Ferreira da Silva, José Paulo de Andrade, Kalil Bittar, Kenarik Boujikian, Luís Carlos Sigmaringa Seixas, Luís Gushiken, Luiz Carlos da Rocha, Luiz Dulci, Luiz Eduardo Greenhalgh, Luiz Inácio Lula da Silva, Manoel Caetano Ferreira Filho, Manuela d'Ávila, Marco Antônio

Veronezzi, Marco Aurélio de Carvalho, Marco Aurélio Garcia, Mariani de Cassia Almas, Marisa Letícia Lula da Silva, Markus Sokol, Michel Temer, Miguel Jorge, Milton Temer, Mino Carta, Moisés Selerges Júnior, Mônica Bergamo, Ottoni Fernandes Júnior, Patrícia Campos Mello, Paulo André, Paulo Bernardo, Paulo Caires, Paulo de Oliveira Campos, Paulo Okamoto, Paulo Villares, Ricardo de Azevedo, Roberto Requião, Rodrigo Tacla Durán, Ronaldo Costa Couto, Sérgio Xavier Ferreira, Valeska Teixeira, Wadih Damous, Valmir Moraes, and Walter Delgatti Neto.

Fernando Morais
Ilhabela, Havana, São Paulo

September 2021

Appendix

An X-ray of the Large Communications Companies' War against Lula and His Party

A study conducted by economists at the Interunion Department of Statistics and Socioeconomic Studies (DIESSE) shows that Brazil suffered more economic damage than direct benefits from the Car Wash investigation, which was led by Judge Sergio Moro, from Curitiba, and the Paraná State Public Prosecutors' Office. According to DIESSE, Brazil lost R$172 billion in investments and 4.4 million workers lost their jobs as a result of paralysis of the large construction companies' public works contracts by order from the judge and the Paraná DA's Office. Civil construction, as we know, is the first and quickest area of the economy to show changes in the labor market. While the Car Wash team's claims that it had reimbursed the national Treasury with around R$4.3 billion confiscated from corrupt businessmen and officials were parroted in the big media outlets, DIESSE showed that during the period investigated by the judge and the ministry, forty times that R$4.3 billion was lost in investments. The sum shows that it blocked the federal government from collecting R$47.4 billion in taxes, half of which would have been collected from the now-unemployed workers' payroll.

But the fact is that the majority of public opinion, according to many studies, seemed inebriated, seeing the judge in Curitiba only as a "champion in the fight against corruption," and not a violator of guarantees and rights that would become blatantly clear with the revelation of his tactics revealed by the *Intercept* and in 7 terabytes of data confiscated by the Federal Police in Operation Spoofing.

An extensive and precise study made exclusively for this book by Manchetômetro (Headline Meter), a Brazilian research institute connected to Rio de Janeiro State University, shows that the lever that for years moved Brazil in favor of Moro's stamping of the word "thief" on Lula's head has names, owners, and public addresses: Brazil's big media companies.

According to a study made at the outset of the Car Wash investigation by the Media Ownership Monitor, an NGO financed by the German government, and by Reporters Without Borders, an NGO headquartered in France with affiliates all over the world, nine of the most influential media outlets in Brazil are owned by the Globo Group (the Marinho family), five are owned by the Bandeirantes Group (Saad family), five by the neo-Pentecostal Universal Kingdom of God Church (owned by "bishop" Edir Macedo), three by the Folha Group (the Frias family), one by the Estado Group (the Mesquita family), and one, *Veja* magazine, owned by Editora Abril (which was owned by the Civita family until it was acquired by Fabio Carvalho, a specialist in and recuperating bankrupt businesses).

This is just a preliminary investigation on the destructive power of the press on public opinion. A thorough, rigorous, and systematic analysis the editorial and political behavior of all of these media outlets during the Car Wash period would demand an effort that would possibly confuse the reader, since there are no terms of statistical comparison, for example, between Globo Group's *Jornal Nacional* TV news program, which averages a 24.7 point audience share, and the main news program on TV Bandeirantes, which averages about 2.5 points according to studies done by Kantar/Ibope (the media research division of the Ibope group that was acquired by the british company Kantar).

Political scientist João Feres Júnior, who holds a PhD from City University of New York and is coordinator of Manchetômetro—a research organization registered with Brazil's National Council of Scientific and Technological Development (CNPQ)—decided to focus his research for this brief study on the audience champions, *Jornal Nacional*, which reaches an average audience of 50 million—around 25 percent of the Brazilian population—*Veja* magazine, which at the time had 1.2 million readers, and the three largest and most influential daily newspapers in the country, *Folha de São Paulo*, *Estado de São Paulo*, and *O Globo* (which, like *Jornal Nacional*, belongs to the Marinho family).

The three newspapers that were analyzed published, on average, more than one daily negative headline about Lula during the period studied. In March 2016, there were 33 negative headlines in a total of 44 publications. In other moments, during the peak months of May and September 2017, the proportion of negative articles cooled down, with 20, compared to 16 neutral articles and 0 favorable to Lula. In April 2018, when the campaign against Lula seemed to pick up, Manchetômetro registered 29 negative headlines against the ex-president, 4 neutral, and 0 favorable.

Figure 1. Behavior of the sum total of articles from three newspapers (*Folha*, *Estado*, *O Globo*) and *Jornal Nacional* from January 2014 to March 2021

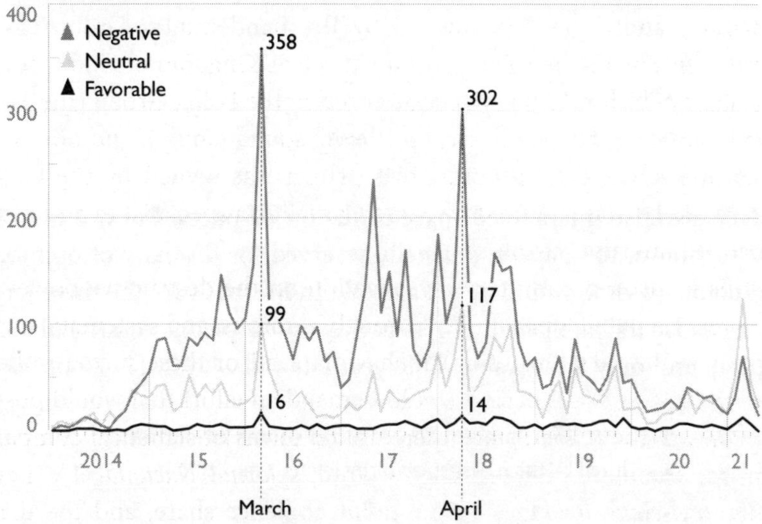

The victory of Bolsonaro in the 2018 elections, contrary to what one might suspect, did not reduce the negative coverage of Lula in the three newspapers, which continued their shocking campaign. In November, the ex-president was the object of 9 openly hostile editorials that referred to him as "the defendant," now that he was no longer a candidate. The rate of negative coverage wasn't much different from the average from 2015–18, a period in which Lula was the target of an average of 30 unfavorable editorials per month—one hammering per day. In peak moments, this average rose to 2 hostile editorials per day. During the three years preceding the 2018 presidential elections, of 2,173 editorials published about Lula in *Folha*, *Globo*, and *Estadão*, only 28 could be classified as positive.

Figure 2. Editorials about Lula in the three main Brazilian daily newspapers

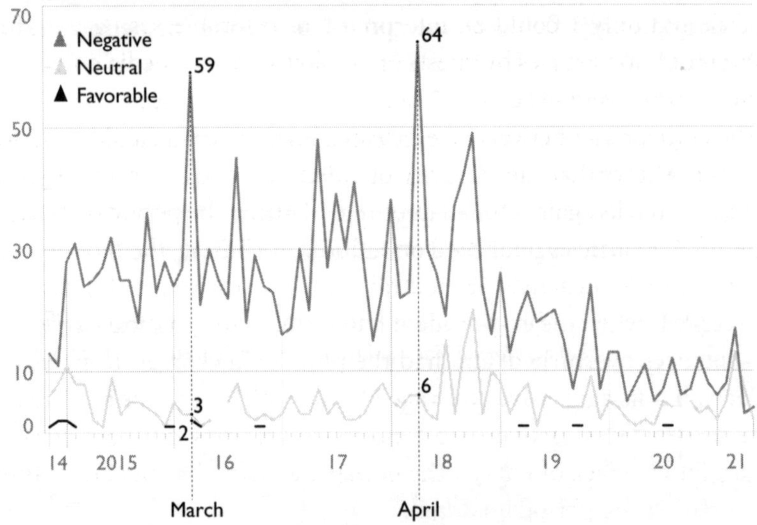

Lula also had guaranteed space in the op-ed pages. But not even in that section of the papers, normally reserved for diversity of opinions and points of view, would he get a break. In March 2016, the three largest newspapers published 114 negative op-ed pieces about Lula, 23 neutral, and only 9 favorable. One year later, in May 2017, 76 opinion

Figure 3. Total number of op-ed pieces written by journalists hired by the newspapers or by invited guest authors

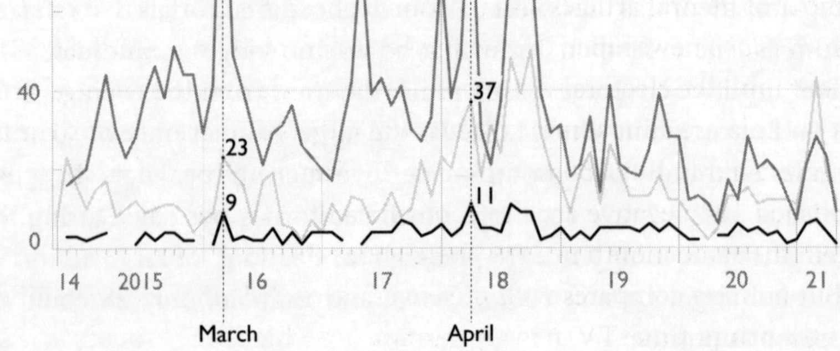

pieces by guest columnists or staff writers massacred Lula, 12 were neutral, and only 1 could be interpreted as favorable. Using the same criteria (opinion articles by guests or employees of the media outlets), in April 2018, 97 were negative, 37 neutral, and 11 favorable.

The comparison between the newspapers in terms of Lula's political treatment shows that the intensity of *Folha*'s coverage was a little lower during its attacks against the ex-president. During the period of its highest number of articles published on Lula, in April 2018, the month of his arrest, it ran 68 negative, 38 neutral, and 13 positive articles. Only in March 2021, when the ex-president had restored his political rights, had his sentences overturned, and had the remaining charges dropped, did *Folha* soften its aggressive coverage of Lula with 72 articles of which 55 were neutral, 11 negative, and 6 positive. This was the least negative month for coverage of Lula by the newspaper owned by the Frias family during the entire period analyzed.

Of the three big national daily papers, *Estadão* was, by far, Lula's most implacable executioner. In it, the number of negative articles was invariably much higher than the neutral ones, and there were almost no favorable articles about Lula whatsoever. Furthermore, during the first month of Dilma Rousseff's second term in office, the paper published 50 negative articles about her. The most egregious example of this endless onslaught of negative coverage would be made by *Veja* magazine, the day before second-round election of 2014, which accused Dilma and Lula of being the heads of a corruption scheme in Petrobras—baptized in the media as the Petrolão. From that moment until Bolsonaro's election, *Estadão* depicted Lula through a growing trajectory of negative coverage. In March 2016, the newspaper owned by the Mesquita family ran 66 negative articles; in May 2017 the number rose to 81. In April 2018, it reached a high of 88, as always accompanied by an irrelevant number of neutral articles and 0 positive ones.

In *O Globo* newspaper, during the period from Dilma's second-round victory until the electoral victory of Bolsonaro, favorable or neutral articles on Lula are almost nonexistent, while the number of negative articles averaged around 50 per month. In March 2016, the daily paper published 100 negative articles about Lula, in May 2017 there were 86, and in the same month in 2018 there were 68.

But nothing compares with the coverage on *Jornal Nacional*, Globo's nightly prime-time TV news program, in which one would at least expect some kind of editorial balance because, according to Brazil's media laws, it is a public concession. During the period analyzed by the team from Manchetômetro, TV Globo's audience saw only 21 positive mentions of Lula, against 705 negative and 403 neutral. In all, *Jornal Nacional* spent 163,529 seconds on negative coverage of Lula during the seven-year period studied. This represents over forty-five hours, or nearly two full days if these stories had run nonstop and consecutively. The sum of all of the favorable coverage, on the other hand, was a derisory 3,374 seconds—less than one hour total.

Figure 4. *Jornal Nacional* coverage of Lula

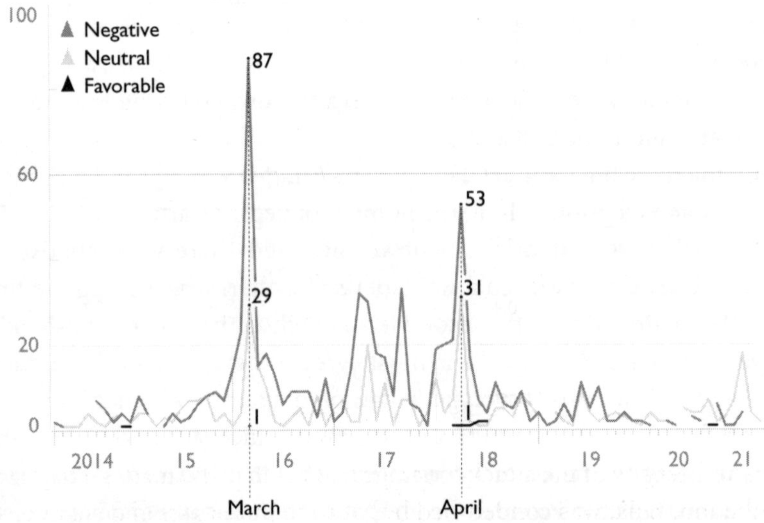

Analysis of coverage in March 2016 on *Jornal Nacional* shows that half of the total airtime that month was dedicated to negative stories about Lula. During the peaks of May and September 2017, the stories were exclusively negative, with 0 being positive.

The methodology and evaluation criteria used in the academic research on media coverage in Brazil and abroad aim to answer the following question: Does the text in question express any position related to the subject or persons mentioned? The portrayal is divided into four categories: positive, negative, neutral, and ambivalent. In April 2018, the month in which Moro ordered Lula's arrest, there was another peak of negative news, now accompanied by an even smaller number of neutral stories. In September 2017, the total number of negative stories on Lula took up 11,769 seconds of airtime, practically ten times more than the neutral stories. If they are summed up, the negative stories on Lula on *Jornal Nacional* that month would be the equivalent of seven straight news programs of one hour each, without commercials. It is as if *Jornal Nacional* viewers spent an entire week that month only watching negative news stories about the former president.

Figure 5. Coverage of Lula on *Jornal Nacional* by amount of airtime

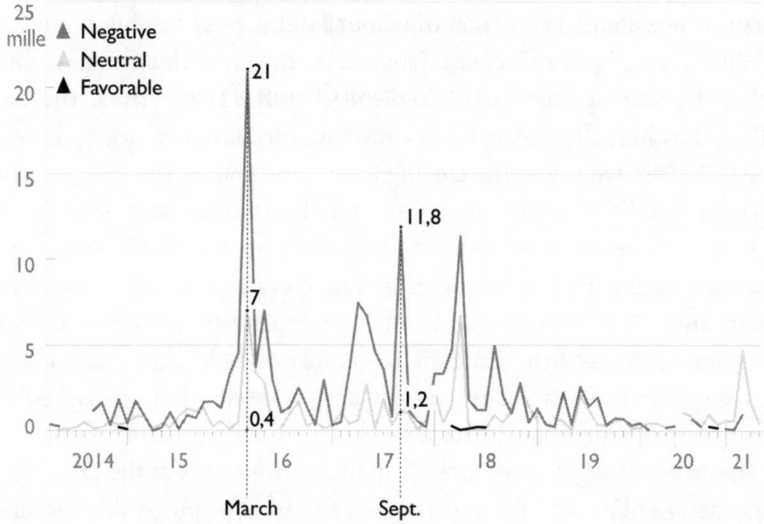

The intensity of the attack coverage had results. The main target of the operation, Lula, was condemned by Moro to nine years and six months in prison on charges that he had received a triplex apartment in the beachside town of Guarujá, on the São Paulo coast, in exchange for favors for OAS, the engineering company that built the building. There was more: Lula was also accused of being the "phantom owner" of a vacation property in Atibaia (a property that belongs to Fernando Bittar, the son of one of Lula's best friends and coworkers from the PT and CUT and who is an important character in this book—Petroleum Workers' Union leader Jacó Bittar).

The Car Wash task force claimed that the dozens of speeches that Lula made around the world were facades to hide bribes paid by beneficiaries of favors from his two terms in office. During the production of this book, the author had the opportunity to watch and record speeches made by the ex-president in North America, Asia, Africa, and Europe. Judge Moro and the prosecutors from Curitiba secretly used information supplied by the US Department of Justice—proven to have come from the FBI and suspected to have been supplemented by the CIA—to build its charges against Lula. Since no reference to this foreign cooperation appears in any of the charges against Lula, Moro and his prosecutors committed a crime under Brazilian law. The ruling against Lula came with an additional sentence—perhaps the most important—because along with depriving him of his personal freedom, it removed the clear favorite from the 2018 Brazilian presidential race, according to all of the public opinion polls.

With a vast base of accumulated data, the investigative task force fueled the war against Lula. Cold and bereft of adjectives, the data collected by Manchetômetro dives into the entrails of the targeted media outlets. Just in what was the closing argument against the charges from Curitiba about the apartment in Guarujá, the Atibaia vacation property, and the "phantom speeches," defense lawyers Cristiano Zanin and Valeska Martins filed—and therefore made available to all of the newspapers and TV networks—a total of 2,960 typewritten pages. Tirelessly, the couple provoked the Curitiba DA's office to hold eighty-eight hearings and pressured the court to hear 228 witnesses that unmasked the farce set up in Curitiba—in vain.

The criminal, legal mess cooked up by Moro, sectors of the DA's office, the Federal Police, and the courts could not have acquired the relevance that it gained without the collusion of the majority of the big media outlets toward a single goal: to end Lula's political career and ostracize him and his entire political party, the PT, from public life, with the infamy of being corrupt. The best example of this conclusion is shown in the final national election poll produced in 2018 prior to Moro's ruling's suspension of Lula's candidacy for the presidency. Held by the Datafolha polling agency, which was hired for the purpose by Globo TV and *Folha de São Paulo* newspaper, from behind bars and barred from speaking to the press, Lula still appeared in the lead, with 39 percent of voter intention, followed by Jair Bolsonaro (PSL, 19 percent), Marina Silva (Rede, 8 percent), Geraldo Alckmin (PSDB, 6 percent), Ciro Gomes (PDT, 5 percent), Alvaro Dias (Podemos, 3 percent), João Amoêdo (Novo, 2 percent), Henrique Meirelles (MDB, 1 percent), Cabo Daciolo (Patriota, 1 percent), Vera Lúcia (PSTU, 1 percent), João Goulart Filho (PPL, 0 percent), and José Eymael (DC, 0 percent). Blank ballots, null votes, "none of the above," and "I don't know" totaled 14 percent. According to the poll, Lula still had more voter support than the total for Bolsonaro, Marina, Alckmin, and Gomes combined. If he had not been in jail and barred from campaigning, everything indicated that Lula would have become the next president of Brazil.

Manchetômetro's analysis of the behavior of Brazil's five most important media outlets during the Car Wash period (2014–21) reveals amazing numbers.

Figure 6. Nearly half of the total coverage of Lula appeared in stories that also mentioned the Car Wash investigation. There are nearly no favorable stories about him, and the proportionately low number of neutral stories remains constant throughout the whole period.

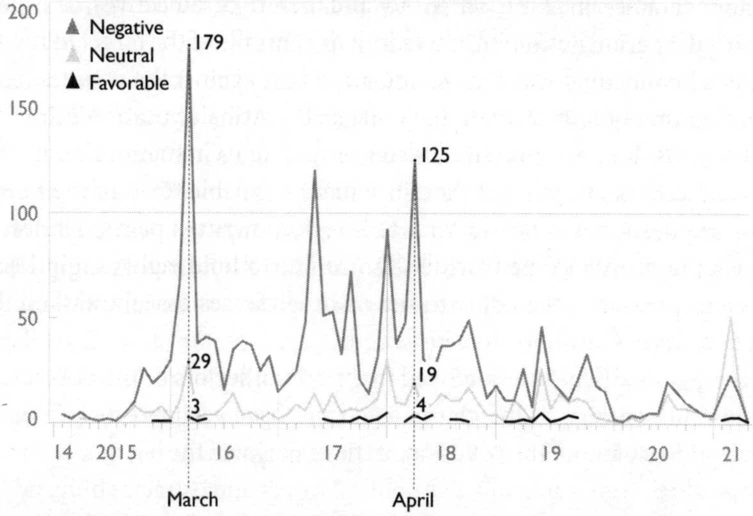

In Brazil's three largest daily newspapers plus *Jornal Nacional*—which averaged around 50 million viewers per night—the peak of the frontal attacks against Lula occurred in five key moments between 2016 and 2021 and culminated with coverage of his arrests and release. In the most scandalously negative moments against the ex-president, the intensity of negative stories exploded. On May 10, 2017, for example, when Lula was personally interrogated by Moro in Curitiba, there were 117 negative articles published in the three newspapers, with only 1 positive and 4 neutral.

Systematic observation shows that during all of the days, months, and years of coverage from these information outlets, the number of negative stories about Lula is far higher than that of neutral or positive stories. This changed in the beginning of 2021, when the neutral stories surpassed the negatives—positive stories at this time were still practically nonexistent. This period coincided with the end of Operation Car Wash, when the Supreme Court reversed Lula's convictions and threw out the remaining charges, restoring his right to run for president and accepting accusations of seven cases of suspicion of bias against former judge Sergio Moro.

On the covers and in the articles in *Veja* magazine, the intensity and the imbalance of the persecution of Lula was equally brutal. During the seven years analyzed, which correspond with the period between April 2014 and April 2021, it ran 87 feature articles about Lula, with 82 negative, 5 neutral, and only 1 positive—ironically, the article that announced Lula's return to electoral politics in 2021, when his political rights were reestablished. During the period examined, the magazine came out with 357 issues, practically all containing negative mentions of Lula. The ex-president's name appeared on one out of every four magazine covers of these editions. In other words, *Veja* demonized Lula in nearly all of its publications.

In 48 covers analyzed, although Lula's image doesn't always appear, there are headlines referring to articles about him inside the edition—among these, only 1 is positive. The communication strategy adopted by the magazine was to shock, as much the readers as people walking by the newsstands, and, for this reason, the art director used all available resources—digitally modified photos, frightening headlines, and slanderous illustrations. If all of the articles were run in sequence, the massacre would last for an entire year's worth of magazines.

Figure 7. Lula on the cover of *Veja*

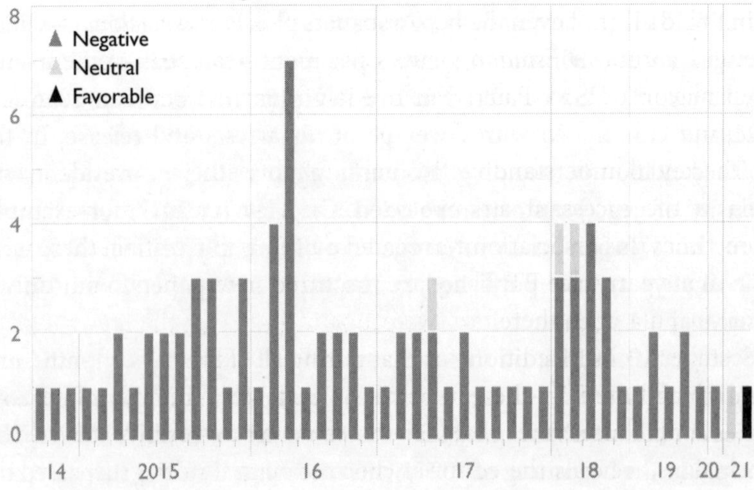

Of the *Veja* cover stories analyzed by Manchetômetro, 35 are negative and have Lula's image in a central position. Seven use smaller photos of him, generally at the top of the cover—in what journalists refer to as a "slash." Of the 35, only 2 were categorized as neutral in the study. One from 2021 is entitled "Game Change," and below in, a subheadline, it says, "In an Attempt to Save Sergio Moro, Minister Edson Fachin Resuscitates Lula, Implodes Car Wash, and Increases Polarization between the PT Leader and Bolsonaro." It is an example of neutral coding, seeing that the implosion of the investigation—in the optics of the magazine—is something negative, as is the polarization between Lula and Bolsonaro.

Another example of a neutral cover page is on issue 2529, from May 10, 2017. The cover shows Lula and Moro stylized as if on a poster for Mexican Lucha Libre wrestling with the words, "The first face-to-face meeting: Moro x Lula." Since there is no clear negative allusion to the PT leader, the researchers on the project classified the headline as neutral. But the fact that the magazine portrayed the judge and the defendant in combat confirms and strengthens Lula's defense team's argument that the judge acted like an adversary, not as a neutral party in the trial.

With this data, we can understand that *Veja* exemplified the campaign of political persecution practiced by the big media. Although he hadn't held political office since 2010, Lula continued to appear regularly on the covers and inner pages of the magazine—something that had never happened in the history of the magazine, which was founded in 1968. It is possible that not even the notorious campaigns against then-president Getúlio Vargas in *Estadão*, or its campaigns against ex-governor and then-mayor of São Paulo Paulo Maluf reached the same level of intensity.

The key to understanding this onslaught of negative coverage against Lula is the incessant attempt to connect his image to corruption. Sometimes this association was made indirectly, through the demonization of his party, the PT. There are magazine covers that do not directly refer to Lula and, therefore, were not included in the study. On the December 10, 2014, edition, for example, the headline, "Car Wash investigation and the PT—the government's party has a lot to explain about the scandal after the charges of receiving bribes during election campaigns," reveals the editorial contortionism to drag the party into the focus of the charges. The editors hid the fact that the political party with the most corruption charges against it in the investigation was the Progressive Party (PP, then led by Piauí senator Ciro Nogueira), which had thirty-three elected official under investigation, including the father-son pair of lawmakers Benedito and Arthur Lira—the latter going on to become president of Congress during the last two years of the Bolsonaro administration. In other moments, the negative image of the PT was associated with direct references to Lula, in texts or images like "10 Years since the Mensalão Scandal," "PT at 35: Species in Faced with Extinction?" and "The Drifting Left."

One selection made by the research team is made up of covers whose only direct reference is to Lula, in which the headlines are comprised exclusively of alarming news that damages his image, such as "Special—Lula and the Law" or "Special Edition—Guilty." In many of these, his face is caricatured in a teratological way, or with graphically produced images of Lula dressed in a 1930s-style striped prisoner outfit, published months before Lula's trial and conviction.

Figure 8. Articles on Lula in *Veja* magazine

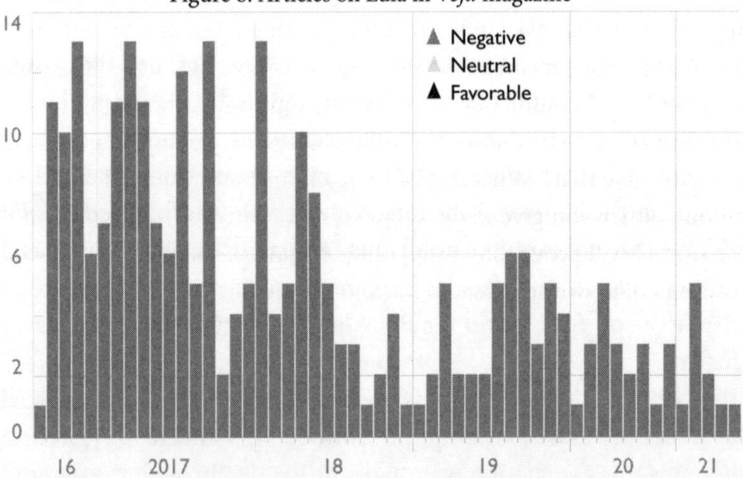

In *Veja*, the opposition to Lula was unbridled and endless, for example in issues in which the ex-president was portrayed in a grotesque and disfigured manner, such as in "The Ruin of PT" and "The Desperation of the Viper." But no cover is as egregious as that of issue 2496, from September 21, 2016, which scandalously plagiarized from a *Newsweek*

cover that depicted the death of Muammar al-Gaddafi, who was lynched and impaled in front of hundreds of cameras. According to the analysts from Manchetômetro, *Veja* attempted to compare Lula with the 1930s outlaw Lampião, who was decapitated by the Bahian military police, who then photographed his head and exposed it to the public for years. Manchetômetro calls attention to the detail that Lula's cranium, on the cover, appears flattened in a way to make him look more like Lampião and adds to the image a fluid running down his face as an "artistic touch," reminiscent of the blood that dripped down the neck of Virgulino Ferreira "Lampião" da Silva's decapitated head in an iconic photograph from the 1930s. In the history of *Veja* weekly news magazine, Lula is the subject most written about.

In a long interview with the journalists Gilberto Maringoni, Juca Kfouri, and Maria Inês Nassif, which was later organized in book form as *A verdade vencera* (The truth will prevail) by Boitempo publishing company, Lula explained how he dealt with the constant attacks:

> This is how they paralyze a government: the rumors start on Thursday. On Friday, things start coming out on the internet, on Saturday, it appears on *Jornal Nacional*, on Sunday it enters the print media and, that night it appears on *Fantástico* (Globo TVs weekly news magazine program) . . . I couldn't take any more of my aides coming in to say, "You are going to be on the cover like this, you are going to appear on the cover like that." What did I decide to do? I told them, "From here on out, either you give me good news or I don't want to know about the story. I will prove that it is possible to govern this country without reading *Folha*, without reading *Estadão*, *Veja* or *O Globo*.

Index

#Nothim (#EleNão), 83
2014 World Encounter of Popular Movements, 22

A Verdade Vencera (book), 289
ABC Metalworkers' Union, 2, 16, 117, 121–2, 163, 172–3, 198, 200, 221, 251, 259
ABC region, São Paulo, 32, 41, 87–8, 105, 109–10, 112, 123, 150, 164, 199, 209
Abi-Ackel, Ibrahim, 110, 127
Abramo, Fúlvio, 234
Abramo, Lélia, 125, 231, 236
Abramo, Perseu, 236
Abreu, Hugo, 193–4
Ação Popular, 236
"Acorda, Maria Bonita," 215
Acre, 255–7, 267
AFL-CIO, 54
Afonso, Almino, 225–6, 228, 230, 234
Afonso, José, 64–5, 229
Agência Pública, 98
Alagoas, 271
Alanic, Jackson Rimac Rosales, 48
Alcione, 110, 247
Alckmin, Geraldo, 9, 66, 84, 284
Alencar, José Almino de, 229
Allende, Salvador, 228
Almada, Gerson, 51
Almeida Prado, Décio de, 125
Almeida, José Maria de, 259
Álvarez, Pepe, 54
Alvez, Wagner Lino, 206, 259
Alzugaray, Domingo, 191
Amado, Jorge, 264
Amaral, Ricardo, 50, 274
amnesty, 205, 212–13, 224, 226–8, 230, 239, 261
Amorim, Celso, 32
Amorina, Henos "Saúva," 234
Andrade, Antônio Carlos Lafayette de, 160
Andrade, Antônio de, 164
Andrade, Joaquim "Joaquinzão" dos Santos, 173, 231–2

Andrade, José Paulo de, 115–16, 274
Andrade, Oswald de, 117
André, Paulo, 5, 275
Angola, 261
Angra dos Reis (nuclear project), 201
Ant, Clara, 5, 271
Antunes, Otávio, 50
April Package, 213
Arafat, Yasser, 159
ARENA (Aliança Renovadora Nacional), 79, 199, 213–16, 220, 224, 239
Argentina, 28, 54, 77, 228, 261
Aritana, Yawalapiti, 193
Army Intelligence Center (CIE), 118
Arns, Cardinal Paulo Evaristo, 120, 122, 192, 238, 244
Arraes, Miguel, 150, 228–9, 243
Arroyo, Angelo, 196
Arruda, Gerson, 90
Arruda, Renata, 90
Arruda, Rubens Teodoro de, 190, 237, 258
Assad, Adi, 51
Assis, Aldimar de, 21
Associação Juízes para a Democracia (AJD), 21
Atibaia (São Paulo), 20, 222, 283–4
Autran, Paulo, 125
Azevedo, Ramos de, 117
Azevedo, Renaldo, 97
Azevedo, Ricardo Messias de, 7, 73, 274, 275

Baggio, Roberto, 89, 100, 274
Bahia, 67–8, 80, 155, 225, 232–3, 264, 289
Banco do Brasil, 38, 51, 125
Bandeirantes TV network, 35, 97, 264
Bannon, Steve, 80–2
Barbosa, Adoniran, 110, 247
Barbosa, Andreia, 9
Bardella, Cláudio, 205, 242
Barelli, Walter, 172, 182, 185
Barros, Ademar de, 177
Barros, Reynaldo de, 264
Barruecos, Chommy, 253
Basic Ecclesial Communities, 164, 207, 220, 234, 238
Batista, Expedito Soares, 237
Belchior, 223
Belgium, 82, 208, 242
Benario, Olga, 53
Bendine, Aldemir, 51
Benevides, Maria Victoria, 125, 236
Bergamo, Mônica, 91–5, 275
Bernardino, Dom Angélico, 24, 186
Betto, Friar, 32, 105, 107, 112, 116, 225, 237, 239, 245, 253, 259, 273
Bettoni, Carlos Alberto, 6
Biavaschi, Magda, 21
Bicudo, Hélio, 125, 258, 263
Biolcatti, Antenor, 167, 181–2
bionic senators, 213
Bittar, Jacó, 206, 234, 255, 260, 263, 267, 274, 283
Blefari, Luis, 113
BNDES (Brazilian Development Bank), 38
Bocklet, Paul, 120
Bolivia, 16, 22, 255
Bolsa Familia, 36
Bolsonaro, Carlos, 83
Bolsonaro, Eduardo, 90

Bolsonaro, Jair, 49, 59, 66–7, 92, 272, 284
Bom, Djalma, 212, 223, 258
Bosco, João, 110, 223, 247
Bosi, Alfredo, 125
Boujikian, Kenarik, 21, 274
Boulos, Guilherme, 8–9, 11, 25, 32, 38, 40, 60, 274
Braga, Cicero, 125
Branco, Galvão, 261
Brandt, Willy, 229
Brant, Fernando, 239
Brant, Vinicius Caldeira, 214, 236
Brasiléia (Acre), 255–6
Brasília, 5, 30, 98, 107, 111, 118, 127, 172, 189, 194–5, 200, 207, 218–19, 221, 227, 231, 240, 245, 247–8, 255–6, 259
Brastemp, 204–5, 220
Brazilian Anti-Communist Alliance (AAB), 214
Brazilian Committee for Amnesty (CBA), 212–13
Brazilian Communist Party (PCB), 55, 106, 123, 168–71, 182, 185, 188, 190–1, 194, 196, 201, 225, 227, 234, 261
Brazilian Constitution, 123, 213, 262
Brazilian Democratic Movement Party (PMDB), 264
Brazilian Development Bank (BNDES), 38
Brazilian First Capital Command (PCC), 51
Brazilian miracle, 172, 201
Brazilian Order of Lawyers (OAB), 91
Brazilian Social Democracy Party (PSDB), 9, 27, 66, 84, 284
Bresser-Pereira, Luiz Carlos, 66–7, 125
Briones, Nicole, 85, 100, 273
Britto, Cezar, 91
Brizola, Leonel, 150, 228, 231, 242, 251
Buarque, Chico, 67, 110, 216, 252, 265, 273
Burrou, Sharan, 54
Buzzfeed, 98

Caetano, Manoel, 23, 55–6, 65, 69, 87, 90, 100, 274
Caetés (Pernambuco), 56, 129–30, 150
Caires, Paulo, 41, 275
Calheiros, Waldir, 238
Câmara, Bishop Hélder, 238
Cambridge Analytica, 81
Campanella, Domingos, 189
Campanholo, Nelson, 167, 181, 245, 259
Campo Grande (Mato Grosso do Sul), 49
Cámpora, Hector, 28
Campos, Augusto de, 125
Campos, Haroldo de, 125
Cândido, Antônio, 125, 231, 235–6, 274
Capibaribe River, 87, 167
Capital (Marx), 214
Cárdenas, Cuauhtémoc, 54
Cardoso, Fernando Henrique, 66, 125, 208, 214–16, 221, 226, 234, 242, 272
Cardozo, José Eduardo, 17, 20, 274
Carnation Revolution, 64, 229
Carone, Edgard, 125

Carta, Luis, 191
Carta, Mino, 176, 191, 242, 248, 275
CartaCapital (magazine), 248
Carter, Jimmy, 228
Carter, Rosalynn, 213
Carvalheira, Marcelo, 238
Carvalho Filho, Luís Francisco, 91
Carvalho, Apolônio de, 231, 236
Carvalho, Beth, 223
Carvalho, Fabio, 278
Carvalho, Flávio de, 117
Carvalho, Gilberto, 32, 112, 274
Carvalho, Herbert, 124
Carvalho, Marco Aurélio de, 21, 275
Casadei, Waldemar, 232
Casagrande, Walter, 264
Casaldáliga, Pedro, 238
Castro, Fidel, 65, 253–4, 265, 267
Catholic Church, 105, 107, 111–12, 117, 164, 174, 206–7, 233–4, 239–40, 244
Cavignato, Osvaldo, 189–90
Ceará, 5, 45, 68, 96, 271
CEBRAP (Brazilian Center of Analysis and Planning), 214, 216
Celebration of the Word, 31–2
Cenimar (Navy Intelligence Center), 107–8, 111, 126
CGT (General Labor Command), 261
Chastalo Filho, Jorge, 51, 56–7, 62, 65, 87, 94, 99–100
Chaui, Marilena, 236
Chedid, Nabi Abi, 242
Chérèque, Jacques, 261
Chile, 89, 228
Chinese Communist Party, 69
Chomsky, Noam, 54
Chrispiniano, José, 50, 75, 100, 274
CIA, 118, 196, 254, 284
CIE (Army Intelligence Center), 118
Civita family, 200, 278
Clean Slate Law, 63
Clinton, Hillary, 80, 82
Coelho, Sebastião de Paula, 186
Cohen, Laurence, 54
Collares, Alceu, 233
Collor de Mello, Fernando, 269, 272
Colombia, 54
Columbia storage and logistics company, 138
Comparato, Fábio Konder, 125
Communist Party of Brazil (PC do B), 32, 70, 123, 196, 225
Congressional Human Rights Commission, 59
Cordeiroi, Miriam, 106
Corinthians (football team), 67, 150, 218, 246, 264
Correia, Rafael, 22
corruption, 3, 51, 95–6, 149, 277, 281, 287–8
Costa e Silva, Artur da, 160, 187, 218, 227
Costa, Gal, 110, 247
Costa, Rodrigo, 43–4, 47
Costa, Rui, 85
Costa, Tito, 218
Council of Financial Activities (COAF), 88–9
Couto e Silva, Golbery do, 118, 191, 194–5, 217, 230, 237, 240–1, 245, 248
Crimmins, John Hugh, 200
Crusoé (magazine), 92
Cruz, Newton, 107

Cuba, 60, 63, 82, 137, 253–4, 265–7, 272
Cuban Revolution, 253
Curitiba, 1, 3, 5, 19, 23, 29, 36, 40, 42, 45, 47–51, 53–6, 58–9, 61–2, 65, 67–9, 72, 76, 85–7, 89–90, 92, 96–8, 103, 165, 277, 284–5
Cursillo movement, 174
CUT (Unified Workers Central), 10, 30, 32, 58, 205, 261, 283
Czarnobay, Lisélia, 5

D'Alema, Massimo, 54
Dallagnol, Deltan, 18, 94–6, 100
Dallari, Dalmo, 117, 123, 126, 238
Damous, Wadih, 12–13, 17, 21, 24, 33, 45, 61–2, 99, 275
Dantas, Audálio, 192, 271
Datafolha, 66, 71, 79, 284
d'Ávila, Manuela, 32, 38, 40, 70, 80, 96, 274
death squads, 111, 258
Delfim Netto, Antonio, 172–3, 185, 204, 242, 274
Delgatti Neto, Walter, 95, 275
Delgatti, Otilia, 95
Demarchi, Walter, 199
Demaria, Emilio Bonfante, 170–1
Democratic Labor Party (PDT), 5, 66, 96, 230, 264, 270, 284
DEOPS, 127
Der Spiegel (magazine), 165
d'Escoto, Miguel, 253
Diadema (São Paulo), 6, 105, 134, 181, 211
Diário da Noite (newspaper), 149
Diário do Grande ABC (newspaper), 159
Diário Oficial, 227
Diário Popular (newspaper), 150
Dias, Erasmo, 120
Dias, José Carlos, 106, 123, 125–6, 238
Dias, Paulo, 251
Dias, Wellington, 17
DIESSE (Interunion Department of Statistics and Socioeconomic Studies), 170, 172–3, 183, 185, 277
Dilermando, José "Ratinho," 109
Dirceu, José, 270, 274
Diretas Já, 83
DOI-CODI, 115, 118, 126–7, 181, 185–91, 194–6, 205, 207
Dominguinhos, 110, 223
DOPS (Department of Political and Social Order), 108, 116, 118, 123–5, 127, 170, 187–90, 212, 226, 236–41, 246, 249–51, 254, 260, 274, 283
Doria, João, 27, 68
Doyle, Hélio, 206, 274
Drummond, João Batista Franco, 196
Duarte, Edgard de Aquino, 238
Duhalde, Eduardo, 54
Dumont, Alberto Santos, 152
Duque, Renato, 51
Dutra, Olívio, 206, 234

Ecuador, 22
Editora Abril, 200, 278
El País (newspaper), 91–2, 94–5, 97
Elbrick, Charles Burke, 226
Eldorado Radio, 244
Engevix, 51
England, 183–215
Escobar, Ruth, 125

Esquivel, Adolfo Pérez, 54
Estado de São Paulo (newspaper), 116, 121, 123, 259, 278
Estado Group, 278
Estado Novo, 229
Europe, 64, 81, 96, 111, 119, 215, 227, 229, 231, 270, 283

Facebook, 66, 81, 83
Fachin, Edson, 7, 30, 55, 98, 274, 287
Fagner, 110, 223, 247
fake news, 22, 79–80, 82, 84, 264
Falcão Law, 263
Falcão, Armando, 263
Fantástico (TV program), 289
Faoro, Raymundo, 125
Farias, Lindbergh, 2, 17, 25–6, 29, 32, 50, 70, 100
Farquhar, Percival, 117
Fausto, Boris, 125
Favreto, Rodrigo, 61–3
FBI, 11, 284
Federal Police, 1, 3, 8, 10–13, 15, 17–24, 28–30, 33–4, 41–3, 45, 47–51, 53–5, 57–9, 61–3, 65, 67, 69, 71, 73, 75, 77, 87–9, 91–2, 94, 98–100, 111, 240, 247–8, 255, 260, 272–3, 277, 284
Federal Supreme Court (STF), 1, 4, 12, 18, 30, 39, 55, 59, 63, 76, 79, 86–7, 92–4, 98–9, 160, 254, 256, 272, 286
Felisberto, Murilo, 176
Fernandes, Florestan, 67, 125, 235–6
Fernandes, Florestan, Jr., 274
Fernandes, Ottoni, Jr., 270, 275
Fernández, Alberto, 77
Fernández, Joséito, 63
Fernandinho Beira-Mar, 49
Ferrador, João (character), 169, 204
Ferreira, Heitor Aquino, 118, 274
Ferreira, Heitor, 127–8
Ferreira, Rogê, 265
Fiel Filho, Manoel, 185, 194, 196
FIESP (São Paulo State Industry Federation), 108, 222, 224, 252
Figueredo, João Batista, 118–21, 128, 194, 196, 206, 217, 221, 223, 226, 228, 237, 241, 246, 248, 262
Fire and Fury (Wolff), 80, 81
Fleury, Sérgio, 111
Flores, Luciano, 18, 87, 92
Folha da Tarde (newspaper), 124
Folha de São Paulo (newspaper), 15, 83, 91, 97, 242, 265, 278, 284
Fonseca, Ariel Pacca da, 195
Força Sindical, 261
Ford, 7, 48, 107, 109, 168, 177–8, 197–200, 202, 205, 209, 220, 242, 259
Fortaleza (Ceará), 5, 271
Fourth International, 234
Fragoso, Heleno, 254, 256
França, Adriana, 65
France, 54, 82, 111–12, 125, 159, 216, 230, 242–4, 261, 278
Francini, Paulo, 125, 242
Franco, Francisco, 230
Franco, Itamar, 270
Free Lula Vigil, 50, 53–5, 57–8, 65–6, 69–70, 74, 89–91, 99–100, 102–3, 107, 260
Freire, Paulo, 125, 236
Freitas, Vagner, 29, 32
French Democratic Confederation of Labor, 111

Friar Betto, 32, 105, 107, 112, 116, 225, 237, 239, 245, 253, 259, 273
Friar Chico (José Ferreira da Silva), 106, 115, 117, 124, 126, 136, 146, 148, 150–1, 155–8, 167–8, 170–1, 174, 179, 182, 186–8, 190–1, 238–9
Frias family, 278, 281
Frias, Otavio, 242
Fris Moldu Car, 143, 151
Frota, Sylvio, 191–2, 195–6
Funaro, Dilson, 242
FUP (Petroleum Workers Union Federation), 41
Furlan, Antonio Osvaldo do Amaral, 216
Fux, Luiz, 92

Gacek, Stanley, 54
Gaddafi, Muammar al-, 289
Galache, Luciano Garcia, 168
Galante, Aron, 199
Galvão, Patrícia "Pagu," 235
Garanhuns (Pernambuco), 129, 241
García Márquez, Gabriel, 89, 256
Garneiro, Mario, 242
Gaspari, Elio, 118
Gato, Marcelo, 170, 172, 183
Gazeta Mercantil (newspaper), 126
Geisel, Ernesto, 118, 183–4, 191–7, 200–7, 217, 227, 243, 263
General Labor Command (CGT), 261
General Motors, 107, 202
Genoino, José, 263
Genro, Tarso, 26
Genu, João Claudio, 49
Germany, 53, 121, 136, 229, 242–4, 261, 270
Gikovate, Febus, 235
Globo TV, 18, 36, 100, 284
GloboNews, 25, 27, 29, 31, 33, 35, 37
Glover, Danny, 54
Godói, Paulo Rui de, 258
Goiás, 263
Góis, Valdomira Ferreira de, 130
Goldemberg, José, 125
Goldman, Alberto, 234
Gomes, Cid, 1, 5, 96
Gomes, Ciro, 66, 68, 284
Gomes, Manuel Anísio, 259
Gomes, Severo, 200
Gonçalves, Paulo Rocha, Jr. (Paulão), 57
Gonçalves, Arnaldo, 206, 232
Gonzaga, Otavio, Jr., 127
Gonzaguinha, 110, 223, 247
González, Felipe, 230
Goulart, João, 25, 143, 216, 227
Gouveia, Antonio, Jr., 126
Grabois, Juan, 54
Graça, Ailton, 32
Granda, Bienvenido, 137
"Grândola, Vila Morena," 64, 229
Greca, Rafael, 58
Grechi, Moacir, 238
Greenhalgh, Luiz Eduardo, 11, 19, 21, 28–9, 33, 70, 100, 212, 239–40, 245–6, 248–9, 251, 254, 256–8, 267, 274
Greenwald, Glenn, 97
Gregori, José, 125
Group of 14, 108, 222, 224
Grünewald, Augusto Hammann Rademaker, 227
Grupo Prerrogativas, 21, 55, 61

"Guantanamera," 634
Guardian (newspaper), 97
Guarnieri, Gianfrancesco, 125, 216
Guarujá triplex apartment, 94, 283
Guarujá, 130–1, 264, 283–4
Guedes, Paulo, 89
Guevara, Che, 224
Guimarães, Nelson da Silva Machado, 254, 256
Guimarães, Ulysses, 261, 269

Haddad, Ana Carolina, 26
Haddad, Ana Estela, 26, 27, 34
Haddad, Fernando, 26, 32, 63, 67, 70, 97, 100, 274
Haddad, Frederico, 26
Haddad, Jamil, 265
Hardt, Gabriela, 91
Havana (Cuba), 253, 265, 275
Heleno, Augusto, 195, 254, 256
Henfil (Henrique de Souza Filho), 204, 211, 229
Herzog, Vladimir, 185, 191–2, 195–6, 205
Hime, Francis, 110
Hoffmann, Gleisi, 1, 29, 32, 50, 67–8, 74, 85, 100, 274
Holanda, Aurélio Buarque de, 125
Holanda, Sergio Buarque de, 231, 234
Holleben, Ehrenfried von, 229
Homeless Workers' Movement (MTST), 8–11, 25, 37
Horta, Murilo Macedo, 222
Houaiss, Antônio, 125
Hoxha, Enver, 225
Hummes, Bishop Claudio, 109, 112, 116, 121–2, 223, 238–40, 245, 249

Ianni, Octavio, 172
IF Metall, 251
IG Metall, 111, 126
Iglesias, Francisco, 125
India, 81, 83
Indonesia, 192
inflation, 172–3, 184–5, 201, 209, 220, 232
Institutional Act 5, 159–60, 173, 209, 230
Intercept, 22, 86, 97–8, 113, 117, 119–23, 125–7, 277
IPÊS (Institute of Research and Social Studies), 126
Iran, 220
Israel, 172
Istoé (magazine), 242
Itaipu hydroelectric dam, 201
Italy, 54, 171, 175, 243–4
Itaú Bank, 126, 135
Ivene (Friar Chico's wife), 186–7, 190–1

Janja (Rosangela da Silva), 67, 72, 99–101
Japan, 119, 126, 185–6, 188, 190, 197, 242–3
Joana (Marisa Leticia's adopted sister), 179, 187
João Ferrador (character), 169, 204
Johnson, Lyndon, 203
Jornal da Tarde (newspaper), 176, 240, 242, 258
Jornal do Brasil (newspaper), 159, 200, 233, 242
Jornal Nacional (TV news program), 35, 278–9, 281–3, 285, 289
Jornalistas Livres, 10

José, Paulo, 125
Juiz de Fora (Minas Gerais), 68, 79
Julião, Francisco, 228–9
Jungmann, Raul, 91
Jutificio São Francisco, 140

Katholishes Büro, 121
Kennedy, John, 269
Kennedy, Ted, 228
Kfouri, Juca, 67, 274
Khrushchev Report, 225
Kok, Einar, 205, 242
Kotscho, Ricardo, 268
Kruger, Hans-Jürgen, 261

labor card, 138, 151, 201, 251
Laerte, 169, 204, 211, 274
Lampião, 289
Lana, Antônio Carlos Bicalho, 238
Landless Rural Workers' Movement (MST), 3, 7, 10, 11, 17, 22, 32, 48, 53, 55, 58, 67, 99, 114, 260
Lapa massacre, 196
Latin America, 77, 86, 150, 164, 228
Lavigne, Rosane, 21
lawfare, 11, 18
Lebanon, 159
Lebbos, Carolina, 59, 86
Leite, Rogério Cézar de Cerqueira, 125
Lembo, Claudio, 214–15, 242
Leme, Alexandre Vannucchi, 238
Lemmertz, Lilian, 125
Lenin, Vladimir, 206, 235
Lenz, Carlos Eduardo Thompson Flores, 63
Levy, Herbert, 126
Lewandowski, Ricardo, 92, 98
Lima Sobrinho, Barbosa, 125
Lima, Alceu Amoroso, 125
Lins (São Paulo), 232–3
Lins, Ivan, 247
Lins, Luizianne, 45
Lira, Arthur, 288
Lobato, Monteiro, 117
Lobo, Aristides, 234
Lombardi, Bruna, 125, 216
Losada, Manuel Piñeiro, 253
Lourdes, Maria "Lurdinha," 182
Lourdes, Maria de (Lula's first wife), 154
Lucia, Carmen, 30
Lula da Silva, Luis Claudio, 7, 20
Lula da Silva, Lurian Cordeiro, 7, 19, 99, 106, 178
Lula da Silva, Marisa Letícia, 17, 19–20, 28, 36, 106, 175, 177–82, 239, 257, 262, 265, 267, 270, 275
Lula da Silva, Marlene Araujo, 20
Lula da Silva, Sandro Luis, 7, 19, 20, 87, 106, 112, 225, 239
Lula da Silva, Thiago Trindade, 99
Lula Institute, 1, 6–7, 9, 26, 28, 50, 139, 205, 271
Lula method of public speaking, 165
Lula's letter to the Brazilian people (2018), 70
Lupi, Carlos, 270
Luster, Luis Carlos, 261
Luz, Bruno, 51

Macalé, Jards, 223
Macedo, Edir, 278
Macedo, Márcio, 6, 17
Macedo, Murilo, 108, 222–3, 242
Maceió (Alagoas), 271

Machado, Edgard da Mata, 125
Machado, Silvio Pereira, 238
Magaldi, Antônio Pereira, 245
Magalhães, Juraci Batista, 259
Magnotti, Edsel, 238, 241
Mago, Athos, 263
Maia, Marco, 45
Mainardi, Diogo, 92, 94
Maluf, Paulo, 108, 116, 127, 186, 213, 216, 217, 287
Managua, 253, 255
Manchetômetro, 278, 279, 282, 284, 287, 289
Mandel, Ernest, 208
Mantega, Guido, 26
Marchezan, Nelson, 242
Marcílio Dias Public School, 131, 134
Marcílio, Benedito, 207, 232
Marcondes, Mauro, 242
Marighella, Carlos, 238
Marinho family, 278
Marinho, Luiz, 29, 30
Marinho, Manoel Eduardo "PT Maninho," 6
Marte Screw Company, 138–41
Martí, José, 63
Martinho da Vila, 247
Martins, Franklin, 51, 226, 228, 270, 274,
Martins, José de Souza, 125
Martins, Paulo Egídio, 242
Martins, Valeska, 17, 264
Marx, Karl, 152
Masetti, Mario, 223
massacre of Lapa, 196
Matarazzo, Ciccillo, 193
Mato Grosso, 193, 262
Matto Grosso do Sul, 49
Mauro, Gilmar, 7
May 12 metalworking shop, 251
May Day 54, 223, 248
MBP-4, 110, 247
McNamara, Robert, 203
MDB (Brazilian Democratic Movement), 170, 199, 207, 213–18, 221, 224–5, 230, 232–4, 239, 243, 239, 243, 264, 269, 284
Medeiros, Edevaldo, 90, 274
Medeiros, Luiz Antônio de, 261
Mélenchon, Jean-Luc, 54
Melhem, José Roberto Fanganiello, 190–1
Mello e Souza, Gilda de, 235
Mellos, Patricia Campos, 83, 275
Melo, Ednardo D'Avila, 187, 193, 195
Melo, Eurídice "Dona Lindu" Ferreira de, 34, 129–38, 144–5, 152–3, 161, 178, 222, 248–50
Melo, Francisco de Assis Correia de, 227
Melo, Ibere Bandeira de, 258
Melo, Misael, 7, 73, 274
Mendes, Bete, 110, 233
Mendes, Chico, 255, 267
Mendes, Gilmar, 98
Méndez, Aparicio, 228
Mendonça, Osmar "Osmarinho" Santos de, 206, 237, 259
Meneguelli, Jair, 259, 261
Menezes, Gilson, 259
Menicucci, Eleanora, 32
Mercadante, Aloizio, 32, 273
Mercador del Rio, Ramón, 208
Mercedes-Benz, 107, 121–2, 150, 169, 209, 220
Mesquita family, 176, 240, 278, 281

Metal Arte, 194
Metalurgica Independencia, 142, 149
Metalworkers of São Paulo and Mogi das Cruzes, 173
Mexico City, 208
Mexico, 54, 81, 164, 184–5, 208, 228
military coup, 25, 110, 126, 149
military dicatatorship, 4, 32, 54, 64, 83, 89, 114, 118, 124, 149, 156, 160, 169–0, 173, 185–8, 191, 193, 199, 201, 205–6, 212–15, 220, 224–7, 229–30, 233–4, 238–9, 254, 258, 261, 263, 269
Military Police, 11–12, 50, 58, 89, 98–9, 106, 108–9, 179, 245, 248, 260, 289
Minas Gerais, 5, 49, 66, 68, 79, 134, 154, 161–2, 176–7, 185, 204, 211, 214, 241, 262
Minc, Carlos, 229
Mindlin, José, 205, 242
Ministry of Foreign Relations, 119
Ministry of Justice, 126
miracle of the vigil, 103
Miranda, David, 97
Modi, Narenda, 83
Moisés, José Álvaro, 236, 242, 260, 274
Monteiro, Afonso, 157
Monteiro, Dilermando Gomes, 109, 195, 200
Montenegro, Fernanda, 125
Montoro, Franco, 213, 230, 242, 264
Morais Filho, Evaristo de, 125
Morales, Evo, 16
Moreira Salles, Fernando, 125
Moreira, Samuel, 12
Morelli, Mauro, 238
Morgado, Camila, 270
Moro, Sergio, 1, 3, 5, 7, 9, 11, 13, 18, 29, 34, 36, 51, 55, 62, 76, 88, 97–8, 272, 277, 286–7
Moura, Edson, 7, 274
Moura, Enilson "Alemaozinho" Simoes de, 206, 223, 237, 244, 258
MR-8 (October 8 Revolutionary Movement), 225-226
Mr. Ze (Marte Screw Company boss), 141
MST (Landless Rural Workers' Movement), 3, 7, 10, 11, 17, 22, 32, 48, 53, 55, 58, 67, 99, 114, 260
MTST (Homeless Workers' Movement), 8–11, 25, 37
Mucida, Izabella, 42, 44, 47
Mujica, José Alberto "Pepe," 22, 54, 59

NAFTA (North American Free Trade Agreement), 81
Nair (Lula's girlfriend), 175
Nascimento, Milton, 239, 265
Nassif, Maria Inês, 289
Natel, Laudo, 213, 216–17, 242
National Association of Automobile Manufacturers (ANFAVEA), 119
National Confederation of Agricultural Workers (CONTAG), 256
National Conference of Brazilian Bishops (CNBB), 245
National Conference of the Working Class (CONCLAT), 261
National Constituent Assembly, 262
National Housing Bank, 161, 178–9
National Information Service (SNI), 107–8, 111, 118, 120, 125, 194, 260

National Security Agency, United States (NSA), 11, 97, 152, 165, 173, 175, 189, 198, 218, 227, 288
National Security Law, 238, 240, 250, 255–6
National Treasury, 3, 119, 277
National Truth Commission, 238
Náutico do Capribaribe (football team), 167
'Ndrangheta, 51
Nepomuceno, Eric, 230, 274
Netherlands, the, 243
Neves, Tancredo, 214
New Brazilian Unionism, 169
New York Times, 204
New York, 186, 204, 221, 228, 260, 278
Newsweek, 288
Nicaragua, 253–4
Niemeyer, Oscar, 270
Nigris, Teobaldo de, 222
Nogueira, Ciro, 288
Nogueira, João, 110
Nogueira, Paulinho, 110
NSA (US National Security Agency), 11, 97, 152, 165, 173, 175, 189, 198, 218, 227, 288
Nunes, Antônio Carlos Félix, 169, 204

O Antagonista (news site), 92–4
O Globo (newspaper), 94, 159, 233, 278–9, 281, 289
"Menestrel das Alagoas," 239
OAS (engineering company), 51, 283
Obama, Barack, 80, 82
October 8 Revolutionary Movement (MR-8), 225–6
Odebrecht (engineering company), 4, 51, 274
Odorico (Lula's maternal uncle),135
Okamoto, Paulo, 5, 45–6, 84, 204–5, 275
Olavo (Lula's friend), 148, 159
Oliveira, Antônio Gonçalves de, 160
Oliveira, Francisco "Chico" de, 242
Oliveira, José Aparecido de, 125
Oliveira, Juca de, 125
Oliveira, Nilo Sérgio "Nilão" de, 255–6
Oliveira, Osvaldo Machado de, 248–50
Oliveira, Raimundo de, 125
Operation Car Wash (Lava Jato), 3–4, 17–18, 23, 34, 36, 41, 51, 55, 60, 76, 79, 86, 92, 95, 97–8, 176, 254, 277–8, 283, 285–7,
Operation Spoofing, 98, 277
Ortega, Daniel, 253
Osasco (São Paulo), 211, 217, 234
Osava, Chizuo, 229

Pahlevi, Reza, 220
Palme, Olof, 230
Palocci, Antonio, 51, 274
Paludo, Januario, 86, 95
Panichi Filho, Armando, 248–51, 273–4
Paolinelli, Alysson, 200
Pará, 260
Paraguay, 201
Paraná, 1, 3, 20, 35, 50–1, 55, 89, 91, 95–6, 98–9, 111–12, 277
Passarinho, Jarbas, 242
Passoni, Irma, 242
Paulo, Igor de, 51
PCB (Brazilian Communist Party),

55, 106, 123, 168–71, 182, 185, 188, 190–1, 194, 196, 201, 225, 227, 234, 261
PCC (Brazilian First Capital Command), 51
PC do B (Communist Party of Brazil), 32, 70, 123, 196, 225
PDT (Democratic Labor Party), 5, 66, 96, 230, 264, 270, 284
Pedroso, Mário, 231, 234, 236
Pelle, Domenico, 51
Pellegrino, Hélio, 236
Pereira, Francelino, 242
Peres, Aurélio, 207, 232
Pernambuco, 32, 56, 109, 129–30, 132, 167, 233, 241
Perón, Juan Domingo, 28
Petrobras, 27, 51, 96, 201, 281
petroleum, 37, 41, 51, 68, 96, 220, 225, 232, 234–5, 283
Petroleum Workers' Union Federation (FUP), 41
Piaui, 17, 31, 206, 288
picket line, 106–9, 114, 137, 140–1, 211, 216, 244
Pimenta, Paulo, 17, 61, 70
Pincus, Gregory, 154
Ping Pong (chewing gum company), 137
Pinheiro Filho, José Adelmário "Leo Pinheiro," 51
Pinheiro, Paulo Sérgio, 125
Pinheiro, Wilson de Souza, 255–6
Pinochet, Augusto, 89, 228
Pinto, Almir Pazzianotto, 168, 242
Pinto, Mahalhaes, 242
Pires, José Maria, 238
Pixinghuinha, 223
Planalto Palace, 118–19, 270
PMDB (Brazilian Democratic Movement Party), 264
Poços de Caldas (Minas Gerais), 161–2, 231–3, 236
Pomar, Pedro, 196
Pomeranz, Lenina, 172
Ponce, Juan, 261
Pope Francis, 22, 54, 77
Pope John Paul II, 164
Portela, Petrônio, 205–6, 208, 242
Porto Alegre (Rio Grande do Sul), 1, 2, 5, 90
Portugal, 64, 229–30, 244, 261
Posadas, Juan, 208
Povo sem Medo (MTST squatters' camp), 9
PP (Progressive Party), 288
PPP (public-private partnership), 26
Prado, Caio, Jr., 125
Prado, Osmar, 32
Praia Grande (São Paulo), 261
Prerrogativas, Grupo, 21, 55, 61
presidential chief of staff, 18, 68, 118, 248
Prestes, Luís Carlos, 53, 170, 188, 225, 227–8, 280
Prestes, Olga Gutmann Benário, 270
Prieto, Arnaldo da Costa, 242
Programa Universidade para Todos (ProUni), 26
Proner, Carol, 21
PSDB (Brazilian Social Democracy Party), 9, 27, 66, 84, 284
PSL (Social Liberty Party), 59, 66, 96, 284
PSOL (Socialism and Liberty Party), 8, 32, 40, 96–7

PSR (Revolutionary Socialist Party), 235
PT (Workers' Party), 1, 4, 6, 55, 67, 71, 84, 197, 206, 224, 230–2, 234, 236, 242, 262, 269
PTB (Brazilian Labor Party), 229–30, 248, 264
O Pulo do Gato (radio program), 115
Putin, Vladimir, 82

Quadros, Janio, 213, 264
Quércia, Orestes, 242

Ramalho, Elba, 110
Rana, Álvaro, 261
Rangel, Flavio, 125
Ratinho Jr., 89
Recife (Pernambuco), 167, 189
Regina, Ellis, 223
Reis, Elias dos, 8, 46
Resil (auto parts factory), 211
retirement pension, 168, 214
Revenue Service, 100
Revolutionary Socialist Party (PSR), 235
Rezk, Antônio, 221
Ribeiro, Darcy, 227–9
Ribeiro, Devanir, 167, 237
Ribeiro, Jacinto, 154, 155
Ribeiro, Marco Aurélio Santana, 273
Rigonatto, Dalter Dimas, 108–9, 245
Rio Branco (Acre), 255
Rio de Janeiro, 2, 19, 21, 29, 41, 61, 80, 83, 96, 100, 170, 187, 189, 195, 217, 225, 227, 255, 262, 265, 273, 278
Rio Grande do Sul, 22, 32, 45, 59, 61, 70, 90, 109, 111, 143, 228, 233
Rocha, Josué, 9
Rocha, Luiz Carlos da, 23, 55–7, 63, 66, 274
Rodrigues, Carlos Eduardo, 7–8
Rodrigues, João Paulo, 8
Rodrigues, José de Souza, 172
Rodrigues, José Honorio, 125
"Rosa," 223
Rosinha, Dr., 50
Rosseti, Disney, 12, 41–3
Rousseff, Dilma, 1, 5, 17–18, 22, 27–8, 31–2, 86, 69–70, 91, 217, 238, 270, 272, 274, 281
Rubens (Lula's half-brother), 133
Russia, 22, 82, 96, 189

Sá, Calmon de, 242
Saad family, 278
SABESP (water company), 16–17
Sabino, Mario, 92
Sachetta, Herminio, 235
Salazar, António de Oliveira, 64, 229
Salem, Armando, 176, 274
Salles, Antônio Pinheiro, 238
Salvador (Bahia), 225, 228
Samoza, Anastasio, 253
Sampaio, Plinio de Arruda, 125
Samper, Ernesto, 54
Sandinista National Liberation Front, 253
Santa Catarina, 262
Santana do Livramento (Rio Grande do Sul), 22
Santiago de Cuba, 60
Santo André (São Paulo), 31, 88, 107, 109-112, 116, 122, 134, 207, 222, 224, 232, 238, 240

Santos (São Paulo), 130–1, 133–4, 144, 153, 163, 170, 173, 185, 228–9, 232, 237, 242, 261, 274
Santos Metalworkers' Union, 170, 232
Santos, Argeu Egídio dos, 163, 185, 197
Santos, Genesio dos, 125
Santos, João Batista dos, 237
Santos, Ricardo Silva dos, 274
Santos, Theotônio dos, 229
São Bernardo do Campo (São Paulo), 5, 15–16, 19, 29, 67, 86, 105, 110, 121, 134, 156, 199, 223, 225, 233, 250, 262
São Caetano do Sul (São Paulo), 150, 156, 168, 186, 222, 224, 250
São Paulo and Mogi das Cruzes metalworkers' union, 173
São Paulo Archdiocese, 31, 33
São Paulo, 2, 5, 9, 11–16, 24, 26–7, 31–3, 41–2, 45, 48–9, 61–3, 67–8, 73, 79, 80, 83, 86–7, 91, 95, 96–7, 99, 107–11, 113, 115–24, 127–8, 130–1, 134–5, 152, 154, 163, 166–7, 172–3, 175–7, 181, 185, 186–7, 189, 191–6, 199, 201, 202, 205, 207, 211, 213–16, 220, 222, 231–4, 236, 239, 241, 248, 255, 257, 259–62, 264–5, 270–1, 273, 275, 278, 283–4, 287
São Paulo's ABC region, 32, 41, 87–8, 105, 109–10, 112, 123, 150, 164, 199, 209
Sarney, José, 66
Satyarthi, Kailash, 54
Scania, 9, 107, 205, 209–11, 251
Schefer, Gastão, 58–9
Scherer, Cardinal Odilo, 31
Schlesinger, Arthur M., Jr., 269
Schmidt, Helmut, 242
Schulz, Martin, 54
Se Cathedral, 192-193, 240
Selerges, Moisés, 2, 5, 10, 16, 41, 44, 46–7, 275
SENAI (National Industrial Apprenticeship Service), 129, 138–41, 146–7, 151, 204
Sepulveda Pertence, José Paulo, 30, 59–60, 256
Sérgio Ricardo, 110, 247
Setubal, Olavo, 243
Sfat, Dina, 257
Sigmaringa Seixas, Luis Carlos, 12–13, 17, 21, 24, 33, 47, 49, 86, 274
Silva, Aristides Inácio da, 130–4, 234, 241
Silva, Fatima Rega Cassero da, 20
Silva Filho, João Maia da, 267
Silva, Genival Inácio "Vavá" da, 61, 86–8, 129, 136, 146, 167, 179, 187
Silva, Guilhermina da, 130
Silva, Jaime da, 129, 150
Silva, João Inácio da, 130
Silva, José Francisco da, 267
Silva, José "Friar Chico" Ferreira da, 106, 115, 117, 126, 126, 136, 148, 150–1, 155–8, 167–8, 170, 171, 174, 179, 182, 186–8, 190–1, 238–9
Silva, José Pedro "Sarrafo" da, 234
Silva, José "Ze Cuia" Inácio da, 129–30, 132
Silva, José "Ziza" da, 129, 133, 135, 155
Silva, Maria "Baixinha" da, 129, 175

Silva, Marina, 66, 284
Silva, Marinete da, 129, 134
Silva, Rosangela "Janja" da, 67, 72, 99–101
Silva, Rubens "Rubão" Teodoro da, 167, 181–2, 198, 237
Silva, Ruth "Tiana" da, 129–32, 145, 150, 159
Silva, Severino Alves da, 209, 237
Silva, Wellington, 31
Silva Teles, Gofredo da, 125
Simão, Azis, 172
Simonsen, Iluska, 124
Simonsen, Mario Henrique, 124, 223, 242
Singer, Paul, 236
Sion High School, 231, 236
Siqueira, Geraldo "Geraldinho," 105, 113, 237, 242, 274
Sirkis, Alfredo, 229
Skromov, Paulo de Mattos, 234
SNI (National Information Service), 107–8, 111, 118, 120, 125, 194, 260
Snowden, Edward, 97
Soares, Airton, 105, 233, 242, 245, 258, 264
Soares, Delubio, 49
Soares, Mario, 229
Soares, Mauricio, 168, 174, 223
Sobel, Henry, 192
Socialism and Liberty Party (PSOL), 8, 32, 40, 96–7
Socialist Convergence (SC), 212, 226
Socialist International, 229
Socrates (football player), 67, 218
Sorocaba railway company, 117
Sousa, Milton "Little Skull" Tavares de, 118, 127
Souza, Emídio de, 6, 12, 33, 41–2, 47, 50, 100, 274
Souza, José Venancio de, 237
Soviet Union, 188–9
Spain, 28, 174
Spektor, Matias, 196
Stalin, Joseph, 208
Stédile, João Pedro, 7, 11, 32, 60, 67, 274
Stone, Oliver, 97, 273
strikes, 10, 22, 32, 34, 105–13, 117, 119–24, 129, 134, 137, 140–1, 147, 160, 167, 169–70, 173, 182, 208–9, 211–12, 219–20, 222–4, 226, 236–40, 243–51, 254, 257, 269
Suárez, Adolfo, 242
Suharto, 192
Super 8, 260
Superior Court of Justice, 21, 75
Superior Electoral Court (TSE), 63, 67, 69, 83, 230–1
Superior Labor Court (TRT), 168, 197
Suplicy, Eduardo, 32, 242, 263
Sweden, 230, 242–4

Teixeira Filho, Afonso, 245
Teixeira Martins (law firm), 17
Teixeira, Paulo, 61
Teixeira, Roberto, 56, 61, 254
Telegram, 96, 119, 121–3, 126, 244
Temer, Michel, 217
Tereza (Lula's girlfriend), 175
The Accidental President of Brazil (Cardoso), 221
Tibiriçá, Beatriz "Bea," 114
Toffoli, Dias, 86–7, 92
Tokyo, 181, 185–6, 188

Toquinho, 110
Torres, Vinicius Ferraz, 210
torture, 4, 108, 115, 118, 126, 132, 157, 171, 181, 185–91, 196, 207, 209, 213, 226, 238–9, 247, 253, 263
Tragtenberg, Maurício, 125
TRF-4 regional court, 2, 5, 21, 30, 35–6, 61–3, 94, 100
Tribuna Metalurgica (newsletter), 169, 172
Troiano, Claudia, 17, 274
Trotsky, Leon, 208
Troyano, Annez Andraus, 172
Trumka, Richard, 54
Trump, Donald, 80–2, 84
Tuma, Rogério, 248
Tuma, Romeu, 116, 118, 127, 226, 239–42, 246, 246–51, 260
Twitter, 83

UGT (Unión General de Trabajadores), 54
unemployment, 147, 150, 152, 181, 232, 251
unionism, 126, 169, 175, 183, 185, 199, 209–10, 224, 242
United States, 81, 112, 154, 192, 228, 244, 254
Universal Kingdom of God Church, 278
Uruguay, 22, 54, 59, 228

Vaccari Neto, João, 4
Vale, João do, 110
Valeixo, Mauricio, 3, 51, 62
Vannuchi, Paulo, 5
Vargas, Getúlio, 2, 25, 183, 196, 225, 229–30, 271, 287
Vargas, Ivete, 230
Vasconcellos, João Paulo, 206
Vatican, 22
Veja (magazine), 37, 97, 176, 200, 206, 230, 278, 281, 286–9
Veloso, João Paulo dos Reis, 242
Venezuela, 81–2, 261
Veronezzi, Marco Antônio, 240, 273
Viana, Pereira, 203
Vicalvi, Roberval, 62
Vicentinho, 5
Victor, Henrique, 245
Vidal, Paulo, 157, 159–60, 163, 168–9, 180, 182, 185, 198
Vidigal, Luis Eulálio Bueno, 242
Vietnam War, 154
Vilardi, Celso, 2
Vilela, Cardinal Avelar Brandão, 239
Vilela, Teotônio, 239
Villares (factory), 107, 151–2, 156–7, 165–6, 168, 181, 202, 239, 241
Villares, Carlos, 242
Villares, Paulo, 202–3, 245, 275
Villas-Boas, Orlando, 193
Visconde de Itaúna Public School, 135
Volkswagen, 107, 121–2, 175, 177–8, 204–5, 219–20
Voz Operaria (newspaper), 194

Wagner, Jaques, 67–8, 85
Wainer, Samuel, 191
Weber, Rosa, 1
Weffort, Francisco, 125, 236, 259
Welter, Carlos, 86
Wey, Anna Maria, 116
WhatsApp, 83, 92
Whirlpool, 204

Willys Overland, 148, 156, 158
Wilma, Eva, 216
Wladimir (football player), 264
Wolff, Michael, 80–1
Workers' Party (PT), 1, 4, 6, 55, 67, 71, 84, 197, 206, 224, 230–2, 234, 236, 242, 262, 269
Workers' Pastoral, 107, 111, 207, 245
World Bank, 172, 203
Wright, Jaime, 192
Wyllys, Jean, 96

Xavier, Livio, 234

Yaconis, Cleide, 125
Yom Kippur War, 172

Zanin, Cristiano, 1, 17, 21, 44, 48–9, 56, 59, 98, 100, 254, 274, 284
Zara, Carlos, 216
Zavascki, Teori, 18
Zé Bettio, 198
Zé Keti, 110, 247
Zerbini, Euriale de Jesus, 212
Zerbini, Teresinha, 212
Ziraldo, 110